Red Bird, Red Power

American Indian Literature
and Critical Studies Series

Gertrude Simmons in 1898, photographed by Gertrude Käsebier. (Gertrude Käsebier Photographs, Division of Culture and the Arts, National Museum of American History, Smithsonian Institution, 69.236.107)

RED BIRD, RED POWER

The Life and Legacy of Zitkala-Ša

TADEUSZ LEWANDOWSKI

UNIVERSITY OF OKLAHOMA PRESS

Norman

Library of Congress Cataloging-in-Publication Data

Names: Lewandowski, Tadeusz, 1973– author.
Title: Red bird, red power : the life and legacy of Zitkala-Ša / Tadeusz Lewandowski.
Other titles: Life and legacy of Zitkala-Ša
Description: Norman, OK : University of Oklahoma Press, [2016] | Series:
    American Indian literature and critical studies series volume 67 |
    Includes bibliographical references and index.
Identifiers: LCCN 2015039588 | ISBN 978-0-8061-5178-6 (hardcover : alk. paper)
Subjects: LCSH: Zitkala-Ša, 1876–1938. | Yankton women—Biography. | Yankton
    Indians—Biography. | Indian women authors—Biography. | Indian women
    activists—Biography. | Political activists—United States—Biography. | Yankton
    Indians—Civil rights. | Yankton Indians—Government relations. | Indians, Treatment
    of—Great Plains. | Indian musicians—Biography. | Women musicians—
    United States—Biography.
Classification: LCC E99.Y25 L49 2016 | DDC 813/.52092—dc23
LC record available at http://lccn.loc.gov/2015039588

Red Bird, Red Power: The Life and Legacy of Zitkala-Ša is Volume 67 in the American Indian
Literature and Critical Studies Series.

1 2 3 4 5 6 7 8 9 10

CONTENTS

List of Illustrations	vii
Acknowledgments	ix
Author's Note	xi
Prologue: An Indian's Awakening	3
1. The School Days of an Indian Girl	17
2. Carlisle and the *Atlantic Monthly*	28
3. Montezuma and the Rebellion	45
4. Uintah	65
5. *The Sun Dance Opera* and the Peyote "Menace"	78
6. New Opportunities, New Trials	93
7. In the Society of American Indians	102
8. In Washington at War	119
9. The Peyote Clash	132
10. Forging a Plan of Resistance	150
11. Oklahoma	163
12. Princess Zitkala-Ša and the National Council of American Indians	173
13. The Final Diaries	184
Conclusion: Zitkala-Ša and Red Power	189
Notes	197
Selected Bibliography	255
Index	267

ILLUSTRATIONS

Gertrude Simmons in 1898 — *frontispiece*

Gertrude Simmons at the Santee Normal Training School, Nebraska, ca. 1890 — 20

Carlisle Indian Industrial School superintendent Richard Henry Pratt, ca. 1900 — 29

"Faculty and Officers of Our School," Carlisle Indian School, 1898 — 33

Zitkala-Ša (reclining), by Joseph T. Keiley, 1898 — 35

Zitkala-Ša (portrait), by Joseph T. Keiley, 1898 — 36

Gertrude Simmons, in mock traditional garb, 1898 — 38

Gertrude Simmons with her violin, 1898 — 39

Gertrude Simmons in profile, photographed by Gertrude Käsebier, 1898 — 47

Dr. Carlos Montezuma and nurses at Carlisle in an undated photo — 48

Zitkala-Ša and William Hanson, ca. 1913 — 84

Old Sioux, or Bad Hand, ca. 1913 — 86

Samuel Lone Bear, photographed by Gertrude Käsebier, 1898 — 90

Arthur C. Parker, ca. 1919 — 104

Members of the Society of American Indians in Cedar Rapids,
Iowa, 1916   112

James Mooney in an undated photo   139

Zitkala-Ša at the Catholic Sioux Congress, 1920   147

Zitkala-Ša being interviewed by Native reporter,
Catholic Sioux Congress, 1920   148

Zitkala-Ša in a publicity photo   174

National Council of American Indians at unveiling of Sitting
Bull statue, 1926   177

Acknowledgments

At the University of Oklahoma Press I would like to thank Thomas Krause, for far too many things to list; Alessandra Jacobi Tamulevich, for seeing potential in the original manuscript; and Emily Jerman Schuster, for all her kind help during the editing process. A big thanks as well to Kirsteen E. Anderson for her meticulous editing work. For assistance during the research process, I would also like to thank Mark Thiel of the Marquette University Archives; Virginia Hanson of the South Dakota State Archives, South Dakota State Historical Society; Richard Tritt of the Cumberland County Historical Society in Carlisle, Pennsylvania; Valerie-Ann Lutz and Michael Miller of the American Philosophical Society; Elizabeth Thrond of the Center for Western Studies at Augustana College; John Gregory Matthews of the Manuscripts, Archives, and Special Collections (MASC), Washington State University Libraries; Kay Peterson of the Division of Culture and the Arts, National Museum of American History, Smithsonian Institution; Daisy Njoku of the Anthropology Archives and Collections, National Museum of Natural History, Smithsonian Institution; Liz Kurtulik Mercuri at Art Resource; Brent Abercrombie at the Indiana State Library; and all the helpful and efficient people, especially Elise Lipps, who work in the L. Tom Perry Special Collections, Harold B. Lee Library, at Brigham Young University. Thanks as well to Jenny C. Freed at Lily Library, Earlham College, as well as the people at the Wisconsin Historical Society and the Beinecke Rare Book and Manuscript Library at Yale University. I thank my mother, Linda Lewandowski, for sending and scanning too many materials to count, and

Jane Vavala of Hinkle Library at Alfred State College, New York, for her generous help in acquiring most of the sources that went into this book. Thanks as well to Doreen Rappaport and Arlene Hirschfelder for taking time to give me advice. I also thank Professor Andrzej Ciuk and Professor Ryszard Wolny, of the University of Opole, Poland, for their support over the past decade. Finally, I thank my wife, Marzena Lewandowski, for her love and support.

AUTHOR'S NOTE

This biography draws on hundreds of handwritten and typed letters, lectures, notes, diaries, and unpublished works. Many of the primary sources contain minor typographical, spelling, and punctuation errors. When I quote these sources, I have corrected such errors in order to enhance readability. None of the original tone or content has been altered. Capitalization of words has been preserved. Words underlined for purposes of emphasis in the original documents are here rendered in italic type. All the emphases appear in the original sources unless otherwise indicated in the notes.

Red Bird, Red Power

Prologue
An Indian's Awakening

In the early spring of 1896, a young woman from the Yankton Sioux Reservation in South Dakota ascended the stage of the English Opera House in Indianapolis to represent Earlham College in the twenty-second annual Indiana State Oratorical Contest. She assumed that she had very little chance of winning, but still spent the night before rewriting and reformulating her thoughts. Despite her harried last-minute alterations and the racial slurs she heard shouted at her as she took the podium, she delivered what was, by any reasonable standard, a remarkable speech.[1]

The young woman commenced in the broadest of metaphysical terms, speaking of the "ascending energy" that "pervades all life" and the "slow degrees" by which "nations have risen from the mountain foot of their existence to its summit." On that summit stood the United States, in all its resplendent glory:

> Out of a people holding tenaciously to the principles of the Great Charter has arisen in America a nation of free men and free institutions. . . . Among its rivers, mountains and lakes, in its stately forests and on its broad prairies, like rolling seas of green and gold, millions of toiling sovereigns have established gigantic enterprises, great factories, commercial highways, and have developed fruitful farms and productive mines. The ennobling architecture of its churches, schools, and benevolent institutions; its municipal greatness, keeping pace with social progress; its scholars, statesmen, authors and divines, giving expression and force to the religious and humanitarian zeal of a great people—all these reveal a marvelous progress. Thought is

3

lost in admiration of this matchless scene over which floats in majesty the starry emblem of liberty.

Just as soon as she constructed this triumphant vision of America, the young woman erased it. "But see!" she entreated, "At the bidding of thought the tide of time rolls back four hundred years. The generations of men of all nations, who have developed this civilization in America, return to the bosom of the old world. Myriad merchantmen, fleets, and armaments shrink and disappear from the ocean. . . . The fleet of discovery, bearing under the flag of Spain the figure of Columbus, recedes beyond the tractless sea. America is one great wilderness again."

In this romantic restoration of the past, this vanished time, smoke from wigwams hung over primeval forests, shouts of hunters resounded throughout the hills, and chiefs imparted legends to the younger generation. Conjuring up images of an ancient people, the young woman spoke of the "forest children" who once inhabited this unspoiled world. Deeply connected to their natural surroundings, they lived in "reverential awe"—seeing the Great Spirit's "voice in the wind," "frown in the storm cloud," and "smile in the sunbeam." Magnanimous by nature, they evinced a naiveté so great that they happily greeted eventual persecutors. "The invasion of his broad dominions by a paler face brought no dismay to the hospitable Indian," the young woman reminded her audience, "Samoset voiced the feeling of his people as he stood among the winter-weary Pilgrims and cried 'Welcome, Englishmen.' Nor did the Indian cling selfishly to his lands; willingly he divides with Roger Williams and Penn, who pay him for his own. History bears record to no finer examples of fidelity. To Jesuit, to Quaker, to all who kept their faith with him, his loyalty never failed." Yet this fraternal attitude could not be sustained. "Civilization" had brought vice, alcohol, and broken treaties, fueling "the Red Man's degradation" and forcing him into pure "desperation."

In a confrontational turn, the young woman outlined the moral correctness of Native retaliation. She challenged her audience with a succession of rhetorical questions:

The White Man's bullet decimates his tribes and drives him from his home. What if he fought? His forests were felled; his game frightened away; his streams of finny shoals usurped. He loved his family and would defend them. He loved the fair land of which he was rightful owner. He loved the inheritance of his fathers, their traditions, their graves; he held them a priceless legacy to be sacredly kept. He loved his native land. Do you wonder still that in his breast he should brood revenge, when ruthlessly driven from the temples where he worshipped? Do you wonder still that he sulked in forest gloom to avenge the desolation of his home? Is patriotism only a virtue in Saxon hearts? Is there no charity to cover his crouching form as he stealthily opposed his relentless foe?

No. Instead, the White Man had been "witness and judge" of Indian conduct during his arrogant push towards Manifest Destiny. Despite centuries of religious and legal development, whites had failed to demonstrate their own supposed humanity, substituting hypocrisy in its place.

The young woman listed the sins. After eight centuries of Christianity in Anglo-Saxon England, they nonetheless "burned the writhing martyr in the fires of Kenith field." The "cultured Frenchman," acting in "the name of religion and liberty," murdered with impunity on the "awful night of St. Bartholomew." During the Reign of Terror, the Seine ran red with human blood. And even worse, the White Man's excesses continue, transplanted onto a new continent where they spread like contagion. "Let it be remembered, before condemnation is passed upon the Red Man," the young woman pronounced in accusatory tones, "that, while he burned and tortured frontiersmen, Puritan Boston burned witches and hanged Quakers, and the Southern aristocrat beat his slaves and set blood hounds on the track of him who dared aspire to freedom." Therefore the "barbarous Indian," unschooled in the ways of civilization, had "brought no greater stain upon his name."

Yet why, the young woman asked, had the white wardens of civilization not served the Red Man? He had been not the beneficiary of paternalism or uplift, but the recipient of an attack that had encouraged "the most debasing influences," so as to drown his "nobler instincts until sin and corruption have well nigh swept them from the Earth." The young woman looked upward to address the very heavens: "To-day the Indian is pressed almost to the farther sea. Does that sea symbolize his death? Does the narrow territory still left to him typify the last brief day before his place on Earth 'shall know him no more forever'? Shall might make right and the fittest alone survive? Oh Love of God and His 'Strong Son,' thou who liftest up the oppressed and succorest the needy, is thine ear grown heavy that it cannot hear his cry? Is thy arm so shortened, it cannot save? Dost thou not yet enfold him in thy love? Look with compassion down, and with thine almighty power move this nation to the rescue of my race." Invoking the presence of God, casting the victory of white civilization as one rooted in military strength rather than adherence to the Gospel, the young woman declared the survival of the Indian a test of religious character. The scope of America's transgression against the indigenous population, she warned, could not be ignored:

"To take the life of a nation during the slow march of centuries seems not a lighter crime than to crush it instantly with one fatal blow. Our country must not shame her principles by such consummate iniquity."

At the heart of this crime lay a burning question. If the United States had "entered upon her career of freedom and prosperity with the declaration that 'all men are born free and equal,'" how, then, could "consistent Americans" refuse equality to "an American people in their struggle to rise from ignorance and degradation?" Prejudice could not prevail, for Indians could only endure with the aid of "enlightened people" bound by the virtuous "obligation of a brother's keeper." In a swift change of tone, the young woman depicted a new future in which the "claims of brotherhood" and "love that is due a neighbor race" reigned, lifting the "threatening night of oblivion" and replacing it with the "olive branch of peace." Hope for this outcome could be found "among the noblest of this country" and "a beneficent government" that had established a system of Indian education offering advancement to its apprentices. With this unexpected note of reconciliation, she concluded her plea: "We come from mountain fastnesses, from cheerless plains, from far-off low-wooded streams, seeking the 'White Man's ways.' Seeking your skill in industry and art, seeking labor and honest independence, seeking the treasures of knowledge and wisdom, seeking to comprehend the spirit of your laws and the genius of your noble institutions, seeking by a new birthright to unite with yours our claim to a common country, seeking the Sovereign's crown that we may stand side by side with you in ascribing royal honor to our nation's flag. America, I love thee. 'Thy people shall be my people and thy God my God.'"[2]

As the young woman spoke her final words that day on the stage of the English Opera House, quoting from Ruth 1:16, her dream of human dignity and unity within one nation was greeted with applause, but also deep insult. As she lifted her head to survey the auditorium, her eyes fell upon a large white banner unfurled by students from a rival college. It displayed the crude caricature of an Indian "squaw," rudely captioned with the word: HUMILITY.[3]

The young woman who delivered the preceding speech, Gertrude Simmons, was born to a Yankton Sioux mother and Caucasian father in the mid-1870s. Better known as Zitkala-Ša (Red Bird), Simmons would become one of the most important Indian rights activists of the early twentieth century. The fight she led was an extension of her ancestors' struggle for recognition and sovereignty. Therefore, it is with these ancestors that her story begins.

Gertrude Simmons began life as a member of the greater Očeti Šakówin, or Seven Council Fires, that make up the Sioux Nation. This people, whose territory once ranged from west of the northern Mississippi River to the Missouri River, includes three major groupings and respective dialects: Dakota, Nakota, and Lakota. Beginning from the east, the Santee (Isanti), or Dakota band, encompasses four subgroups: the Mdewakantonwan, Sisitonwan, Wachpekute, and Wachpetonwan. The Yankton (Ihanktonwan) and Yanktonais (Ihanktonwanna), often referred to as Nakota, meanwhile inhabited a triangular area flanked by the pipestone quarries at the source of the Des Moines River down to the junction of the Big Sioux and Missouri Rivers. Finally, the roaming Lakota, or Tetons, to the west, with their populous Oglala, Brule (or Sičangu), Minniconjou, Oohenopa, Sihasapa, Hunkpapa, and Itazipčo (or Sans Arcs) subgroups, boasted the largest numbers.[4] The Yankton Sioux were the first in the Seven Council Fires to reconcile formally with the U.S. government. In 1858 they settled on their own reservation on the southeastern border of present-day South Dakota, electing not to participate in Sioux conflicts with whites. Even as struggles against intrusions continued, the Yankton consistently supported peace efforts. Nonetheless, they acutely felt the psychological and emotional consequences of the violence surrounding their territory.[5]

By the time of Gertrude's birth, the Sioux had been coping with white encroachment for many decades. Under treaties in 1837 and 1857 the easternmost Dakota had given up considerable lands on both sides of the Mississippi, whereas the Lakota had experienced greater success maintaining territorial integrity. In 1866 Red Cloud and Tasunkakokipapi (both Oglala) led an effective effort to prevent the U.S. Army from building a road through traditional hunting grounds on the Powder River. The resulting Treaty of Fort Laramie (1868) guaranteed the Lakota lands west of the Missouri, including the Paha Sapa, or Black Hills, on a newly established Great Sioux Reservation. The treaty also secured promises of material assistance and declared the Powder River area to the west free from further infringement as "unceded" Indian territory—"so long as the buffalo may range thereon in numbers sufficient to justify the chase."

The situation rapidly changed. In 1874 Lt. Col. George Armstrong Custer led an expedition into the Black Hills, verifying the existence of gold there and precipitating a flood of fifteen thousand white prospectors. Following an army order for all Lakota to retreat to the Great Sioux Reservation,

Sitting Bull (Hunkpapa) and Crazy Horse (Oglala) defied the U.S. military.
On June 25, 1876, Custer and the Seventh Cavalry invaded a large Lakota
and Cheyenne encampment. They were quickly routed in a counterattack
led by Crazy Horse. But the Battle of the Greasy Grass, or Little Big Horn
Creek, was a short-lived victory. The U.S. Army prevailed only months later,
ending both large-scale military conflict in the Northwest and off-reservation
life for the majority of the Sioux. Sitting Bull retreated to Canada with a small
group of his followers, only to return and surrender four years later and, for
a time, join William "Buffalo Bill" Cody's Wild West Show. Crazy Horse was
fatally wounded in captivity when he refused to submit to imprisonment.
In the wake of the war the remaining Sioux leaders, disarmed and under
threat of starvation, signed a settlement with Congress that relinquished
the Black Hills and the right to hunt farther westward.[6]

The loss of the Powder River hunting grounds was in some sense a mere
formality. By the end of the 1870s, the bison that had so long offered sustenance had been mostly wiped out by white hunters in a deliberate attempt
by the U.S. Army to gain control of Indian populations. As one of the archi-
tects of the policy, Gen. Philip Sheridan, wrote, "If I could learn that every
buffalo in the northern herd were killed I would be glad. The destruction of
this herd would do more to keep Indians quiet than anything else that could
happen, except the death of all Indians."[7] By 1910, herds that had once numbered thirty million were reduced to just five hundred.[8] With the buffalo
destroyed, a new era commenced, marked by a different set of challenges
for Indians on reservations. In 1887 the Dawes Severalty Act became law.
Meant to induce a rapid transition from hunting and gathering to an agrar-
ian economy, it partitioned 118 reservations into individual landholdings on
which "competent" Natives could practice farming, assimilate, and eventually become citizens. Instead, the act mainly resulted in the distribution of
"surplus" territory for white settlement and the further loss of the indigenous land base, about 86 out of 138 million acres, by 1934. Worsening matters, at the behest of cattle ranchers and railroad executives, the U.S. government moved to divide the Great Sioux Reservation into smaller units under
the Standing Rock, Cheyenne River, Rosebud, Lower Brule, and Pine Ridge
agencies. The additional infringement left many Sioux longing for a restoration of the past. In the late 1880s the Ghost Dance movement arose, led by a
Paiute messiah named Wovoka. His message of peace promised to join all
Native peoples living and dead in a future of prosperity free from whites,
who would forever disperse as the buffalo they killed returned.[9]

The Ghost Dance spread rapidly among the Sioux, attracting the attention
of an inexperienced agent, Daniel F. Royer, on the Pine Ridge Reservation.[10]

Fearing that he was witnessing the early stages of a violent uprising, Royer appealed for help. When U.S. troops arrived at Pine Ridge and Rosebud in October 1890, more than two thousand Brules and Oglalas congregated and headed north to a plateau in the Badlands called O-ona-gazhee. After the killing of Sitting Bull in a botched arrest attempt by a group of Indian police on December 15, more Hunkpapas, Minniconjous, and Brules followed. One band of 340 led by the Minniconjou Big Foot, under-provisioned and struggling against inclement weather, returned rather than press onward. They were intercepted by the Seventh Cavalry and forced to camp at Wounded Knee Creek. The majority, including women and children, survived only one day longer, perishing in the Wounded Knee massacre on December 29. Though many assembled at O-ona-gazhee had already begun returning to reservation territory, they stopped in protest upon hearing of the massacre. Others soon joined them, expanding their numbers to four thousand, including five hundred Cheyenne. A U.S. Army show of force in the form of five thousand soldiers soon compelled surrender. On January 15, 1891, the group made an orderly march to Pine Ridge, ending Sioux military struggles.[11] Such was the backdrop of Gertrude Simmons's childhood and adolescence.

The Sioux who had resisted returned to an existence of subsistence farming and government rations. This new life was distinguished by undernourishment, material scarcity, and a decline in population. As unwilling wards of an often indifferent government, they faced a society in which many whites held to the refrain "the only good Indian is a dead Indian." Indigenous nations had few allies save Christian peace groups and the Board of Indian Commissioners, created during the Grant administration to curb endemic corruption in the Department of the Interior's Office of Indian Affairs (also called the Bureau of Indian Affairs [BIA], Indian Office, or Indian Bureau). The Indian Rights Association (IRA), the foremost among the Christian peace groups, was founded in Philadelphia in 1882. This largely Quaker organization drew support from smaller evangelical Protestant groups, such as the Women's National Indian Association (1879) and the Boston Indian Citizenship Association (1879).[12] The latter's most famous member, Helen Hunt Jackson, had authored the groundbreaking *A Century of Dishonor* (1881), which exposed the long history of injustices perpetrated by the U.S. government on the Native population. Jackson put forth a radical notion. "The great difficulty with the Indian problem," she wrote, "is not with the Indian, but with the Government and people of the United States."[13] Working in cooperation with the Board of Indian Commissioners and the Office of Indian Affairs, reform groups attempted to ensure humane treatment, publish investigative reports, and organize publicity campaigns designed to highlight the situation of America's autochthonous populations.[14]

Yet the IRA's mission statement—"the complete civilization of the Indians and their admission to citizenship"—contained a crucial implication, predicated on the erasure of Native cultures through a program of assimilation.[15] The IRA lauded the Dawes Act, for instance, for having "thrown wide open the door to Indian citizenship" by attempting to break up communally owned land and make Indians into industrious farmers.[16] Christianization, they held, was synonymous with civilization.[17] Seeing little value in "savage" indigenous ways, the IRA likewise viewed the re-education of children as the crucial salve, a requirement of ascension to a higher plane of existence. On this point, none agreed more with these "Friends of the Indian" than Capt. Richard Henry Pratt, an influential figure who in the late 1870s and 1880s pioneered the concept of off-reservation Indian education.

In 1879, with the aid of government funding, Pratt founded the first off-reservation Indian boarding school in Carlisle, Pennsylvania, under the motto "Kill the Indian, and save the man." Pratt described the assimilationist philosophy behind the Carlisle Indian Industrial School in an 1883 article for the *American Missionary*. "It is plain," he wrote, "that the real hindrance to Indian progress is found in their being kept entirely separated from the other masses of our population . . . made to feel they are a separate people and must remain so forever. . . . To overcome these difficulties the Indian mind and the mind of the public as well as Congress must be educated to grant them the enlarged privileges accorded to other races. The boy will never learn to swim until he goes in the water, and the experiences of industrial life and civilized life through its associations will determine for the Indian and the white the true status."[18]

By his own admission, Pratt had no respect for Native ways of life. As racially enlightened as he was, ethnocentrism informed his work. At Carlisle, Pratt hoped his wards would shed their supposedly inferior cultures, religions, and languages, and become "refined, educated, cultured beings" who would eventually bear the title of American citizen.[19] In an often-repeated analogy Pratt compared his education of Indians to domestication of wild fowl. He claimed he had once enlisted his barnyard hen to tend a nest of wild turkey eggs. When hatched, the young chicks were smoothly integrated into farm living and never escaped back into the wild. The experiment proved that any feral animal "only need[ed] the environment and kind treatment of domestic life to become a very part of it."[20]

Though Pratt's concept of the eastern boarding school was soon largely replaced by less costly, on-reservation schooling, institutions like Carlisle and the Haskell Institute in Kansas (founded 1884) remained models. A system of government-supported schools was created across the United States in the waning years of the nineteenth century. Educational curricula promoted Christianity and the eradication, for ostensibly benevolent purposes, of Native civilizations.[21] As touted by Yankton Reservation agent J. F. Kinney in 1887, "Education cuts the cord which binds [Indians] to pagan life, places the Bible in their hands, and substitutes the true God for the false one. Christianity in place of idolatry, civilization in place of superstition, morality in place of vice, cleanliness in place of filth, industry in place of idleness, self-respect in place of servility, and, in a word, humanity in place of abject degradation."[22] Pratt was inclined to more diplomatic expressions, such as the need to recognize "the unity of the human race" within "our national family."[23] Nevertheless, the Indian schools project coupled with the Euro-American belief in corporal punishment often produced infelicitous consequences.

Many of the Indian students who attended boarding schools suffered greatly. Upon their arrival, school officials subjected children to an instant and jarring immersion into white culture and language. At many institutions the children's hair was shorn, their traditional garb burned, and before-and-after pictures taken to document the transformation. School authorities arbitrarily changed students' names and those who persisted in speaking Native tongues were sometimes beaten. Indian boarding schools generally featured strict military-style discipline, regimens determined by the clock (an entirely useless, foreign apparatus to Indians), and unpaid outwork in local communities.[24] Homesickness, malnutrition, poor living conditions, and lack of immunity to European diseases caused frequent premature deaths. Of the seventy-three children taken from the Shoshone and Arapaho Nations between 1881 and 1884, twenty-six survived their schooling.[25] The compulsory indoctrination into white culture, meanwhile, produced a generation of graduates who experienced a complex and harrowing limbo of disrupted identity. One such person was Gertrude Simmons.

Gertrude was about eight years old when, evidently tempted by missionaries' stories of boundless apple orchards and an exciting train ride, she left her mother's tepee by the Missouri River for White's Manual Labor Institute, a Quaker-run boarding school in Wabash, Indiana.[26] For Gertrude this event began a long course of white schooling (and resultant cultural alienation) that ended with two years of study at another Quaker institution, Earlham College in Richmond, Indiana. As a freshman student, Simmons was chosen to represent Earlham at the State Competition for College Orators, where she delivered "Side by Side"—the speech that commences this biography. The oration serves as a highly suitable introduction to the literary and political works of Zitkala-Ša (pronounced Zit-KAH-la-shah), meaning "Red Bird" in the Lakota dialect of the Siouan language. Simmons took the name around 1898, making for some uncertainty about what to call her in this biography. With the exception of an approximately two-year period (1900–1902), Simmons went by Gertrude or Gertie. After she married in 1902, Simmons took her husband's surname, Bonnin, but continued to use Zitkala-Ša for most of her publications and certain public appearances.[27] The majority of printed material identifies her as Zitkala-Ša, the name that reflects her Sioux heritage.[28] This book stays within the Zitkala-Ša tradition, though prior to 1900 it refers to her as either Gertrude or Simmons, in order to reflect her age.

The name Zitkala-Ša first came to prominence with a series of semiautobiographical exposés on Indian boarding schools for the *Atlantic Monthly* in 1900. A little more than two years earlier, Simmons had secured a post at the Carlisle Indian Industrial School after withdrawing from Earlham, in part due to illness and in part to a need to support herself.[29] Her experience in Pennsylvania swiftly convinced her of the wrongness of Pratt's approach and the hollowness of its promise. In 1899 Simmons left for Boston to study violin. There she published her three-part literary rejoinder to the white world and Indian education: "Impressions of an Indian Childhood," "The School Days of an Indian Girl," and "An Indian Teacher among Indians." In these stories—highly critical of the Christian assimilationist project, White's Institute, Carlisle, and by implication groups such as the Indian Rights Association—Simmons lamented the cultural alienation forced upon her and other boarding school pupils. Though highly sentimental by modern standards, the *Atlantic Monthly* series quickly made Simmons, or Zitkala-Ša, the toast of Boston literary society but an enemy of Pratt's. Defying criticism from the Carlisle press, she continued to publish politically oriented stories and critical statements in the *Atlantic Monthly, Harper's Monthly,* and *Everybody's Magazine*. The pieces helped Zitkala-Ša find an audience for her compilation of traditional Sioux tales, *Old Indian Legends,* published by Boston's Ginn & Company in 1901. As a whole, her early works constituted a critique that overturned white discourses of civilization, gender, and religion to reveal the hypocrisy of the Euro-American perspective on Native peoples.

For Zitkala-Ša words were not enough. In the early 1900s she rejected her burgeoning career in Boston for a return to Yankton, where she hoped to directly engage the issues raised in her writings. She also broke with her fiancé, the illustrious Yavapai physician and activist Dr. Carlos Montezuma, in part over his staunchly assimilationist views. Instead, she married another Yankton, Raymond Telephause Bonnin, an Indian Bureau employee with greater respect for traditional culture. In 1902, Bonnin's work took the couple to the Uintah and Ouray Reservation (Commonly called the Uintah Reservation) in Utah, home to the Northern Ute Nation. There, Zitkala-Ša gave birth to her first and only child, Raymond Ohiya Bonnin. At Uintah, the Bonnins became extremely frustrated attempting to assist the Ute community within a context of demoralization and corruption. Zitkala-Ša did not actively pursue writing projects, but eventually found expression through an artistic collaboration with a Mormon music teacher, William Hanson. Together they composed *The Sun Dance Opera* (1913), a meld of Sioux melodies and western musical forms based on the Plains Indians' most significant religious ceremony, the Sun Dance. During this period Zitkala-Ša's religious life took another direction. After publicly condemning Christianity in the early 1900s, she made a surprising conversion to Catholicism after spending the winter of 1909–10 at the Standing Rock Sioux Reservation. In Utah, she also began an anti-peyote campaign in reaction to peyote's growing popularity among the Utes. Discounting any religious uses for what she considered a dangerous drug that led to moral degradation, Zitkala-Ša lectured to women's groups and temperance associations across the Midwest, hoping to achieve statewide bans.

The Bonnins' lives changed dramatically after Zitkala-Ša joined the Society of American Indians (SAI) in 1914. The organization, formed in 1911 by progressive Indians on a racially conscious self-help platform, allowed Zitkala-Ša to reemerge into the vanguard of Indian activism as a community center organizer, as SAI secretary-treasurer, and as writer and editor for the *American Indian Magazine* (*AIM*). In order to further her work, she and Bonnin moved to Washington, D.C., in 1917. There Zitkala-Ša expanded her anti-peyote crusade at the federal level by allying herself with Pratt and the IRA (the very people she had disparaged in the early 1900s) and sparring with the eminent pro-peyote ethnologist James Mooney before a congressional subcommittee. Other causes also captured her interest. In the late 1910s, Zitkala-Ša vociferously advocated for the extension of citizenship to Native peoples by promoting Indian participation in World War I. Zitkala-Ša left the SAI in 1919 after the peyote issue split the membership. She nonetheless continued her citizenship crusade with the support of the nondenominational Christian General Federation of Women's Clubs (GFWC), a nationwide association founded in 1892 via the consolidation of two suffrage groups. At GFWC gatherings Zitkala-Ša often performed and lectured in buckskin dresses, while promoting the notion that she was the granddaughter of Sitting Bull in order to gain media attention.

In 1921 Zitkala-Ša published *American Indian Stories* and *Americanize the First American: A Plan of Regeneration*. The first indicted white society for its treatment of Native peoples; the second outlined a map for tribal self-determination within the United States. Soon thereafter with the support of the GFWC and John Collier's American Indian Defense Association (AIDA), Zitkala-Ša investigated numerous crimes, including murder, carried out against Oklahoma's Five Civilized Tribes by politicians, judges, and businessmen seeking to profit from oil-rich Indian lands. The resulting pamphlet, *Oklahoma's Poor Rich Indians* (1924), is credited with helping to spur the Meriam Report (1928), whose recommendations led to substantial reforms within federal Indian policy in the 1930s. In 1926, Zitkala-Ša and her husband founded the National Council of American Indians (NCAI). The organization eventually represented numerous nations, including the Sioux, Apache, Cheyenne, Ute, Navajo, and Pueblo, in efforts to secure legal protections that had long been denied and create an inclusive, intertribal political movement that could achieve democratic sovereignty within the United States. During the NCAI's existence it was the only Native-run lobbying group in the United States. When Zitkala-Ša died in 1938, the NCAI died as well.[30]

Notwithstanding her once high profile, Zitkala-Ša spent her last years depressed and uncertain if she had made any beneficial impact. In death she was quickly forgotten and remained so for the following half century. Only in the mid-1980s were *Old Indian Legends* and *American Indian Stories* reissued, generating renewed scholarly interest in her work.[31] Early criticism focused on the supposedly "liminal" character of Zitkala-Ša's life and writing. She was declared a "cultural ghost" who fatefully betrayed her birth culture and lived an endlessly "schizophrenic" existence, too influenced by her white education to present a consistent critique of white society or even to know her place in the world.[32] During the late 1980s, into the 1990s and even the first decade of the twenty-first century, other scholars put forward critical, assimilationist interpretations of Zitkala-Ša. Here she was depicted as "selling out" by cooperating with figures such Pratt, using her "exotic" Indian identity to promote causes among white female patrons, practicing Christianity, fighting against peyote, and attacking Mooney (the proclaimed "champion of religious freedom").[33] By the late 1990s, however, new scholars had begun to counter liminal and assimilationist analyses with bicultural readings of Zitkala-Ša's work. They generally argued that her Yankton communal values and knowledge of the white world enabled Zitkala-Ša to form a compelling critique of American society that asserted the validity of her Sioux heritage.[34]

It is unsurprising that Zitkala-Ša's work has provoked such differing readings. Her task was a complex negotiation, her historical circumstances limiting. As an indigenous woman in early twentieth-century America, Zitkala-Ša was bound by political, racial, gender, ideological, and discursive restrictions that, in many ways, she managed to overcome. She faced objectification within white society as an exotic female specimen of a supposedly dying race, a preconception she sometimes used to her advantage. Though disenfranchised for much of her life, she achieved political influence through white women's groups that, at her urging, sought to guard the interests of Native peoples. On her own, she attempted to organize indigenous women for the purposes of community self-help. Much of Zitkala-Ša's work as a public intellectual also occurred at a specific time, the Progressive era, when ideas of almost ineluctable societal advancement through organization, problem-solving, anti-corruption reforms, and prohibition prevailed. Zitkala-Ša and many of the early twentieth-century Native rights activists who founded the SAI, such as Montezuma, Charles Alexander Eastman (Santee), and Arthur C. Parker (Seneca), felt that the path to recognition depended on demonstrating that indigenous peoples could thrive in American society, if given a chance. For these "Red Progressives" determined to ameliorate conditions, part of this project meant at times showing how Indians could move "forward" by learning English and becoming American citizens. Indians could thus prove that they were the equal of whites in intelligence, ability, virtue, patriotism, and during World War I, battle.[35] Criticism of U.S. society, meanwhile, often had to be couched in mollifying terms to sway, rather than offend, white audiences.[36] Because Zitkala-Ša's activism often fell within these confines, the ensuing assimilationist interpretations are understandable.

Yet considering the remarkable dedication of the Red Progressives, Zitkala-Ša foremost among them, any blanket assimilationist classification, with all its negative connotations, does not offer a fruitful approach.[37] Nuance is vital. Zitkala-Ša's conception of the Indian's role in American society had at its heart a necessary and deep connection to indigenous identity—and a deeply critical view of white society. Her concern, especially in the 1920s and 1930s, was, as she put it, "regenerating" her peoples.[38] This project was neither an attempt at cultural absorption nor merely an assertion of the validity of Sioux heritage. Instead, Zitkala-Ša's activism was most often a declaration of supremacy and demand for autonomy.[39] Throughout her work it is possible to discern within the intermittent expressions of liminality, Victorian moral control, and conciliatory gestures to white discourses, the tenets of a sustained ideology of Native self-determination.

After Wounded Knee there was little chance for a restoration of traditional ways. The military defense that had temporarily sustained sovereignty was no longer an option for the Sioux. Zitkala-Ša was one of a new generation of Sioux resistance fighters who sought protections using the tools that her historical period offered. Through writing, rhetoric, organization, lobbying, and activism, she ably formulated a response to white rule very similar to that of subsequent generations. During the Red Power era of the early 1970s, the American Indian Movement (AIM) and intellectuals such as the Yankton writer and activist Vine Deloria, Jr., famously trumpeted a similar platform, forcefully criticizing U.S. society and government, and making demands that had at their heart a call for Indian cultural renewal and political independence. Zitkala-Ša's positions, though often misunderstood and derided, were little different. This fact is particularly evident in two of her unpublished writings, "The Sioux Claims" and "Our Sioux People" (1923). Ultimately, Zitkala-Ša's proto–Red Power grand vision encompassed abolition of the Indian Bureau; conservation of Native land bases; equality and at times superiority of indigenous cultures versus Euro-American culture; preservation of distinct values, virtues, and beliefs; self-defense through U.S. citizenship and Constitutional rights; democratic tribal self-determination on an equal footing with the federal government within the United States; grassroots organization; and an intertribal identity for those Zitkala-Ša termed "the First Americans."[40] These stances define Zitkala-Ša's life and legacy. She was, as this biography argues, a forerunner of Red Power.[41]

CHAPTER 1

THE SCHOOL DAYS OF AN INDIAN GIRL

Gertrude was the last child of Taté I Yóhin Win (Reaches for the Wind, or Every Wind), a Yankton woman likely born sometime between the mid-1820s and 1830. In 1830, the Yankton began ceding their territory, which would be reduced by millions of acres over the subsequent two-and-a-half decades. As a result, Taté I Yóhin Win's life became one of transition and hardship. Her first marriage was to a French-Canadian fur trader named Pierre St. Pierre. The union produced two surviving children—sons Henry, born around 1849, and Peter, born approximately four years later—and perhaps other children who did not survive infancy. The St. Pierre family resided at the confluence of the Missouri and Big Sioux Rivers, where other French traders had settled with their Yankton brides. St. Pierre, who was likely older than his young wife, died in 1853, leaving his twenty-something widow and sons with no means of support. In the wake of this misfortune, firstborn Henry was taken in by white settlers, while Peter, just a baby, found refuge with Taté I Yóhin Win at her brother's camp.[1]

For the next five years Taté I Yóhin Win remained unmarried. She took a new husband in 1858, the same year as another turning point in Yankton history.[2] That year, her tribespeople signed a treaty with the U.S. government giving up 11.5 million acres of land in exchange for a 430,000-acre reserve, though they retained access to the pipestone quarries (see prologue).[3] Taté I Yóhin Win's second husband, an Anglo named John Haysting Simmons, perhaps compared poorly with St. Pierre. Simmons eked out a living as a manual laborer and occasionally drank to excess. Nonetheless,

Taté I Yóhin Win took the name Ellen Simmons and kept it to the end of her life. This second marriage was longer-lasting than the first. Over sixteen years the couple produced several offspring, two of whom survived: a boy named David, born around 1866, and a girl born some time after. What role Peter St. Pierre played in the family is unknown. Peter was about twenty when John Simmons died in 1874, leaving Ellen once more to appeal to her family for assistance. Her brother, now significantly older, could offer little help. Unable to survive by hunting game, he, his family, Ellen, and her two youngest children headed on foot to the Yankton Agency in Greenwood, Dakota Territory, to apply for U.S. government rations.[4] They arrived there in 1874.[5]

Once camped, Ellen Simmons's small daughter, exhausted from the four-day journey, became ill and died. Shortly after this all-too-common tragedy, Ellen married a Frenchman named Felker, described as a "worthless fellow" by his contemporaries.[6] This assessment was likely accurate. Simmons soon dismissed Felker after he beat David—as the Sioux deemed corporal punishment of children inexcusable—but the brief marriage resulted in another pregnancy.[7] Ellen gave birth to a girl in the winter of 1875–76. The birth date recorded in the notoriously unreliable Yankton census was February 22, though the year of birth varies.[8] It is unclear whether Felker stayed (or even lived) long enough to witness his daughter's arrival. Regardless, he had no part in raising her. Ellen quickly erased Felker's faint memory by bestowing the surname Simmons on her child, Gertrude.[9]

With the departure of Felker, Gertrude's childhood became female-dominated. Even the brother who had traveled to Greenwood with Ellen Simmons in 1874 seems to have perished before or shortly after Gertrude's birth, leaving a widow and one daughter.[10] Gertrude's half-brother David, meanwhile, spent just two years or so near Greenwood before leaving for boarding school. In 1877, he enrolled in the Santee Normal Training School, thirty miles away in neighboring Nebraska.[11] Founded by Alfred L. Riggs and dedicated to the education of the Sioux, Santee was a leading institution among missionary schools.[12] In 1878, around age twelve, David left again, this time for a three-year course of study at the Hampton Institute in Virginia, an institution established for freed slaves after the Civil War. David was among the first group of American Indians to study there.[13]

Despite no immediate fraternal or paternal presence, Gertrude thrived. Yankton elders provided a nurturing, communal atmosphere, as did Gertrude's aunt and older cousin. Though dependent on rations, these women and Ellen Simmons led a basically traditional lifestyle that Gertrude would later characterize as idyllic.[14] At age six, not long after David had returned from Hampton, Gertrude began attending a Presbyterian bilingual school at the Yankton Agency.[15] Two years later she made her own trip east. As she told the story later, Gertrude was seven when missionaries appeared at Yankton looking to recruit pupils for White's Manual Labor Institute, a Quaker-run boarding school in Wabash, Indiana. Her curiosity roused by their stories of boundless apple orchards and an exciting train ride, Gertrude gladly agreed to leave her mother's tepee on the banks of the Missouri.[16] Though Ellen Simmons had allowed her son David to leave for Hampton and had likely converted to Christianity by this point, she had deep reservations about sending her last-born away.[17] For obvious historical reasons Ellen generally abhorred and distrusted whites; yet her family's living situation offered few other options. The Sioux means of sustenance had been obliterated along with the buffalo herds, and those living at Yankton were largely confined. Government agents often pressured parents to give up their children to eastern boarding schools, withholding rations and using soldiers for purposes of intimidation.[18] Ellen Simmons, aware that the future looked increasingly dismal, decided to relinquish her daughter temporarily in the hope that it would enable the girl's survival. By marking an "X" on consent papers furnished by the Quaker missionaries, Ellen signed away the right to raise her daughter for the next three years.[19]

When Gertrude left for Indiana, seven hundred miles from home, she had no conception of what awaited her. Her destination, White's Institute, had been founded as an orphanage for children of both whites and Miami Indians, whose tribe had originally occupied the area around present-day Indiana and parts of Michigan and Ohio. Seeking financial stability during one of the economic recessions that plagued nineteenth-century America, the institute opened an Indian school in 1883, gaining it a federal subsidy of $167 for each pupil boarded. Instruction began with twenty-three students, the majority recruited from Yankton and Pine Ridge.[20] Gertrude arrived in February 1884, expecting to exist happily under "a sky of rosy apples."[21] Instead, the foreign environment and immediate homesickness reduced her to tears.[22] The grounds at White's did in fact contain 150 apple trees, but a year after Gertrude arrived the orchard began to die off.[23]

The semiautobiographical piece Gertrude later wrote for the *Atlantic Monthly* depicted White's unfavorably. She condemned the school's "iron routine" punctuated by random beatings. She described the violent cutting of her hair and how the faculty inspired fear of the devil in religion class. Most wrenching was the death of a friend, one of two girls from Gertrude's class who perished from the neglect inherent in the Quaker "civilizing machine."[24] Unsanitary conditions and a lack of indoor plumbing often

Gertrude Simmons in a group photo with other pupils at the Santee Normal Training School, Nebraska, ca. 1890. Gertrude is standing in the back row, third from the right. (Courtesy of the Center for Western Studies, Augustana College, Sioux Falls, SD)

resulted in cases of trachoma, a potentially blinding eye disease, while malnutrition also contributed to illnesses.[25] White's, unlike some other government-funded schools, was probably not an entirely nightmarish place, but it demanded levels of organization and discipline that Indian students found pointless. The children rose early in the morning to a day dominated by roll calls, ringing bells, and a tight schedule of instruction, housecleaning, and farmwork.[26] This government-mandated curriculum was designed to produce male farmers and female homemakers skilled in the domestic arts. Meanwhile, the Quaker faculty actively sought to convert the students to Christianity and stamp out Native religious beliefs in order to "raise the religious character of the pupils to a higher standard."[27] This ethnocentrism permeated all school instruction. Gertrude heard much about the supposed superiority of white civilization over Indian ways.

After three years at White's, eleven-year-old Gertrude finished her course of study. According to her later account, upon returning to Yankton in early March 1887, she resumed her old ways and style of dress.[28] Gertrude continued her studies at the Presbyterian school for the next year and a half, then began boarding at the Santee Normal Training School in 1889, but returned home less than a year later.[29] Now a teenager, Gertrude found it increasingly difficult to cope with life at Yankton. The years divided among her birthplace, Wabash, and Nebraska, and the clash between white schooling and long-established Sioux ways had taken a toll. Gertrude, caught between old and new, domestic and foreign, began to feel an alienation from her surroundings that strained her relationship with her mother. Ellen Simmons could not offer comfort to a daughter who felt she could not find a place at Yankton.[30] Seeking escape, Gertrude left for White's again in December 1890—the same month as Sitting Bull's killing and the Wounded Knee massacre.[31] By then White's boarding school had grown into what the local paper called "the most important and interesting enterprise in Wabash County."[32] During Gertrude's second stay she proved an exceptionally talented student, excelling in writing, oration, and music. Her abilities in voice, violin, and piano were likely discovered by a local Quaker woman, Susan B. Unthank, and fostered by private study. Gertrude also made friends. In 1891 a fifteen-year-old Lakota named Thomas Marshall enrolled at White's. Seven years later he would propose to Gertrude. At the start of 1893 school officials sent Gertrude on a recruiting mission to the Yankton and Pine Ridge Reservations, where she managed to sign up twenty-nine new students. There is no record of how she felt about removing them from their parents. The following year, 1894, a fourteen-year-old Yankton boy named Raymond Telephause Bonnin arrived at White's, perhaps as a result of Gertrude's recruitment efforts.[33] Raymond, too, would later propose to Gertrude.

In her last year at White's, Gertrude's duties widened. The school had become insolvent, so much of the staff was let go. Gertrude and her friend Thomas Marshall, now age nineteen, stepped in to teach, care for the younger pupils, and tend to the bookkeeping. In June 1895, as her crowning achievement at White's, Gertrude gave a stirring commencement speech entitled "The Progress of Women." Her declaration of the necessity of granting equal rights to women reflected the belief in female equality that had long marked Quakerism. Gertrude exhorted, "half of humanity cannot rise while the other half is in subjugation." The *Wabash Plain Dealer* lauded her oration as a "masterpiece, never surpassed in eloquence or literary perfection by any girl in the country."[34] Soon after Gertrude graduated, White's liquidated its Indian school.[35] Meanwhile, Gertrude was soon set to enter another Quaker institution, Earlham College, in Richmond, Indiana. Her mother, however, rejected the idea, pressuring her daughter to return home and make a life at Yankton.[36] Gertrude neither obeyed nor even went back for a short visit. Instead, she spent the summer with the Unthanks while teaching music to earn money. The Unthanks were educated music lovers and evidently quite prosperous. They gave Gertrude much support. She addressed them affectionately as "Aunt Sue" and "Uncle Joe."[37]

Miss Simmons arrived at Earlham College in the autumn of 1895, the sole Indian student on a campus with a little less than five hundred co-eds. Though this fact might have made matters uncomfortable at times, Simmons was in little danger of being ostracized. Native and black students had studied at Earlham before. The college, especially for its time, boasted a remarkably tolerant atmosphere rooted in a perceived history of friendship between Quakers and Native peoples. Also noteworthy was Earlham's attitude toward co-education. Male and female students, the vast majority coming from the educated middle classes, studied much the same curriculum, ate together, and even inhabited the same dormitory—albeit in separate, single rooms. This is not to suggest any relaxed, casual mingling between the sexes, however. Students were expected to conduct themselves with stiff formality and address one another as Mister or Miss. Yet Earlham had welcome advantages. The campus featured indoor plumbing, quality food, and what was likely an unprecedented degree of privacy for Simmons. At Earlham she had an expense account. Who furnished the funds is unknown, but perhaps it was the Unthanks.[38] The increased comfort allowed Simmons to concentrate on her studies, which included courses in subjects from English and elocution to biology, zoology, Greek, and Latin. Simmons became almost a straight-A student the first trimester, excelling in English subjects but receiving a B in biology.[39] For her thesis, Simmons planned to translate a series of traditional Sioux stories into Latin. In her spare time, she took up tennis.[40]

Miss Simmons was a very sensitive young woman with a very slim figure. A fellow student, Chalmers Hadley, recalled that she was as "slender as Minnehaha," in a morbid reference to Longfellow's starving heroine in the epic poem *The Song of Hiawatha* (1855). Hadley also remembered that Simmons did her best not to disturb the "fluffy dandelion heads which she did not wish to injure" as she walked across campus. Her sensitivity to nature extended to what other Earlham students probably regarded as pests. In the spring and autumn evenings Simmons, rather than studying, "sat in darkness to protect the moths, which fluttered through the open windows, from burning their wings in the lighted gas jet."[41] Simmons later depicted her college years as lonely, trying, and marked with remorse over disobeying her mother. She wrote that when in her solitary room she spent most of her time weaving, close to tears, regretful at not returning home. She also

lamented the "scornful and yet curious eyes of the students" and her decision to stay on "among a cold race whose hearts were frozen hard with
prejudice."[42] Hadley recollected that Simmons's "relations with other students were pleasant but somewhat distant."[43]

A different picture emerges from the pages of the college newspaper,
the *Earlhamite*. While Simmons likely felt a certain isolation on campus, on
paper she was an extremely active and popular student. Judging from the
Earlhamite, the sum of her activities must have left little time for weaving.
Shortly after arriving, Simmons joined the G Clef music club and began ap-
pearing in school recitals, on and off campus. Her performances included
the piano solo *Rondeau Brillant*, by Weber, and the vocal duet "Drift, My
Bark." She also became a member of the Phoenix Society, a literary club at
whose meetings she played piano. The only serious trouble Simmons seems
to have encountered in her first semester was related to her eyesight. In December the *Earlhamite* mentioned that she and another student had made a
trip to Cincinnati "to have their eyes treated."[44] Otherwise, Simmons was,
seemingly, an immediate and remarkable success. In the early winter of 1896
she entered Earlham's oratory contest with the women's rights speech delivered at White's, retitled "Side by Side." Though a female freshman competing against male sophomores, juniors, and seniors, Simmons decisively
bested her opponents. The panel of judges, made up of Earlham alumni,
awarded her 512 points (eighteen more than the second-place finisher) on
the basis of thought, composition, and delivery. The February *Earlhamite*
commented: "Her delivery was pleasing, and her voice, though not strong,
was clear and distinct." Simmons's fellow freshmen, as an expression of
pride in her accomplishment, hosted a reception for her following the win.
Meanwhile, the senior class, stunned at their loss, "retired to the library . . .
and consoled themselves with oranges."[45]

Thanks to her victory, Simmons was chosen to represent Earlham at the
statewide oratory competition in March. Held in one of Indianapolis's
grandest structures, the English Opera House and Hotel, the annual contest presented a much bigger challenge. Simmons also had a legacy to protect. A female senior had represented the college the year before, winning
first place.[46] Nevertheless, Simmons decided to take a huge risk. Perhaps
believing she had little chance of winning, or perhaps having long wres-
tled with feelings that she felt compelled to express, Simmons rewrote
"Side by Side" (the speech that begins this book) into a forceful argument
for Indian equality.[47] She had witnessed the effects of American expansionism. Her life till then had been one of transition and cultural dislocation.
She would now reveal in public the profound anger that she had suppressed

within her for years, and defend her people against a society that had killed them and expropriated their land in the name of God and civilization.

Even though by now she was used to public speaking, the scene that awaited Simmons in Indianapolis must have been intimidating. Accompanied by more than one hundred Earlhamites, the young woman left on the morning of Friday, March 13, for the seventy-three-mile train ride. When she and her companions reached the city, they found the streets overflowing with students from five rival colleges—DePauw, Hanover, Franklin, Butler, and Wabash—all proudly displaying their school colors. The competition took place that evening in a hall packed with more than a thousand rowdy spectators. Though scheduled to start at 8:00 P.M., the proceedings were delayed when a fight broke out between Earlham and Butler students. Butler students, occupying the top balconies, had strung two lines high across the opera house. On one they attached a large blue-and-white umbrella, which they "continually raised and lowered over the heads of the other delegations" to cause irritation. On the other wire they began to hang banners. The first, innocuously, declared "Butler on Top." The second mocked DePauw, the perennial favorite, with the figure of a man representing "conceit." The third—directed right at Simmons—depicted "an overdrawn caricature" of an Indian "squaw," captioned with the word "Humility." Earlham's delegation was seated in the left orchestra. When some Butler boys momentarily left their post, a DePauw student sneaked in and cut the line suspending the umbrella. As it fell to the floor, Earlham's loyal attendees pounced, ripping it to shreds. Butler responded with a raid on the orchestra. The ensuing scuffle had to be broken up by two policemen. The tension-filled competition finally got underway at quarter to nine.[48]

According to Simmons's account, she entered after the Butler-Earlham tussle and was unaware of the banner ridiculing her.[49] News reports indicate that she took a seat in the front row with the other contestants, all of whom faced the stage for the duration of the contest. The six judges seated nearby were formidable. They had traveled in pairs to Indianapolis from Harvard, Yale, and Vanderbilt. Five speakers preceded Simmons, each developing popular themes of Christian virtue and American expansion, democracy, and progress. "Christianity Reasonable" denounced the scientific, abstract notion of God in favor of "the person of Christ." The patriotic, crowd-pleasing "Indiana; a Century of Progress" closed with a shameless proclamation: "The highest test of a country is the character of its men, and the typical American is found, not in the East or South, but here, in grand and glorious Indiana!" One oration lauded the "new divine right" of American democracy. Another extolled the influence of Christianity in American governance.

When the penultimate speaker took the stage, his "forced pronunciation" and incoherent ramblings wearied the crowd, who grew increasingly restless and distracted as the beleaguered orator struggled to finish.[50] It was then, in that moment of frayed concentration and exhausted patience, that Gertrude Simmons, a small, black-haired figure, stood up to take her turn. Throughout the evening she had sat uncomfortably. Many present had "gazed upon [her] with curiosity"—perhaps a euphemistic description of racist heckling. As she walked up to the podium, the response from the audience was noticeably cooler than for the other contestants.[51]

Despite all the distractions, when Simmons commenced her opening ode to the "marvelous progress" of the United States, very quickly "the audience was all attention."[52] Her speech's tone perfectly matched that of her competitors; her voice was small, but her delivery captivating. How would her listeners react when the oration turned confrontational? Simmons stood before a thousand white Americans, speaking of life before European contact, then pointedly illustrating the cruel "invasion" that had come from overseas. She described the utter devastation of Native families, societies, and civilizations; the patriotic justification for the Red Man's retaliation; and his status as the land's "rightful owner." She described the horror of American slavery, Christianity's history of murder and torture, and the willful hypocrisy directed at victims of white oppression. She asked the wardens of religion and civilization why they had attacked, instead of aided, Indian peoples, and whether more violence was all that would follow. There, before the audience, she begged God in heaven to come to the rescue of her race.[53] The audience sat hushed and unprotesting as she rigorously overturned every prevailing national narrative of America. Their attention, in fact, only heightened. As Simmons concluded with her call for reconciliation, applause began, swelling gradually into a "tumultuous" ovation.[54] One judge was observed drying tears from his eyes. After several moments of silence, he announced, "When it comes to oratory, I place the Indian girl far above the college boys every time."[55]

It was during this burst of appreciation that Simmons looked up to see what had been hanging above the opera house throughout the evening: the "squaw" banner. Waiting for the judges' decision while the white sheet dangled "insolently in the air," she seethed inwardly at the show of intolerance.[56] Her forbearance was rewarded when she won second place.[57] A judge from the South, outraged at "Side by Side's" critical allusion to slavery, prevented Simmons from taking first by scoring her dead last in the "thought" category.[58] Contemporary accounts, however, declared Simmons the true victor. The *Indianapolis News* praised her "power as an orator" and stated that she had won the "vote of the hearts of the hearers." The *Earlhamite* also noted, "The tumultuous applause which burst from the audience as [Simmons] closed, showed she had won their hearts."[59] The audience had listened and cheered. But had they understood? What had they been willing to hear?

Full reprints of "Side by Side" appeared in the *Earlhamite* and in the Santee School newspaper, the *Word Carrier*. Yet the speech's critique of white civilization was mostly ignored. Larger papers covering the oratorical contest, the *Indianapolis News* and *Indianapolis Journal*, chose to dwell on the aesthetic aspects of Simmons's performance. Purposefully or not, they misrepresented her central points. In "Cheers for the Indian Maiden" the *News* highlighted Simmons's physical features, specifically how her countenance "showed in delicate but firm lines the cut of the Indian face" and her "well-shaped" hands displayed a "deep copper color." The paper also reported that "the slight, dark-skinned girl" kept her audience rapt: "Her voice was clear and sweet; her language was that of a cultivated young woman, and her pronunciation was without a trace of a tongue unfamiliar with English. Her manner was real, womanly and refined." The *News* summarized the content of "Side by Side" more or less faithfully, white brutality included, while simultaneously describing Indians as lacking "the advantages of civilization and Christian teaching." The reporter noted that "[Simmons] spoke effectively of the cruelty of the Indian in the forests of America at the very time that witches were being burnt at Salem." Ultimately, "Side by Side" was cast as a paean to the benefits that had "resulted from a Christian spirit toward the Indian."[60]

The *Journal*'s review was much the same. It constantly returned to the subject of Simmons's physical attributes, labeling her "the pretty young Indian woman" who appeared "much better looking than the pictures of the average Indian." The paper praised her voice as "wonderfully pleasing, being musical." As to the "dramatic" effect of "Side by Side," Simmons's "pleading for her people" was put down to "excellent elocutionary training"—to be viewed as a performance rather than a legitimate call for Native rights.[61] These types of generally obtuse objectifications of Simmons as an exotic curiosity would continue throughout her life.

Even so, Simmons's success at the Indianapolis college oratory contest was something to savor. Earlham's oratory coach, Edwin. P. Trueblood, greeted Simmons at the Richmond train station on her return. She stepped into a specially prepared, horse-drawn carriage "brilliant with college colors" and escorted by "mounted attendants." At Earlham, the student body greeted Simmons with cheers at the campus gates, which had been decorated in her honor. Her fellow Earlhamites led her into the students' parlor, where, later that day, she was officially praised at a special reception. A poem describing her experience in Indianapolis was read, while partygoers passed around an upside-down umbrella filled with candies. The college president sent a congratulatory telegram. At the evening's end, "Miss Simmons expressed her appreciation of all that had been done, and of the kindly feeling which had been shown." Everyone present voiced their affection with "an Indian yell expressive of victory" that they had learned for the competition.[62]

Simmons had achieved major recognition. Shortly thereafter, however, she began to show signs of serious exhaustion. Perhaps the physical collapse was caused by the draining excitement of the oratory win or the psychological stress arising from her divided loyalties between worlds at this time. Too unwell to remain on campus, she was sent to the home of a local family to convalesce. The *Earlhamite* reported in April 1896: "Miss Gertrude Simmons spent the last week of the term at Knightstown, resting from the excitement and anxiety incident to the contest. Miss Simmons worked faithfully and well for her college, and she certainly deserved the little respite from college duties."[63] In May, Simmons returned to campus to help found *Anpao*, a student magazine.[64] When the summer came, she traveled back to Wabash, presumably to stay once again with the Unthanks.[65] She returned in the fall but did poorly in the first trimester, earning an A in Latin and Cs in two other courses. She rebounded in the second term, receiving four As, but in her third term Simmons seems to have received credit for only one class.[66] In January 1897, the *Earlhamite* published one of her poems, "A Ballad," written on an indigenous theme.[67] No other information on her activities appeared. Simmons's health evidently remained frail. For the remainder of her life she would experience periods of illness with lung infections, fatigue, and stomach illnesses.[68]

The extended bout of sickness ended Simmons's college career after her sixth trimester. A desire, or perhaps a need, to support herself financially also played a role.[69] Ashamed to return to Yankton for fear of her mother's rebukes, she resolved to direct her talents toward Indian education.[70] In 1897, at age twenty-one, Miss Simmons secured a position at Richard Henry Pratt's Carlisle Indian Industrial School in Pennsylvania.[71] In the heat of the Indiana summer she boarded another eastbound train.

CHAPTER 2

CARLISLE AND THE
ATLANTIC MONTHLY

When Simmons began her journey to eastern Pennsylvania in the summer of 1897, Carlisle, her destination, had been in operation for eighteen years and was the most famous Indian boarding school in the country. Its founder, Richard Henry Pratt, promoted his institution as a beacon of hope for America's indigenous populations. Born in Rushford, New York, in 1840, and raised in Logansport, Indiana, Pratt experienced a carefree childhood until the sudden murder of his father forced the then thirteen-year-old to support the family with a string of menial jobs. Pratt joined the Union Army in 1861. When the Civil War ended, he returned home to settle down. But a quiet life with his new wife was not for him. In 1867 he accepted a commission as second lieutenant in the Tenth U.S. Cavalry, an African American unit. In 1875, Pratt found himself guarding Indian prisoners of war at a St. Augustine, Florida, army fort.[1] With the aid of two teachers from New England, he developed a course of education designed to inculcate in them the rudiments of white civilization. Persuaded by the prisoners' progress that indigenous peoples were—somewhere deep inside—like whites, Pratt sought to continue and expand his program nationwide. During a period when politicians and officials in Washington were eager to remove the Indian threat that hindered settlement, Pratt was able to convince U.S. Secretary of the Interior Carl Schurz to establish Carlisle in an unused army barracks.[2]

Pratt's institute could not be described as a comforting place, despite its comparatively enlightened mission. Designed to eradicate all vestiges of

Captain Richard Henry Pratt, superintendent of the Carlisle Indian Industrial School, at his office desk, ca. 1900. (Courtesy of the Cumberland County Historical Society, Carlisle, Pa.)

Indian cultures from its wards, the school's program killed the Indian inside by breaking down students' nascent understanding of themselves through ridiculing indigenous ways. The school magazine, the *Indian Helper*, typically denigrated the "wild reservation man's . . . hideous costume of feathers [and] paint." Carlisle also spoke openly about the necessity of killing the Native spirit: "It is this nature in our red brother that is better dead than alive, and when we agree with the oft-repeated sentiment that the only good Indian is a dead one, we mean this characteristic of the Indian. Carlisle's mission is to kill THIS Indian, as we build up the better man."[3] The school's narrative thus judged all that was Christian and white as good, and all the attributes that marked indigenous peoples as constituting heathenism. In order to achieve the desired transformation, Carlisle faculty deliberately renamed children to strip them of their former identities, barred them from speaking their Native tongues, and convinced them that their cultures were bellicose (and inferior) with lectures that blamed white aggression on unprovoked Indian violence.[4] Living conditions, particularly during the first years, were dreary. Students even lacked beds, and breakfast consisted of bread and water.[5] The nature of the environment is best indicated by an incident that occurred a year after the school opened. A friendly visit by Brule Sioux Chief Spotted Tail, who had personally turned over some of his tribe's children to Pratt on a recruiting trip, quickly developed into an escape attempt. After witnessing the misery and homesickness among the children he had sent, Spotted Tail returned to Carlisle, gathered his children, grandchildren, and another young relative, and exited under the protection of his entourage. Pratt, overwhelmed and fearful of a mass escape attempt by the remaining students, was stymied. He recovered in time to send his men after a few homesick children who had run away during the confusion. One small Oglala girl found hiding in a train car in Harrisburg was returned, screaming and weeping hysterically.[6] Such incidents did not alter Pratt's beliefs. (His version of events described Spotted Tail's children and grandchildren begging to remain at Carlisle.)[7] The captain persisted in his conviction that total immersion in white culture offered the most humane course to "civilization," economic independence, and religious rebirth for the "Red Man."

Pratt's military background shaped the character of Carlisle, where students wore uniforms, marched, and performed drills. He stood as the highest authority—known as the ever-watchful "Man-on-the-band-stand." To Pratt, civilizing the Indian meant, in part, quashing what he perceived as indolence and willful waywardness, and replacing it with the values of self-sufficiency and deference. The *Indian Helper* explained, "Only reasonable things are asked of our boys and girls, and the word to be learned in every instance is O-B-E-Y. Obedience saves much time and energy. The Man-on-the-band-stand would have his boys and girls guard against INSOLENCE. No young person can afford to use INSOLENCE as a weapon of defense, especially when he knows that he is in the wrong."[8] Students who disobeyed were sentenced to confinement in the guardhouse—a punishment administered in some cases by juries of older students.[9] Spiritual salvation, meanwhile, came in the form of the Christian gospel preached at the campus chapel. An 1895 article on Carlisle in the *New England Magazine* recorded that many "moral and religious influences are brought to bear on the pupils . . . moral teaching is made part of the social life, and enters into all activities of the school."[10] In light of such treatment, it is unsurprising that the Oglala Sioux writer and intellectual Luther Standing Bear, one of Carlisle's most illustrious graduates, spent his first years at the school convinced that he might be killed at any moment.[11]

Carlisle's graduation rates were notoriously low, 12.5 percent.[12] Compliant students eventually earned diplomas. For boys this signified that they had learned a trade, such as farming or blacksmithing. They could then, in theory, join American society in every way the white man's equal, or return to their reservations to assist their home communities.[13] For female students, Carlisle's stress on Christian virtue went in lockstep with the Victorian Cult of True Womanhood, whose values of piety, purity, obedience, and domesticity were thought entirely foreign to the homes of "savage" Indians. Consequently, Carlisle aspired to break the bonds between generations of Native women in favor of domesticity.[14]

Pratt considered the remaking of indigenous girls into honorable women as not only an aim in itself, but as vital to the success of his entire project. Transforming Native females was the route to reforming Indian males, and without honorable women, acculturating males was pointless. As Pratt wrote, "Of what avail is it that the man be hard-working and industrious, providing by his labor food and clothing for his household, if the wife . . . makes what might be a cheerful, happy home only a wretched abode of filth and squalor?"[15] In consequence, Carlisle scheduled a heavy measure of domestic labor, from baking and sewing to laundering and maid work. Students were often outsourced to provide free services in local homes. Also fundamental was expunging the Indian female within the girls. Carlisle encouraged girls to reject and discard traditional practices inherited from their mothers and grandmothers. Severing this familial bond was a necessity, Pratt observed, because, "It is the women who cling most tenaciously to heathen rites and superstitions, and perpetuate them by instructions to their children." Due to their radically different modes of existence, indigenous women were stereotyped as "stupid" and sexually "lewd."[16] Successfully remolding Native girls in the image of genteel womanhood, then, was a paramount accomplishment. As one educator from Simmons's alma mater, White's Institute, described it, "There is nothing . . . we observe with greater pleasure than the improvement of the girls in womanly grace and virtue from year to year, and their constant training in household duties."[17] Indeed, when Simmons arrived to take up her post at Carlisle in July 1897 she must have appeared the very paragon of cultured, submissive Victorian femininity, perfectly adapted to and "tamed" in all manner of white ways. That impression would not last long.

Simmons spent just one month at Carlisle before being sent to Yankton in August to recruit new students.[18] On her arrival there the deprivation shocked her. She found her mother in a state of misery, living alone in a dilapidated, drafty home.[19] Others fared little better. The Sioux reservations

had been inundated by squatters laying claims to land under the Dawes
Act. Simmons, her mother, and her brother David had received adjoining
allotments, but overall Yankton had lost land with the imposition of a
farming regime. Government agents discouraged former migratory practices associated with hunting-and-gathering subsistence. Many Yanktons
found themselves forced to lease lands to whites in order to make a living.[20]
David Simmons, however, evidently did well as a farmer.[21] He married a
woman named Victoria, probably in the early 1890s, and by 1897 had two
children, a girl named Irene and a boy named Raymond.[22] Nonetheless, during this period the population at Yankton declined precipitously to less
than two thousand due to European diseases such as chicken pox, measles,
and influenza.[23]

Acutely aware of the crisis afflicting her people, Simmons left Yankton
agitated. She returned to Carlisle in September and opened the academic
year with a lecture entitled, "The Achievements of the Red and White Races
Compared." According to the *Indian Helper*, she presented "a most thrilling
and earnest appeal to the youth of her race to show to the world by their
earnestness of purpose that the history of the Indian has been wrongly
written, and that their motives as a people have been misunderstood."[24]

Over the next eighteen months Simmons did her best to support Pratt's
mission. She began singing at school ceremonies and soon thereafter assumed leadership of the all-female Minnehaha Glee Club. The *Indian Helper*
assiduously detailed her activities, which included class shopping trips
in town and the occasional poetry reading.[25] Simmons also revived her
friendship with Thomas Marshall. He had come east to enroll in Dickinson
College in Carlisle town. When not attending classes, Marshall resided at
Carlisle school, where he supervised the boys' dormitories.[26] While Marshall and Simmons grew closer, she made friendships with others as well.
On her twenty-second birthday the Carlisle faculty threw her a surprise
party in the teachers' parlor, replete with "delicious cream and cake." The
Indian Helper reported that "a host of Miss Simmons's friends" indulged in
"laughter, song, games and other merriment."[27]

In late April 1898 Simmons wrote her Wabash friends, "Aunt Sue" and
"Uncle Joe" Unthank. She informed them that "the change of work has
made it possible for me to gain several pounds," and that she had begun to
teach: "I am considered a good teacher and have been asked to teach here
next year. Of course I am glad that it is so but I do not mean to lose sight of
College for the sake of money-making." There was, however, an exciting
prospect on the horizon. Simmons told the Unthanks that she had been
selected as a violin soloist for a planned tour by the Carlisle Indian School

"Faculty and Officers of Our School." This photograph appeared on the Christmas greeting card for 1898, printed in the *Indian Helper*, December 23, 1898. Gertrude Simmons is in the front row seated on the stairs, third from the left. Pratt is in the back row, inside the column on the right. (Courtesy of the Cumberland County Historical Society, Carlisle, Pa.)

Band in the fall. It was sure "to be a great thing." She closed, "With much love, Your Indian niece."[28] Though Simmons apparently did enjoy aspects of her work, many of her relationships, and the activities at Carlisle, the school's ideology clearly exacerbated her inner conflicts. Four months earlier, in the sixth-year class she taught, she had held a subversive debate on "whether or not the treatment of the Indians by the early settlers caused King Phillip to make war." The choice of subject matter demonstrates that Simmons's resistance to the principles of white education was increasing with every passing day. The *Helper* reported, "There was a degree of life manifested on the part of the speakers gaining the floor, that was refreshing, and arguments pro and con that would have done credit to the higher grades. [The judges] decided that the best argument was on the negative side."[29] In other words, the settlers were absolved of responsibility for the conflict. More recent historical analysis blames not the Natives for their refusal to adopt Christian norms in the face of Puritan inclusiveness and generosity, but the Puritans for appropriating land and not respecting indigenous rights.[30]

When Carlisle's spring semester ended in July Simmons was briefly free to pursue other interests; she began studying violin in earnest under the tutelage of Leipzig Conservatory graduate Professor Taube, in Harrisburg. A month later Simmons traveled to New York City. There she stayed in the home of Gertrude Käsebier, easily the most famous female photographer in the United States.[31] Käsebier had an interest in indigenous peoples, having grown up in the West among Indian playmates. In 1898 she embarked on a project of photographing the Native performers in Buffalo Bill Cody's Wild West Show. A handsome young Oglala Sioux named Samuel Lone Bear became one of her favorite subjects.[32] He and Simmons would later cross paths.

Simmons likely met Käsebier either in Manhattan during a Carlisle school trip to Buffalo Bill Cody's Wild West Show, or perhaps at one of Käsebier's photographic exhibitions in Philadelphia. The two women became fast friends. Throughout August, Simmons posed for a series of portraits taken by Käsebier and her colleague, Joseph Keiley. Keiley's efforts focused on Simmons's perceived exoticism and sensuality. (Prints of his portrait of her sold for a thousand dollars in 1900.)[33]

Käsebier's series revealed Simmons's duality in contrasting images. In one photograph Simmons stands in (mock) traditional garb, seemingly scanning the horizon, vigilant against white encroachment. In the other, violin in hand, she appears the quintessence of accomplished yet docile Victorian womanhood. Juxtaposed, the portraits make an interesting statement on the tensions Simmons sometimes felt within herself.[34] Incidentally, Simmons's first recorded use of the name Zitkala-Ša appears written on the back of one of these portraits.[35]

Simmons returned to Carlisle at the end of August.[36] She was followed shortly thereafter by Käsebier's son, Frederick, who, apparently smitten, had been sending her letters.[37] In October the *Indian Helper* mentioned that "Mr. F. W. Kasebier [sic], 201st Regiment N.Y. was Miss Simmons's guest on Thursday evening."[38] Though Frederick may have arrived with high hopes, they were soon dashed. Sometime between October and January, Simmons's relationship with Thomas Marshall deepened and the couple became engaged. One might have thought that Simmons's future now seemed clear. Her career would continue at Carlisle, she would marry, and the Marshalls would settle into domestic life in the East. Instead, by the beginning of 1899 Simmons had left Pennsylvania. Encouraged by Käsebier to explore the limits of her talent, she headed for Boston to study violin, supported by a

Zitkala-Ša, by Joseph T. Keiley, 1898. Glycerin-developed platinum print (National Portrait Gallery, Smithsonian Institution/Art Resource, NY, NPG.2006.10)

grant from the commissioner of Indian Affairs.[39] Marshall must have been chagrined. Nonetheless, the engagement continued.

Boston offered Simmons an opportunity to partake of the erudite atmosphere an eastern metropolis could offer. Throughout 1899 she trained privately with Eugene Gruenberg, an eminent Austrian violinist and teacher

Zitkala-Ša, by Joseph T. Keiley, 1898 (printed 1901). Photogravure. (National Portrait Gallery, Smithsonian Institution/Art Resource, NY, S/NPG.79.26)

employed at the New England Conservatory of Music. Simmons obviously had talent or Gruenberg would not have accepted her as a pupil. But at twenty-three, she was competing against younger students with more experience. Simmons was apparently never able to meet the standards for acceptance into the Conservatory, though she did attain superior proficiency.[40] Boston also stimulated her greatly. She quickly established herself among the city's elite through an acquaintance with the eminent photographer Fred Holland Day, whom she likely met through Käsebier. Day introduced Simmons to many prominent figures, most importantly Joseph Edgar Chamberlin, known as "the dean of Boston journalists."[41]

In late April, four months into her Boston stay, Simmons received sudden word that her fiancé had died of measles. The Carlisle press wrote of Marshall, "The life of one of the most promising and unselfish as well as most dear to a loving family and to a wide circle of friends is thus inscrutably taken." Simmons sent a "large and beautiful wreath of white roses" to be placed upon his grave.[42] She subsequently received support and sympathy from those at Carlisle, yet the death was another upheaval in her young life.[43]

Marshall's passing, so far from his home, may have provoked Simmons to reflect even more deeply on the dislocations she had endured in becoming "civilized." As spring turned to summer she began to write of her experiences. Chamberlin aided greatly by giving Simmons a place to write in his summer home and encouraging the newly appointed editor of the *Atlantic Monthly*, Bliss Perry, to publish her work.[44] The magazine had a reputation for raising issues of racial and social inequality and featuring diverse contributors.[45] Perry accepted Simmons's submissions. The resulting series of semiautobiographical installments—"Impressions of an Indian Childhood," "The School Days of an Indian Girl," and "An Indian Teacher among Indians"—appeared in the *Atlantic Monthly* in January, February, and March of 1900. Wanting to be recognized as Indian, Simmons signed the stories "Zitkala-Ša."[46] Her use of the name signaled a genuine psychological and spiritual rebirth.

The same year Simmons's series, a "political autobiography" of sorts, appeared, the Indian population registered its lowest ever census figures, supporting the popular white conception that Indian peoples were headed for extinction. Ethnologists, scrambling to record indigenous stories and artifacts, were among the few who lamented their passing.[47] Even the *Atlantic Monthly*'s cultured subscribers, many of whom were perhaps sympathetic to the idea of Indian domestication, had for decades been exposed to harrowing fictitious accounts of "red savagery." Simmons's readers, then, largely accepted such paradigms. Editor Perry, meanwhile, knowingly risked offending some of the magazine's audience by publishing critical accounts of Quaker Indian schools and of Carlisle. Nonetheless, he decided to allow Simmons a forum in the interest of the greater goal of "cultural recognition for ethnic groups."[48] Simmons's risk was of course much greater. Her articles would be closely read by those involved in Indian education. Any controversial statements could severely jeopardize her position within that insular world. But she did not hold back. The *Atlantic Monthly* series amounted to a cathartic indictment of white America's ethnocentrism that overturned

Gertrude Simmons, in mock traditional garb, photographed by Gertrude Käsebier in New York City, 1898. (Gertrude Käsebier Photographs, Division of Culture and the Arts, National Museum of American History, Smithsonian Institution, 69.236.103)

Gertrude Simmons with her violin, photographed by Gertrude Käsebier in New York City, 1898. (Gertrude Käsebier Photographs, Division of Culture and the Arts, National Museum of American History, Smithsonian Institution, 69.236.108)

dominant discourses by suggesting that whites, rather than their Indian wards, required enlightenment in the values of civilization.[49] With the trilogy's publication, Simmons, or rather Zitkala-Ša, became the first Indian woman to write about her own life without the aid of an editor, interpreter, or ethnographer.[50] Fittingly, she took the opportunity to reestablish her eroded identity and assert the validity, if not superiority, of her birth culture by putting—as Amelia Katanski writes—"a human face on the wrongs done to Indians at the turn of the century."[51] And though Zitkala-Ša's stories mixed autobiographical fact and biographical fiction based on the lives of peers, they held true to the core of her (and others') journey into the white world.[52]

In "Impressions of an Indian Childhood" Zitkala-Ša begins her life story on the Dakota plains, in some places embellishing and adding literary touches. Cleverly, she draws on biblical motifs to upend the temptation of Eve in her own experience: Christian missionaries lure her, the young Gertrude, from her Edenic home on the Yankton Reservation.[53] In this dying oasis she lives happily with her mother near the banks of the Missouri River, "a wild little girl of seven" with no fear but that of "intruding" on others—an implicit criticism of white encroachment. Federal policy has assailed the Sioux domestic sphere. Gertrude's father (in the article a Sioux warrior rather than a white man) and uncle have been killed, while her sister has perished after forced removal to the reservation. Survivors are keenly aware that their culture may not outlast their children's lives. They are all victims of the "heartless paleface," whom Gertrude's mother describes as a "sickly sham" in comparison to "the only real man"—the "bronzed Dakota." The misfortunes of the Sioux family shift the perspective of the contemporary white reader to the "wild" Indian girl—reversing the narrative of the Indian aggressor.[54]

Yet Gertrude is anything but "wild." She emulates the cultural accomplishments of her mother, a caregiver and beadwork artist who teaches the values of modesty, self-discipline, and respect for elders and their traditions—a radical departure from white stereotypes of the crude, lewd "squaw."[55] Still, the small family's life is torn asunder when Gertrude is fooled by "two paleface missionaries." The men promise her a ride on the "iron horse" to a place with a "great tree where grew red, red apples." The apples, while referencing the Book of Genesis, also take on another shade of meaning: their skin is red, their inside white, which is the goal of assimilation.[56] Ultimately, the enticements are too much to bear for the impressionable child. Despite her mother's protestations she foolishly yields to the missionaries' trickery, betraying her culture for knowledge of the white world. Gertrude's mother objects but finally relents, understanding that her daughter will "need an education when she is grown, for then there will be fewer real Dakotas, and many more palefaces." On the day of her departure Gertrude walks, covered in her traditional blanket, to the carriage that will take her to the train station. Her excitement quickly dissipates. She is overcome with tears at the separation from her mother. Once you leave Eden, there is no going back.

Gertrude's journey east continues in "The School Days of an Indian Girl."[57] On the train all sorts of passengers rudely scrutinize her. Their stares bring her to the brink of tears as she goes farther and farther into "civilization," represented by the denuded trees, transformed into lifeless telegraph poles, that line the railroad.[58] When Gertrude arrives at the school grounds, the scene vividly recalls many Indian children's first exposure to the entirely alien world of boarding school. Standing outside, she beholds cold, imposing buildings and shining bright lights on "icicled trees" surrounding them. Her first instinct is to flee. She is scooped up by a woman who makes her a "plaything" and will not unhand her. Gertrude is incensed, preferring to be treated as a "dignified little individual." Such misunderstandings, which result from the great cultural divide between the missionaries and their wards, will only worsen. Reduced to sobbing, Gertrude is comforted by an older Sioux girl, who puts her to bed that evening. As the story unfolds, it achieves a total reversal of the white-as-civilized, Indian-as-savage discourse. Gertrude finds herself consistently violated at the hands of the school's missionaries, who attack every aspect of her personality and culture. In one episode Gertrude is treated like a "little animal," violently shorn of her hair by wardens who scalp at will. She hides under a bed and tries to resist by kicking and screaming, to no avail. Her hair comes off, causing the loss of her "spirit."[59] In another scene, her friend is beaten merely for playing in the snow and failing to explain herself in English.

To Gertrude, life at the boarding school becomes a set of arbitrary rules that limit the children's freedom for no concrete purpose. The ostensible "civilization" is in fact an environment of random restrictions and physical punishment. Threats of damnation are used to keep behavior in check, causing Gertrude such consternation that she has a harrowing nightmare in which she is chased by the devil. She takes her revenge on a children's Bible the next morning, scratching out his "wicked" eyes. Equally damaging is the school's "iron routine," which denies the autonomy, respect, and individual attention Sioux mothers provide. Caught up in a "civilizing machine" that ignores the children's true needs, Gertrude's friend succumbs. The small girl dies with the Bible in her hands as a missionary looks on.[60]

The "paleface woman" is not the Indian girl's savior, but an accomplice in her murder.[61] The scene mocks Christianity as not truth but "superstitious ideas," subverting the religious foundation of white schooling.[62] As such, Christian nurture is an oxymoron that leaves Gertrude and her friends unfit for true civilization.

The greatest harm manifests itself when Gertrude returns home years later, only to find that her thinking has been so distorted she cannot resume her old ways. Gertrude lives a sadly liminal existence. Trapped between white and Sioux aspects of her identity, she helplessly "hang[s] in the heart of chaos, beyond the touch or voice of human aid." Boarding school has, as intended by federal policy, effectively broken the bond between mother and daughter. Gertrude is unable to communicate with the woman who so carefully raised her. Boarding school has also altered the character of life on the reservation. There are "no more young braves in blankets and eagle plumes, nor Indian maids with prettily painted cheeks." There is little else for Gertrude to do than to leave once more. Against her mother's wishes, she returns east and eventually continues her education at Earlham College. There she experiences profound loneliness, but overcomes harsh demonstrations of intolerance at the oratorical competition in Indianapolis to win second prize. It is a Pyrrhic victory. Her message of reconciliation, "Side by Side," is greeted with the "squaw" banner, representing a crescendo of white racism.[63] Approbation from some among the colonizers, the sympathetic judges and classmates, cannot fill the void caused by disrupted identity and cultural dislocation. Gertrude senses only her mother's disapproval. She knows that estrangement from her ancestral roots has taken away a part of herself.

In "An Indian Teacher among Indians" Gertrude Simmons completes her process of awareness to opposition.[64] She falls ill after the oratorical competition. Stubborn "pride" prevents her from returning home. Instead, she goes east—farther into white civilization. Simmons decides to direct her energies into "work for the Indian race." She takes a post at Carlisle, identified only as "an Eastern Indian School." When the superintendent (Pratt) taps her for a recruiting trip in the West, Simmons has the chance to visit her mother. She returns to find that Yankton has become a "refuge for white robbers," who have settled on the other side of the Missouri. Her mother warns, "My daughter, beware of the paleface. . . . He is the hypocrite who reads with one eye, 'Thou shalt not kill,' and with the other gloats upon the sufferings of the Indian race." As Taté I Yóhin Win sends her curse out across the Missouri toward the dots of campfires that burn with gross impunity, Simmons understands that she must fight for her lands and heritage. She returns to Carlisle, but the job is intolerable. Incompetence is everywhere about her, from an "opium-eater" teacher to an "inebriate pale-face" doctor so ineffective that his Indian patients suffer preventable deaths. Another instructor delights in torturing "an ambitious Indian youth" by calling him a "government pauper." All this is sanctioned by Pratt, a "Christian in power." When government inspectors turn up, he puts on a phony presentation of students' work worthy of the "sickly sham" Simmons's mother spoke of years before. Simmons finally comes to a full realization of her wayward path: "For the white man's papers I had given up my faith in the Great Spirit. For these same papers I had forgotten the healing in trees and brooks. On account of my mother's simple view of life, and my lack of any, I gave her up, also. I made no friends among the race of people I loathed. Like a slender tree, I had been uprooted from my mother, nature, and God. I was shorn of my branches, which had waved in sympathy and love for home and friends." No longer a healthy tree, Simmons is "a cold bare pole . . . planted in a strange earth"—much like the row of identical telegraph lines that flew by the train window on her first trip east at eight years old. Pratt's young wards, "a small forest of Indian timber," are headed for the same fate.

Psychologically and spiritually unmoored, Simmons quits her post and relocates to "an Eastern city." There she is able to gain some distance from the past. Her memories of white visitors to Carlisle only stoke her resentment. "In this fashion," Zitkala-Ša writes, "many have passed idly through the Indian schools during the last decade, afterward to boast of their charity to the North American Indian. But few there are who have paused to question whether real life or long-lasting death lies beneath this semblance of civilization." This equation of spiritual and cultural death with the process of assimilation evokes the memory of physical death at Wounded Knee only a decade before. White "civilization"—nothing more than a set of rules that justifies punishment for the veneer of order—is not a new life for the Indian, but rather his imprisonment and death. "Wild" does not denote "savage," but "free." "Civilization" denotes a sorry "enslavement."[65]

The dangerous, defiant stance Zitkala-Ša took in the *Atlantic Monthly* series exposed her to potential censure and condemnation. She had attempted to shatter conventional thinking, but the question remained whether contemporary white readers could comprehend her stories' moral implications. Just as with "Side by Side," Zitkala-Ša's semiautobiography earned praise but did not influence white America's thinking on the "Indian question."[66] Yet, despite their subversive content, the writings won critical acclaim. Zitkala-Ša became the toast of the Boston literati, who were eager for more.[67]

Within months, *Harper's Bazar* featured Zitkala-Ša in the column "Persons Who Interest Us." *The Outlook* included her in an article, "The Representative Indian." In both cases, however, the pieces focused exclusively on Zitkala-Ša the person, dismissing, ignoring, or refusing to grasp her critique. *Harper's* column marveled at Zitkala-Ša's "beauty and many talents," noting that, "Her first progress towards civilization was made at a Friends' school in Indiana." Before, she had been "a veritable little savage, running wild over the prairie and speaking no language but her own." A brief assessment of her stories spoke merely of Zitkala-Ša's "artistic feeling" and "rare command of English."[68] The *Outlook* article, penned by Jesse W. Cook (a teacher at Carlisle and friend of Zitkala-Ša's), opened with the question of when Indians, an "undigested, unassimilated part of the body politic," would "become Americanized and be of use to the world." Interspersed among praise for Zitkala-Ša's "unusual musical genius" and writing, Cook described reservation Indians as existing in a "stage of barbarism." His article ended with the statement that Indians had "to live *with* the people whose ways they must adopt" as the only route to "a higher order of civilization."[69]

The only reviewer of the period to actively engage Zitkala-Ša's message was literary critic Elizabeth Luther Cary (probably not widely read). In "Recent Writings by American Indians" (1902), Cary characterized Zitkala-Ša's stories as an illogical revolt against civilization, permeated by "a kind of melancholy that forces sympathy." In Cary's judgment there was no objective reason either to feel sorry for the Sioux girl, given to "childish revenge," or to understand her unwillingness to adopt white ways. "Many of her grievances," Cary complained, "are those which only an intensely sensitive nature would nurse and remember, and, after many years, record." The problem was not Indian boarding schools, but Zitkala-Ša herself. Cary did at least extol the "richness" and "truly compelling eloquence" of Zitkala-Ša's prose. "Strange, pathetic, and caustic," Cary wrote, "[her] phrases burn themselves into the reader's consciousness"—even if little else did.[70]

Zitkala-Ša's message had been ignored or criticized. Her great allure remained that of the "civilized savage."[71] Nevertheless, she had found her calling. She would use her notoriety to write of the wrongs she had witnessed and experienced. Richard Henry Pratt, however, would not suffer Zitkala-Ša's criticisms in silence.

CHAPTER 3

MONTEZUMA AND THE REBELLION

In February 1900 Carlisle's *Indian Helper* made a brief, cryptic allusion to Zitkala-Ša's recent literary debut: "The people's eyes whom Zitkala Sa [*sic*] alludes to in her *Atlantic Monthly* article might be called a pair of stares."[1] Whatever this meant, the tone of general disapproval reverberated in Carlisle's other periodical, the *Red Man* (published for the public, rather than students and graduates). An editorial therein regretted that Zitkala-Ša "did not once call to mind the happier side of those long school days, or even hint at the friends who did so much to break down for her the barriers of education and custom, and to lead her from poverty and insignificance into the comparatively full and rich existence that she enjoys today." Attempting to defend Carlisle's honor and purpose without insulting its renowned employee, the *Red Man* continued, "We do not feel that the home-sick pathos—nay more the underlying bitterness of her story will cause readers unfamiliar with the Indian schools to form entirely wrong conclusions. Her pictures are perhaps not untrue themselves, but taken by themselves, they are misleading."[2] These generally restrained, reasonable comments were the opening volley in what would soon become a larger, more vituperative campaign to discredit Zitkala-Ša as a reputable chronicler of Indian education.

There was perhaps little objective reason to believe that the *Atlantic Monthly* series could do any real damage to Carlisle or effect change in federal Indian policy. Nevertheless, many of Zitkala-Ša's former teachers were so incensed that they expressed their consternation in an article for the

Minneapolis Journal. Pratt, who hated bad press, also took the articles personally. Joseph Edgar Chamberlin had previously tried in vain to assure Pratt
that Zitkala-Ša was not being malicious. "Throughout it all," he wrote, "she
has been animated with no other feeling toward you than one of respect and
full confidence. But she had resolved to lay bare her heart, feeling that to do
so was not only the best *art*, and the basis of the best literature, but that it was
also best for her own people and their education." Pratt was unmoved. He
told Chamberlin of the "great deal of feeling throughout the Indian service
against Miss Simmons for [her] writing," adding that her "shortsighted-
ness" was impeding the "cause of right Indian education." Nursing his anger, Pratt promised to stay silent on the matter—though he justified his
stance on Indian education by conjecturing where Zitkala-Ša would be without white schooling: "But for those she has maligned, she would be a poor
squaw in an Indian camp, probably married to some no-account Indian."[3]

Despite the tensions caused by the *Atlantic Monthly* series, Zitkala-Ša's
long-planned tour of the Northeast with the fifty-three-piece Carlisle Indian School Band was finally about to get underway. She traveled back to
Carlisle in early March to prepare.[4] Pratt now had an ulterior motive. He
clearly hoped to squelch any further public rebellion by maintaining relations with Zitkala-Ša. Referring to Zitkala-Ša's presence on the tour through
analogy with the harrowing Indian captivity narratives that fascinated
nineteenth-century readers, Pratt wrote to a colleague, "I believe in captur-
ing her and keeping her on our side if possible."[5] Zitkala-Ša's answer to the
controversy was simple. In April the *Red Man* printed her defense: "To stir up
views and earnest comparison of theories was one of the ways in which I
hoped ["Impressions of an Indian Childhood"] would work a benefit to my
people. No one can dispute my own impressions and bitterness!"[6]

The Carlisle band's performances featured violin solos by Zitkala-Ša and
a charged dramatic recitation of "The Famine" from Longfellow's *Song of
Hiawatha*. The fringed and beaded buckskin Zitkala-Ša wore while presenting the latter showcased her physical allure and histrionic abilities. The
Trenton Daily Gazette registered incredulity at her accomplished recitation:
"Any criticism of the concert that failed to take note of the wonderful performance by Zitkala Sa [*sic*], a charming young Indian woman who must
have surprised everybody with the power of her declamatory force would
be incomplete. Her recitation was 'The Famine' from Hiawatha. Her beginning scarce kept the attention. She warmed and as the lines called for
the exposition of the passions the young girl's dramatic power grew till it
became marvelous. She held every ear and the recourse frequently to hand-
kerchiefs told how great an effect she was exerting over her audience. She

Gertrude Simmons in profile, photographed by Gertrude Käsebier in New York City, 1898. (Gertrude Käsebier Photographs, Division of Culture and the Arts, National Museum of American History, Smithsonian Institution, 69.236.104)

Dr. Carlos Montezuma and six unidentified nurses at Carlisle on the steps of the school hospital. (Courtesy of the Cumberland County Historical Society, Carlisle, Pa.)

was applauded to the echo."[7] Other reviews confirmed the triumph. At the Memorial Association in Washington Zitkala-Ša reportedly "took the audience by storm," the ovation so tremendous that she was forced to return for curtain calls. At concert's end she was escorted into the auditorium, where Longfellow's daughter waited to greet her. A command performance for the McKinleys at the White House followed the next evening. At its conclusion, First Lady Ida McKinley personally presented Zitkala-Ša with "a large bunch of beautiful English violets."[8]

Zitkala-Ša's appearances with the Carlisle Indian School Band were to climax with a performance at the Paris Exposition of 1900. Unfortunately, the school could not raise sufficient funds for the voyage.[9] Instead, Zitkala-Ša spent the summer at Yankton with her mother before returning to Boston in the fall.[10] It was on the Carlisle tour, however, that Zitkala-Ša first encountered Dr. Carlos Montezuma, then acting as the band's "team doctor."[11]

Montezuma's route to Carlisle was circuitous and dramatic. Born to a Yavapai family in present-day Arizona in the mid-1860s, he was kidnapped at around age five by the Pima tribe during a brutal massacre, and sold for thirty silver dollars to an Italian immigrant named Carlos Gentile. Gentile raised the boy as his son, bestowing on him the surname Montezuma after the last of the Aztec chiefs. Over the next decade young Montezuma crisscrossed the country with Gentile, eventually settling in the home of a Baptist pastor, William H. Steadman, in Urbana, Illinois. By 1889, Montezuma had graduated from Chicago Medical College and hoped to open a private practice. Due to the prevailing climate of racism, an indigenous doctor, even an exceptionally talented one, faced obstacles in attracting patients. After his first attempt at establishing a practice in Chicago failed, Montezuma had no recourse but to work for the Indian Service as a physician on reservations and at boarding schools in North Dakota, Nevada, and Washington, before moving on to Carlisle from 1893 to 1896. In Pennsylvania, Montezuma became close to Pratt and a supporter of his goals. He lectured widely promoting assimilation. In return, Carlisle teachers treated Montezuma as an "honored guest."[12] He was likewise cited in periodicals as walking proof that Indian assimilation could introduce valuable members into white society.[13] Then about thirty-five years old and one of the most famous Indians in the United States, Montezuma would soon become a significant figure in Zitkala-Ša's life.[14]

Not long after the Carlisle band tour concluded and Zitkala-Ša had left for Yankton, the June issue of the *Red Man* featured a literary critique of her *Atlantic Monthly* stories. It charged that "many of the incidents are purely fictitious and often the situation is dramatically arranged to produce the desired effect." Seeking to deflect her criticisms, the article painted the aspiring author as an ungrateful prodigal daughter who had employed tawdry literary techniques to illicit sympathy among uninformed readers. The *Red Man* deplored the "conventional berating" of "the paleface," mocked the death of Zitkala-Ša's sister in "Impressions" as "simply dramatic fiction," and suggested that the idea of white settlers occupying reservation land was absurd. Most galling, however, according to the article, was Zitkala-Ša's "contempt and disgust" for her former benefactors. This attitude showed her to be "a person of infinite conceit"—a fact illustrated by her "passionate and ill-tempered" behavior as a child, when "she is dragged out from under a bed kicking and scratching wildly." Consequently, "Nothing is good enough for her. She is utterly unthankful for all that has been done for her by the pale faces, which in her case is considerable. It would be doing injustice to the Indian race whose blood she partly shares to accept the picture she has drawn of herself as the true picture of all Indian girls. They average far better."[15]

The same issue of the *Red Man* contained "Two Sides of Institution Life," an article describing all boarding schools as afflicted by some degree of "loneliness" and "lovelessness." This truth, though unfortunate, constituted no reason to discount the entirety of Carlisle's work. Comparing indigenous children to "deafmutes," the "blind," and the "feebleminded," "Two Sides" insisted that no large institution serving such a disadvantaged group could be expected to "give the personal touch, the individual atmosphere of the ideal home." Yet boarding school represented a vast improvement over "the homes of the Indians," which "fall so far below our own standard as to be wholly out of the question as a nursery for our future citizens." In closing, the article strongly recommended that Zitkala-Ša appreciate, rather than assail, the removal of Native children from "an environment of dirt, poverty, mental stagnation, and unmoral if not actively immoral influences."[16] How this attack affected Zitkala-Ša is unknown. The combined *Red Man and Helper* made another critical allusion to her work in September 1900. "Hunt for the South Side" accused Zitkala-Ša of "sitting on the cold side of a hill" and remembering only the "gloomy scenes and the dark pictures in life."[17]

Obviously undeterred, Zitkala-Ša pushed forward with both her writing and her personal life. The Boston publishing house Ginn & Company commissioned her to produce a children's book of Indian stories, and she began a new relationship. Sometime in early 1901 Zitkala-Ša passed through Chicago on her way to Boston. There, as she later phrased it, she had an "unexpected meeting" with Carlos Montezuma.[18] Soon thereafter, despite his loyalty to Pratt, Montezuma began feverishly courting Carlisle's most vocal critic. In mid-February he sent a tentative letter. It arrived just as Zitkala-Ša was in the middle of composing a short story. Montezuma (almost all of whose letters have been lost) asked about her future plans and whether she would again be coming through Chicago. He also gingerly inquired if she had recovered from her fiancé Marshall's death, almost two years prior. Zitkala-Ša responded, "The sad affair of which you hint was not an easy matter to deal with. But the power of depressing influences is only temporary." She further explained that she planned to divide her time between teaching and writing. She was already arranging to return to Yankton in the spring. There she planned to teach at a reservation school and collect stories from elders. She closed her letter with the kindest of words: "Let me wish the day's sunshine may enter your soul—I am your Friend, Zitkala-Ša."[19] Very soon after Zitkala-Ša's posted this missive, her first fictional story, "The Soft-Hearted Sioux," appeared in the March 1901 *Harper's Monthly*.

"The Soft-Hearted Sioux" examined the effects of missionary education on a sixteen-year-old boy who returns to his reservation "a stranger" in "foreigner's dress" after spending nine years at boarding school. Having internalized Christian teachings, or Christ's "soft heart," he is determined to convert his family and tribe but is denounced by the medicine man and made an outcast. Lacking both the tribe's support and indispensable hunting skills, the boy and his family face starvation. Urged by his ill father to hunt, the boy kills a cow owned by a neighboring white rancher. Pursued as he runs home carrying a flank of meat, the boy manages to kill the rancher and escape. His father, however, expires before receiving the life-giving sustenance. Having failed to fulfill the demands of both the "civilized" and "savage" worlds, which have simultaneously cast him as Christian missionary and Indian warrior and hunter, the boy leads his mother to the medicine man's new camp and turns himself in to white authorities. Receiving no mercy from his "soft-hearted" Christian captors, the boy faces death like a Sioux warrior, unafraid.[20] Like the *Atlantic Monthly* series, this story disputed the value of missionary education, asking how high a price indigenous peoples must pay for assimilation.[21]

Predictably, "The Soft-Hearted Sioux" failed to inspire sympathy at Carlisle. Zitkala-Ša wrote to Montezuma that Pratt had denounced the story as "trash" and her as "worse than Pagan." Having learned of his censure through back channels, Zitkala-Ša was furious. She described Pratt as "woefully small and bigoted" and ridiculed his "imposing avoirdupois." "I won't be another's mouthpiece," she promised Montezuma, "I will say just what *I* think. I fear no man—sometimes I think I do not fear God. But I do respect the conscious spirit within me for whose being or going I cannot account." There had been approbation from other quarters that certainly mattered more than Pratt's criticism. "The 'Atlantic Monthly' wrote me a note in praise of the story," Zitkala-Ša mentioned, while, "An intelligent literary critic says my writing has a distinguished air about it—others say I am covering myself with glory!" *Harper's* had also accepted another of her stories, "The Trial Path." Hence, Zitkala-Ša could confidently announce, "I am bound to live my own life!"[22]

Pratt's public response to the "The Soft-Hearted Sioux" was excoriating and, like his earlier attacks, aimed at Zitkala-Ša personally. On April 12, the *Red Man and Helper* printed a rejoinder on the front page (reprinted from the Santee school's *Word Carrier*) that pronounced the story "morally bad," condemned its depiction of Christianity as a "travesty," and harped on the ostensible defects of Zitkala-Ša's character.[23] The venom was palpable. "All that Zitkalasa [sic] has in the way of literary ability and culture," the review began, "she owes to the good people, who, from time to time, have taken her into their homes and given her aid. Yet not a word of gratitude or allusion to such kindness on the part of her friends has ever escaped her in any line of anything she has written for the public. By this course she injures herself and harms the educational work in progress for the race from which she sprang. In a list of educated Indians whom we have in mind, some of whom have reached higher altitudes in literary and professional lines than Zitkalasa [sic], we know of no other case of such pronounced morbidness."[24]

Though Zitkala-Ša should have expected the reaction, it sickened her. In another letter to Montezuma she branded Pratt a poor exemplar of "Christ's teachings." "See the Helper!" she exclaimed, "This is the way Pratt loves me!" But in the face of such opposition, she remained true to her strongest beliefs. "I must live my life," Zitkala-Ša stated to Montezuma, "I must think in my own way (since I cannot help it). I must write the lessons I see. . . . I have a place in the Universe, and no one can cheat or crowd me by a single hair's breadth. Just the same I feel sick way in my heart. . . . Shall I continue in my work or shall I keep still? If I had no confidence in you—I would not write this letter. I will recover from this nausea caused by the crude morality of those who would be critics of my art. But I am ill at this moment. Ah—I rise. I lift my head! I laugh at the babble! I dare—I do! I guess I am not so sick after all."[25] The criticism had stung but also inspired her. If Pratt intended to halt her pen, his denunciations had the opposite effect: Zitkala-Ša resolved to continue writing.

Montezuma was doing plenty of writing as well. By mid-April he had already declared his love.[26] His urgency was no doubt piqued by Zitkala-Ša's long line of admirers, whom she teasingly cataloged. This letter, posted in March, reveals a young woman skilled in the art of flirtation, experiencing all the glory and possibilities of youth:

> I shall never tell you in so many words if I love you or not. If my giving you the preference to a long list of applicants conveys no meaning to you, words would be sounding metals only. Race has little to do in the man who is to win me. . . . On my list are these—
> 1 a well-known German violinist
> 2 a Harvard professor
> 3 a Harvard Post Graduate
> 4 a Well-Known writer of today
> 5 a man of a prominent New York family
> 6 4 Western men scattered from Montana to Dakota

She added, "I have not counted any of last year's nor those previous, for it would be too long a task. I write all this stuff to show you there are other men who can give me as much as you could." The stiff competition she inventoried was not the only obstacle to Montezuma's vision of wedded bliss. Zitkala-Ša was not overly impressed by his credentials and valued her own independence. "I do not care about a doctor's profession more than those of the others," she flatly informed him, "In truth music, art and literature are more in line with my own. I raise both hands to the great blue overhead and my spirit revels in a freedom no less than the vast conclave! I am free! I am proud! I am chosen! I caper to no world of pygmies nor a pigmy god!" Closing the letter Zitkala-Ša scrawled what could be regarded classic hard-to-get lines: "Do not attempt to meet me. I am gone entirely out of your reach."[27] Though such teasing and bold pronouncements may have contained elements of giddiness, serious undertones signaled a deep conflict between the would-be couple.

From the start, two major issues precluded a happy union between Zitkala-Ša and Montezuma—though both parties, often in a spirit of genuine respect and affection, attempted to overcome them. The first was Zitkala-Ša's refusal to submit to a secondary, dependent role as doting, obedient wife, what she termed as "a fine horse to draw your wagon." She pressed Montezuma on the issue, disdainful of his hopes for a future of conventional domesticity. "Feed your horse," Zitkala-Ša taunted, "shout its pretty name! You love that horse, don't you! Feeding and stroking won't buy me! I am now puzzled for what you would marry me. Were you planning a Charity Hospital under the guise of matrimony?"[28] And in all fairness, she did warn him: "I am too independent. I would not like to have to obey another—never!"[29] Zitkala-Ša had come to embody many of the ideals of the educated, professional New Woman, who needed no man to define her and demanded her place in the public sphere.[30] The place and purpose that Zitkala-Ša saw for herself presented the couple's second problem.

Montezuma wished Zitkala-Ša to move to Chicago, where he was making another, more successful attempt at private practice. Zitkala-Ša conceded that city life did boast the "artificial tastes" of Euro-American society that to her had become "second nature." But, using her skills as a writer and teacher to benefit Native peoples took priority.[31] This project required living in Yankton, whether or not Montezuma came along. His refusal to consent provoked a number of outbursts. "Perhaps the Indians are not human enough to waste your skill upon!" Zitkala-Ša wrote in a fury, "Stay in Chicago. Do! I consider my plan a more direct path to my high ideals. It will be a test of character but I shall not stay away for cowardly fears. If I succeed—it is genius. If I fail—it was due time to undeceive those who credit me with genius! In the meantime I am what I am! I owe no apologies to God or men!"[32] Montezuma rejected the idea of again practicing medicine for the Indian Service, finding the conditions unacceptable.[33] This despite Zitkala-Ša's suggestion that he "could do a vast deal of good by filling the position of Agency physician."[34] Moreover, there were other aspects to this disagreement.

Zitkala-Ša saw assimilationist boarding schools, with their stress on vocational training, as merely promoting Indian enslavement in the agricultural sector. "I will never speak of whites as elevating the Indian!" she told Montezuma, "Until Colonel Pratt actively interests himself in giving college education to Indians I cannot say his making them slaves to the plow is nothing other than drudgery! And drudgery is hell—not civilization! If Carlisle expects the Indian to adapt himself perfectly to 'civilized' life in a century she must admit that the Indian has powers which entitle him to a name better than Primitive!"[35] Aiding the Indian's lot, therefore, had to be accomplished on-reservation and from a different perspective.[36] In stark contrast, Montezuma argued that only a decimation of reservation life could transform the "savage," which was imperative by whatever means necessary. One of his lectures asked the question, "What right have we to take away a child from its Indian parents?" Montezuma's answer was, "It is done every day by the courts in cases of white children whose parents are incapable of taking care of them. You can never civilize the Indian until you place him yet young (and the younger the better) in direct relations with good civilization. When you do this with judgment, you will succeed and make him a useful citizen of the Republic."[37] Zitkala-Ša was mystified by this stance and Montezuma's fervid support of Pratt. In her letters she tried to convince Montezuma of his own intrinsic worth as a Native, rather than as a "civilized savage" saved by the powerful balm of white education. "I resent Carlisle's talking of you as it does," she complained, "Its talk—boasts—of you as a savage Apache and now an honorable physician in Chicago—the result of Education!! I guess if the character was not in you—savage or otherwise—education *could not* make you the man you are today. It was not that you were Indian—nor that civilization was an irresistible power—but because in an unusual measure the Great Spirit of a Universal God was and is in *you!*"[38] Montezuma, who had been raised by whites almost his entire life and had imbibed their prejudices, largely repudiated these notions. But still, Zitkala-Ša and the doctor planned a rendezvous.

In the spring of 1901 Zitkala-Ša traveled from Boston to the Fort Totten Agency, on the Devil's Lake (now renamed Spirit Lake) Sioux Reservation in North Dakota. Before she boarded the train at 1:00 P.M. on May 8 she warned Montezuma, "I am a delusion and a snare. . . . I swear I am not yours! I do not belong to anybody."[39] Zitkala-Ša arrived in Chicago the next evening at 5:25, having endured an almost thirty-hour journey, and Montezuma greeted her. What happened next is open to speculation. Four days later, however, Zitkala-Ša had resumed her journey. On May 13 she stepped aboard another train in St. Paul, Minnesota. Once settled in her carriage, she took out a pen and paper. Montezuma was on her mind. The car swayed from side to side, making it hard to write. Nonetheless, tender words flowed: "Last night I placed my beautiful red rose on part of my pillow. This morning I awoke but my rose would not be aroused—you were and are now wondrously kind to me. I know it—and appreciate it too. How comes it to pass—I wonder. So long I've wandered hither and thither—careless of others as they were of me. I fear there is some error in all of this—. . . Did you know last evening I wished I had not to leave you? As I think of you I desire for you only."[40]

Zitkala-Ša reached Fort Totten many hours later. By returning to the reservation and continuing her literary career, she hoped to meet the responsibilities of personal fulfillment, family, and culture.[41] On May 28, she wrote Montezuma again, displaying far less passion. Zitkala-Ša explained that she would stay in Yankton for one year. If Montezuma did not want to suffer a long engagement, he could marry whenever and whomever he chose.[42] Yet just two days later she missed him dearly, admitting that she wanted to return to Chicago before moving on to Yankton.[43] By early June they were discussing their wedding.[44]

At Fort Totten, Zitkala-Ša began interviewing elders for a second volume of stories requested by Ginn & Company. In letters to Montezuma she explained what a nice time she was having with the "old folks."[45] Nevertheless, she still had not told her mother of her impending return. Zitkala-Ša also mentioned that to the rest of her family, her brothers, she was only a "myth," having been gone for so long.[46] Recalling family memories, she told Montezuma the meaning behind her self-given name. "I have a half brother whose name is Simmons," Zitkala-Ša explained. "Once my own father scolded my brother; and my mother took such offense from it that eventually it resulted in a parting—so as I grew I was called by my brother's name—Simmons. I bore it a long time till my brother's wife—angry with me because I insisted on getting an education said I had deserted home and I might give up my brother's name 'Simmons' too. Well—you can guess how queer I felt—away from my own people—homeless—penniless—and even without a name! That I choose *to make* a name for myself and I guess I have made 'Zitkala-Ša' known—for even Italy writes in her language!"[47] At the end of June Zitkala-Ša traveled to Yankton.[48] Once in Greenwood, she elected not to live in Ellen Simmons's summer tepee. Instead, she rented a room at the Greenwood Agency, where she wrote and worked on proofs of *Old Indian Legends*.[49]

In returning, Zitkala-Ša had resolved to stay and aid the mother she once abandoned so willfully. "I must live with her," she told Montezuma, "and show her each day a practical demonstration of my love for her."[50] This act of cultural preservation and filial appreciation, however, failed to revive the once-strong relationship. Continuous squabbling produced distressed missives to Montezuma: "This very night that I write I have been need-lessly tortured by Mother's crazy tongue till all hell seems set loose upon my heels. And I feel wicked enough to kill her on the spot or else run *wild*."[51] Given the mood in South Dakota, it is unsurprising that the doctor resisted Zitkala-Ša's requests that he move there and, eventually, her cold ultimatums—"If we marry—it will be when you have carried out my wish [to come to Yankton]—not before. . . . What do you say to that?"[52]—and in-sulting threats—"Let me wish you success in your chosen world and work. Mine lie in places 'barren and foreign' to your acquired taste."[53]

Montezuma should have heeded these letters. While he was far away in Chicago Zitkala-Ša began to reacquaint herself with Raymond Bonnin, whom she had known at White's Institute seven years prior. Susan Rose Dominguez conjectures that Zitkala-Ša's older brother, David, may have re-introduced the pair at a Greenwood Agency social. They began riding horses together regularly in August. Conversing in their native language, they found that they shared much in common. Since leaving White's, Bonnin had attended the Haskell Institute in Kansas from 1896 to 1898, returning to South Dakota to claim an allotment and work as a clerk in the Indian Ser-vice.[54] Raymond's father, Joseph Barnebe Bonnin, had been born in Paris in 1840. He had come to Canada with his family as a boy, but immigrated to the Northwest Territory at age twenty-five. There he became a prosperous prospector and trader. In 1868 he married Emeline Picotte, daughter of the Frenchman Joseph Picotte, one of the first traders to travel up the Missouri River, encounter the Yankton Sioux, and marry into the tribe.[55] Like Zitkala-Ša, then, Bonnin was of mixed lineage, boarding school educated, and a prom-inent citizen. Though baptized Catholic as a boy, perhaps by traveling missionaries, Bonnin no longer attended church.[56] Instead, he remained dedicated to the betterment of indigenous peoples and appreciative of his family's cultural traditions.[57]

By the end of August Bonnin and Zitkala-Ša had grown close. She began wearing one of his presents, a ruby ring. Montezuma had also been warned that he was "not alone in the race." But even so, Zitkala-Ša, capriciously, gave him another chance. "You say you love me—Others boast the same. How shall I know which is the deepest interest and genuine? But at last. I have concluded to try you once again." Montezuma sent an engagement ring, which she accepted.[58] Juggling two lovers did not, seemingly, distract Zitkala-Ša too greatly from her work. When struck by writer's block, she only needed to recall Pratt's criticisms, which spurred her on. "Pratt has used his pull against me," she wrote in a September letter to Montezuma, "because my think is not his think—nor my ways—his ways! and just the hate of him fires me to work again even when I would most like to fold my hands."[59] *Old Indian Legends* came out a month later, featuring illustrations by the Winnebago artist Angel DeCora Dietz.[60]

Though marketed as a collection for younger audiences—"the blue-eyed little patriot" and "the black-haired aborigine" alike—*Legends* constituted both an assertion of Sioux cultural resilience and a critique of encroachment on indigenous lands. This attack commenced in the preface with Zitkala-Ša's allusion to *"our* country's once virgin soil" and America's new "second tongue" (emphasis added). The perspective destabilized white territorial primacy, while the book's stories, or *ohunkankans,* created a narrative arc dwelling upon the Sioux relationship to nature, the threat of Euro-American intrusion, and the treacherous temptations found in modern society.[61] In *Legends* the trickster Iktomi, a "spider fairy," is repeatedly punished for disrupting the natural order; badgers, who represent Indians, are robbed by a boorish bear, who stands in for violent, acquisitive whites; Blood Clot Boy, a Sioux avenger, saves the badgers from their invader; Iya, a gluttonous "camp-eater," disguises himself as a baby to infiltrate and swallow up Sioux settlements; Old Double Face, a kidnapper of Sioux children, sings sweetly as he tortures (much like missionaries); and finally, a rabbit foolishly gives up his eyes to enjoy an easier life dominated by technology.[62] *Legends* ends with a victory for the Sioux in which harmony is restored, external foes are defeated, and a rebirth is achieved. The collection remains highly significant for its translation of purely oral Sioux tradition into English.

The debut of *Old Indian Legends* in October 1901 coincided with the publication of Zitkala-Ša's "The Trial Path" in *Harper's Monthly.* Like *Legends,* this short story spoke to the necessity of perpetuating the oral storytelling traditions of the Sioux, and of the role of elders in safeguarding and passing down knowledge. In "Trial Path" a grandmother tells her granddaughter of two men who once fought for her affections—a fight in which one died. Rather than execute the murderer the tribe's chieftain devises a trial in which the man must survive a ride on a wild pony. He succeeds, is reintegrated into the community, and eventually marries his lover. Just as the grandmother is about to impart the "sacred knowledge" that gives ultimate meaning to the events, the granddaughter drifts off to sleep.[63] The story functioned as a call for the Sioux, and Indians in general, to learn and internalize the tales and teachings of their elders. Appreciation of the past was necessary to withstand the onslaught of forced assimilation and preserve the spiritual remnants of a threatened culture.[64]

Montezuma, meanwhile, was trying to preserve the remnants of his threatened engagement to Zitkala-Ša. He had been warned again in October of his competition. "I have a friend out here," Zitkala-Ša wrote, "who claims all I can give by the laws of natural affinity."[65] Apparently Montezuma did not take the strong hint seriously. He still hoped to marry, but instead of seeking a compromise, Montezuma seems to have resorted to bullying tactics. Around the New Year the romance became increasingly tumultuous. Zitkala-Ša's letters contain brutal tirades that reveal tremendous frustration, followed by remarkably loving reconciliations. On January 1, 1902, she wrote:

> My Dear Dr. Montezuma,
>   If you are so sure you are my superior, that I am a fake—do not resent losing so worthless an acquaintance.
>   I feel sorry for you—that your own indiscretion centered your regard upon such a wretch as I am! (God is my only judge!) He knows me and my struggles better than my best and finest mortal friend!—In His eyes I would be doing you a greater wrong to marry you than to have done as I have. Do not think I made my reply in a trifling mood—for there are many [illegible] by the way; and it was not the easiest thing I've done—to live up to my best judgment. Do not feel reckless and revengeful! Live on in your brave way. Live up to your highest conception of God's creatures. I am striving but Oh—dear—it is hard—so hard—I wish sometimes that I was dead.[66]

Yet just two weeks later Zitkala-Ša wrote again, calling Montezuma "My dearest heart of hearts" and complaining sweetly that she did not receive an expected letter.[67]

It was around this time that Zitkala-Ša's life could have changed dramatically. On January 25 she confided to Montezuma: "By the way I have not told you that a two year old baby (whose mother was an old school chum of mine—who has recently died)—is offered to me. It was [illegible] dying request. Her husband invites me to visit the old home to see the child at least. . . . The matter has weighed heavily on my mind—Finally after many haltings—I have decided not to accept such a care when I have my old mother already on my shoulders. Still I wish I had been able to give my time to such a task. That would mean my giving up my writing, and that is out of the question." One wonders, however, how much the decision bothered her. In the very next line she asked, ever so coyly, for a "favor." Montezuma was kindly bid to look for some drape material "with Japanese dragons on it" (which Zitkala-Ša had previously noticed in a store in Boston). The purpose was to make her mother's house "a little cozy."[68]

The fleeting prospect of motherhood disregarded, the regular conflicts and reconciliations between Zitkala-Ša and Montezuma were unsurprising. They were both dynamic and attractive people who disagreed profoundly. Zitkala-Ša remained adamant that Native peoples should reject white society and be "masters of [our] circumstances" who must "claim our heritage."[69] This meant accepting no interference from whites under the guise of charity, an idea Montezuma found absurd.[70] That January Zitkala-Ša had made an overt political statement against the assimilation movement and the U.S. government in general. In the *Boston Evening Transcript* she compared Indian children on reservations to "prisoners of war," beleaguered by an educational "experiment" imposed from Washington.[71] She had already sarcastically expressed the same sentiments to Montezuma in a (partially) furious letter on white civilization's treatment of indigenous peoples: "I wish to see larger than trifling details in a question like that of the powers of years to produce the flower of civilization. It is a sad thing to see one's race practically prisoners of war—Bound like babies—and must have a permit for every move! It is heart-rendering to see a government try experiments on a real race—If like physicians they would first try [like a] big vivisection, their wonderful theories on lower creatures like cats and dogs, then the Indian, I might not feel it so keenly at times! Say—try starving out life by feeding insufficient unfit food to cats, then having found the best death rate, try it in earnest upon the old Indians on these Reserves."[72] One can guess at Montezuma's reaction.

How much the two differed is best revealed in a remarkable letter Zitkala-Ša wrote in June 1901. It criticized white society, designating "civilization" a "temporary world" in which education teaches one to "master" a set of "conveniences." The outcome is imprisonment in the ruts of a dull, mechanized existence: "The majority of men and women are hopelessly treading drudgery mills and that is called civilization? To be compelled to work when you do not wish it—is drudgery—not civilization. . . . I prefer to be stone-dead than living-dead! The intellectual class of the so called civilized is a small minority! The majority are drudges—after so many centuries if the Anglo Saxon can produce so small a flower—by what magic do you expect a primitive Indian race to become civilized—and not drudges!? I would rather have [Indians be] all intellectual artistic men and women but if I place them as primitive as you do—I would have no right to expect so much—save the right of being disappointed." Zitkala-Ša did not mean, however, that sovereign indigenous peoples should reject white society entirely, but only take their place in its highest echelons: "But I do expect the Indian to compete with the highest minds in every branch of pursuit of today—And this is my reason—I consider the Indian spiritually superior to any race of savages, white or black—I call the Indians' simplicity of dress and freedom of outdoor life—wisdom which is more powerful than that of the hot house flower of which your large city can boast!" With greater wisdom, Zitkala-Ša continued, came a greater exercise of morality, expressed in the Indian's "own self respect and honor to keep unwritten laws."[73] This was a life and legacy worth maintaining against the attack of white civilization. In one letter from April 1901 she wrote to Montezuma, evidently in all seriousness, "Oh! how I'd like to return to olden times!"[74] In another she suggested that it was a "grander thing to live among the Indians."[75]

There were personal and moral, as well as political, reasons for Zitkala-Ša's decision to remain outside American society. While feeling it "selfish and cruel" to abandon the elders on the reservations, she also still carried a strong sense of obligation toward her mother.[76] Additionally, she had taken on more work as a teacher at the Crow Creek Agency school.[77] In April 1902, Zitkala-Ša and Montezuma were still fighting over whether he would apply for a position at Yankton or she would move to Chicago. Zitkala-Ša had almost given up on the relationship.[78] But in May they were again on cordial terms. Montezuma wrote to compliment Zitkala-Ša on her latest story, "A Warrior's Daughter," published in *Everybody's Magazine* in April.[79]

"A Warrior's Daughter" is best viewed in the context of Zitkala-Ša's belief in equality of the sexes, much on display in her letters to Montezuma during this period.[80] The two had sparred over her overt refusal to adopt a submissive position within their proposed marriage. They stumbled on another philosophical disagreement over what role women should play in a future Indian rights organization that both wished to establish. While Montezuma was adamant that such associations should be exclusively male or female, Zitkala-Ša expressed revulsion at his misguided insularity. "For spite," she warned him, "I feel like putting my hand forward and simply wiping the Indian men's committee into nowhere!!! No—I should not really do such a thing. Only I do not understand *why* your organization does not include Indian women. Am I not an Indian woman as capable to think on serious matters and as thoroughly interested in the race—as any one or two of your men put together? Why do you dare to leave us out? Why? Sometimes as I ponder the preponderous [sic] actions of men—which are tremendously out of proportion with the small results—I laugh. It is all more waste of time than we pause to realize. It is as Emerson says—a game of 'Puss with her tail'—no more!"[81] These beliefs in sexual equality, or even female superiority, clearly inform "A Warrior's Daughter."

"A Warrior's Daughter" subverted and defied conventional literary renderings of femininity in its presentation of Tusee, a tough and wily Dakota woman who daringly rescues her helpless male lover, who has been captured after participating in a raid. Approaching the enemy camp, Tusee seduces and dispatches her lover's foe, then disguises herself as an old woman and carries her exhausted lover away into the night.[82] The daring rescue demonstrates the ability of Native women to match and exceed the power and intellect of any man. This oppositional statement to the dominant Victorian Cult of True Womanhood likewise defined Native women outside of white society's restrictive proscriptions, perhaps signaling that by 1902 Zitkala-Ša intended to fight for, or rescue, indigenous peoples on her own terms.[83] She had, however, tired of fighting with Montezuma over their relationship. Raymond Bonnin had won "the race."

As South Dakota's *Tyndall Tribune* reported on May 10, 1902, Zitkala-Ša wed Bonnin in a civil ceremony in the home of mutual friends near Standing Rock.[84] There is no hint in Zitkala-Ša's correspondence with Montezuma that the wedding was imminent. The doctor must have been shocked. He had invited Zitkala-Ša to Chicago in April. Zitkala-Ša's response was extremely friendly. She politely declined, but asked Montezuma whether he knew of any specialist in Chicago who could examine an old violin that she had just found. "By the way," she also mentioned, " 'The Atlantic Monthly' has just accepted a little scribble of mine—'Why I am a Pagan.' I imagine that Carlisle will rear up on its haunches at sight of the little sky rocket! ha! ha!"[85] She was bidding favors and complaining of Pratt. All seemed normal. The next moment she was married.

Judging from Zitkala-Ša's post-marriage letters, Montezuma's initial reaction was half-disbelieving. He pointed out that his financial situation promised a better life than Bonnin could offer and evidently suggested that Zitkala-Ša could return to him. She reminded Montezuma that she possessed lands valued at six thousand dollars. Money was no inducement.[86] Montezuma, rejected again, insisted on having his ring back. Zitkala-Ša,

however, had carelessly lost it. The correspondence devolved into recrimi-
nations throughout June and July. "Did I not once return that infernal
ring?" Zitkala-Ša wrote in angry script, "Who used his powers of persua-
sion to cause me to wear it again? You did—you upright blameless man!
Have you forgot how you contradicted me every time I told you I thought it
useless to consider matrimony?"[87] But Montezuma would not relent, sending insulting, accusatory missives. "And now," Zitkala-Ša wrote back, "you
fume about like a chicken with its head cut off knowing nothing of what
you strike against!" She reminded him. "I am proud—fearless and as independent as you."[88] Montezuma was so angry that he later considered suing
Zitkala-Ša for the cost of the ring—seventy-five dollars.[89] Their relationship
would only be repaired a decade later.

As if to prove her pride, fearlessness, and independence, at the beginning of the year Zitkala-Ša had published "The Indian Dance: A Protest
against Its Abolition," in the Boston Evening Transcript. The article bordered
on the truly scandalous in its defense of the naked form. It opened with
Zitkala-Ša confronting an imaginary settler complaining of Indians dancing nude as he hacks away at the icy Missouri River with an axe. Zitkala-Ša
ponders the European male's impulse to imprison the body and stop Natives
from practicing their religious dances. She describes corseted white women
gliding about to orchestral music as "gauze-covered barbarism"—perhaps "a
martyrdom to some ancient superstition which centuries of civilization and
Christianization have not wholly eradicated from the yellow-haired and
blue-eyed races." Faced with such foolishness, Zitkala-Ša mounts a waiting
pony and rushes out onto the plains, which "restore to [her] the sweet sense
that God has allotted a place in his vast universe for each of his creatures,
both great and small—just as they are."[90] Entering the debate, Pratt countered Zitkala-Ša's celebration of the human body. Carlisle reprinted her story
in its official newspaper, but branded "the savage dance . . . the greatest possible hindrance to Indian progress."[91] But "The Indian Dance" was only a
prelude to Zitkala-Ša's "Why I Am a Pagan," which appeared in the Atlantic
Monthly in December 1902. Zitkala-Ša had penned this piece as a retort to
criticism of "The Soft-Hearted Sioux."

"Why I Am a Pagan" begins in Yankton, where Zitkala-Ša has returned
and purged herself of the values of white schooling. She describes the
"loving Mystery" that crosses all "racial lines" to create "a living mosaic of
human beings." In her home, she is confronted by a Native preacher, who
hopes to covert her. The man, though he speaks "most strangely the jan-
gling phrases of a bigoted creed," is still "God's creature." Yet Zitkala-Ša
disappoints him by disregarding his warnings about hell. When a church

bell rings in the distance, the preacher, a slave to the white man's religion, beats a hasty retreat to deliver his afternoon sermon. As Zitkala-Ša watches him disappear down the path she reflects on his foolhardy visit and directly addresses her critics: "The little incident recalled to mind the copy of a missionary paper brought to my notice a few days ago, in which a 'Christian' pugilist commented upon a recent article of mine, grossly perverting the spirit of my pen." "Christian pugilist" was an allusion to the *Word Carrier*, which first criticized "The Soft-Hearted Sioux," and to Pratt, who had reprinted the review. Rebelling against this disparagement, Zitkala-Ša had chosen a different religion, seeking consolation, guidance, and divine contact in nature. "If this is Paganism," she concluded, "then at present, at least, I am a Pagan."[92] At the time Zitkala-Ša wrote this declaration of Native religion's superiority, "Paganism" was the missionary community's derogatory epithet for indigenous beliefs, considered a godless, "savage" religion.[93] Zitkala-Ša, the graduate of a Quaker boarding school, had publicly undermined the basis of missionary involvement in Indian education by re-embracing the very belief system they sought to eradicate.

But whether Zitkala-Ša had really rejected Christianity is ambiguous. Her letters to Montezuma during this period, for instance, do not explicitly suggest so. In one she admits that she "rarely if ever attend[s] church."[94] In other letters, she discusses God using phrases such as "ever buoyant Master Spirit." In one, she states, "Personally—I have so universal a spirit that I can go to nature in either East or West and find enjoyment."[95] It is plain, however, that Zitkala-Ša had become disgusted at the way Christianity was often wielded against indigenous peoples. "Why I Am a Pagan," therefore, rejected conciliation with the white world.[96]

Rejecting any notion that full assimilation into American civilization was desirable, Zitkala-Ša sought independence from the ideological confines of her white education. This project entailed the preservation of traditional ways and remaining tribal lands, the only place where direct engagement with those ways could occur. She had come to several core conclusions, many of which fit within a proto–Red Power paradigm: her culture was superior to the mechanized rut of white civilization; Indians were held "prisoners of war" by a transplanted society and were in need of a self-run, inclusive intertribal organization to defend them against its onslaught; aspects of Christianity and Euro-American civilization that wrongly denigrated valuable Native cultures had to be countered; indigenous participation in the white world should be on an equal footing, with Indian access to the highest realms, not merely the life of drudgery and cultural erasure promoted by the boarding school system; and finally, indigenous women had power. They, like men, needed to stand up in defense of their heritage. The last aspect seems to have sprung from the resilience and wisdom Zitkala-Ša's mother had demonstrated as a Yankton woman, Quakerism's belief in sexual equality, and the ideal of the educated, independent New Woman that appeared at the end of the nineteenth century. Thus, as foreshadowed at the end of "The Indian Dance," when Zitkala-Ša flees on her pony to escape the whites attacking her culture, the young writer abandoned the East.

In the latter half of 1902 Bonnin received a new post with the Office of Indian Affairs on the Uintah and Ouray Reservation in Utah, at a salary of $600 a year.[97] In December, the Bonnins went westward. Zitkala-Ša had given up her cosmopolitan life in Boston, Montezuma's Chicago, her music, and her literary career, all to begin, as she wrote in "An Indian Teacher among Indians," her "work for the Indian race."[98]

CHAPTER 4

UINTAH

The Bonnins arrived at the Uintah and Ouray Reservation, home to the Northern Ute Indians, in the winter of 1902.[1] By that time the Utes' former lifeways had been permanently destroyed by a conjunction of Spanish settlement, French exploration, and westward American migration that had made survival off the land increasingly difficult. Trapping and bison hunting had wiped out game, while whites had appropriated water sources. Worsening matters, the Utes had a series of skirmishes with the U.S. Army after the Mexican-American War in 1848. The combatants negotiated a treaty in 1849 that allowed U.S. citizens free passage through Ute lands—if confined to a route of authorized trading posts and military forts. Subsequently, a steady stream of Mormons, eleven thousand by 1850, began to disrupt Ute territory en route to present-day Utah. Prospectors also appeared in search of gold. Their arrival provoked numerous small-scale confrontations and a deadly measles epidemic that decimated the Ute population.

In an attempt to aid settlers, particularly the Mormons, President Lincoln created by proclamation the Uintah Valley Reservation in northeast Utah, the first reserve for the Utes. Lincoln's action offered them no respite. The Homestead Act of 1862 quickly increased settlement, agriculture, commercial hunting, and mining operations on Ute lands. Seeking a way to cope with external pressures, the Tabeguache (Uncompahgre) Ute, led by Chief Ouray, signed their first treaty with the U.S. government in 1863. With the stroke of a pen, they agreed to give up ancestral lands in present-day eastern Colorado and migrate west. Although other Ute bands continued to resist, another treaty in 1868 created the Consolidated Ute Reservation along the western Colorado border, meant for all remaining groups. As more settlers poured westward and became more vociferous in demanding Indian removal, Ouray's Utes were driven northwest to present-day Utah, surrounded, territorially confined, and forbidden to hunt. Meanwhile, the steady stream of Mormon settlers did not abate. Ouray died in 1880, the same year the Uintah and Ouray Reservation was created. His widow, Chipeta, remained a highly respected figure on the reservation. Utah became a state in 1896.

The year the Bonnins arrived at Uintah, the U.S. government began coercing the Utes to divide their lands into allotments of forty or eighty acres. Unallotted land was quickly opened to white settlement. (The Bonnins, too, purchased land.) Despite Ute protests, by 1909 more than 3½ million acres had been lost to homesteaders, who far outnumbered the Utes. Having never had a tradition of farming, Utes who did take allotments rarely chose to live on them. The BIA punished those who refused to adopt white lifestyles or send their children to school by withholding rations. Isolated and overwhelmed by the white tide, many Utes became mired in poverty. Diseases such as diphtheria, chicken pox, and tuberculosis stalked a people that viewed modern medicine with suspicion, and their population underwent a steep decline. Basic security, meanwhile, was so tenuous that the Ninth Calvary, stationed at Fort Duchesne, regularly patrolled to prevent raids and arson. Many Utes bitterly opposed the BIA, and the threat of rebellion was omnipresent; in fact, some Utes tried to stage a rebellion at Uintah in 1905, during the time the Bonnins were there.[2] All of Zitkala-Ša's letters from Utah reflect this period of wrenching transition. They describe the reservation as a violent place populated by land speculators, opposing religious factions, and corrupt BIA agents who treated the Utes with contempt, and conspired against her and her husband for material gain. Zitkala-Ša's stay at Uintah was thus a difficult trial, in which, as Leon Speroff puts it, "the commitment of her youth was severely tested."[3] She wavered between a steely determination to aid the resident indigenous population and a desire to escape them.

On May 28, 1903, Zitkala-Ša gave birth to her only child, a son named Ohiya (Winner), whose English name was Raymond, after his father.[4] Taking very little time off to recover, the new mother sought work as a teacher at the government-run Uintah Boarding School at Whiterocks, where the Bonnins initially established their home.[5] Founded in 1885, the school was a typical Pratt-style institution. Students dressed in uniforms and short hair was a requirement. In 1901 a measles outbreak there killed seventeen out of a full student body of sixty-five. The school quickly became so un-popular that in 1904 the reservation superintendent began paying parents to enroll their children.[6] Though Zitkala-Ša boasted very high qualifica-tions, the BIA repeatedly ignored her letters requesting employment. Per-haps Zitkala-Ša's relatively recent criticism of Indian schools in the *Atlantic Monthly* had blackballed her at the BIA. Unwilling to sit idle, Zitkala-Ša took the initiative. Fortuitously, she found a collection of brass instruments shipped to the school years before for a music program that had never been funded. Requisitioning the instruments, she formed a children's band that gave local concerts. She also attended to the older population with a basket-weaving course and lectures on hygiene, run out of her home.[7] Not until 1905 did Uintah Boarding School temporarily hire Zitkala-Ša (at $600 a year), when an instructor abruptly resigned. Reservation authorities quickly sought a replacement, but the new teacher failed to appear as promised. As a result, Zitkala-Ša was rehired in March 1906.[8] Displaying more empathy for the students than her white colleagues did, she was able to lessen some of the harsher elements of rapid-assimilation-style instruction.[9]

Bonnin meanwhile established himself as an agent. Responsible for buying provisions for the Utes, ranging from fencing materials to cattle, he often challenged white suppliers when he felt the tribe was overcharged.[10] To-gether, the Bonnins started compiling family histories of each of the Ute bands on the reservation, advising on treaty issues, and handling Ute cor-respondence with the U.S. government.[11] Efforts to aid those on the reserva-tion extended into the Bonnins' personal life. After they got settled, their household expanded to include an orphaned Ute boy named Oran Curry and an elderly, homeless Sioux called Bad Hand, or Old Sioux, who had been subsisting off small game. Local legend had it that Old Sioux was the centenarian cousin of Sitting Bull. At the Battle of Little Big Horn he had been shot in the hand, after which he relocated to present-day Utah and became a recluse.[12] Old Sioux would live with the Bonnins for fourteen years.[13] (Bonnin's mother, Emeline, however, died back in South Dakota on March 30, 1904.)[14]

Zitkala-Ša still had an offer from Ginn & Company to publish more In-dian stories, yet oddly, she did not actively pursue the opportunity. She did continue to write, but even though she recorded traditional stories and prepared them for submission, she never sent them to Boston.[15] Only one, "Shooting of the Red Eagle," appeared in the Haskell Institute's *Indian Leader* in 1904.[16] The situation at Uintah must have been difficult for Zitkala-Ša. On the reservation there was little room for the personal artistic expression or cultural fulfillment she had experienced in her twenties. The only luxury seems to have been her piano, the centerpiece of her modest home.[17] Zitkala-Ša cultivated engaging company to escape ennui. Although she taught hygiene classes to Ute women and socialized with them, Ute culture was largely foreign. Consequently, she gravitated toward the Mormon population, which better reflected her tastes and level of education.[18] Mormons, unlike typical Euro-Americans, believed that Indians, or "Lamanites," were "a people of great promise and genealogy."[19] Zitkala-Ša began to develop a wider social life, participating in events organized by the Church of Latter-day Saints (but not converting to the religion) while teaching and studying piano, sometimes in the nearby town of Vernal. She also began work as an Indian Service clerk in 1907, and made trips to Salt Lake City when time allowed.[20] But as soon as Zitkala-Ša befriended members of one religious group, she came in conflict with another.

In 1893 the Episcopal Church opened a mission and subsequently established chapels in several locations at Uintah. Though the church attracted few Utes, more Episcopalians arrived in the summer of 1909, intending to set up a mission school, a first for the reservation, with the support of Commissioner of Indian Affairs Francis Ellington Leupp.[21] It soon turned out that the would-be teachers had designs on the government-run Uintah Boarding School at Whiterocks. They began to effect a merger of sorts with official support from the reservation hierarchy. Likely seeking a civil servant for the job of school superintendent, the agent in charge offered Bonnin the position. He initially resisted due to the religious conflict, but after consideration, he accepted for reasons that are unknown. Bonnin's salary as a property clerk had been raised to $1,100 per year, exactly his salary for the new post.[22] As it turned out, the appointment was a disaster. Such a disaster, in fact, that Zitkala-Ša sought aid from an unlikely source: Richard Henry Pratt. When and how they mended their relationship is unclear, but by 1909 Pratt had become her new confidant. In a letter posted from Whiterocks on July 9, addressed to "My dear friend," Zitkala-Ša explained the situation to her erstwhile employer and enemy.[23]

The letter complained of the "experiment" of putting the reservation school "under church control" (with "Episcopal" in parentheses). In particular, Zitkala-Ša expressed concern over how "detrimental" the situation had been to Bonnin, who had been undermined from the start. She wrote, "Employees began at once to resent being under an *Indian*; the matter grew worse—until they referred to me as an 'Indian Squaw.' They absolutely refused to obey Mr. Bonnin's legitimate instructions and the Agent, whose wife is a strong Episcopalian, failed to give Mr. Bonnin any support. Mr. Bonnin preferred changes and the Agent withheld them. . . .

My husband has served the Government 6½ years and rendered efficient service. He is an Indian. He needs the work and is a willing worker. I cannot understand, how in the name of Christianity anyone should try to down him in this work. These Church people who are making the trouble never took a Civil Service Examination, all but one knew nothing about Indian work." The lack of proper qualifications aside, the racial slur gives a good indication of how many whites working on reservations viewed their Native colleagues. The entire episode, meanwhile, illustrated how the BIA bureaucracy, controlled by such whites, often prevented the airing and rectification of various legitimate grievances. Zitkala-Ša complained that Bonnin had been forced to accept the Episcopalian interlopers' appointments even though they threw the school into disorder. Bonnin's superiors blamed him for the mess. "It seems to me," Zitkala-Ša wrote in her characteristically metaphorical language, "like hobbling a horse and pounding him over the head because he has no speed!"

Matters eventually came to a head when Bonnin called for an investigation and the agent conspired to have him transferred. Zitkala-Ša planned a trip to Washington, D.C., in order to protest in person. Afterward she was to travel to Philadelphia and confer with Pratt. On the way, however, she ran into an old (unidentified) friend, who promised to raise the matter with the BIA, and consequently she missed her appointment with Pratt. Concerned that Pratt might have felt slighted, Zitkala-Ša wrote reassuringly, "I had wished to see you because I knew you are always the Indian's friend. I wanted to get your advice." The letter closed, "I hope I have not worried you with our tale of woe. With greatest esteem, Gertrude Simmons Bonnin."[24] If Pratt was moved by the "tale of woe" to intervene in some way, his actions were ineffective. By that point he had lost his former influence. In 1904 he had been removed from Carlisle due to his vigorous public opposition to the Indian Bureau.[25] In the end, the Episcopalians took control of the school.[26] Bonnin then quit the Indian Service in the fall of 1909, and his family left Utah for the Standing Rock Reservation in North and South Dakota. Zitkala-Ša started work at Fort Yates, the headquarters of the reservation, as an issue clerk.[27]

The time at Fort Yates had a profound and lasting influence on Zitkala-Ša's life. There she became involved with the reservation's long-established Benedictine Catholic mission. The mission sponsored several Catholic Sioux Congresses at Standing Rock Sioux Reservation, the first in 1891, the summer following the Wounded Knee massacre. These religious gatherings in some ways substituted for the Sun Dance, which the federal government had banned.[28] In later correspondence Zitkala-Ša wrote of the "wonderful work" done by the nuns and three Catholic priests at Standing

Rock. One priest, Father Martin Kenel (known as Father Martin), became her friend and religious advisor. The collective devotion Zitkala-Ša witnessed largely mitigated her former distaste for Christianity. She put it simply: "I was converted."[29]

This was a remarkable about-face for a woman who seven years earlier had made a name for herself denouncing the influence of missionaries on Indian reservations. Yet in one way Zitkala-Ša's conversion was not entirely contradictory. In the early twentieth century the Catholic Church frequently opposed federal Indian policy. Zitkala-Ša's involvement with the Church also gave her a sympathetic and influential ally in Washington, D.C.: Father William H. Ketcham, director of the Bureau of Catholic Indian Missions (founded in 1874) and member of the Board of Indian Commissioners.[30] For the next seven years Zitkala-Ša would try to enlist Ketcham's help in a number of causes, both personal and religious.

The Bonnins must have been happy at Standing Rock. Zitkala-Ša was successful at her post as issue clerk, and her family was among fellow Sioux and Catholics. It is a mystery, then, why after only six months they returned to Utah in the spring of 1910. The only incentive, gleaned from Zitkala-Ša's letters, is that they had previously bought a claim with the intention of starting a ranch, and did not want to abandon it.[31] On her return, Zitkala-Ša took up an entirely different pursuit: bringing Catholicism to the Utes. In May she wrote Ketcham the first of many letters. "Pardon the liberty I take," it began, "in thus addressing you for the sake of humanity." Zitkala-Ša explained that she and her husband were "educated Sioux Indians" formerly employed by the Indian Service, now farming "on a claim" at Uintah. Recounting her conversion to Catholicism, Zitkala-Ša expressed her sincere desire to convert others: "I long for these Utes to have the opportunity to learn of God as our Catholic Church teaches." She mentioned that an Episcopal church had been established in Uintah, but related with regret that "these Utes still continue their Annual Dances—'the Bear Dance' in the early Spring and the 'Sun Dance' the first of July. Sunday is not observed by the Indians because it is usually a dance day." There was only one hope left. "I firmly believe," she asserted, "only the Catholic Church can reach these benighted Utes." The letter went on to suggest a place for a mission or church in an abandoned building that once housed a government school. Zitkala-Ša concluded with a declaration of faith: "I fervently trust my appeal for help from our Church for these Indians shall not be in vain."[32] Yet, she did not post her missive immediately.

The next day Zitkala-Ša wrote to Father Martin, expressing what appears to be profound loneliness. "In this wilderness, closely fortified by the

Rockies, there seem to be no real Christians, or civilized men," she lamented. Instead, the "majority of the white people are Mormons," while the "Utes are yet groping in Spiritual Darkness." Describing Uintah as a "Godless country" overrun with speculators in league with corrupt BIA agents, Zitkala-Ša begged Father Martin to aid her in establishing a Catholic church. She warned him that the Utes, "if left in their ignorance and demoralization, would never go forth to seek Christ; and thus the Light will have to be brought to them." In words that would have greatly pleased her teachers at White's Institute, Zitkala-Ša continued, "I am so anxious for this benighted people to reap the benefits of knowing and serving the only true God, as I have been greatly benefited." To these ends, she enclosed the previous day's letter to Ketcham, asking that Father Martin forward it along with an introduction.[33]

Zitkala-Ša's expression of dismay at the Utes' practice of the Sun Dance is surprising. Just a few months later she attended the ceremony at Uintah with her husband. On the last day, among the crowd, they bumped into William Hanson, a Mormon music teacher whom Zitkala-Ša had met around 1908.[34] Hanson had lived in Utah almost all his life. Born in Vernal in 1887 to a farming family, he had studied at Brigham Young University for two years in his late teens. In 1907 Hanson left to perform his duties as a missionary for the Church of Latter-day Saints in several northern states. Upon his return he secured a post at the local high school, Uintah Academy.[35] Throughout these years he cultivated a deep interest in indigenous cultures. According to Hanson's later account, Zitkala-Ša showed great enthusiasm for the Sun Dance, freely explaining its history and meaning. Soon thereafter, she suggested that they create an opera based on the ritual. Composed over the subsequent 2½ years, *The Sun Dance Opera* would debut in early 1913. Unfortunately, few details of the collaboration exist. Only Zitkala-Ša's correspondence with Kenel and Ketcham remains as the primary record of her life in 1910–12.

As Zitkala-Ša had requested in her May 1910 missive, Father Martin wrote Ketcham at the beginning of August.[36] The two-month delay was likely a result of the Catholic Sioux Congress being held at Fort Yates in June.[37] Kenel's letter introduced the Bonnins as "the best educated Indians I have ever met," told of Zitkala-Ša's conversion, and singled out her devotion: "While here she became a Catholic—her husband was baptized a Catholic— she was one of the most earnest converts I ever saw, and both conducted themselves as model Catholics, and we were very sorry to lose them." At the end of his letter, Kenel repeated Zitkala-Ša's earnest appeal for a Catholic presence at Uintah.[38]

Father Ketcham, then traveling in the Southwest, did not personally respond. However, Charles S. Lusk, secretary of the Bureau of Catholic Indian Missions, did. He wrote directly to Zitkala-Ša, assuring her that her
plea for the Utes would "rouse great sympathy" in Ketcham's "heart and
mind" and compel him to "do all in his power to provide religious facilities
for them." But unfortunately, Lusk warned, "the financial resources of the
Bureau are somewhat limited, and consequently, we may not be able to render any material help at this time."[39] Three weeks later Lusk wrote again, at
Ketcham's behest, to suggest that Zitkala-Ša contact the bishop of Salt Lake
City, Lawrence Scanlan, who would be in a better position to offer practical
assistance.[40] In the fall Zitkala-Ša wrote as instructed, but received no reply.
Undeterred, she again wrote Father Ketcham to press her case in January
1911, urging him that the Utes required "the Light that the Catholic Church
can give them."[41] Ketcham sent back a short, formal answer, agreeing to
write the bishop himself. In the meantime, he asked Zitkala-Ša to make an
informal census of unconverted souls at Uintah.[42] About a week later, she
duly furnished a "crude map" of the territory, indicating where the population of "about 1000" Indians lived. Highlighting the urgency of the situation, Zitkala-Ša emphasized the depths of degradation into which the Utes
had fallen. "The Utes show no interest in Spiritual Life," she explained, "They
are governed largely by superstitions. They are immoral. They waste all their
time in gambling; some drink intoxicants. Even the School Children, who
should know better, after leaving school, are living lives of immorality." But
the greatest problem for Zitkala-Ša was perhaps sexual relations among the
Utes. Such "marriages are not legal," and yet they seemed unaware of the
danger. "They do need help," she told Ketcham, "but do not know it. I hope
and pray for their conversion."[43] The bishop of Salt Lake apparently did not.
Ketcham soon sent word to say that he, too, had been ignored by His
Excellency.[44]

In March of the same year Zitkala-Ša found herself begging the Catholic
Church's assistance in a personal, rather than religious, matter. Her family
was experiencing financial hardship due to expenses incurred by their
venture into commercial farming, and as a result, Bonnin had reentered
the Indian Service. He was working as a clerk at the agency office in Whiterocks, eight miles away from home, while Zitkala-Ša, nine-year-old Ohiya,
and Old Sioux stayed at the ranch. Bonnin badly wanted the position to be
made permanent. His predecessor had been earning $1,200 a year, an aver-
age salary for a civil servant, but the steady income would help his family's
finances greatly. Zitkala-Ša hurriedly wrote Father Martin: "I beg of you to
be patient with my request—if it appears—bold: but knowing of no one

else who really would take interest in our small affairs, I turn to you—as once I did at Yates." She requested that Kenel contact Ketcham, who had enough influence in Washington to secure both the post and the salary for her husband. "I have prayed that God would give us a way to earn the necessary money," she wrote, "and we trust this is to be the answer."[45] Kenel and Ketcham, to their credit, promptly intervened, but with mixed results. Bonnin was appointed property clerk just a couple of weeks later; but his salary was set, unfairly, at only $1,000 per annum—less than he had been making when he quit the Indian Service in 1909.[46] It was a typical act of BIA inequity.

The Bonnins soon learned that a financial clerk had convinced his superior to arrange the pay cut, which allowed the clerk to maintain his own salary at the more generous sum of $1,600 a year. Nonetheless, Zitkala-Ša poured out her gratitude to Father Martin in a long, effusive letter, though she simultaneously expressed dismay at the financial clerk's "trimming off someone else's salary to save his own."[47] For the Bonnins, Uintah was always an uncertain place where white agents sometimes plotted against them or treated them with disdain.[48] These persistent slights appear to have nurtured within Zitkala-Ša a feeling of persecution and suspicion that would affect her later in life. The letter to Father Martin also showed that the Bonnins were eager to leave Utah. Bonnin had been offered a superintendent's position in Banning, California, a year prior, but was unable to accept due to his financial circumstances, most likely arising from the purchase of the ranch. Now prepared to lease their property—comprising eighty acres, four buildings, and a cellar—the Bonnins hoped that Father Martin could find them a job on a reservation with a Catholic mission. "I want so much to be near our church," Zitkala-Ša told him, "I want to bring my boy up *in the church.*"

Given their run-in with the Episcopalians and the machinations of white agents, it is unsurprising that Zitkala-Ša viewed God, the Catholic church, Father Martin, and Father Ketcham as all she had to depend on. This conviction manifested itself in the same letter to Father Martin, where she described an episode that revealed her seriousness about Catholicism and her reliance on a divine presence:

> This week has been one of wonderful nearness of God, our Father. I scarce know how to tell it. Yet I have tried your kind patience often with rehearsals of my troubles; Now I want to tell you of our numerous blessings.
>   You know Mr. Bonnin is working in the Agency—8 miles away. Ohiya, the Old Sioux and I have been alone on the Ranch—the past three weeks. Monday I was overtaken by Grippe [flu]. The severe pain in my lungs made me fear Pneumonia. I rose at 2 O'clock in the morning and sat by the fire.

I felt very ill and very lonely. Then I did remember that God was ever present! That all the Saints of Heaven would hear my prayers! I wondered why the weakness in me had been so Strong? Why I thought first of human help which is uncertain at the best! While God and Heaven never fail!

I prayed for help—as the child and the feeble old man were dependent on me for their daily care. I returned to bed and slept. Since then I have improved rapidly. I am up now and feel quite well.

This belief that God offered protection was reinforced shortly after when the Bonnins desperately needed money to pay off a substantial debt of $550. With no other recourse they hired a lawyer to sell a portion of their land—a decision that almost ended in disaster. In the hope that a perceived lack of interest would allow him to make the purchase at a reduced price, the lawyer never advertised the sale.

The Bonnins learned of the lawyer's deception, but the debt was still due. Having been "saved from this Attorney's snare," "like a miracle" Bonnin unexpectedly inherited the exact amount required from the sale of his mother's estate. Just after they received the news, a "Cattle man from Colorado" offered to buy their cattle for the generous price of $745 (about $18,000 in present terms). "These manifest Divine aids when the test of our strength physical and mental and Spiritual had about reached its limit," Zitkala-Ša declared to Father Martin, "makes us feel more devout, more humble in the Sight of God." And she was certain Father Martin's prayers had helped. Concluding the letter, she expressed a desire to go to confession. Before sealing the envelope, she enclosed a five-dollar donation.[49] Zitkala-Ša also thanked Ketcham: "It is a revelation of God's infinite mercy," she wrote, "to the smallest of His creatures, myself and husband. My heart is full of gratitude to Him for giving us friends like You and Father Martin. . . . It inspires us to more zealous efforts to live as behooves true children of our Church."[50]

Father Martin acted quickly on Zitkala-Ša's request for employment outside Utah. He alerted Ketcham, who three weeks later informed the Bonnins of vacant positions for a teacher and housekeeper at an Indian day school in San Juan Pueblo, New Mexico. The area boasted a Catholic church with two priests. Ketcham proposed that Bonnin teach and Zitkala-Ša fill the subordinate post. The combined salary would be $1,140.[51] Though Ketcham's intentions were good, Zitkala-Ša surely must have been insulted at his suggestion that she accept a housekeeping position. She politely offered her family's "sincerest thanks," but explained that she had attended college, been a teacher, and held responsible clerking positions within the BIA bureaucracy. Office work was preferable for a woman of her education, she explained, while her husband had "a view to fitting himself for an Executive position." She thanked Ketcham once more, begged his patience, and confided the hope that he could find use for them elsewhere.[52]

Even as Zitkala-Ša was seeking to leave Utah, she had not given up on her mission to bring Catholicism to the Utes. In the spring of 1911 she took up the cause again, bolstered by the arrival of Mrs. Davis, "part Indian" and "loyal Catholic," who had come to Zitkala-Ša for music lessons. In a letter to Ketcham, Zitkala-Ša noted that two other Native women, graduates of the Haskell Institute in Kansas, had also arrived on the reservation. Both professed the Catholic faith. They, along with several other Catholic families who had recently migrated there, "eighteen souls" in total, seemed to portend "the beginning of a future Catholic Mission for these Utes and the rest of us." Her letter described recent events at Uintah that underlined the pressing need for intervention: "These Utes are in great need of rescue. About two months ago, an aged Ute woman, blind, deaf, and very feeble, was the victim of a terrible brutality. Someone stole into her wigwam and cut a large chunk of flesh from her thigh! . . . The offender has never been found though the Agent made some attempt to find him. Secretly, we fear it was the heathen craze of a Ute Medicine man. They have been known to use Human Flesh in their medicines." And that was not all. "Again," Zitkala-Ša wrote, "one of the Agency Policemen has been living with a little girl, who is not 12 years old, as his wife." Though the policeman was fired, the sorry incidents were proof of the "very sad condition of these Utes."[53]

There is no indication that Ketcham was moved by these horrors. His main anxiety seems to have been over "the Catholics in your vicinity who are not attended." The bishop of Salt Lake showed no such concern. He continued to ignore Ketcham's appeals.[54] In mid-October, however, two opportunities presented themselves. The military post at Fort Duchesne had been abandoned and there was talk of relocating the Whiterocks Agency. Perhaps the Catholic Church could establish a presence there before the government took over once again, Zitkala-Ša suggested. Further, two positions in the Uintah Boarding School had also become vacant, and perhaps a priest could be sent to fill one or both.[55] Ketcham looked into the matter and even wrote the bishop of Salt Lake again. Finally, he concluded there was "no hope" of securing a suitable candidate for the boarding school positions, and gave up. He did not mention any possibility of taking over the military outpost.[56] Zitkala-Ša's vexation at not securing a priest was compounded two months later, in February 1912, when the Bonnins got word of a possible opening in the Indian Service at Fort Yates, paying $1,200 a year. They dashed off a letter to Ketcham.[57] He replied that they had been misinformed.[58]

Such minor frustrations were nothing compared to the serious trouble that erupted a few months later, in May. Earlier in 1912, Zitkala-Ša had placed a bid on forty acres of reservation land.[59] The purchase was apparently made under a fee patent scheme, introduced by the Burke Act of 1906, which allowed Indians deemed "competent" to sell allotments awarded under Dawes Act without the requisite twenty-five-year period during which the land was held in trust by the U.S. government.[60] Zitkala-Ša paid $810, "all cash." The secretary of the interior appeared to have approved the sale on February 17. Ten days later Zitkala-Ša assumed control of the land. By spring the Bonnins had cleared and plowed thirty acres at the cost of six dollars apiece. Seeded in anticipation of the summer harvest, the land was leased to another party. Then suddenly, in May, Zitkala-Ša received a letter from the Indian Office stating that she was required to re-deed the land to the original owner. As the wife of a civil servant and Indian Service employee, she had not been eligible to buy the land in the first place. The letter contained an official ultimatum: give back the land (which would mean breaking the lease, paying damages, and losing the money spent on improvements), or Bonnin would have to resign his job. Zitkala-Ša, as she regularly did when in trouble, wrote Ketcham. She related the dire situation, that she had not been in error, and that she did not want "to incur the displeasure of the Government." It was another example of callous treatment by the BIA, she concluded. "I hate to say it," Zitkala-Ša complained, "but it looks to me like the Government, in this case favors the conservative, ignorant Indian, giving him all protection to the point of disregarding the industrious, ambitious 'educated' Indian." This was the "usual case," because most Indians sold, rather than improved, their lands. "I really believe," she added, "that if Indians were encouraged to buy lands, it would be a material advantage to the entire race." Even though Bonnin had given up his post the day before Zitkala-Ša finished the letter, she trusted that Ketcham could intercede to get him reinstated.[61]

Ketcham was absent from Washington when the desperate dispatch arrived, but fortunately, the bureau secretary, Lusk, immediately saw to the matter. He contacted the Indian Office and obtained a promise from the chief clerk to investigate.[62] Zitkala-Ša sent Lusk a long letter in reply. Along with her thanks, it contained a litany of complaints about how the Indian Office had treated her and Bonnin: "Somehow these officials hate to ever admit a mistake which is plainly theirs! They shield one another! There is no hope for an Indian to look to them for justice." In a final insult Bonnin was summoned to remove his family's belongings from the BIA housing in Whiterocks, which they had moved to a year earlier. Bonnin's last check was withheld until he completed a full inventory of all the government property originally provided. The "insult heaped upon injury to us," Zitkala-Ša wrote, was "hardest to bear."[63]

With the intervention of the Bureau of Catholic Indian Missions, Bonnin was reinstated to the Indian Service some seven months later.[64] Despite the more or less happy ending, the whole incident represented a larger trend that Zitkala-Ša had witnessed all her life. Her husband's forced resignation and the threatened loss of her land were merely part of the historical problem of the U.S. government relentlessly cheating Indians. She remarked to Ketcham: "It is hard to have to stand helplessly by while we behold the graft carried on in the political game in Washington, D.C.—My case, like many others, is last because it is insignificant—The incentive to the political world is graft and not justice. Were I a man, I'd gather together all the Indian votes in our United States—then perhaps—my appeal for justice would have some consideration."[65] This was a bold idea that Zitkala-Ša would later try to realize.

CHAPTER 5

THE SUN DANCE OPERA
AND THE PEYOTE "MENACE"

There is no evidence in the Bureau of Catholic Indian Missions records to suggest that Zitkala-Ša and Father Ketcham corresponded between August 1912 and March 1913. The likely reason was the busy run-up to the premiere of *The Sun Dance Opera*. Zitkala-Ša and William Hanson unveiled their collaboration in Vernal, Utah, in February 1913, to an enthusiastic reception.[1] The National Indian Association later reported in its newsletter that "Indians and whites drove in from forty miles around" to attend the event.[2] It was a notable success. But how did it take form?

Dissecting *The Sun Dance Opera*'s composition is problematic. Zitkala-Ša left no written record of her work, while Hanson left a substantial account in his memoir, *Sun Dance Land* (1967). One would think Hanson's book would resolve any problems pertaining to the opera's genesis. Instead, the opposite is true. Over time Hanson appears to have consistently minimized Zitkala-Ša's role and expanded his own—presumably to feed his ego. At the time the opera was composed Zitkala-Ša boasted a vastly superior musical education and, of course, knowledge of Native music. Though she was likely responsible for the major share of the first performance, the original score was quite basic. Much of the opera's allure rested on the songs of the Ute performers and their elaborate costumes.[3]

Hanson's highly embellished *Sun Dance Land*, when filtered for plausibility, does retain some value as a source. He describes Uintah as a dismal place populated by dispirited Utes, once free, now conquered. Fort

Duchesne, labeled the "Hell Hole" by local civic leaders and clergy, is little more than a magnet for gambling and prostitution. There, U.S. soldiers drink to excess, and homicides occur with such regularity that the center of town, called the "Strip," features its own cemetery exclusively for the murdered. While this depiction is perhaps sadly accurate, Hanson's recollections sometimes defy credibility. His Old Sioux, in particular, is a suspicious creation. Cast as "the 101 year old hero of Custer fame and a full cousin of Sitting Bull," Old Sioux has supposedly spent fifty years as a recluse—a mathematical impossibility when one looks at the dates in question. Old Sioux is only coaxed out of his dwelling in a cave by the Bonnins' promise that the whole world is now at peace and "Uncle Sam" is no longer angry with him. To reassure Old Sioux, the couple spontaneously concocts a ritual in which a "solider boy" surrenders his military jacket to the curious old gent, who happily wears it for the rest of his days. In another episode Old Sioux, dismayed that Bonnin has forgotten to bring home the traditional Sunday roast beef, deftly slaughters and dresses two skunks, which he proudly places in the icebox.

Sun Dance Land's description of *The Sun Dance Opera*'s creation is similarly dubious. In the book's first pages Hanson downplays Zitkala-Ša's contribution in an oddly contradictory manner. "I especially acknowledge the great help of Mrs. Bonnin who became a full *collaborator* in recording and producing the Sun Dance Opera," he writes. Hanson continues, "She skeletoned the story"—suggesting that hers was an ancillary contribution. Likewise, Hanson states that at the premiere Zitkala-Ša "assisted and directed"—an oxymoronic phrase. As for the particulars of the collaboration on the opera, Hanson's nostalgic (and unrealistic) account takes place over just two days, during which Zitkala-Ša explains the Sun Dance's rituals and introduces the opera's main melodies. Hanson tells of an evening in the Bonnins' cabin in the woods, "enhanced by the flickering light of candles and the fireplace," whereupon "Mrs. Bonnin got out her violin but could not transcribe the difficult redman chants. She hummed and strummed the themes on her violin while I improvised at the piano and immediately put them on the blank music pages." In reality the writing of the libretto and composition of the music took a little more than two years. But minus the temporal compression and sentimental mood-setting, Hanson's sketch of the method they used appears logical. He at least gives some indication of more work being done. In the ensuing months the Bonnins were apparently frequent houseguests. They repaid these invitations by regularly "assisting" Hanson in his work. One aspect of Hanson's book, however, rings true: Zitkala-Ša's

Sioux-centrism. Once the Sun Dance had been chosen as a theme, she insisted upon the Lakota, rather than the Ute version (the Yankton were not
known as great devotees of the ceremony). The Sioux, she stated, were her
"first love." Other Plains Indians had "borrowed" the ceremony.

Despite *Sun Dance Land*'s general unreliability, it does offer one major
point of interest—its portrayal of Zitkala-Ša's manner and views. Hanson's
recollections show that although Zitkala-Ša had converted to what she would
have branded a "white religion" in the early 1900s, her perspective on the
failings of white society had not changed. Hanson writes, "For her lectures,
Zitkala-Ša always appeared in her gorgeous full dress of buckskin, beads,
and feathers. Her two long braids of hair hung to her knees. . . . She always
reminded her white-man audiences of the current and past history, of the
unfair intrusion of immigrants and of the Government upon an unsuspecting and weak aborigine. She boldly condemned the American people for the
constant use of force and intrigue in the conquest of the red-man-inherited
and occupied territory. She grasped every opportunity to criticize the 'Acquisitive white conquerors of the simple, roaming natives.' "

Both Bonnins shared this perspective and retained pride in their indigenous heritage. Hanson recalls that they "extolled the deep-seated national emotions and dreams their people maintained about the 'old time
culture' of their forefathers." They likewise insisted that Natives "did not
know immorality until after the white invasion." Instead, "Courting among
lovers was modest; was controlled by selective customs; and was not accompanied by the brazen love-petting exhibitions so often seen today."
This concern over sex outside marriage was a well-established refrain in
Zitkala-Ša's writings to Father Ketcham.

Importantly, *Sun Dance Land* also contains a statement by Zitkala-Ša on
compulsory assimilation, wholly consistent with the views she articulated
many times in her writings: "It seems to us, who know much about white
man practices, that it is quite presumptuous for your Indian Agencies, in the
face of all of their questionable habits, to assume so much as to try to forcibly substitute new standards upon this unwilling race. How much better
would be their replacement?" This outlook is underscored by the conten-
tion that Indians are "nature-made," "inherently religious," and possessing
of "a child-like (Christ-like) faith."[4] If the general thrust of Hanson's characterization is accurate, it helps one better understand why Zitkala-Ša, who in
May 1910 lamented to Ketcham that the Utes still practiced the Sun Dance,
chose the ritual as an operatic vehicle. Because she retained respect for
Native religions, especially those associated with the Sioux, she wanted to

demonstrate their worth to white audiences. Hanson's motivation for collaborating with her on the opera, meanwhile, sprang from his desire to preserve the culture of what he assumed was a vanishing race. He writes in *Sun Dance Land* that "aboriginal songs, the rituals, the habits" were "doomed to oblivion in the *natural* processes which were rapidly allowing the policies of the white man to have complete power and domination of America."[5]

An examination of the Sun Dance itself sheds further light on the opera's historical relevance and ultimate purpose. It is thought that the Sun Dance was first performed by Plains Algonquians in the early sixteenth century, after which it spread quickly throughout other Plains nations by means of cross-fertilization. By the late eighteenth century the Sun Dance had become the most important and elaborate ceremony practiced on the plains, though different groups invested the ritual with their own meanings, forms of expression, and mythology. Generally, the Sun Dance features ceremonial dancing, singing, and music, all performed for onlookers who sit in a specially designated area. Individuals who choose to dance forego food and drink for the duration, and beforehand usually vow to fulfill a range of activities from leading a successful hunt to taking revenge on enemies in war.[6] The central physical element is a pole culled from a sacred tree, which stands in the middle of the Mystery Circle, or Hoop. The Mystery Circle is, in turn, surrounded by a sweat lodge used for purification and tepees where participants prepare. Stretching over several days, usually four, the Sun Dance unfolds in dramatic re-creations of war, abduction, torture, and escape. An Intercessor oversees the dance, acting as an intermediary between Earth and the Great Spirit. He is assisted by other holy men and a host of other tribal members who fulfill functions such as leading the dancers and seeing to the items, such as pipes, used in the ceremony. A woman of status is sometimes chosen to give dancers moral support during their sufferings.[7]

For the Sioux the Sun Dance has been called the "essential method of communicating with Wakan Tanka" (often translated as the Great Spirit). In their version of the ritual the bison takes a central role. An effigy of a bison is hung from the sacred tree, and a bison skull serves as an altar. Dancers endure piercings through the skin and sometimes under the muscle. Bison skulls may be attached to the piercings with tethers, in which case dancers drag them around the Mystery Hoop four times. The skin may tear open, signifying the most important part of the dancer's sacrifice. Those who are pierced may alternatively be tied to the sacred tree, to then pull away until either the skin or the tether breaks. Pieces of flesh are subsequently given as offerings or signs of thanks. Ultimately, these days of deprivation, fasting, and bodily pain demonstrate that the dancer has offered his body, or himself, so that his prayers may be answered.[8]

Notwithstanding that at least twenty Plains nations practiced the Sun Dance as their primary annual ritual, by the twentieth century it had, at least officially, vanished. Government agents and missionaries condemned the ceremony as extravagantly savage, "barbaric, wild and heathenish." And because the Sun Dance could sometimes gather fifteen thousand Indians together at one time, the ritual seemed to pose a threat of Indian rebellion. Therefore, in 1881 the federal government banned the Sun Dance on the Pine Ridge Reservation. Two years later the ritual was declared illegal nationwide. Washington subsequently outlawed all Native religious practices in 1884. The Sun Dance, nonetheless, continued, either underground or with the knowledge of reservation superintendents, even though the Department of the Interior reiterated the ban in 1904.[9]

As the 1800s waned the primary focus of the Sun Dance altered in response to the increasing outside pressures associated with white control. Whereas in the 1850s the ceremony was often performed to ensure a good bison hunt or victory in war, in later years it sought to heal anxiety caused by the painful adjustments to reservation life, new epidemics, and population decline brought on by white contact. When the Wind River Shoshone, for instance, were confined to reservations, they no longer went to war or hunted bison. As their numbers decreased, shamans began to modify the traditions of the Sun Dance. They eliminated the ceremonial hunting and war aspects, concentrating instead on the themes of curing the sick and maintaining unity in the face of demoralizing circumstances. Dancers underwent their tests of endurance to heal the sick and ameliorate social ills. The Sun Dance therefore became a "redemptive movement" that sought to enable participants to "live in this world and struggle for the good of all, rather than withdrawing from it," and at the same time to "suppress narrow individualism in favor of broad collective ends."[10]

The Sun Dance Opera was radical in several ways. Before its premiere Indians had appeared only in spectacles such as Buffalo Bill Cody's Wild West Show, where they performed for white audiences in America and Europe, or in the American pageants of the mid-1800s.[11] The pageants often commenced with short plays in which Native actors (or whites impersonating Natives) happily ceded their lands, then quickly exited to make room for virtuous white settlers. Such pageants expounded on the proud themes of settlement, community building, western expansion, and development. Neither of these depictions could be characterized as especially accurate or flattering to Indians. With reference to representations of Indians in American pageants, the critic Virginia Tanner commented in 1909, "America has never done the Red Man justice. It remains for her in Pageantry to finish him off completely."[12]

By the early 1910s some operas had been written on indigenous themes. Arthur Nevin's mythical *Poia* (1910) featured a disfigured Blackfoot named Poia, who due to his deformity is unable to wed the princess Notoya. He finally wins her hand after he saves the Sun God's son, Morning Star. Near the opera's end Notoya is stabbed by the evil villain, Sumatsi. In death, she and Poia find eternal life with the Sun God. Whereas *Poia* was more Wagnerian myth in an aboriginal setting than indigenous story, Victor Herbert's *Natoma* presented the tale of a Native heroine in California during the Spanish colonial period. *Natoma* premiered in New York in 1911, starring the famed soprano Mary Garden. In this opera, Natoma, after killing her mistress's vile suitor, commits herself to Christianity and life in a convent rather than take flight and join her own people.[13] Finally, Giacomo Puccini's western-themed opera, *La Fanciulla del West*, written for the Metropolitan Opera in 1910, included the outrageously stereotyped characters Billy Jackrabbit and his "squaw" Wowkle. *The Sun Dance Opera*'s celebration of Native religion and heroic characters was not only a contrast to previous representations of Indians, but also an unprecedented artistic breakthrough anchored in the assertion that indigenous cultures had value. It is now considered "the first Native opera."[14]

The Sun Dance Opera unfolds at the pipestone quarries in the vicinity of Yankton. The libretto centers on a love triangle involving the heroic Sioux Ohiya (named after Zitkala-Ša's son), his Ute love interest Winona, and a young Shoshone man named Sweet Singer. Winona's father, a Ute chief, chooses Sweet Singer to lead the musicians in the upcoming Sun Dance. Ohiya pledges to win Winona's hand by taking part in the grueling ceremony and carves a flute that he uses to court her. Sweet Singer also makes his intentions clear, offering Winona's father gifts to win him over. Winona, however, has eyes only for Ohiya, who completes his dance in the last act as Sweet Singer conveniently dies and disappears with the "Witches of the Night." All rejoice as the Ute chief presents his daughter to Ohiya at the opera's end.

The first performances of *The Sun Dance Opera*, in Vernal, Utah, featured twenty-three musical numbers in three acts. Hanson led the orchestra and a small, Euro-American chorus. Classically trained whites played the leads. The Utes made major contributions by fashioning authentic costumes for the performances, singing traditional songs, dancing, and performing

Zitkala-Ša and William Hanson, ca. 1913. (Courtesy of L. Tom Perry Special Collections, Harold B. Lee Library, Brigham Young University, Provo, Utah)

representations of the Sun Dance (including the ritualized piercings done by the Sioux).[15] The Bonnins' adopted grandfather, Old Sioux, led some of the dances and distinguished himself as a principal performer. Significantly, white and Indian students from Uintah Academy were enlisted to perform together. After the initial performances in Vernal, *The Sun Dance Opera* was revived several times into 1914. The Brigham Young University Music Department in Provo staged a new production with a chorus of one hundred and a sizable orchestra, which toured from May to December. Performances took place in Salt Lake City and smaller towns across the state, in some cases featuring an introductory lecture by Zitkala-Ša on the religious beliefs behind the opera. Reviews in local papers were consistently enthusiastic.[16]

Only one lengthy review remains from the Vernal premiere of *The Sun Dance Opera*, written by Professor N. L. Nelson of Brigham Young University, for Salt Lake City's *Deseret News*. (A truncated version was later reprinted in *Musical America*.)[17] Nelson's thoughts are noteworthy because they reveal how the opera affected listeners' perceptions of indigenous peoples. He writes, "This opera does not follow conventional lines, depicting the Indian in the dime novel fashion so familiar to the world in drama and moving picture shows. On the contrary, it is a sympathetic portrayal of the real Indian—a conscientious attempt to depict the manners and customs, the dress, the religious ideals, the superstitions, the songs, the games, the ceremonials—in short, the inner life of a people hitherto but little understood." Nelson's reaction, however, might have been partly inspired by his recent acquaintance with Zitkala-Ša. He describes her as "one of those rare spirits whom God sends, now and then, among lowly peoples to lift them to higher planes." Nelson also took care to mention that Zitkala-Ša lived in a "modern home," rather than a tepee. A revelation, certainly.

Nelson's review also tells of Zitkala-Ša's "mission to bring about a more sympathetic understanding between her people and their white neighbors." Importantly, he quotes her directly with respect to the religious aspects of the opera. Zitkala-Ša's remarks demonstrate that despite her conversion to Catholicism, she wished to emphasize that indigenous beliefs had equal value. "I have been trained . . . in the concepts of the Christian religion," she states, "but I do not find them more beautiful, more noble, or more true than the religious ideals of the Indian. Indeed, if one allows for a change in names, the two sets of concepts are much the same. I should not like to see my people lose their ideals, or have them supplanted by others less fitted to influence their lives for good." These sentiments, coming from a highly articulate and cultured Native woman, made a profound impression on

A portrait of Old Sioux, or Bad Hand, the Bonnins' adopted grandfather, dressed for a performance of *The Sun Dance Opera*, ca. 1913. (Courtesy of L. Tom Perry Special Collections, Harold B. Lee Library, Brigham Young University, Provo, Utah)

Nelson. He confides to his readers, "That our brothers and sisters of the desert have such a spiritual background to their lives, was a complete revelation to the writer, and makes him feel the need of meeting them on the plane of a nearer social and spiritual equality."

Regarding the opera's musical qualities, Nelson offers little critical acumen. He admits that he lacks education in this respect, but appears greatly impressed by what he has witnessed: "The music was particularly thrilling. Without being a connoisseur of the divine art, and therefore incapable of passing judgment from an art standpoint, the writer was conscious throughout, from the first notes of the overture to the closing chorus, of a quality that every little while set up a quivering in his spine." This quaintly expressed excitement was stoked with "spectacular effects and climaxes," marked by "vivid stage effects" and "color and variety of movement." More important, however, is Nelson's assessment of the libretto's representation of Native peoples and religion. In this respect he is won over, declaring that the "theme of this opera is certainly a noble one," which "appeals to a sentiment deeply imbedded in the consciousness of the western world . . . the feeling that the Indian has been deeply wronged because not understood." These are, arguably, progressive views.

Judged solely by Nelson's enthusiastic comments, *The Sun Dance Opera* achieved Zitkala-Ša's professed goal of establishing a greater sympathy for Native culture among (at least some) whites. Contemporary assessments of *The Sun Dance Opera* have been more circumspect. While scholars have noted its significance as a statement on the validity of indigenous religion, they point out the inauthentic elements, some misleading representations of the ceremony, and the inherent hazards of adapting indigenous cultures for white audiences.[18] Nevertheless, it is important to highlight the context in which the Sun Dance evolved on the Uintah and Ouray Reservation and how *The Sun Dance Opera* acted as a mediating influence.

The Northern Utes were the first of the Ute tribes both to encounter the upheaval of reservation life and to practice the Sun Dance. They adopted the ritual from the Wind River Shoshone in 1889 or 1890, approximately the same time the Ghost Dance movement was reaching its climax and imminent destruction at Wounded Knee. During the brief period when the Utes were taking up the Sun Dance, they curtailed the Ghost Dance, holding it at night as an additional ritual when they performed the Sun Dance. Interestingly, despite the Department of the Interior's ban on Native rituals, Uintah Reservation officials often knew about Sun Dances, but did not report them to the commissioner of Indian Affairs. During his tenure, Superintendent Robert Waugh only once, in 1894, mentioned "orgies" and "heathen rites" with "barbarous features." These judgments were not necessarily about the Sun Dance, as Waugh could have been referring to the Bear, Blanket, or Tea Dances performed by the Utes. Even though peyote had begun to appear on Uintah by the early 1910s, many Utes saw the Sun Dance as the one true religion and were willing to flout the government ban to preserve and practice it. Unlike the Sioux, they performed the dance without piercings, but dancers still endured three to four days of hunger and thirst to gain spiritual power. Groups then traveled around the reservations bringing gifts to their hosts and holding feasts.

In 1911, about one-third of the Uintah Reservation took part in the Sun Dance. That year, the ceremony was performed as a cure for "the great white plague" (tuberculosis). "They believe," an article in the *Denver Republican* explained, "that it will prevent sickness and death in their lodges, and long before their white brothers knew a preventative for tuberculosis these Indians were exercising in the sunlight and carrying out methods which twentieth century scientists prescribe for consumption." The unnamed reporter also wrote that Ute men danced around the sacred pole for seventy-two hours without food or water, with only a willow twig in the mouth for sustenance. Chipeta also played a role: "Old Chipeta, the oldest living Ute squaw, who will be the feature of every celebration on the western slope this summer, has witnessed scores of these annual sun dances and her unfailing weather predictions are only surpassed by her prophesies as to which braves will be the next to die. She has undying faith in the sun dance and for three weeks before the great fete spent her time with the younger generation of braves, whipping them into line with her sharp tongue and making them adhere to the teachings of the tribe."[19]

In 1913 the Sun Dance on the Uintah Reservation drew hundreds. That year the ceremonial gathering took on a political tone, with many leaders giving speeches highly critical of the U.S. government.[20] When interpreted in this context, *The Sun Dance Opera* takes on an added political dimension of defying white society's attempts at suppression. A cultural dimension also emerges, in which the opera elevates a religious ritual that whites declared "heathen" and "barbaric" into the realm of western high art. In this case the medium is a large part of the message.[21] In 1914, the same year *The Sun Dance Opera* premiered in Salt Lake City, the Uintah superintendent once again forbade the Utes to perform the ceremony. The Utes disregarded him. They held the Sun Dance as usual in the same place they still hold it today, four miles south of Whiterocks. The superintendent did not report the matter to Washington.[22] The idea of white audiences across Utah being induced to applaud Ohiya's exploits in the Sun Dance, then, appears rather subversive—even within the limits of the opera's Euro-American elements. Pertinent as *The Sun Dance Opera* was to the religious rights of indigenous peoples, soon after its debut Zitkala-Ša redirected her attention to curbing, rather than promoting, a different strain of Native religion.

In 1914, an Oglala Sioux, Samuel Lone Bear, arrived in Dragon, Utah, seventy-five miles from Fort Duchesne. Lone Bear was born in 1879 and attended Carlisle for five and a half years, from 1892 to 1897. Afterwards he joined Buffalo Bill Cody's Wild West Show, sitting for several portraits by Gertrude Käsebier in 1898 and touring Europe from 1902 to 1906. Lone Bear was a handsome and charismatic man. During his time as a performer he mastered trick roping and horse riding. When he returned to the United States, Lone Bear began an itinerant life. He fathered a child with a white Chicago woman, but did not marry her. By 1910 Lone Bear was traveling through South Dakota and Nebraska, leaving a trail of petty crimes, seductions, confidence schemes, and unpaid debts. He had also begun to accumulate multiple aliases: Pete Phillips, Peter Phelps, Sam Loganberry, Chief S. C. Bird, Leo Old Coyote, Leo Okio, and perhaps most famously, Cactus Pete.

When Lone Bear reached Dragon his multiple charms endeared him to Dick Sirawap, father to two teenage daughters named Ella and Sue. Lone Bear moved into Sirawap's home and, beginning in short order, impregnated both his girls a total of five times—the youngest at the age of thirteen. One summer, while still Sirawap's guest, Lone Bear took another young girl, Mary Guerro, across state lines to Nebraska. There he kept her as a sexual prisoner and impregnated her. Utah authorities jailed Lone Bear, but because no witnesses were willing to testify against him, the court eventually set him free.

Despite his criminal behavior Lone Bear represented himself as a missionary. Preaching the benefits of peyote, he introduced the Utes to a ritual called Cross Fire.[23] His influence grew after he helped Ute Chief John McCook alleviate his rheumatism. McCook was the brother-in-law of Chief Ouray, whose widow, Chipeta, remained highly esteemed. Impressed that Lone Bear had healed one of Ouray's extended family, many Utes began using peyote.[24] Within just eighteen months of Lone Bear's arrival, estimates were that half the Northern Utes, including many leading citizens, were attending weekly gatherings. Peyote buttons began being sold in Dragon, where McCook lived, and rumors circulated that its use had caused several deaths. The Utes' responses were varied: some rejected peyote; others incorporated peyote into older religious practices; others followed some of the Christian religions practiced by settlers; and others remained committed to the Sun Dance.[25]

Though new to Uintah, peyote use was first recorded by the Spanish more than four hundred years prior among Indians in the north of present-day Mexico.[26] (Its use may extend back more than five thousand years.)[27] In the seventeenth and eighteenth centuries peyote spread northward, taking

Samuel Lone Bear as a young man, photographed by Gertrude Käsebier in 1898. (Gertrude Käsebier Photographs, Division of Culture and the Arts, National Museum of American History, Smithsonian Institution, 69.236.032)

hold among the Coahuitec, Hopi, and Taos Pueblo in what is now the American Southwest. Peyote functioned to ease and heal illness, protect the user, and bring on spiritual visions. A differing form of Peyotism arose toward the end of the nineteenth century among the Comanche, Kiowa, and Wichita Plains Indians, who developed peyote use into a religious movement that in part responded to the disruptions of white intrusion.[28] These nations created distinct, organized rituals within designated spaces accompanied by songs; feasts; and paraphernalia such as feather fans and drums.[29] This form of the Peyote religion became prevalent after the demise of the Ghost Dance movement, spreading especially among the Navajo, Winnebago, Paiute, and to a degree, the Sioux. It was, in essence, a peaceful countermovement.

Peyotism derives its significance from preserving ancient beliefs, worshiping the Great Spirit, healing not only the body but also spiritual and cultural existence, understanding the possible weaknesses that allowed whites to prevail, finding goodness even in one's oppressors, and in particularly, creating social solidarity in the face of cultural destruction. Such solidarity was meant to unite all indigenous peoples through intertribal bonds.[30] Importantly, many of Peyotism's rituals and beliefs were drawn from Christianity. Some followers even identified themselves as Christians. Many of the Peyote religion's promoters, meanwhile, were graduates of Carlisle or Haskell.[31]

Though one might have expected Zitkala-Ša to support such a movement, her reaction was hostile when peyote arrived on the Uintah Reservation. She was not alone. In 1916 Uintah Chief John Duncan, alarmed at peyote's spread and Lone Bear's tawdry exploits, contacted Standing Bear, a prominent Sioux at Pine Ridge, where peyote had also gained a foothold. Duncan asked Standing Bear "to find out about the peyote medicine." He also explained the situation at Uintah: "We don't know about this medicine, we are afraid of it but this fellow [Lone Bear] is fooling lots of my Indians. . . . They say it is something about God. . . . He has been here two years now. . . . The Sioux fellow told the Utes that if any of them are sick or poor . . . if they eat this medicine they will get well and fat again."[32] Duncan's fears were natural. Before the 1910s the Ute had no experience with peyote. To Duncan, just as to Zitkala-Ša, peyote use appeared to revolve not around any spiritual tenets, but around Lone Bear's noted lack of moral probity.[33] Standing Bear likewise opposed peyote use, and later that year would make a special trip around Uintah to speak against it, accompanied by Zitkala-Ša.[34]

In the meantime Lone Bear, like the religious charlatan he was, took every opportunity to relieve the Utes of their money. His favorite scheme involved selling tokens that supposedly possessed supernatural powers. These activities outraged Zitkala-Ša. As she observed the growing use of peyote, she branded the cactus a "menace" and began to agitate among women's groups for a state ban.[35] Zitkala-Ša had found a new crusade, which would continue and intensify over the following decade.

CHAPTER 6

NEW OPPORTUNITIES, NEW TRIALS

In 1911, Zitkala-Ša's former fiancé, Dr. Carlos Montezuma, helped found the Society of American Indians (SAI), the first Native-run Indian rights group in the United States. Montezuma, possibly influenced by his romance with Zitkala-Ša in the early 1900s, had experienced a change of heart. Now in the forefront of progressive Indian rights activism, he was agitating furiously for the abolition of the BIA and reconnecting with his identity as an indigenous person.[1] It would not be long until Montezuma and Zitkala-Ša would meet again.

The SAI, originally the American Indian Association, was formed under the leadership of Fayette Avery McKenzie, a sociologist at Ohio State University. Born in 1872, McKenzie had not only experience working in government Indian schools, but also a PhD from the University of Pennsylvania and a firm conviction that indigenous peoples could "catch up" with whites.[2] His *American Indian in Relation to the White Population in the United States* (1908) argued that America's Native peoples could be rapidly integrated into white society through a comprehensive program that eliminated Native cultures and encouraged education, allotment, and citizenship.[3] In his courses at Ohio State McKenzie often focused on the "Indian question," inviting prominent Native Americans such as Montezuma to lecture before his students.[4] Montezuma and McKenzie developed a close relationship based on their shared desire to "inaugurate a strong movement, which by its dignity, [would] possess and exert a great power in the interests of the natives of America." They made their first, unsuccessful attempts at establishing an

association in 1908 and 1909. The duo eventually managed to bring together a temporary executive committee in 1911. They organized a founding conference on Columbus Day (October 12, 1911) in Columbus, Ohio—a
symbolic gesture.[5]

The SAI's guiding principle was "native leadership . . . based on race rather
than on tribe." Its goal was "to encourage Indian leadership, promote self-
help, and foster the assimilation of Indians while encouraging them to
exhibit pride in their race."[6] Although whites could join as associate members, only people of indigenous descent could enjoy full membership with
voting rights.[7] Membership in either category cost two dollars per annum,
plus an additional dollar for a subscription to the SAI's *Quarterly Journal*.[8]
SAI membership largely consisted of middle-class professionals, most of
whom had attended off-reservation boarding schools, practiced Christianity, accepted general assimilationist imperatives, and went by both Native
and Euro-American names. Many had attended Carlisle and endorsed
Pratt's assimilationist model.[9] Pratt himself appeared at the SAI's 1912 conference to deliver a speech condemning the BIA, on-reservation schools,
and Wild West shows. (Zitkala-Ša's friend, Father Ketcham, spoke as well).[10]
Yet unlike Pratt's mission, the erasure of Indianness was not an SAI priority.
Instead, members advocated adjusting to new circumstances rather than
completely remaking racial and cultural identity, and designated aspects of
indigenous cultures, such as art, for preservation.[11] The original conference
call, for instance, stated that the "Indian has certain contributions of value
to offer our government and our people."[12] Later SAI mission statements
also spoke of the need to "present in a just light the true history of the race,
to preserve its records, and emulate its distinguishing virtues."[13]

The original SAI membership included many noted American Indians,
such as Chief Henry Standing Bear (Oglala); BIA Supervisor Charles E. Dagenett (Peoria); Episcopal priest Sherman Coolidge (Arapahoe); and Henry
Roe Cloud (Winnebego), the first person of indigenous descent to graduate
from Yale University. Yet arguably, the SAI's three most important founding members were the Santee physician and writer Charles Alexander
Eastman, the Seneca archaeologist Arthur C. Parker, and the Omaha lawyer
Thomas L. Sloan.[14]

Eastman, or Ohiyesa (Winner), was of mixed lineage. His father, Many
Lightnings, had been captured and imprisoned in 1862 while fighting
the U.S. Army; his half-white mother died in childbirth. Assuming the
boy's father had also died, an uncle raised the boy in the traditional manner until he was fifteen. It was then that Many Lightnings, pardoned by
Lincoln and now a practicing Christian who called himself by his deceased

wife's last name of Eastman, unexpectedly reappeared. From that point, Charles Eastman entered the Santee Normal Training School (where Zitkala-Ša also studied). The first day was so jarring he fled. But after recovering from the initial shock Eastman proved a brilliant student, eventually graduating from Boston University Medical School. He took a post on the Pine Ridge Reservation just in time to tend to the survivors of the Wounded Knee massacre. The killings left him horrified. Further disgusted by the poor conditions on reservations and the blatant indifference and corruption of the BIA, Eastman resigned, took up private practice in Minneapolis, and began to write and lecture.[15] By the time he helped found the SAI, Eastman had become an internationally known author. His many books—*Indian Boyhood* (1902), *Old Indian Days* (1906), *Wigwam Evening—Sioux Tales Retold* (1909), *The Soul of the Indian* (1911), and *From the Deep Woods to Civilization* (1916)—all dealt with his early life among the Santee Sioux and documented their stories, concepts, and values.[16]

Parker's background differed greatly from Eastman's. He was born on the Cattaraugus Reservation in Iroquois, New York, to a prominent family. Arthur C. Parker's grandfather, Ely S. Parker, was the first indigenous person to hold the position of commissioner of Indian Affairs (under Grant). Parker considered entering the seminary in his youth, but eventually gravitated toward anthropology. Though he never finished university and worked for only a short time in museums and libraries, at the age of twenty-five Parker secured an archaeological post at the New York State Museum after competing in an open exam. A distinguished career in academia followed, during which he brought renown to the museum for his pioneering work on the Iroquois.

Lastly, Thomas L. Sloan hailed from the Omaha Reservation in Nebraska. After graduating from Hampton Institute and studying law in Cincinnati, Ohio, he returned home to use his legal skills to represent Indian interests. Each man—Eastman, Parker, and Sloan—would serve as president of the SAI, though the divisive issue of peyote would later put the pro-peyote Sloan in conflict with his colleagues. Before these differences surfaced, however, the SAI briefly flourished, growing to 619 members in 1913.[17]

The SAI was male-dominated. In 1912, there were 66 women among the 219 active members.[18] Two notable women attended the first conference in 1911, however. The first, Laura Cornelius (later Cornelius Kellogg), was an extraordinary character. An Oneida born in Wisconsin, she graduated from an Anglican school.[19] Her experience was so unhappy that she vehemently rejected the boarding school model. At the opening conference Cornelius proposed that reservations be transformed into "industrial villages," or cooperative endeavors in which the participants would hold stock.[20] She was later touched by scandal when Parker accused her of "dancing almost in the nude for the benefit of Indian people," and bilking several businessmen out of their money for use in helping reservation Indians. As a result, Cornelius was barred from the SAI in 1913.[21] She would subsequently publish the Red Progressive tract *Our Democracy and the American Indian* (1920).[22] The second woman, Marie Baldwin, came from a long line of distinguished Chippewa from the Turtle Mountain Band in North Dakota. Her grandfather, Pierre Bottineau, had reportedly assisted the Lewis and Clark expedition, while her father, Jean Baptiste Bottineau, had grown wealthy through real estate and fur trading. Bottineau later moved his family to Washington, D.C., where he became a lobbyist for his people and advocate of assimilation. Baldwin exemplified this ideal, and was also a dedicated suffragist. After attending Catholic school, she earned a master's degree in law from Washington College of Law, then went to work for the Indian Bureau as an accountant in the Education Division. Baldwin served as the SAI's treasurer for several years—until she eventually came into conflict with Zitkala-Ša.[23]

Though the Bonnins had been invited to join the SAI, the years after 1910 were not an opportune period for them to take on additional responsibilities.[24] In late 1912 and early 1913, Zitkala-Ša's work on *The Sun Dance Opera* consumed a great deal of time, keeping her away from her home and family. Then in February 1913 the Bonnins moved to Fort Duchesne, where Bonnin assumed a property clerk position at the new agency.[25] The Bonnins also badly wanted to leave Utah, even though Zitkala-Ša had made some progress in her quest to bring the Catholic church to Uintah. In a letter to Ketcham, dated March 2, 1913, Zitkala-Ša reported that the bishop of Salt Lake had finally sent a priest, Father Ryan, to Whiterocks during Easter in 1912 to hear confessions. The Bonnins gave Ryan fifty dollars (a substantial portion of their yearly income) but never heard from him again. Quite charitably, she opined that the good father was probably too "busy" to maintain contact. Otherwise, things were going well; Zitkala-Ša told Ketcham that the acting Uintah supervisor was allowing her to aid Bonnin in clerical work.

Still, Zitkala-Ša desired to move elsewhere and have Ohiya educated by those who shared her religion. "I feel," she wrote, "that I must place my boy in a Catholic School. Mr. Bonnin and I do not seem to be able to get out of this country; and our boy is growing fast. He is nine." Seeking advice, she asked the father to recommend a boarding school.[26] Ketcham replied less than two weeks later, unsure whether he was meant to suggest white or

Indian schools. He mentioned several possible "white colleges" in the West.[27] Zitkala-Ša wrote back on March 19, concerned over possible racism and financial considerations. "We are not able to pay a high tuition," she reminded Ketcham, "and perhaps the fact of his Indian blood would prove a subtle hindrance to him—in a White School—So perhaps an Indian School (Catholic) is the best." Zitkala-Ša asked him to suggest such schools, stressing the importance of the matter while appealing for his forbearance: "I beg you to have further patience with me and my continual writing."[28]

Soon after this letter was written, Zitkala-Ša's preoccupations with securing a priest and attending to Ohiya's education were dwarfed by domestic troubles she and Bonnin encountered. Her frequent absences to stage *The Sun Dance Opera* put considerable strain on the marriage. Much more damaging was her budding friendship with a former BIA financial clerk named Asa Chapman, who had many times been a guest in the Bonnins' home. By April 1913 Bonnin clearly felt he was losing his wife. A loud quarrel ensued; Zitkala-Ša and Ohiya moved to a neighbor's; and worse, a fellow agent accused Bonnin of being physically abusive.[29] The matter would be made glaringly public within the BIA administration several months later, causing much humiliation and prompting Zitkala-Ša once again to turn to Ketcham for assistance.

In early May, just weeks after the fight, Zitkala-Ša and Ohiya boarded a train for the long journey to Westerville, Ohio, where Maud Russell, an old friend, awaited them.[30] Zitkala-Ša planned a stop in Chicago, where Montezuma lived. The doctor, now age forty-seven, was courting a twenty-five-year-old, Romanian-born, German-speaking woman named Marie Keller, whom he would marry four months later.[31] In Chicago, Zitkala-Ša's thoughts turned to her old love. Perhaps spontaneously, she telephoned Montezuma. The call was Zitkala-Ša's first step toward mending the relationship and joining the SAI.

On May 13, Zitkala-Ša posted a letter to Montezuma. Twelve years earlier to the day she had written Montezuma from a train carriage, revealing her feelings for him. Now she revealed that she was deeply unhappy, despite her opera's success. Even disregarding her recent marital difficulties, her situation was ironic. A decade earlier Zitkala-Ša had rejected the life of conjugal tedium Montezuma seemed to offer, yet she had become entrapped in even more limiting circumstances. Her letter was remarkably different in tone than the youthful orgies of self-confidence she had written in her twenties:

My dear Dr. Montezuma,
    The real joys in Life we get only in little "nips"—as you said last night. With some of us those "nips" are few and far between. But really—sometimes

the thing we desire had we got it—may have proven anything but a *joy*. In all sincerity I want to say that you had a narrow escape—but you *escaped*. I was not worthy because I did not recognize true worth at that time.

Permit me to say that I am one of your admirers—It does not really matter one way or another to you—because I am not great as you are. However, I wish you to know that I would like to be counted as one of your friends. I humbly beg your forgiveness for my gross stupidity, of former years—which was not relieved by my misfortune to lose what I could not replace. I have never passed through Chicago since that time and I could not go through now without putting forth an effort—no matter how hard—no matter if you might have refused to see me—I had to try to see you.

The telephone conversation obviously rekindled former feelings of intimacy. After expressing regret that they could not meet in person, Zitkala-Ša divulged her profound dissatisfaction with domesticity and reservation life: "I seem to be in a spiritual unrest. I hate this eternal tug of war between being wild and becoming civilized. The transition is an endless evolution— that keeps me in a continual Purgatory. My duty as mother and wife—of course keeps me in the West; but now I can hardly stand the inner spiritual clamor—to study, to write—to do more with my music—yet *duty* first! Rip Van Winkle slept twenty years! but my sleep was disturbed in half that time. I wonder if I may sleep again, Gertrude Bonnin."[32]

As the letter suggests, years of home life, the falling out with Bonnin, and her involvement in *The Sun Dance Opera* appear to have fully resuscitated in Zitkala-Ša a desire to strive for greater accomplishments. Within a very short time she took measures to alleviate her turmoil and seek intellectual engagement. In Ohio, she began studying piano at Otterbein University in Westerville, practicing six hours a day. Six weeks later she traveled to Nauvoo, Illinois, to enroll Ohiya in the Spalding Institute for Small Boys, a Catholic boarding school staffed by Benedictine sisters.[33] Though Ketcham had recommended other Catholic schools at Pine Ridge and Rosebud, Zitkala-Ša did not take his advice.[34]

Zitkala-Ša clearly desired her son to have a Catholic education, but just as clearly she desired more freedom to pursue activities outside of the home now that her adopted son, Oran, had grown old enough to largely look after himself.[35] On June 23, Zitkala-Ša wrote Montezuma from Burlington Station in Omaha, Nebraska. The long letter gives another view into her frustrations. "I am taking my boy to school," Zitkala-Ša told him, "I know it is necessary to educate him but this knowledge does not make it any easier to *leave* him." However her ambitions could not be satisfied, nor her potential reached in the present circumstances. "I want to earn a diploma in Piano Music some [*sic*] of these days," she explained, "You know I have a great desire to finish things I had once started. . . . I studied a piano piece which is considered one of the most difficult things written for the piano. Prof. Grahill said I had talent. I am not bragging but simply telling you the encouragement I have along my line of study." Yet the most pressing issue in Zitkala-Ša's life appeared to be a need for more independence. She stated bitterly that she had to leave once again for home: "I am returning to Utah because Mr. Bonnin insists upon it. I shall continue my study at home and try to go every summer to some place to study under a real first class teacher of music. I am telling you all this because I want you to know that I intend to improve my mind." This personal desire was difficult enough to fulfill. Her domestic life precluded larger commitments. "I fear I won't be able to attend the Indian association—even though it should chance to meet in Denver," she explained to Montezuma. "It is not that I lack interest or even public spirit—but my *duties* seem to limit me to the home—for the time, at any rate."

Zitkala-Ša then made a discreet request. She asked Montezuma to send her news of his activities anonymously, hinting that her marriage might not bear the strain of a letter from an illustrious old flame. "I should count it a special favor if you would send me copies of your lectures and articles published—should you feel so inclined—now and then—I will not be in a position to receive any letter—even though it might be ever so impersonal—as I know you would have made it. In view of this—I would be glad to know of your work through an occasional copy of something you've 'done gone and said.' Should I do anything—I'll let you know—but I doubt my doing anything worthwhile for some time to come as I shall have to spend so much time in practice and teaching, too." She closed, "Let me wish you continued successes. Yours sincerely, Gertrude Bonnin."[36]

Unfortunately, in September the Bonnins' life at Uintah began to unravel further. In early October Zitkala-Ša sent Father Ketcham a four-page, typewritten letter that described their predicament. First she related that Bonnin had requested a raise. The supervisor, Jewell D. Martin, originally approved it. The Indian Office, however, rejected it, suggesting that Bonnin be given a clerical assistant instead. Zitkala-Ša badly wanted the position to increase her family's income, but a rival Catholic, an older woman named Jennie Burton, then teaching at the Whiterocks school, had expressed interest in the job. Complicating the matter was the domestic dispute that had occurred in late April—Zitkala-Ša called it a "private family misunderstanding"—which had become very public. Charges had been "filed maliciously" against Supervisor Martin for covering up the squabble.

The man responsible was another agent, Fred A. Baker, who reported to the Indian Bureau that Bonnin had broken Utah law "by assaulting his . . . wife Gertrude Bonnin in a jealous rage over the alleged attentions to her by Asa C. Chapman." Bonnin's actions, Baker stated, had "cast discredit upon the Indian Service." Understandably, Zitkala-Ša felt threatened by the possibility that her family's reputation would be besmirched, not only in Washington, but among the Ute community and others on the reservation. Not only would her personal reputation suffer, but if the allegations were taken seriously in Washington, they might preclude her from being considered for the position of Bonnin's paid clerical assistant. As Zitkala-Ša had done many times before, she enlisted Ketcham's help. "Father," she confided, "we did have untold unhappiness in our little home, in Apr. on account of an unreasonable jealousy that caused my husband to act imprudently." But, she emphasized: "I AM INNOCENT OF ANY IMMORAL ACT." "My mistake was showing too much interest in literary conversations with a man [Chapman] who came frequently to our home." Strengthening her defense, she accused Baker of making the accusations of assault "upon hearsay," stating in a handwritten addition to her typewritten: "Mr. Bonnin never assaulted me! G. B."

Baker's complaint forced Supervisor Martin to write an explanation to the commissioner of Indian Affairs in Washington. Martin reported that a "quarrel" did occur in April, and that Zitkala-Ša and her son had taken refuge at a neighbor's home. The neighbors in turn informed him, and he "went immediately to Mr. Bonnin's home to talk with him and ascertain whether or not there was any foundation for his reported jealousy." The remainder of the report exonerated Bonnin of any guilt. According to Martin, the heart of the issue was that during gatherings at the family home, Bonnin "felt that Mrs. Bonnin had manifested too great an interest in the musical and literary tastes and culture of Mr. A. S. Chapman." Bonnin "feared that she was coming to appreciate Mr. Chapman more than himself and that he felt in danger of losing her affections." The row had broken out when Bonnin "upbraided" his wife, who, angered at his suspicions, responded in kind. Bonnin did not believe that his wife had been unfaithful, Martin made clear, but "he was genuinely grieved" that his wife might prefer another man. Martin completely and unreservedly vouched for the Bonnins, citing his "long and intimate acquaintance" with them and expressing certainty that Mrs. Bonnin and Chapman had not had an affair, both being "models of rectitude." The sympathetic superintendent concluded by assuring the commissioner that the misunderstanding had been entirely resolved. "Mr. and Mrs. Bonnin prize each other as never before," he wrote, having "successfully weathered that matrimonial storm." After a talk with Martin, Bonnin had even once again accepted Chapman as a friend. Though Martin supported her husband unreservedly, Zitkala-Ša still feared Baker would cause trouble. Baker had promised to personally take up the matter with Commissioner of Indian Affairs Cato Sells in Washington. Zitkala-Ša begged Father Ketcham to speak to Sells on her behalf and dispel the falsehoods that Baker was circulating. Likely feeling quite isolated, she wrote, "I have no other one to whom I may turn at this hour of trial." [37] Martin's report, however, evidently satisfied the commissioner. Baker's onslaught does not seem to have produced any consequences other than embarrassment.

Though Bonnin had been officially cleared, Zitkala-Ša must have been exhausted by the end of 1913. The year had begun with the exhilarating premiere of *The Sun Dance Opera*, which had brought something close to the public recognition she had enjoyed in the early 1900s. Yet she had suffered much as a consequence. Ohiya was at boarding school, relieving some pressure yet simultaneously inviting a sense of loss. At home Zitkala-Ša had to contend with a suspicious, discontent husband, not to mention the further distress of her marital difficulties becoming fodder for a fellow agent intent on doing damage. These events would have discouraged anyone, but Zitkala-Ša was determined to move forward. She was heartened by the interest of a Catholic priest, Father C. Poirier, whom she had met in the spring of 1913. Poirier had visited Uintah and subsequently planned a long stay in Fort Duchesne at the Bonnins' home for the autumn. "We are grateful," Zitkala-Ša wrote Ketcham, "that God has answered our prayers for a Priest." The Bonnins were looking forward to introducing Poirier to a young man they had converted to the church, who was "now studying the Catechism."[38] Along with promoting Catholicism among the Utes, Zitkala-Ša also planned additional performances of *The Sun Dance Opera* for 1914. Yet, other issues eventually took precedence. Instead of investing her energies into the opera or her piano studies, Zitkala-Ša was moved by the "public spirit" she had written of in the June letter to Montezuma. She turned her focus to the SAI.

CHAPTER 7

IN THE SOCIETY OF
AMERICAN INDIANS

Zitkala-Ša joined the advisory board of the Society of American Indians in 1914.[1] According to the *Wagner Post*, on Christmas Day of that year, Ellen Taté I Yóhin Win Simmons died. Her funeral was held at the Presbyterian church in Greenwood, South Dakota. The *Post* listed her age as ninety and described her as "one of the most respected Indian women of this reserva-tion." Accordingly, the service was very well attended. No available sources from this time, or any other, reveal Zitkala-Ša's thoughts on her mother's passing. From the obituary it is not even clear that she attended the funeral.[2] Bonnin's father, Joseph, died a little more than a week later, on New Year's Day 1915.[3]

After dealing with these deaths Zitkala-Ša's first order of business was a grassroots initiative to create a Ute community center. This effort coin-cided with the arrival of a new superintendent at Uintah in 1915, Albert H. Kneale. In his memoir, *Sun Dance Land*, Hanson recalls Agent Kneale with fondness: "He was a conscientious and broadminded man of experience, sympathy, and sound judgment."[4] Zitkala-Ša's letters depict a much different man. Nevertheless, in 1915, with Kneale's permission, Zitkala-Ša comman-deered an empty warehouse at Fort Duchesne to use for a community center. There, she formed a female sewing group to make clothes for the destitute and organized a meals program—"a practical demonstration in domestic science"—as she called it. It was also a practical demonstration of female indigenous self-help. On days when government rations were issued the center provided shelter during inclement weather.[5]

At the 1915 SAI conference in Lawrence, Kansas (September 28–October 3), Zitkala-Ša presented a paper on her community center work. She was duly praised by the membership.[6] The SAI even published a special notice in its journal asking that any useful supplies be directed to Uintah: "Members and friends having books, sewing materials, surgical bandages, good pictures and articles useful in this work of promoting industry, sanitation, cheer and pleasant homes, should send them to Mrs. R. T. Bonnin, Fort Duchesne, Utah."[7] The Fifth Annual SAI Platform, adopted in 1915, called for better schooling and definition of Indians' legal status, an opening of the courts to tribal claims, and improvements in hygiene inspection, while also asking the U.S. government to "look with favor upon the Community Center plan" of Zitkala-Ša's.[8]

In the summer of 1915 Zitkala-Ša began corresponding with Arthur C. Parker, then SAI secretary-treasurer. They quickly formed a friendship that produced many letters. Parker cordially sent the Bonnins several copies of the SAI *Quarterly Journal*. Parker explained that because the periodical was a public organ, only certain "opinions" could be "discussed without fear." Other matters, "for diplomatic reasons," had to be debated in "executive councils."[9] Zitkala-Ša wrote back to compliment Parker on his journal contributions and to press her case for a new strategy of "utilizing the large numbers of Adult Indians . . . and Returned Students" to fortify the SAI. Her idea was to create an on-reservation presence that would educate the potential rank and file. "It is a work that the educated owes to his untutored kinsman," she argued, "whether appreciated or not."[10] Parker replied that Zitkala-Ša had "struck upon a good idea." He stressed, though, that Indians had to show their willingness to prove themselves "thrifty and progressive" in order to gain the attention of whites in government. This project involved resuscitating "the old independent racial pride and desire to achieve." Parker encouraged Zitkala-Ša to move forward, regardless of "ignorant Indians or cynical whites." "If some talented woman like yourself, who has the vision and initiative should gather about her a company of the adult Indians and returned students for heart to heart talks, there can be no doubt that much good would result."[11]

Flattered by his praise, Zitkala-Ša sent Parker some of her poems, which he promised to publish in the SAI journal. Parker had just returned from the annual Indian Rights Association and Board of Indian Commissioners conference in New Paltz, New York, where he could see firsthand that the SAI was attracting serious attention among the BIA and the reform community. Parker reported that the commissioner of Indian Affairs, Cato Sells, was "very anxious about the publicity we give matters in the Quarterly."

Arthur C. Parker, ca. 1919. The image is taken from the pamphlet *American Indian Freemasonry* (1919), to which Parker contributed.

Zitkala-Ša's community center work, which Parker said he "took special pains to explain," also received Sells's endorsement. Parker was convinced that such on-reservation centers held the key to progress:

> We are striking the needed space long left empty in service to the Indians. The governmental mission is right and proper for the government, if administered well. The church mission of course is divinely commanded, but heretofore

there has been no social mission dealing with the people as social creatures and recognizing primarily their human cravings. Both the church and the state have attempted to perform this function. The world's history has shown that there is disaster when any people so far surrender its social regulation that they are governed by either the church or the state entirely. There is a loss of freedom and initiative. I therefore believe that the plan, of which you are to be the head has some of the most tremendous possibilities that any movement has heretofore had in the line of Indian uplift. Be of good courage.[12]

With Parker's support, Zitkala-Ša advanced in the SAI hierarchy. In 1915 she joined the board of the *Quarterly Journal*, shortly thereafter becoming a contributing editor. The SAI distributed the journal to public libraries, historical societies, and subscribers, with the mission to provide "a medium of communication between students and friends of the American Indian."[13]

By early 1916, Zitkala-Ša was firmly in vanguard of the Native rights movement. "The Indian's Awakening," published in early 1916 in the *American Indian Magazine* (*AIM*), as the *Quarterly Journal* was renamed, announced her return. The lengthy poem (here excerpted) charted Zitkala-Ša's feelings of duality, alienation, and ultimately, triumph. She commenced with the traumas of missionary schooling:

> I snatch at my eagle plumes and long hair.
> A hand cut my hair; my robes did deplete.
> Left heart all unchanged; the work incomplete.
> These favors unsought, I've paid since with care.
> Dear teacher, you wished so good to me,
> That though I was blind, I strove hard to see.
> Had you then, no courage to frankly tell
> Old race-problems, Christ e'en failed to expel?
> . . . .
> I've lost my long hair; my eagle plumes too.
> From you my own people, I've gone astray.
> A wanderer now, with no where to stay.
> The Will-o-the-wisp learning, it brought me rue.
> It brings no admittance. Where I have knocked
> Some evil imps, hearts, have bolted and locked.
> Alone in the night and fearful Abyss
> I stand isolated, life gone amiss.

Despairing at her half-transformed identity, Zitkala-Ša asks:

> Oh, what am I? Whither bound thus and why?
> Is there not a God on whom to rely?

A divine voice sings to her of the "wondrous host of cosmos," God's "shifting mosaic." Closing her eyes she prays, beholding in her mind the "harmonious kinship" of all things. She mounts a horse and rides into the realm of the spirits, far away from the "reptiles and monsters, war, graft, and greed" that dominate the white world. She arrives in a place of astounding beauty, marked by azure seas and skies. Ancestors who have passed on happily await her in the presence of the Great Spirit:

> Hark! Here is the Spirit-world, He doth hold
> A village of Indians, camped as of old.
> Earth-legends by their fires, some did review,
> While flowers and trees more radiant grew.

Zitkala-Ša registers astonishment at the sight: "Oh, you were all dead!" she cries to her kinsmen. "One of the Spirit Space" answers that they are "souls, forever and aye," who now populate the heavens as stars in a long chain of memory. Having learned everything possible from life, they now reside in eternity. The departed soul addresses her:

> O hear me! Your dead doth lustily sing!
> Rejoice! Gift of Life pray waste not in wails!
> The maker of Souls forever prevails!

At that, she is transported back to reality, heartened, inspired, and determined to fulfill her new mission.

> Direct from the Spirit-world came my steed.
> The phantom has place in what was all planned
> He carried me back to God and the land
> Where all harmony, peace and love are the creed.
> In triumph, I cite my joyous return.
> The smallest wee creature I dare not spurn.[14]

The poem was credited to Zitkala-Ša, a name that Mrs. Bonnin had not used in more than a decade. The gesture reaffirmed her Sioux identity and signaled that she had returned to making the same criticisms, expressing the same concerns, and exhibiting the same pride in her heritage.

"The Indian's Awakening" also revealed how Zitkala-Ša's presence in the SAI was somewhat of an anomaly. Her veneration of the old ways and "romanticized accounts of Indian heritage," as Speroff puts it, often ran counter to the general progressive, assimilationist goals of the membership.[15] The language of this poem was reminiscent of "Why I Am a Pagan," and her antagonism to Christian education and the "reptiles and monsters, war, graft, and greed" of white American civilization harkened back to the *Atlantic Monthly* series. Yet above all, "The Indian's Awakening" proclaimed Zitkala-Ša's determination to revive the greatness of the indigenous past in order to achieve a new future. To accomplish this, the SAI had to directly affect national Indian policy and Indian lives. Part of this project meant work at the reservation level—the same notion Zitkala-Ša advocated to Montezuma in the early 1900s when she argued that a return to tribal lands was necessary to defend Native interests and improve conditions.

Improving conditions, albeit very slowly and incrementally, is exactly what Zitkala-Ša's community center had begun to accomplish in the winter of 1915–16. Several letters to Parker described the work at length and the satisfaction it provided her. That the community center was largely a female effort pointed to Zitkala-Ša's belief in the power of indigenous women to effect positive change. By then sewing classes were being offered in both Fort Duchesne and another town, Randlette. The women who attended spent one meeting "entirely for making warm garments for a crippled woman at Ouray Sub-Agency." The elderly woman was "so pleased" that she spontaneously admitted her desire for Zitkala-Ša's help: "She told my interpreter that she almost asked me to sew her warm garments at the Issue day, one month ago. I told her that though she did not permit herself to speak her wish, I heard her with my heart." The sewing circle provided its services without charge but expected beneficiaries to reimburse them for the cost of materials.

In a well-equipped and heated government building, Zitkala-Ša organized a group of young Ute women to cook lunches for those who traveled to Fort Duchesne to receive subsistence and paychecks on Mondays. The lunch program primarily aided the poorly paid Ute Indian Service employees. Previously, they had been expected, out of hospitality, to feed fellow tribesmen when they arrived in town. "The beauty of it is," Zitkala-Ša told Parker, "that all the food is prepared and served by Indian women. To encourage them to assume responsibility; and to arouse their spirit so that they are not afraid of hard work, self denial nor fatigue, this is what rejoices me." She added that Agent Kneale's wife visited these meetings and "helped us royally." The atmosphere of community self-help seems to have inspired others. In Randlette a local woman offered the use of her sewing machine. The act of generosity made Zitkala-Ša "feel like singing."[16] The need was also great. By late February the sewing group had "more requests from our old grandmothers and grandfathers, for sewing necessary garments than we can do at present." But Zitkala-Ša anticipated that the sewing circles would eventually grow enough to meet the needs.[17] She soon had plans to open another center in Whiterocks.[18]

What Zitkala-Ša was accomplishing with her work, especially the Monday lunch service, is all the more impressive when one realizes that she was largely self-funding it. She explained to Parker: "The flour, sugar, coffee, boiling meat and dried fruit (for pies), and lard, I have paid for with my own money, . . . until the small gains on the lunches, shall accrue sufficiently to reimburse me. I hope someday, our Society will have money for this work. Because I do so firmly believe in it, I would sacrifice in order to get this field opened for our Society." To Zitkala-Ša, this sacrifice was justified by the positive response from the local community. "Many, many men and women," she reported, "wish to shake hands with me, wherever I go. They *know* my heart is tender for them. That I am not afraid to show them true sympathy. I would not harden my heart to these poor human creatures for fear that a half a dozen of them might try to work upon my feelings. . . . I try to cheer them, joining them in little jokes or funny stories; I look upon their degradation and poverty, as only temporary conditions. So we laugh and get busy trying to make some useful thing out of what is in our reach. Later desire for better things will grow; and learning 'to do' for themselves and helping the infirm, and aged, they will continue to advance."[19]

This hope for the future was tempered by the growing use of peyote at Uintah. Two of Zitkala-Ša's winter letters to Parker mention its influence. "There is one very sad thing I must report," she warned, "peyote has been introduced among these Utes; and it seems that some of the men who had always been considered 'good, sensible' Indians have fallen among its victims."[20]

Seeking to curb the spread of peyote, Zitkala-Ša began to lecture throughout Utah, Nevada, and Colorado on its evils. Soon she had the support of such groups as the Women's Christian Temperance Union.[21] She insisted to Parker that if the governor of Utah would only take action against "this dreaded peyote," the Utes could be "saved."[22] Still, Zitkala-Ša's anti-peyote campaign did not detract from her community work. When spring came the government warehouse/community center at Fort Duchesne was transformed into a local chapter of the SAI. Monthly meetings focused on issues such as boosting school attendance, promoting child welfare, and organizing community activities. Though the meetings were held under the auspices of the SAI, the organization provided no financial assistance.[23] It was perhaps just as well. Zitkala-Ša ultimately saw the community center effort in widely inclusive terms. As she wrote, her goal was "uniting and welding together the earnest endeavors of various groups of educators and missionaries."[24] The work, however, was very slow and frustrating. Though Zitkala-Ša expressed pride and gratification in her work in many of her letters to Parker, she also spoke of greater forces on the Uintah Reservation that frequently thwarted her.

Since the Bonnins' arrival in Utah, they had witnessed the Utes' rapid dispossession. In 1905 President Roosevelt had taken more than one million acres of Ute land to create the Uinta National Forest Reserve. Other lands were requisitioned for development and settlement. By 1909 the original reservation of 4,000,000 acres had dwindled to a dispersed collage of only 360,000 acres, with one-third still set aside for allotments. The BIA's ostensible goal was to make farmers out of the Utes. To that end, the newly established Office of the United States Indian Irrigation Service at Whiterocks commenced the Uintah Indian Irrigation Project in 1906. Unsurprisingly, the Utes benefitted little. Mormons were hired for most of the construction work, and only 3 percent of labor costs went to Ute workers—even though the irrigation project had been funded by the sale of their land. Those Utes who wanted to farm resided on only a minor portion of the land irrigated, 11,000 acres out of a total of 88,000 served by the new ditches. The government subsequently charged Utes for water rights, even if they were not farming. Failure to pay resulted in forfeiture of their land. By 1916 the troubles caused by the irrigation project were considerable. Individual irrigation projects carried out by Utes were rendered useless as larger government-built canals increasingly siphoned off available water. Chipeta, then approximately age seventy and blind with cataracts, wrote Commissioner Sells with Agent Kneale's help. She insisted that something be done to rectify the water situation. The request was completely ignored. Kneale later suggested that Sells send Chipeta a gift for keeping her people pacified. Sells proposed furniture. Kneale gave her two shawls instead.[25] Water would have been better.

The gift of two shawls revolted Zitkala-Ša, as did the engineered water shortage and other BIA chicanery occurring around 1916.[26] She complained to Parker of how the Utes had been cheated out of their own monies, which had been appropriated to build and maintain local bridges, one on a state highway. There was also a bill in Congress intended to requisition Ute grazing lands for white ranchers. Zitkala-Ša wished that the SAI had better access to Senate reports in order to act as a legislative watchdog. What disturbed her most on a daily basis, however, was the treatment Utes suffered from whites:

Think of a bigoted petty-political appointee and his wife [the Kneales, one presumes], neither over educated, unrefined, selfish and about as crude as a mud fence, posing as tin gods; and the subordinates, poor Whites, fall down to worship at their feet.

Then when an Indian comes into sight, these prostrate ones, rise up like lords to domineer over him. Poor Lo thinks he must submit to the US Government, so he acts like a whipped cur when he wishes to ask about his own money.

This outrageous condition provokes me. I grow weary of the tin gods, the false worshipers and the subservience of the Indian.

I am restless with the query "What shall I teach, where shall I begin, in order to restore the Reservation Indian to his native independence?"

The answer to this question was elusive, the environment hostile. Zitkala-Ša explained, "The Reservation Worker must go through fire and water; walk upon swords and handle fragile glass while striving to evoke harmony, real harmony, from this mess of Reds and Whites, good, bad, and indifferent."[27]

Also problematic was the lack of transparency within the BIA administration. Zitkala-Ša told Parker that "data from the Indian Office relative to amounts of Indian funds, proposed expenditures and payments to Indians" were unavailable. The SAI had to take steps in order to gain oversight, she argued, or they would continue to be "kept In the Dark."[28] Zitkala-Ša also stressed that SAI leadership should get involved locally, aiding Indians who were often illiterate and required direct assistance. Influencing white reformers was not enough; a tangible presence counted more. "I am more than ever convinced that this is a field too long overlooked," she argued to SAI Vice President Estaiene DePeltquestangue, "and it is our first duty, to make an effort toward uplift work among our reservation Indians, ourselves; and in our own way."[29]

Following her own advice from a year prior, Zitkala-Ša created a project aimed at enlisting students returned from boarding schools. Her local SAI chapter had inducted almost seventy-five such members by mid-1916. Determined to keep doing her "Indian-best," Zitkala-Ša hoped soon to reach one hundred.[30] Informing the younger generation about national Indian issues, she told Parker, could produce "untold benefit to the Reservations" and, of course, the SAI. "Then we will grow strong," she forecasted, "We will see hundreds come into the main society. This is what I desire most." In this way the SAI could provide an alternative to the Indian Service for new graduates seeking to aid their peoples. Vital information from Washington, in the meantime, had to be furnished by a new "supplement to the Indian Magazine" directed at "the Reservation Indians whose English vocabulary is very limited and powers of concentrated thinking still in the bud," as Zitkala-Ša quaintly phrased it. She ended the letter, "My heart and my soul (such as they are) are in this work."[31]

Zitkala-Ša could articulate her hopes, ideas, and often, chagrin, privately to Parker. In public forums, she began to display greater restraint. Perhaps Parker's previously expressed reluctance to discuss openly certain "opinions" influenced her. Zitkala-Ša had tremendous respect for Parker. She even offered to take over some of his work as secretary when he briefly fell ill in February 1916.[32] Even five years after the SAI was founded, the idea of an Indian-run organization was still highly novel and treading cautiously was advisable. Therefore, in promoting her community center Zitkala-Ša praised the "self-sacrificing missionaries" who worked on the reservations. Her expression of gratitude, however, politely stressed the need for self-help first. In "A Year's Experience in Community Service Work among the Ute Tribe of Indians" (1916) Zitkala-Ša wrote, "We have awakened, in the midst of a bewildering transition, to a divine obligation calling us to love, to honor our parents. No matter how ably, how well others of God's creatures perform their duties, they never can do our duty for us; nor can we hope for forgiveness, were we to stand idly by, satisfied to see others laboring for the uplift of our kinsmen. Our aged grandparents hunger for tenderness, kindness and sympathy from their own offspring. It is our duty, it is our great privilege to be permitted to administer with our own hands, this gentle affection to our people."[33] Such language and the religious concerns it reflected certainly contrast with the criticism in "The Indian's Awakening." But just as Zitkala-Ša began to advocate outward cooperation and diplomacy, relations within the SAI were beginning to sour.

The 1916 SAI annual conference in Cedar Rapids, Iowa (September 26–October 1), was poorly attended. SAI President Sherman Coolidge opened the proceedings touting a fruitful "union of strength and harmony." Montezuma instead caused tensions by advocating the abolition of the BIA. He likewise complained that the SAI seemed more interested in talking than taking action, and urged those present to "get on the right road." Montezuma was soon in the midst of a vocal disagreement over whether one could be both a BIA employee and a loyal Indian. Phillip B. Gordon, a Chippewa Catholic priest, came to his defense. Gordon maintained that being a member of the SAI and working for the corrupt Indian Office were irreconcilable. Coolidge, Marie Baldwin, and Zitkala-Ša, however, defended the notion that one could do good within the BIA, as the latter put it, "from a sense of duty." Zitkala-Ša argued that those who worked in the "wilderness," meaning on the reservations, "give the kind of help that money could never

Members of the Society of American Indians in Cedar Rapids, Iowa, September 29, 1916.
Zitkala-Ša is in the front row holding a large hat. Pratt is standing farthest to the right.
This photograph appeared in the *American Indian Magazine* (July–September, 1916).

buy." She instead advocated creating conditions that would eventually
make the BIA irrelevant. An embattled Montezuma eventually conceded that
though he opposed the BIA "as a system," he did not oppose the many individuals who worked for it.[34] As if to further emphasize her point, Zitkala-Ša's
address on the conference's third day reported on her successful community
center work.[35]

The 1916 gathering was most notable for the SAI's first public statement
against peyote. Pratt was the main force behind it. He presented a speech
imploring the membership to adopt a resolution in favor of the Gandy Bill,
proposed by South Dakota Representative H. L. Gandy, meant to outlaw peyote possession and trade. Some protested, but the resolution passed and
peyote use was officially condemned—to Zitkala-Ša's delight.[36] She had invited S. M. Brosius of the Indian Rights Association to Uintah to investigate
the influence of peyote there and had furnished information that would be

used in the IRA's 1916 Annual Report.[37] Zitkala-Ša's lecture tours in the Midwest by this point had also yielded results. That year the General Federation of Women's Clubs subsidized the publication of *The Menace of Peyote*. This pamphlet, written by Zitkala-Ša, detailed the "indiscriminate use" of the drug, its negative impact on infant mortality and crime rates, and the "moral and physical degeneracy" it purportedly encouraged.[38]

Zitkala-Ša was also quick to use the SAI to fight her anti-peyote crusade. Her anti-peyote poem "The Red Man's America," published in the *American Indian Magazine*, criticized the lack of a federal ban. The takeoff on Samuel Francis Smith's "My Country 'Tis of Thee" began with an assertion of territorial primacy, and went on to allude to violent foreign tyranny:

> My country! 'tis to thee,
> Sweet land of Liberty,
> My pleas I bring.
> Land where OUR fathers died,
> Whose offspring are denied
> The franchise given wide,
> Hark, while I sing.
>
> My native country, thee,
> Thy Red man is not free,
> Knows not thy love,
> Political bred ills,
> Peyote in temple hills,
> His heart with sorrow fills,
> Knows not thy love.

After referencing the Gandy Bill—"Let Gandy's Bill awake / All people, till they quake"—the poem concluded with an appeal for "just human right" not merely from the U.S. government, but from the "Great Mystery."[39] Zitkala-Ša's activism and writing, even when aimed at cultivating white support, always had a highly critical edge.

The 1916 SAI conference proved a great personal success for Zitkala-Ša. She was elected secretary and her friend Arthur C. Parker, then in his early thirties, was elected president. Zitkala-Ša was also interviewed by the *Cedar Rapids Evening Gazette*. The resulting article, "Indian Woman Has Accomplished Much for Uplift of Race," showed the difficulties in communicating effectively with the white press. The *Gazette* described Zitkala-Ša as "an Indian woman of great culture and refinement," but erroneously noted that she was "married to a white man." This was more than sloppy reporting. In language typical of the times the *Gazette* stated: "Mrs. Bonnin left the civilization of the east to go into the desert of Utah that she might bring unto the untamed Utes the message of the white man."[40] This characterization of her work revealed a pervasive unwillingness among Euro-Americans to think outside familiar narratives of westward expansion, white civilization, and Indian savagery.

Her use of the SAI for her own ends notwithstanding, Zitkala-Ša surely was an asset to the organization. The *American Indian Magazine* heralded her election as secretary with these words: "She lives for one great ideal, the complete liberty of her race and for this end she devotes every minute of her life without compensation. We believe that she is the most remarkable Indian woman living, and yet she is the most unassuming."[41] Whether unassuming or not, Zitkala-Ša was the only person within the membership who could rein in an increasingly impatient Montezuma. Shortly after the conference he quit, then publicly criticized the SAI for its refusal to call for the abolition of the Indian Bureau. Zitkala-Ša placated him with a masterful letter of conciliation:

> My dear good friend;
> . . . I know you are doing all in your power to help our race.
> It saddens me, that in our earnestness for a cause, we do not take time to study our various views and manage some way to unite our forces. All Indians must ultimately stand in a united body, for their own protection.
> . . . Publicity is one of the necessary things; and you are right in trying to enlighten the public. So far, so good. I would like to beg you not to make reference to the Society of American Indians, in an unfriendly way. You, yourself are not unfriendly. What if today, they seem to you, to do things wrong, be charitable, for we all must learn, day by day, how best to meet the problems of life. . . . May I speak for the Society? We do value your membership in our society. We know and see the things you do; it is simply a difference in the method of working out a solution. . . . If you could, if you would, Doctor, Listen to the plea of one, heart and soul, in this work of Indian liberation, you would resolve, never more to print one word against your Society of American Indians. You would show them *charity*. . . . You are brave and strong. We want you to shield and help guide us, wayward though we appear; we do not want you to deal impatiently with us; or to emphasize our shortcomings to the world. Who is without fault?
> So Doctor, I beg you, be kind to us; You will see that after all we are true to our race. We have not sold out to the Bureau. We are eager and anxious for preparatory work to be done, that we may live to see the Bureau abolished.
> Consider this letter, confidential. It is a personal letter and unofficial.[42]

Swayed by such tactful diplomacy, Montezuma soon renewed his membership.[43]

But mending tiffs was not Zitkala-Ša's main concern. At the end of 1916 she was bursting with ideas, thrilled to be in the forefront of activism, and searching for new ways to aid the SAI cause. That winter Zitkala-Ša wrote Commissioner Sells, requesting that he allow SAI members to visit reservations. "Such a permit," she explained, "would satisfy those in authority on Indian reservations [and] it would serve to identify the bearer that he was a true representative of our society; and seeking to co-operate with all uplift work for humanity."[44] Sells's response was cool. "You are advised," he stated, "that it is against a long established policy of the Indian Office to issue general permits to visit Indian reservations, and that it is not desired to establish a contrary precedent." Yet Sells did promise that if Zitkala-Ša sent a list of reservations, he would send letters of introduction.[45] Nothing came of the effort, which Zitkala-Ša apparently hoped to link with a membership drive. She suggested to Parker that official three-person SAI delegations be sent to reservations to recruit new members, and also proposed an alliance with an unidentified organization established among the Sioux tribes.[46]

Zitkala-Ša made a striking proposal for gaining greater attention from the white population, as well: "Someone," she told Parker, "should write an 'Uncle Tom's Cabin' for the American Aborigine." The Indian agent, after all, was much like "the slave killer," Legree. Nonetheless, Zitkala-Ša opined, "The task would be too difficult for an Indian. The perspective is entirely too close. I can hardly write a few pages of a report on conditions in one agency, without being nearly consumed with indignation and a holy wrath." Inspired by this "holy wrath," Zitkala-Ša bombarded Parker with so many ideas that she apologized for writing "so frequently." Such was her passion: "I am determined that our work for the Indian race shall not drag because of any negligence on my part."[47] Determination, however, was not enough. Zitkala-Ša's idea of SAI community centers branching out to connect all reservations did not come to fruition—not as a result of any "negligence" on her part, but rather of the failure of others to replicate her model elsewhere and of a lack of concrete, material support from the SAI. The organization, bogged down by growing factionalism, simply did not have the financial means.[48]

There was more to be depressed about as well. The Bonnins' time in Utah was about to come to an awful climax in a series of nasty affronts that illustrated the callousness and indifference of the Kneales and the BIA white power structure. The first slight was relatively small. Ohiya had returned from boarding school just as the Kneales had arrived to take charge at Uintah. Zitkala-Ša wrote Father Ketcham that Mrs. Kneale had started an Episcopalian Sunday school. Zitkala-Ša overheard her say, "Anyone who does not go to church is no friend of mine."[49] Considering that her family had moved into the same building as the Kneales, in government housing at Fort Duchesne, Zitkala-Ša thought it wise to send Ohiya.[50] She soon regretted it. "At first," she related to Ketcham, "since we have no Catholic church, I sent my boy, 13 years old, to [Mrs. Kneale's] Sunday school. Each time he would come home with 'Mamma at Sunday School they say there is no hell.' 'We don't have to go to confession, we can just pray to God' etc. etc. I decided not to send my boy anymore." Offended, Mrs. Kneale had her husband take it out on Bonnin, who was forced to do extra work at the agency. Mrs. Kneale then told the other students that Ohiya, who had been the only Indian at the Sunday school, could not come to the planned Christmas celebration, even though Zitkala-Ša had contributed money for the tree.[51] It was just as well that Ohiya missed the party. Not long before, two of his classmates had called him "You son of an Indian bitch."[52]

Having to shield Ohiya from Episcopalian persecution was but one misfortune. As Christmas approached Zitkala-Ša informed Parker: "My charge to keep, that poor old homeless Sioux, whom I have cared for these fourteen years is very sick. He occupies a room in my house. I hear him groaning. . . . Poor old soul, he looks to me for everything. I have to coax him to take the Doctor's medicine; and again to eat the broth I have prepared for him."[53] By mid-December Old Sioux had died. Many Utes visited him while he was infirm, and also assisted with the burial. No whites, however, bothered either to visit or to attend the funeral. When informed of Old Sioux's passing, "Some acted surprised. No sympathy, no aid, no Christianly kindness, was shown; Just a faint flicker of surprise disturbed momentarily, the serenity of their self-conceit, for do not they go to church on Sunday?" Just after the funeral service, when Zitkala-Ša was "about worn out with fatigue," came the next blow. "Mr. Parker," she warned, "if you had previous engagements, cancel them. Lock your door and resign yourself to this letter." The following story unfolded.

Around November, Ohiya had started taking care of a burro owned by a Ute who lived in Dragon. The Ute was due to come for the animal when the opportunity presented itself. The burro resided behind the government house shared by the Bonnins and the Kneales. Ohiya played with it daily. This "very innocent pastime" was soon to turn ugly. On the eve of Thanksgiving, two burros belonging to a white neighbor got into the Bonnins' backyard pen late at night. Ohiya's adopted burro began to bray, and Bonnin was forced to let it free to stop the ruckus. Just as Bonnin returned to bed, he heard Kneale coming down the stairs. The next morning Kneale claimed to

Bonnin that he had merely driven the burros away. Ohiya began searching the area for his lost pet. That afternoon he returned home in tears. "Mamma," Ohiya reported, "the hotel people say Mr. Kneale killed my burro." Zitkala-Ša was in disbelief. A day later the burro, dead and bloody, with three bullet holes in its hide, turned up in a nearby barn. "It is an outrage," Zitkala-Ša told Parker, "that such a deed be committed by a Government official; that in free America, there is a community that must take such out-lawry in silence, from one who is supposed to be their example." Not long after the discovery of the burro's death, its Ute owner appeared to collect it. Shocked by what had occurred, the man started asking "why the Whiteman's burros were not killed when his was killed." The Ute community expressed equal anger.

Zitkala-Ša's lengthy letter (nine pages typewritten) recited a litany of other complaints: Kneale's poor treatment of Bonnin, the case of a pregnant Ute woman turned away from the local hospital, accusations that Kneale had taken bribes to allow the peyote trade, how Mrs. Kneale asked her for a donation of coffee for a whites-only Christmas supper ("Oh yes, I gave the coffee! Bit my tongue almost in two."), and how Kneale, who controlled the whole reservation with a clique of favored agents, was persecuting her due to the success of her volunteer work. Weeks later Kneale led a raid on the SAI community center, enlisting the resident police chief to unlock the doors and remove the tables for use somewhere else on the reservation. His wife had done the same earlier in the year, requisitioning plates without permission or advance notice.[54] Parker could only respond with sympathy and vague promises of help. "My conception of the horrors of intensive life on a reservation under domination grows," he wrote, "My heart is full of sympathy for you and Mr. Bonnin and all the poor people who suffer. You are very brave in the face of all these disagreeable things. . . . I am considerably agitated over the unpleasant turn of affair at the Agency and the action of the Superintendent. The high handed action on the burro affair is a revelation of the man. How can I help you without hurting you? I'm going to try in a diplomatic way. I have friends in Congress."[55]

Those "friends" did not help and Kneale was not yet finished. He followed up the community center break-in by arrogantly admitting at a Ute council meeting that he had killed the burro. Those present were stunned. The burro's owner, incensed, demanded $20. Kneale offered him $2.50, claiming that he had done the community a favor by getting rid of the "nuisance." Although the Ute man refused the money, Kneale shoved it into his pocket, declaring, "take this money, you are my friend." Even worse, Zitkala-Ša had discovered that Kneale had been working with a Mormon farmer, John

Hyslop, on a scheme to deprive the Utes of their grazing land by breaking it up into allotments, to be sold to whites. Zitkala-Ša reported some of this perfidy to the BIA, though she was certain that Kneale's "gang" would stand up for him and explain all the misdeeds away.[56]

At the beginning of 1917 a disheartened Zitkala-Ša wrote to Parker, "Every Indian who has attempted to do real uplift work for the tribes gets stung. No wonder that he quits trying; goes back to the blanket, and sits in the teepee like a boiled owl." She added, "I have not sense enough to stop. Wouldn't know if I was killed; and the chances are I wouldn't know then, being dead."[57] On the other hand, the future, for once, looked encouraging. Zitkala-Ša's election to the post of SAI secretary at the 1916 conference proved key. The position was much better accomplished in Washington, D.C. After the long and frustrating tenure in Utah, the Bonnins decided to move. In the spring of 1917, they left Fort Duchesne with Ohiya.[58]

CHAPTER 8

In Washington at War

Leaving Utah must have been a tremendous relief. Though the Bonnins bore a self-imposed responsibility to the Utes, dealing with the Indian Bureau had become so exasperating that they often felt "driven to commit some act of desperation." Zitkala-Ša explained to Father Ketcham, "We love our people and are able to help them—for after fourteen years—we have *earned* their confidence. But we are weary and very worn out with the unjust and petty persecutions of political appointees who would make the Goddess of Liberty to blush—could she get one peep into the despotic reign of pinheads! [BIA officials] on an Indian reservation." Zitkala-Ša also confessed that, as of late, she had been "so very much discouraged" that she could not bring herself to pray. Her agony was the result of BIA machinations that she felt had consistently thwarted her and her husband's efforts. "And yet the very cause of persecution," she noted, "has been because I was doing work to advance real uplift work for my race."[1] This sense of being persecuted for her work, incubated in Utah, would persist throughout her involvement with the SAI.

Moving to Washington, D.C., allowed Zitkala-Ša to become a prominent player in the reform movement. The Bonnins arrived in May, shortly after Zitkala-Ša had traveled to California, where she gave a speech at the Sherman Institute, an Indian school. In it she blamed generically labeled "people" for spreading peyote use on reservations.[2] According to the *Friends' Intelligencer*, the "very impressive address before the student body of six hundred" detailed "the degenerating effect of the death-dealing Peyote upon

her people."[3] The *Riverside Daily Press* also reported on the lecture under
the headline: "Mrs. Gertrude Bonnin Wants Indian Reservation Put on
Map—Wants Drug Habit Wiped Out."[4] Once in the capital, the Bonnins
rented an apartment at 707 Twentieth Street, near Dupont Circle, where
Zitkala-Ša promptly established a second SAI office. An office had previously been established in the Barrister Building, but she preferred to work
from home.[5] The transition to Washington initially proved difficult. Within
a few months, Zitkala-Ša came into open conflict with fellow SAI member
and treasurer Marie Baldwin.

Both Zitkala-Ša and Baldwin were Catholics who agreed on the issue of
peyote. Nonetheless, tensions were almost inevitable. Baldwin was the
only other high-profile woman in the SAI, and in stark contrast to Zitkala-Ša,
was of privileged upbringing. As part of the old guard, Baldwin conceiv-
ably felt threatened by Zitkala-Ša's swift rise. The latter, in turn, may have
felt insecure about taking on a more important post in a new city and pressured to make a grand success of it.[6] Zitkala-Ša's decision to establish a new
SAI office irritated Baldwin, who wished to retain the old one.[7] They also
differed on abolition of the Indian Bureau. Baldwin, though employed as
an accountant in the BIA Education Division in Washington, had begun a
vocal crusade to dissolve the Indian Office immediately and push for total
Indian assimilation. Together with Montezuma and Father Phillip Gordon
(elected chairman of the SAI advisory board in 1916), she had leveled much
criticism at SAI intransience on the matter. Zitkala-Ša, despite all her negative experiences in Utah, advocated for a more measured bureaucratic
transformation. She also worried that Gordon had influenced the Bureau of
Catholic Indian Missions to secretly declare the SAI an enemy organization.[8]
If forced to choose between the two, Zitkala-Ša had assured Parker, "I
would stand by the SAI to the end, . . . I would not go back on the efforts of
my race, even if I had to quit my church."[9]

Treasurer Baldwin was slow to read her correspondence. Her post, like
that of secretary, was unpaid, likely diminishing her enthusiasm. Since assuming the position of secretary in Utah, Zitkala-Ša had repeatedly complained to Parker about Baldwin's lengthy response time and failure to send
needed materials.[10] Not long after the 1916 SAI conference Zitkala-Ša had
insisted to Parker that because of Baldwin's inattention, it was a "mistake"
to re-elect her. "While she has an enviable location, by being in Washington," Zitkala-Ša conceded, "she is uninterested. She has not the time. By her
neglect, my work is hindered. . . . If the Treasurer cannot help furnish me necessary data; I do not intend to go to sleep, waiting for her!!"[11] One letter contained the closing, "That Chippewa ought to be snatched baldheaded for not

sending the complete membership list, with addresses."[12] Once in Washington Zitkala-Ša began opening mail officially addressed to the SAI, but meant for Baldwin in her capacity as treasurer. When Baldwin received paperwork that clearly indicated her letters had been read, she made a vague threat to sue. Zitkala-Ša, fully aware that Baldwin held a law degree, quickly became convinced that a plot was afoot to destroy her work within the society.

Just before the planned SAI conference in 1917, Zitkala-Ša wrote to Pratt about the situation. The letter, typed on official SAI stationery, demonstrates the obsessive suspicion that had developed out of Zitkala-Ša's experience at Uintah (not to mention the society's emergent factionalism). "Dear friend of the Indian, General Pratt," she began, "It is my desire to restore the SAI to its original purpose, but without an active number of supporters, I feel like a grain of sand against an organized army of cunning crooks. Still a grain of sand can stop the smooth running of gigantic machinery. It's knowing when and where to lodge this bit of insignificant sand." Zitkala-Ša went on to explain the Baldwin debacle in detail. "The latest annoyance to interfere with my work," she continued, "is a demand from the Treasurer for Treasurer's letters *with their envelope.* Doesn't it sound queer? I have given her my signed itemized statement of all dues and moneys that come through this office; and was my understanding, as well as Mr. Bonnin's that she did not want me to wait for her on official mail as her personal mail was never sent to the Society Office." Zitkala-Ša further claimed to have a letter from Baldwin stating, "I do not do justice to the position of Treasurer because it is impossible for me to do even the little amount of work that I do."

To support this allegation, Zitkala-Ša maintained that only after letting Baldwin's letters pile up for a week did she begin opening and itemizing them. When Baldwin retaliated by threatening to sue, Bonnin spoke to her by telephone, explaining bluntly that though his wife was happy to sacrifice for the SAI, the couple would not put up with a "government suit." Baldwin, Bonnin added, was at liberty to come at any time to collect her mail. "Isn't this some experience?" Zitkala-Ša asked Pratt. Her closing statements revealed a paranoid desperation: "I need strength and wisdom to cope with the various little schemes and games of the enemy of the Indian race," she told him. "I need the backing of all people truly concerned for the Indian, for the enemy would like to make quick work of me. I can see it licking its chops for conference time. So it grieves me that you are still holding to the idea of not attending this year. I do not know when we needed you more."[13] Zitkala-Ša, however, did fine on her own.

Mere hours after Baldwin removed her papers from the SAI office in early June, Zitkala-Ša stridently but deftly pleaded her case to Parker.

Complaining of Baldwin's actions, she pummeled Parker with a run of rhetorical questions: "Is this the plan? Just where do I come in? Is my service
nothing? Is my sacrifice nothing? Who said so?" She excoriated Baldwin for
wasting SAI money, lacking devotion, ignoring pressing duties, and perhaps even being a BIA spy. Zitkala-Ša also reminded Parker of the free
services she was rendering as secretary. This led into an ultimatum: recognize her apartment as the official SAI office and fund the rent appropriately—
otherwise her family would be forced to leave Washington. These demands
were justified by her greater dedication. "It is due to me, as Secretary,"
Zitkala-Ša insisted, "and more because I have sacrificed more than Mrs. Baldwin, for the sake of the SAI cause."[14]

Throughout the summer and fall the struggle escalated. In September,
Zitkala-Ša wrote to Parker: "The Treasurer's utter failure to give me the
monthly statements of the Society's financial status, has kept me in the dark."
She went on to point out that she had brought in approximately a thousand
dollars in new membership dues, lecture fees, and magazine sales. The only
just solution was for Parker to have the SAI Executive Council meet and declare her secretary-treasurer.[15] The same month in a letter marked "Personal
and Confidential," Zitkala-Ša complained at length about Baldwin's perceived deficiencies and "strange behavior." Parker received another ultimatum: "Either recognize the Secretary's wishes or the Treasurer's. . . . I am
writing wildly, no doubt, because I feel wild. I will work better without the
Treasurer's bothering me. If she is too important, she claims she was one of
the first members; 'that while Mrs. Bonnin is trying to work for the Society,
she is only a newcomer'; she [Baldwin] is an ancient, antique member, a
queer fossil of the Society of American Indians, then I had better cease my
work. I am throwing myself away if this is the case. And misleading my
best friends."[16] Baldwin tried to counter by claiming that she had done
some of Zitkala-Ša's work, to no avail. Zitkala-Ša's theatrical street fighting
won out. "Mr. Parker," she dramatically announced, "before I leave Washington for lack of money, I'll camp in a tent on the river somewhere . . . I
did not come to Washington to spend my time and strength, in a disagreement with a [sic] Mrs. Baldwin. If you remember, I need to save my strength,
as my heart is bad at times; Of course, it is never any good. They say the
only good Indian is a dead Indian."[17]

Parker sided with his loyal secretary by recognizing her office.[18] The incident cemented their friendship. He and Zitkala-Ša began addressing each
other cutely as "Dear Seneca President" and "Dear Sioux Secretary."[19] The
feud between the two women, however, would continue until mid-1918,
when Zitkala-Ša finally deposed Baldwin and triumphantly took the dual

post of secretary-treasurer. Though Parker had chosen sides, he commented, "Both have been petty and spiteful. And no women will ever make a good secretary, bad as I was in some ways. Women officers will scrap."[20] Parker might have noted that men, too, "will scrap." The Zitkala-Ša–Baldwin tiff was of minor significance compared to the catastrophic events unfolding overseas.

On June 28, 1914, the Great War had begun in Europe and quickly devolved into a bloody stalemate of futile trench warfare along the Marne River. Responding to isolationist public opinion, President Wilson initially opposed a domestic military buildup, supporting a public policy of neutrality. He ran his 1916 presidential campaign on the slogan, "He kept us out of war." Even the sinking of the RMS *Lusitania* in 1915 by a German U-boat had not drawn the United States into the conflict, though it killed more than one hundred American passengers and swayed public opinion against Kaiser Wilhelm II. Soon after Wilson's reelection in 1916, however, his tone changed markedly. His 1917 inaugural speech stressed, with regard to the war: "Our own fortunes as a nation are involved, whether we would have it so or not." Berlin had resumed its policy of unrestricted submarine warfare in January 1917 in an attempt to break the blockade of German ports. After the destruction of American vessels in March and the sensational publication of the Zimmerman note, a telegram in which the German foreign minister offered to cede U.S. territory to Mexico in exchange for its support, in early April the United States finally entered World War I.[21] Declaring war invited not only challenges abroad, but importantly, skepticism at home. The political climate Wilson created to overcome domestic opposition inevitably influenced the work of Native activists within the SAI. In the context of wartime dangers, the society sought to exploit potential opportunities for advancing the cause of indigenous peoples.

In order to reconcile Americans to the war effort, the Wilson administration created the innocuously named Committee on Public Information (CPI). Headed by former newspaper man and police commissioner George Creel, this propaganda organ was responsible for selling the war through pamphlet distribution, magazine advertising, and patriotic speeches delivered by "Four-Minute Men." The war was expertly cast as a noble struggle to democratize the world. American citizens responded zealously to the propaganda offensive, which played up reports of the Huns' atrocities, encouraged unquestioning loyalty to the state, and urged all within U.S. borders to become "100% American." Taking the initiative, vigilantes horsewhipped pacifists, persecuted labor unions, and harassed and even lynched German Americans.[22] The federal government and the media legitimated such

actions, in particular those of the American Protective League, which cooperated with the U.S. Bureau of Investigation (BOI) to spy on, harass, de-
nounce, and illegally arrest anyone evading the draft or exhibiting unpatri-
otic behavior.[23]

The wartime environment created official ideological and political restrictions on free speech. The Espionage Act of June 15, 1917, established
criminal penalties and prison sentences for antiwar activities, while the Sedition Act of May 6, 1918, did the same for those found guilty of "disloyal,
profane, scurrilous, or abusive language" toward government institutions
and American symbols such as the flag.[24] The latter description would easily have encompassed Zitkala-Ša's "A Sioux Woman's Love for Her Grandchild," written for *AIM* in 1917. The poem depicted Custer's proverbial "Last
Stand" from the perspective of an elderly Sioux woman who refuses to
abandon her lost granddaughter as U.S. troops advance. The grandmother
makes her own last stand as a cavalry unit overwhelms her encampment.
Zitkala-Ša painted a chilling image:

> Fleeing from the soldiers startled Red Men hurried
> Riding travois, ponies faced the lightnings, lurid
> 'Gainst the sudden flashing, angry fires, a figure
> Stood, propped by a cane. A soul in torture
> Sacrificing life than leave behind her lost one.
> Greater love hath no man; love surpassing reason.[25]

This strong antimilitary statement—not to mention Zitkala-Ša's acerbic
play on the patriotic hymn "My County 'Tis of Thee" in "The Red Man's
America," published in the same year—surely qualified as subversive.

The new government intrusiveness did not end with prohibitions on public expression. War meant conscription. In the first forty-five days after the
declaration, only seventy-three thousand men volunteered for active duty—
far short of the one million deemed necessary for battle overseas.[26] In short
order, Congress passed the Selective Service Act of 1917. CPI head George
Creel hailed the idea behind the draft: "Universal training will jumble the
boys of America all together, shoulder to shoulder, smashing all the petty
class distinctions that now divide, and prompting a brand of real democracy."[27] Petty racial distinctions, especially concerning those of African
descent, were another matter. The question of Indian participation in the
Great War, however, was naturally of great relevance to both Native populations and SAI leaders.

Much to the SAI's disappointment, Commissioner Sells came out in favor
of segregated Native American units. Parker vocally rejected the notion,

controversially stating that "segregation has done more than bullets to conquer the red man." He also stated that segregation would perpetuate stereotypes, relegate American Indians to a lesser position, and preclude indigenous soldiers from proving that they could serve side by side with whites, every part their equals. Underscoring editor Parker's objections, *AIM* branded racially segregated units "walking reservations."[28] Zitkala-Ša was equally opposed to Sells's position. She confided to Parker that an Indian regiment sent to the front "would appear . . . an intended annihilation of the Red Man; for in one fray the INDIAN regiment would be wiped off the earth." As for all-black units, Zitkala-Ša posited, "Secretly I wonder if it is not a cute idea to reduce the Negro population." In an allusion to the political climate she quickly added, "This sounds like treason, so you better not quote me, unless you want me hung."[29] Certainly this last sentence was a joke, but one that reflected the political reality. Jesting aside, Zitkala-Ša was deeply passionate about the issue. When it appeared that an all-Indian battalion would be created she wrote Parker again, furious at the idea: "Shame upon the . . . Walking Reservation. . . . Indian Battalion! Why those false words hide the greatest scheme to utterly annihilate the Red Man, by a whole-sale slaughter!"[30] More maddening was the idea that such regiments would be officered by whites, who Zitkala-Ša felt would take all the "glory." Segregated black units were to be led by black officers, compounding the affront. Zitkala-Ša could only declare, with a dash of racism, that the Indian's "strength of character and nobility has been admitted verbally to be far superior to the Colored race."[31] It was therefore some relief when the War Department decided that segregated units, at least with respect to Indians, were unworkable.

The Selective Service Act required all men between the ages of twenty-one and thirty-one to register for the draft. Sells acted immediately by forming small draft boards on selected reservations, made up of the superintendent, the chief clerk, and a physician. Though noncitizens and those with unclear citizenship status were supposed to be exempt, such requirements were soon waived. Perhaps surprisingly, there was no widespread Native resistance to the reservation draft. Instead, many volunteered for reasons ranging from patriotism to opportunities for economic advancement (a soldier's average salary totaled $528 annually; the average for an Indian amounted to only $92). The warrior traditions in some tribes were also important, as was a general renewal of Indian pride sparked in part by service in the war effort. The BIA furthermore heavily promoted military service as a route to assimilation. The cumulative effect was a swell of registration. By the war's end between twelve and thirteen thousand indigenous men had served in some capacity, an astonishing 25 percent of the adult, male Native population—as compared to 15 percent of all other adult American males. Off-reservation boarding schools, in particular, supplied large numbers of young men.[32]

Once the issue of segregation had been settled, the SAI gave in to the patriotic fervor. SAI members joined either out of belief in the conflict or in the hope that participation would encourage the U.S. government to grant citizenship to Indians.[33] Generally speaking, the SAI also saw the war as a means to win greater respect and appreciation for Indian competence.[34] Parker joined, and Bonnin willingly enlisted at Fort Meyers, Arlington, Virginia, one month following the declaration of war in April 1917. After completing officers training camp, he received a second lieutenant's commission in March 1918. Too old to be shipped overseas, Bonnin served in the Food Provisions Unit of the Quarter Master Corps in Washington, D.C. The money must have helped his family's finances considerably. He was honorably discharged with the rank of captain two years later.[35]

There is no clear documentary evidence of Bonnin's motives for volunteering. Only one of Zitkala-Ša's letters sheds some light on the matter. Despite the Bonnins' great disillusionment with the BIA, they felt proving the Indian's worth justified the sacrifice. "Sometime," Zitkala-Ša wrote Pratt, "I hope I may have the pleasure of telling you all the interesting details of how my husband after fourteen years of service in the Indian Service, was about to be persecuted to desperation; and how when he offered himself as an American, and took the tests required by the training camps, he was commissioned while thousands of others failed to qualify. This shows how the Indian Bureau smothers good Indians. I am happy that my husband could make a test case to strengthen our arguments, to say nothing of his loyalty to our America."[36] The "test case" remark appears most revealing. It demonstrates how Zitkala-Ša and many others in the SAI sincerely believed Indian participation could sway white public opinion and secure Indian rights. Then, in the midst of wartime, when the opportunity to achieve progress at home seemed so ripe, the SAI's activities began to stall.

As it turned out, the 1917 SAI annual conference (where Zitkala-Ša was certain she would be devoured by "the enemy of the Indian race" who had been "licking its chops") never occurred. Plans were underway in July to hold the conference in Oklahoma City, with the theme "The American Indian in Patriotism, Production, Progress."[37] However, ostensibly out of respect for those serving in the war, the executive membership voted to cancel the meeting.[38] As secretary, Zitkala-Ša sent out a letter explaining that due to "the fact that our President and our First Vice-President are under army orders; and many of our members are in the ranks, serving our country," the conference had been "postponed." She acknowledged the "disappointment" many might feel because of the decision, but assured members that "the cause of the Indian will be advanced a hundred fold by our sacrifices for the greater world freedom."[39] In truth, Parker likely had ulterior motives for suggesting cancellation. Aside from the potentially divisive issue of the war, the ongoing peyote controversy had decisively split the membership. Debate over the abolition of the Indian Bureau, led by Montezuma, also remained a prickly issue. Zitkala-Ša had finally come to agree with the doctor's somewhat extreme position, which forced her to publicly defend her stance to more moderate factions.[40] "I am not a radical," she wrote to the *Tomahawk*. Yet she insisted that any system emanating from Washington would be a "political hydra" responsible for "all the oppression of the past."[41] Freedom from government control through the protections of citizenship became Zitkala-Ša's new cause.

Montezuma loudly protested the decision to cancel the 1917 conference. Convinced that the BIA had intervened to stop discussion of the war, he wrote in his newly founded Native rights journal *Wassaja*, "As an Indian, [I think] the meeting of Indians to discuss their welfare is more important than the war (even though we are called savages)."[42] Few agreed. Parker, in contrast, authored a declaration of war on the Axis on behalf of the Onondaga Nation and even created a spy network to ensure that New York Native peoples registered for service.[43] Through the SAI, Parker also hoped to bring attention to indigenous contributions to the war effort. Following his lead, in the *American Indian Magazine* Zitkala-Ša promptly highlighted how aboriginal patriotism justified the granting of citizenship. However rational the strategy, its implications, in hindsight, give considerable pause. Though Indian service opened up new rhetorical possibilities, at least on the surface it blindly (or opportunistically) supported rabid patriotism and the unprecedented human destruction that was World War I. Was there a better alternative? In the context of that time, probably not.

In some sense, Zitkala-Ša's public support for the war was unsurprising. The idea that militarization could remedy America's social problems was shared by progressives who supported intervention. This was an unfortunate trap into which many intellectuals stepped, and into which Zitkala-Ša leaped. But with regard to the legal status of Indians, there appeared good reason. In July 1917 Arizona Representative (later Senator) Carl Hayden introduced H.R. 5526, which would have extended citizenship to all Indians, released tribal monies, and closed tribal rolls. It did not pass, but in January 1918 Representative Charles D. Carter of Oklahoma proposed H.R. 9253, calling for citizenship and release from BIA wardship for "competent Indians." Though Carter fought for the bill over the next three years, it failed.[44] These legislative acts, however, spurred on activists to argue the cause— Zitkala-Ša foremost among them.

Throughout 1918 Zitkala-Ša produced a series of war-themed writings for *AIM* that mixed patriotic declarations with implicit criticism of white society. Invoking principles of democracy so prevalent in wartime propaganda, she forcefully advocated a fulfillment of the touted-but-unrealized American promises of liberty and justice for all. "As America has declared democracy abroad," she pointed out, "so must we consistently practice it at home." Citing the military service of various members of the SAI, Zitkala-Ša boasted that Indians abroad had "intermingled their blood with that of every other race in the supreme sacrifice for an ideal." If they were "good enough" to fight, they must also be "good enough for American citizenship now."[45] One of her key points was that even though the indigenous population had been decimated to only three hundred thousand, Indians were loyal Americans. Native women were producing clothing for "our brave soldiers," while Native men had volunteered on a larger scale than their white brothers. "Were patriotism like this to sweep through our entire population of millions," Zitkala-Ša proudly proclaimed, "we would have in a day, an invincible army of twelve and a half million men."[46]

These knee-jerk paeans to patriotism, offering no real sense of reflection, were in sharp contrast to Zitkala-Ša's critical poems from 1917, "The Red Man's America" and "A Sioux Woman's Love for Her Grandchild." More importantly, her laudatory odes to patriotism now appear unfortunate in light of how Indians were treated during the war—not to mention the ultimate futility and moral vacuity of World War I itself. Native American soldiers in Europe suffered a 5 percent mortality rate, compared to a 1 percent mortality rate military-wide. Some tribes even suffered death rates as high as 10 to 14 percent due to exposure to disease and to commanders who felt Indians should carry out more dangerous, stereotypical roles as scouts and messengers.[47] In many respects Zitkala-Ša's hawkish praise for obedient Indian participation in the war undercut the decisive bite and moral core of her Native rights advocacy during this period.

In retrospect, Zitkala-Ša's response to the war compared poorly with Montezuma's. Eight months after the U.S. declaration of war, Montezuma founded the League for the Extension of American Democracy to the American Indians, with a primary cause of abolishing the BIA. Montezuma also expressed much more openly the chasm between Washington's democratic pronouncements and the reality of reservation life.[48] In June 1917 (the same month the Espionage Act passed), he audaciously asserted in *Wassaja:* "We hear on all sides that America must maintain her true spirit of democracy, we must see that all men are treated on an equal footing, equality and human rights must be upheld. . . . Indian Bureauism is the Kaiserism of America toward the Indians. It enslaves and dominates the Indians without giving them their rights. It is praise-worthy for a nation to hold up to the world such a high standard of justice. But the question may well be asked, 'Why does this liberty-loving country discern injustices across the sea, and close its eyes to the same thing at home?' Does this not show that America has failed at home?"[49] Unlike Zitkala-Ša's patriotic tracts, these arguments displayed both moral forcefulness and consistency in revealing the fundamental moral irony of Indian participation in the war. Courting even more danger from government censors, Montezuma argued that the drafting of Indians into the military was a clear "wrong."[50] Socialist leader and three-time presidential candidate Eugene Debs was charged in the summer of 1918 with publicly advocating draft evasion. He was swiftly sentenced to federal prison.[51]

Given Montezuma's views, it is little wonder that the federal government took notice of him. Montezuma was first targeted by the American Protective League, then spied on by the BOI. Fearing repercussions, he issued a written statement partially recanting, restating, and sanitizing his positions. A now-declassified U.S. military intelligence report on Montezuma accuses him of publishing his journal "with a view to inciting insurrection and disloyalty among the Indian tribes." Documents also show that the BOI looked with suspicion on his German wife and "strong-minded" German mother-in-law, who had supposedly instilled in Montezuma the belief that "Germany is alright and Uncle Sam is all wrong."[52]

Given the very real danger government censorship represented to voices of dissent, one can look with greater understanding upon the tightrope walk Zitkala-Ša performed in 1917–18. As her letters to Parker and Pratt (quoted earlier) reveal, she had conflicting feelings, eternal suspicions, and burning hatreds toward the U.S. government, the BIA, and World War I. In a letter to Parker dated July 28, 1917, when the question of all-Indian units was still being debated, Zitkala-Ša wrote, "This terrible war is maddening. Will there be anything left after the war?"[53] But though her balancing act may have smacked of blunted morality, she did sincerely view the war as a unique occasion to gain protections for Indians and to some extent begin to rectify past wrongs.

In the spring of 1918 Zitkala-Ša started preparing for the annual SAI conference under the 1917 slogan, "Indian Patriotism, Production, Progress."

She signed the conference announcement "Yours for the Indian Cause," which would become her tagline for years to come.[54] She meant these words to be taken literally. Throughout the summer her conference preparations were hampered by a new and unlikely addition to her household, a destitute army veteran named Madoniawaybay. Zitkala-Ša explained to Parker: "I have an unusual tax upon my own strength, for after successfully getting a Non-English speaking Indian out of the Army with an honorable discharge, finding suitable work for him here in the city; I have had to make a 'camp bed' for him on the SAI office floor; and give him his breakfasts and evening dinners. When you remember I have no maid, you know I am putting myself out quite a bit for my unfortunate brother. However, I am a strong believer in backing up one's convictions with every ounce of life that the good God gives. Madoniawaybay's home is in Ft. Peck, Montana; he is over 32 years old. He is interested in learning to drive auto-trucks. That will be remunerative business for him. He begins his study of English in the night school very soon. I am seeing about that."[55] Fortunately, Madoniawaybay made excellent progress in his studies. He soon found a day job at five dollars a week, secured work as a railroad brakeman, and opened a bank account. Six weeks later Zitkala-Ša reported that Madoniawaybay was "very much elated with himself" and was "looking well."[56]

The 1918 SAI conference took place in Pierre, South Dakota, on September 25–28. There, Zitkala-Ša presented a motion to lobby President Wilson to include an Indian delegation in the planned peace conferences in France. Though the idea had originally been Montezuma's, no one else among the mere twenty-five active members in attendance expressed any interest.[57] The SAI conference, in fact, had been arranged mostly on Zitkala-Ša's initiative. Parker did not attend because of work.[58] Without his loyal secretary's efforts the gathering probably would have been cancelled as in 1917.[59] With Parker absent, Charles Alexander Eastman was elected SAI president. Baldwin was forced out as treasurer, and a victorious Zitkala-Ša took the dual post of secretary-treasurer and soon after became editor of *AIM*.[60] Baldwin retaliated by taking months to transfer the SAI funds to her nemesis. In mid-October, Zitkala-Ša informed Gordon: "The former Treasurer has not turned over to the new Treasurer the Society's books, documents, check books, rubber stamp; nor the balance of Society Funds deposited in the bank by her during her term of office."[61] In December, Zitkala-Ša was still complaining to Montezuma: "If [Baldwin] hoped to block work by hanging on to a few dollars, she has miscalculated—as work is going on!"[62]

That December, Zitkala-Ša was still convinced that an Indian presence at the Paris Peace Conference could somehow lead to Indian citizenship and self-determination at home. She wrote Montezuma that the chances of "securing full citizenship for the American Indian" depended on their "heroic sacrifice in the war for democracy." Therefore, the "psychological time" had come to press for Indian claims. She exhorted SAI members to send telegrams to Wilson, but to no effect.[63] Her own telegram stated that the SAI wished "representation" in Paris, "immediately."[64] Futile though the project may have been, Zitkala-Ša's intent was to draw attention to the plight of indigenous peoples within America. In Europe, of course, the smaller nations and ethnic groups were finally to receive rights of self-determination at the war's end.[65] Why not in America? Zitkala-Ša would continue to ask this question in the coming years.

Some resolutions proposed at the 1918 conference succeeded. Because those present were mostly the radical members, for the first time the SAI officially agreed to call for the liquidation of the Indian Bureau—even though some prominent members were still bureau employees.[66] Montezuma's dramatic address, "Abolish the Indian Bureau," must have fired them up.[67] Members against the measure were left disgruntled. Attendees also decided that at the war's end they would focus on bettering the "legal status and condition" of Native peoples. This meant, in particular, a strong push for citizenship.[68] Though the poor turnout might have been explained by the war, in truth the SAI was rapidly disintegrating due to factionalism and dismay over its ineffectiveness. That year they had even failed in an effort to keep Carlisle Indian Industrial School in operation. Citing the war emergency, the U.S. Army appropriated the buildings for use as a hospital three weeks before the SAI conference.[69] Another issue had also hurt solidarity within the SAI: peyote. Blocs for and against had emerged. In the midst of exploiting international developments in the name of the Native cause, Zitkala-Ša had not neglected the "menace" she encountered at Uintah.

CHAPTER 9

THE PEYOTE CLASH

Just as the "menace" of peyote had drawn the attention of the SAI, the Indian Rights Association saw a swell of anti-peyote campaigning in the mid-1910s. The IRA and Board of Indian Commissioners met annually at a Quaker-run resort in New Paltz, New York. Set on placid Lake Mohonk nestled among green hills and sheer cliffs, the hotel was the site of what has been termed a "holy war" that sought to suppress Native beliefs in favor of, as William Willard phrases it, the "construct of Anglo-conformity."[1] In 1914 Fred H. Daiker, the Indian Bureau's chief of law and order, gave a speech entitled "Liquor and Peyote a Menace to the Indian," which assured those present that the BIA was seeking legislation to suppress use of the cactus. Peyotists were referred to as "mescal fiends."[2] Conference attendees, meanwhile, proposed a resolution broadening the existing reservation ban on alcohol to include peyote. Any arguments pertaining to religious freedom were dismissed "as a cloak to cover its general use by the Indians."[3] Several SAI members in attendance, including Charles E. Dagenett, Henry Roe Cloud, Marie Baldwin, and Arthur C. Parker, supported the action. They knew that other full members supported the faith, while many white associates disapproved. During the following two years the story was much the same. The IRA became increasingly concerned that Peyotism, or the Peyote religion, was a dangerous movement, and might become more attractive to Indians than Christianity. As a result, IRA conference platforms promoted a ban.[4]

In 1916, the IRA's annual report featured material furnished by the Bonnins on peyote's spread in Utah. In a letter to S. M. Brosius of the IRA (who
had visited Uintah at their request) they made a series of claims: peyote
brought out "the baser passions," encouraged the Utes to "reject the teachings of Church," and had caused twenty-five deaths in two years.[5] Considering Zitkala-Ša's actions in the early 1900s, she was now courting odd company. Her continuing relationship with Pratt can be explained by their
personal history, but the IRA and the Board of Indian Commissioners, which
since the 1870s had actively placed missionary groups on reservations, sym-
bolized everything she had so openly spurned in her youth. Zitkala-Ša's resolve to effect a ban on peyote had clearly tempered her attitude toward cooperation with such groups.

Parker attended the Mohonk conference in 1916. Afterwards he reported
to Zitkala-Ša: "You will be glad to know that your war on peyote is not
without results. At Mohonk your letter was presented in Committee and the
IRA quotes your petition." Parker however warned, "The fight is a bitter
one. Some very clever Indians are fostering the use of the drug." Showing
an intense interest in the issue, he requested more information on peyote
use at Uintah.[6] Zitkala-Ša quickly replied. Her letter singled out Chief John
McCook, "formerly a grand old man," as most prominent among the "Peyote leaders."[7] McCook had been her target for some time.

In early November 1916, while still living in Utah, Zitkala-Ša had taken a
little trip. She, her adoptive son Oran Curry, Standing Bear from Pine Ridge,
and his wife rented a rig; borrowed some government horses; and headed to
Randlette. They had sent word for all "leaders of peyote" to meet them.
When they arrived, Standing Bear gave a speech in Sioux, which Zitkala-Ša
translated into English. Curry then translated it into Ute. Standing Bear explained how the Sioux at Pine Ridge had deemed peyote dangerous and
had voted to reject it. They were now doing all they could to curb its use.
The assembled Utes listened politely, expressed their views, and suggested
that Zitkala-Ša and her party travel to Dragon, where they could call on the
"chief peyote man," John McCook. McCook was Chipeta's brother. He was
quite well-to-do, the owner of many head of cattle and sheep. In old age he
began to suffer from rheumatism. Peyote—his "medicine"—helped alleviate the pain. Sam Lone Bear acted as McCook's procurer. Lone Bear had
reportedly become wealthy from his growing client list. Many Utes had
sold their farm animals and traded their possessions for his peyote.

Just a few days after the meeting in Randlette, McCook and Chipeta received Zitkala-Ša and her entourage. Sitting in her hosts' home, Zitkala-Ša

attempted to persuade them of peyote's nefarious influence. Standing Bear gave his speech once more. Chipeta appeared sympathetic. McCook resisted. "When Washington told us to stop gambling," he remarked, "I told my people to stop it. When Washington told us that whisky was bad; I told my people not to use it." But, he stated, "As long as we can get this medicine, I think we will continue the use of it." Zitkala-Ša warned McCook that there were efforts underway to outlaw peyote. Brushing aside any consequences of continued peyote use, McCook answered that he would visit Pine Ridge, perhaps soon, to consult with the Sioux chiefs Standing Bear had mentioned. Zitkala-Ša left disappointed. When she brought the matter up with Kneale the results were no better. Kneale told her: "Let them fight it out among themselves."[8]

Zitkala-Ša reported the November encounter to Parker. Two months later she told him that matters had worsened. "Utes are taking their school children to peyote meetings," she wrote, "and a teacher told me yesterday that certain children were not themselves at all, for they were using peyote."[9] Engaging the issue, however, had begun to exhaust her: "Peyote! Why I dream peyote. I have made so many typewritten copies of my peyote data, which I am sending to people who are taking active interest in the matter, that my fingers fairly ache. . . . This peyote prohibition is something that has gone too long without attention [and] requires immediate action. Every year's delay means that much more difficulty in curbing the spread."[10] Despite her fatigue, Zitkala-Ša viewed her anti-peyote campaign almost as a divine mission. She had recently acquired "some strong data against peyote," which she believed had been given to her "for a purpose."[11] Even if she could not convince McCook and the Utes to stop using peyote, she was confident in her ability to persuade white reformers to take measures to halt its spread. She turned her disappointing day in Dragon into an article for the *American Indian Magazine*, "Chipeta, Widow of Chief Ouray with a Word About a Deal in Blankets" (1917).

This article described the visit to McCook's home. Zitkala-Ša established Chipeta as an important and sympathetic figure, explaining that she was the widow of Chief Ouray, "a red patriot who had many times saved the lives of white settlers and who had in many an emergency saved his tribe from disaster." Chipeta's exploits matched her husband's and deserved recognition from Americans. Zitkala-Ša cited her "wild rides through the hills," during which she "risk[ed] her own personal safety to give warning to her white friends of impending raids." Yet the curse of peyote had fallen upon Chipeta and her brother McCook. Both had been "deceived into the use of a dangerous drug." Zitkala-Ša recounted the meeting in Dragon where

McCook refused to listen to arguments. A barrage of questions circulated in her mind: "Did you ever try giving a serious talk or lecture to an audience that was more or less under the influence of a drug? In such a case what results may you expect? Did you ever hear of an evangelist addressing a class of drug users who in their abnormal condition were helplessly unable to receive his message? What do civilized communities do with their drug victims? Do not they legislate for the protection of society and for the protection of the drug user?" In the midst of these searching queries Zitkala-Ša was filled with a "great longing" for a "message from the Great White Father telling his red children that peyote was bad for them." Swift federal intervention was required, she concluded, lest the degradation continue.

The article then threw another tactical punch. Zitkala-Ša reported that in honor of Chipeta's and Chief Ouray's honest and loyal dealings with the federal government over the past decades, Washington officials proposed a gift. But rather than receiving something of real value to the Utes, such as a guarantee of water rights, the title to a quarter million acres of land for future generations of Ute, or a much-needed ban on peyote, Chipeta was instead presented with "a pair of trading store shawls," paid for with interest generated on Ute money. The shamefully dismissive token, coupled with Washington's refusal to confront the peyote epidemic afflicting Native peoples, stood in contrast to the illustrious widow's naive trust in the Great White Father's goodwill—"Poor unsuspecting Chipeta, loyal friend of the whites in the days when Indian friendship counted!"

Zitkala-Ša's depictions naturally beg examination. From a strategic perspective she accomplishes her aim, inspiring shame and perhaps indignation in contemporary white readers sympathetic to the Indian cause. Yet at the same time questions arise regarding her article's paternalistic attitude, undercutting of tribal sovereignty, and representations of Chipeta and McCook. The series of questions, particularly those that mention the evangelist "addressing a class of drug users" who are "unable to receive his message" and the duty of "civilized communities" to prevent addiction through legislation, indelicately suggest that peyote hinders the conversion of the "uncivilized" Indian to Christian norms. Chipeta and McCook meanwhile appear diminished by Zitkala-Ša's simplistic rendering.[12] Chipeta (White Singing Bird) was in truth a woman of keen political shrewdness, highly instrumental in her husband's chiefdom. For more than six decades she was the spokeswoman for the Ute people. A harsh critic of the federal government, she railed against broken treaties and the policies that left her tribe without the water, land, and game necessary for the survival of traditional ways.[13] Zitkala-Ša knew these facts as well as anyone; but in order not to complicate matters and to justify legislative intervention, she chose a discourse of hapless, misguided Indians versus cruelly neglectful whites.

Collective protest and lobbying against peyote continued. In 1916 U.S. Representative H. L. Gandy of South Dakota introduced a bill in Congress prohibiting its use. It was ignored despite Indian Bureau support.[14] The federal government did, however, prohibit the sending of peyote via the Postal Service.[15] Zitkala-Ša, then campaigning in Utah, Nevada, and Colorado, was more effective. In 1915 she persuaded Utah State Senator Don Colton to propose a bill banning peyote in Utah. She argued "that white citizens were protected against harmful drugs by state legislation, why then was it not the state's imperative duty to protect its Indians against this harmful peyote?" Colton's assistance so pleased her that she recommended him for membership in the SAI.[16] Zitkala-Ša was also able to persuade organizations such as the National Mothers' Congress, the Anti-Saloon League, and the Women's Christian Temperance Union to sponsor anti-peyote bills that became state laws in 1917.[17]

During this period Zitkala-Ša consciously used her Native ancestry to generate interest, giving piano recitals and speeches for white patrons and activists in a collage of indigenous clothing and accouterments—what some scholars have termed a "tribal mélange."[18] She wrote Parker of one such event in California: "Have been asked to speak and give a piano solo, in the most popular church in Pasadena, Mar. 14th, [1917] all in Indian dress. I have agreed, for in this case the use of Indian dress for a drawing card, is for a good cause." Zitkala-Ša nevertheless worried that her choice might be controversial. "No doubt," she continued, "there may be some, who may not wholly approve of the Indian dress. I hope it does not displease you. Even a clown has to dress differently from his usual citizen's suit. In News papers, italics are resorted to, with good effect."[19] Parker was not displeased. Instead, he announced his "gladness" at Zitkala-Ša's "effort to break down the Peyote traffic."[20] The "tribal mélange," however, would soon come under fire from a different player in the peyote debate.

The peyote controversy reached a climax on February 21, 1918, when the House Subcommittee on Indian Affairs began hearings on a bill proposed by Congressman Carl Hayden of Arizona, who wished to extend existing liquor laws to include peyote. Zitkala-Ša, in her roles as anti-peyote activist and SAI secretary, was summoned to testify.[21] In advance of the subcommittee hearings, on February 17, the *Washington Times* ran a long story, "Indian Woman in Capital to Fight Growing Use of Peyote Drug by Indians." The article incorrectly identified Zitkala-Ša as a "relative of the great Sitting Bull" (a claim she likely made herself in an attempt at self-promotion).

Furthermore, it sloppily called Zitkala-Ša by the alternating first names "Gertrude" and "Charlotte," and offered this description together with a photo of her in traditional dress: "Highly educated, speaking English fluently, she combined the simplicity and directness of her race with the polish of a college graduate." Though the end of the profile contained some of Zitkala-Ša's statements on the "mental and physical evils" of peyote, the body provided sensational claims (not attributed to her, though she may have been the source) regarding the drug's use: "The Indians cling to [peyote] in many cases as a gift from the deity—some thinking it will give them a sight of the deity himself—and all regard it as a great medicine and intoxicating stimulant. In order to secure its uninterrupted use, it has been claimed that it has been used as a kind of sacrament in the Indian religious ceremonies, but we know that in these feats [sic], which last all night, its use leads to the wildest intoxication and all kinds of orgies in which men, women, and even children take part to the degradation of their minds."

The article also recounted several fantastic peyote-induced hallucinations and actions. The concluding interview emphasized the drug's capacity to remove "all moral restraint." Zitkala-Ša likewise dismissed pro-peyote arguments based on religious freedom as irrelevant due to "the fact that it is used in a way which outrages decency and induces intoxication and degeneracy." Only addicts and "those who profit from this vice," she argued, "plead for its retention."[22]

This last claim was an exaggeration. Though the majority of SAI members opposed peyote use, opinions were split on the issue.[23] One prominent member, Thomas Sloan, had traveled to Washington to testify on behalf of Peyotism's legitimacy, while President Charles Eastman had come to speak against it. Eastman and Zitkala-Ša found a stalwart ally in Pratt, with whom she dined on the Monday before the hearings. Later that week, Zitkala-Ša wrote Parker, "You can imagine how busy I am preparing for the fray. One good thing there are able people on this side."[24] Among them was Father Ketcham, due to attend the hearings to question witnesses in his capacity as a member of the Board of Indian Commissioners. On the opposing side was a formidable antagonist: the eminent ethnologist James Mooney, employed at the Smithsonian Institution. Mooney was determined to defend the peyote rituals he had studied for almost three decades.

Born in Richmond, Indiana, in 1861 to Irish immigrants of modest means, Mooney had, since childhood, been fascinated by indigenous peoples. Richmond was the location of Earlham College, whose Quaker community instilled in him the need to support Native rights. It was a lesson he took very seriously. Mooney's 1878 high school valedictory address stressed that studying tribal cultures was imperative for there to be any hope of establishing and perpetuating a humane Indian policy. As a young man, Mooney became increasingly involved in Irish politics, forming a U.S. chapter of the National Irish Land League in support of Charles Parnell's efforts to aid small farmers back in the old country. Yet he never relinquished his interest in indigenous cultures. Mooney studied every ethnology book available to him at Earlham, and conducted his own amateur studies. When he became disillusioned with the factionalism of the Land League, Mooney left to pursue his first love. In 1885, after three years of trying to get his foot in the door, he was hired as a volunteer, then a paid employee in the Smithsonian Bureau of Ethnology. There his career advanced quickly through his extreme dedication.[25]

By the time Mooney was set to testify before Congress on behalf of peyote in 1918, he had completed extensive studies of the Cherokee, Cheyenne, and Sioux, and of the Ghost and Sun Dances.[26] Invited to an SAI meeting in 1914, Mooney declined, citing ill health, but sent a backhanded word of encouragement: "Your organization seems to hold the promise of good for the Indian, if it can secure the cooperation of the intelligent fullblood leadership."[27] Mooney's post at the Smithsonian was a powerful one. In large measure, men like him determined how the educated, reading public in the United States perceived Natives, because most of the available information derived from the Smithsonian Bureau of Ethnology and just two other museums. A central aspect of ethnology in that era was ranking peoples on a scale from "primitive" to "civilized."[28] Mooney would display this prejudice during the hearings. Despite holding the same prejudices, groups like the IRA felt only mistrust and suspicion for the Smithsonian and its ethnologists' support of "savage" ways.[29]

Mooney first encountered peyote in 1891 while doing fieldwork among the Kiowa in Oklahoma. He subsequently explored peyote use throughout the Southwest, amassing volumes of information that earned him a name as an authority on the subject. Certain that attempts to prohibit peyote use were misguided, Mooney believed that peyote ingestion deserved the status of a religious sacrament. Oddly enough for peyote's chief defender, Mooney's testimony evinced obvious ethnocentrism at every turn. His main arguments lay in demonstrating that peyote use led to the rejection of alcohol and that the Indians who used it had reached a higher plane of quasi-Christian civilization. On the first day of the hearings Mooney testified before the subcommittee: "The Indians are now largely civilized; they are becoming citizens; they are educated, and they travel about and take an interest in each other." Contact with white society had however been

James Mooney in an undated photo. (Courtesy of the Anthropology Archives and Collections, National Museum of Natural History, Smithsonian Institution, NAA INV 02862900)

detrimental to the health of many young men, who looked to peyote as a cure for a range of European illnesses. "The result," Mooney continued, "is that the young men, not the older uncivilized ones, but the younger, middle-aged and educated men, have taken up the peyote cult and organized it as a regular religion, beyond what they knew before among various tribes. In some tribes they have their own church houses, built at their own expense." Because Peyotism was now a "regular religion" practiced by the educated and "civilized" generation, it merited recognition.

In support of this claim, Mooney characterized the peyote ritual as complemented by Christian-like prayer and a communal dinner that was a wholesome "family affair." At length, he described the ceremony practiced by the Kiowa and Comanche: "The Indians of the same neighborhood assemble at the home of one of their number—whole families together—late Saturday afternoon. They come in wagons, or now even in automobiles. They have their supper together in picnic fashion, the women doing the cooking while the men prepare the peyote tipi and the children play about. . . . The men go into the church or tipi, set it up for this purpose, about 9 o'clock at night. The meeting is opened with a prayer, after which four peyotes are handed around to each participant and eaten. After that they take a small drum and a rattle, the usual Indian accompaniment to singing, and sing hymns, and at intervals say prayers in which they mention quite frequently the name of Jesus and their Indian name for God, both which names they now know well." What follows is "nothing that can be called an orgy," but instead a "baptismal ceremony" and celebratory feast in which all participate. Mooney stressed that no women or children ever took peyote, unless stricken with illness. This, too, he noted, found justification in the Christian gospel: "In thus praying over the sick the Indian worships only literally the Bible injunction: 'Is any man sick around you, let him bring in the priests of the church and let them pray over him, anointing him with oil in the name of the Lord, and the prayer of faith shall save the sick man and the Lord shall raise him up.' "[30]

Reading Mooney's testimony peppered with assimilationist imperatives, modern scholars may wonder why he has been declared the "champion of religious freedom."[31] Mooney was a nominal Catholic who saw many similarities between Christianity and Native religions.[32] But far from advocating Peyotism from any indigenous perspective, he undermined the very idea of sovereign traditions in his description of the religion as a crude imitation of Christianity. Responding to questions from congressmen, Mooney specified Peyotism's purportedly transitional nature in a statement that cogently summed up his ethnocentrism, even racism, based in an evolutionary paradigm. "It is not a Christian religion," he stated, "but it is a very close approximation, and, in my opinion, as Indian religions and Indian psychology go, it is as close an approximation to Christianity and as efficient a leading up to Christianity as the Indian, speaking generally, is now capable of. By a process of evolution the Indian has interwoven with this peyote religion the salient things of Christianity. I have been present at the peyote ceremony where they put down a church hymn book and sang prayers to Jesus Christ in the Indian language. You could catch the name of Jesus constantly through the prayers, and they use the Christian cross sign very often in it. In other words, this is the Indian approximation to Christianity, coming through the channels to which he is accustomed." After delineating this steady march towards "civilized" worship, Mooney reiterated that "the peyote religion forbids the use of whisky," and those who practice it are "temperate tribes." Peyotism, in sum, was a route to religious and behavioral assimilation. (Sloan's brief testimony entirely supported Mooney's assertions that peyote curbed alcoholism.)

In the midst of pedantically making his case, Mooney suddenly launched into a verbal assault on Zitkala-Ša, whom he refused to acknowledge by name. Referring to the recent piece in the *Washington Times*, Mooney attempted to undercut his opponent's authority as a spokeswoman for indigenous peoples by attacking her "tribal mélange." "The article," he stated with withering sarcasm, "is accompanied by a picture of the author, who claims to be a Sioux woman, in Indian costume. The dress is a woman's dress from some southern tribe, as shown by the long fringes; the belt is a Navajo man's belt; the fan is a peyote man's fan, carried only by men, usually in the peyote ceremony."[33] Mooney's criticisms, however, fell flat. The representatives evinced little concern over fashion.[34] The boorish, ad hominem attack turned out to be, as Mooney biographer L. G. Moses puts it, a "tactical blunder."[35] Zitkala-Ša's testimony was respectfully received the following day.

Zitkala-Ša's strategy for neutralizing Mooney was two-pronged: first to refute his experience as an ethnologist, second to relate the effects of peyote on reservations from her observations as a former resident. She promptly questioned the legitimacy of Mooney's testimony, citing his obvious status as an outsider and intermittent observer. "Ethnologists who go out to visit these [peyote] meetings cannot stay there day after day, month after month, year after year," she explained, "and when they make their visits those little meetings are prearranged. I have been a school-teacher too long not to know that when I have a class recite before a visitor that immediately the air is charged with a certain restraint. We know that is human nature, and in these Indian meetings that are visited, when the Indians know that an ethnologist intends to write it down, they naturally cannot help feeling a sort of restraint, and I dare say that they do not do the things at those times that they are in the habit of doing." Only someone in close contact with reservation life, such as herself, could accurately judge peyote's influence.

Zitkala-Ša stated that she had seen firsthand the effects of the cactus's spread throughout the Midwest. Though she admitted lacking specific knowledge of the actual ceremonies, comparative ignorance was irrelevant. Her personal account could perhaps not be entirely refuted. "I lived among the Utes of Utah for 14 years," she reminded the subcommittee. "I visited the Utes in their homes until I knew them all; I seemed to be related to them and seemed to be one of them. . . . When peyote was first introduced among them, during the last two years, I saw my friends victimized, and that hurt my heart. I did not know the technical term of peyote; I never saw the thing grow, but common horse sense told me that the indiscriminate use of a powerful drug was dead wrong." To illustrate the dire effect of peyote at Uintah Zitkala-Ša abandoned her "own personal sense of modesty" and spoke directly of the "orgy" issue, describing a possible case of rape in which a young woman was ravished under the influence of peyote—by none other than Samuel Lone Bear. Rape was an obvious consequence of a drug that could "excite the baser passions." Plus, that drug could be lethal.

Without presenting bothersome printed evidence, Zitkala-Ša claimed that peyote had already caused "at least 30 deaths" among the Utes. She punctuated the statistic with the case of a man in Dragon who had purportedly taken an overdose and gone mad. The highly dramatic scene was a good lesson for Mooney in the art of theatricality. "He became wild," Zitkala-Ša declared, "tearing his clothing off he jumped into a deep mud hole. There before a crowd of onlookers of whites and Indians he dove [sic] his hands into the soft mud; then he jumped up to his feet and wildly grabbed handsfull of the mud and smote himself with it. Before anyone could help him he died in a few minutes, before this crowd of eye witnesses."[36] Whether the story had any truth is unknowable. Regardless, it grabbed her listeners' attention. Zitkala-Ša then targeted Lone Bear—a man who had been accused of a list of crimes ranging from theft and forgery to confidence schemes, and who would eventually go to federal prison for his sexual predation.[37] She told of how Lone Bear sold phony peyote licenses for five hundred dollars and devised all manner of scams to wrest money from the gullible. In one "graft upon the superstition of the Utes," Lone Bear had sold twenty "magic crosses" made of cheap metal. He advised the new owners to hide their crosses away and look at them only after a period of time. If the crosses had tarnished, this was "an evil omen" that death was near. Ingesting peyote was the only remedy. Preying on such superstitions, Lone Bear was able to make a handsome profit and keep many in his thrall.

Zitkala-Ša's stories mesmerized the congressional subcommittee. Employing no mean degree of good old-fashioned barnstorming, she summoned her declamatory powers for a final plea that underscored peyote's potential as a destructive force. "Now, in conclusion," she stated before the assembled politicians, "I would like to say that humans are humans, and human nature is the same regardless of color. . . . This habit of using peyote is not going to be limited to the red man alone, and we already see it spreading out among the white men. Colorado mothers have been told that the soldiers on the Texas border are using peyote and have become alarmed, and I have heard of white people substituting [peyote for opium] when opium could not be secured. . . . [T]his menace is going to spread . . . like wildfire, and we need now to protect all the citizens of America by quenching that little spark, because it will be easier now than later." Zitkala-Ša thus effectively linked the issue of peyote to the prospective degeneration of white society. One subcommittee member, Representative John N. Tillman, praised her as "one of the most intelligent witnesses we have had before us."

Though Zitkala-Ša was a Catholic, she entirely avoided the issue of Christianity in her testimony. She only declared her religious affiliation on being directly questioned. When asked how Christians regarded peyote use, Zitkala-Ša stated that there was no religious issue involved and no specifically Christian perspective worth examining: "I suppose that [Christians] would be [against peyote] on the ground that they would oppose anything that was demoralizing. I do not believe . . . that this opposition can be represented as being made because of a difference in religions. It is not that, because even Indians who are Christians become addicted to the habit of using peyote right along." Therefore, while Zitkala-Ša (like Mooney) obviously endorsed traditional Victorian Christian morals, such as premarital chastity and temperance, religion was, at least according to her testimony on the day, immaterial. Only the effects of the cactus, not religion, mattered. When answering related questions on temperance issues Zitkala-Ša claimed that peyote and alcohol were "twin brothers" that did nothing but "undermining work" that harmed the family unit and broke up homes.

Zitkala-Ša's testimony was followed by Eastman's. Supporting her assertions, the Sioux doctor labeled peyote use under religious auspices a mere "subterfuge" that allowed continued harm to the Indians. His testimony was, however, hardly the crescendo. The most incendiary testimony that day came from Pratt, now retired as a brigadier general. He fired a barrage at Mooney, and by extension the ethnological community, accusing them of promoting religious use of peyote for their own professional purposes. Though he admitted his knowledge of peyote was "confined almost entirely to hearsay," Pratt had plenty to say. He accused the Bureau of Ethnology of "never [having] been helpful to the Indians in any respect" and of wasting public monies on their own pet projects. "You will be unable to find," he charged, "if you go through all of the Indian tribes, where they [the ethnologists] have taken the Indian by the hand and said, 'My brother, you can become a citizen of the United States.'" On the contrary, "the ethnologists always lead the Indian's mind back into the past." Also on display was Pratt's well-established tendency to make personal attacks. He brought up a long-past incident in which Mooney had been wrongly accused of hiring a former Carlisle student to "find an Indian who would submit to having his back slit, the skin lifted and thongs put in his back" to be attached to cattle skulls. Mooney then took photographs as the man ran around. The ethnologist, infuriated, condemned the statement as "an absolute falsehood." Pratt would not relent. He quickly made the further charge that ethnologists like Mooney had been wholly responsible for originating both the Ghost Dance and peyote use, declaring, "You ethnologists egg on, frequent, illustrate, and exaggerate at the public expense, and so give the Indian race and their civilization a black eye in the public esteem."[38] This was, without doubt, Pratt at his least politic.

In May of 1918 the House Subcommittee of the Committee of Indian Affairs published its report, "Prohibition of the Use of Peyote among Indians," which strongly recommended a ban. Zitkala-Ša's testimony was quoted under the title "Peyote Causes Race Suicide." A statement by Father Ketcham appeared as well. He wrote that after numerous conferences with Kiowas and Quapaws "discussing the question [of peyote] and trying to view it from every possible angle," his "personal friendship for these tribes in particular and for the Indian people in general" made it impossible for him to condone peyote. Despite Mooney's efforts, the report concluded that any objections to a peyote ban on religious grounds were risible: "The claim, stoutly maintained, that these . . . night orgies in a closed tent polluted with foul air, should not be outlawed because of the religious character of the ceremonies should receive scant credit."[39]

In the interim before the bill came to the floor for a vote, Zitkala-Ša contacted Pratt: "I suppose," she wrote, "you have heard that the Peyote Bill (H.R. 3614) has reported out of committee favorably. This makes me very happy indeed; and I want to thank you again for your very able assistance at the hearings. Now I feel I must redouble my efforts, with a view of having this Bill enacted into law." (The Pratts and Zitkala-Ša had become very close friends by this point, spending evenings together in the company of Elaine Eastman, Charles Eastman's estranged wife.)[40] A month later, Zitkala-Ša wrote President Wilson, begging him to "send a word of encouragement to our Congress to act promptly and favorably upon peyote legislation."

Enclosed with the letter were the text of the bill, the subcommittee report, and a list of progressive women's organizations that backed the legislation.[41] It was referred to Commissioner Sells, who had already promised his support. Zitkala-Ša expressed her gratitude, perhaps too effusively:

> It made me very happy when you so kindly told me my appeal to the President in behalf of the Peyote legislation had been turned over to you. I realize that our great president looks to your own good judgment in forming his course of action. I am thankful that this letter was brought to your own personal attention. When this matter is finally approved I shall feel greatly indebted for your able stand on this question. It will not be the first act of true kindness to the Indian on your part, for I remember with gratitude your attitude against Indian units; and that today our Indian soldier enjoys the close comradeship of our White Americans, because of your views on that subject.[42]

Sells warmed to the superfluous flattery. He promised "to aid the peyote legislation in every way possible."[43]

Mooney, meanwhile, put his efforts into circumventing any potential legislation. In October 1918, he helped establish the Native American Church of Oklahoma in hopes of gaining legal protection for the ceremonial use of peyote. Its charter read, "This corporation is formed to foster and promote the religious belief of the several tribes of Indians in the state of Oklahoma, in the Christian religion with the practice of the peyote sacrament."[44] Mooney's actions naturally infuriated Zitkala-Ša. She wrote Pratt once again (on official SAI stationery), complaining that the "so-called peyote church" was meant "to evade possible peyote prohibition." Seeking a decisive counterpunch, Zitkala-Ša searched her mind for a way to attack Mooney directly. She formulated an assimilationist response that Pratt, or any other white sympathetic to the anti-peyote cause, would readily endorse: "Mr. Mooney as I understand, is paid by the Government for his services along ethnological lines. This work takes him into the heart of Indian communities. It appears that he takes advantage of these field trips to encourage peyote eating among the tribes. . . . As the future of the Indians means less to him than the past, he appears to cater to their wishes, that he may the more easily extract Indian lore for his books." Zitkala-Ša's target was not "Indian lore," but rather suspicions about Mooney's research. She felt truly concerned with both the Indian's past and future, so long as neither included peyote. Her letter continued, "In view of the foregoing, do you not agree that the attitude of this man is detrimental to the progress of Indians; and that some prompt action should be taken to disarm him of his government position; that if he goes into the field he will not appear to have the support of the government for his peyote propaganda but must go as an individual, upon his own merit?"[45] Pratt enthusiastically agreed. Soon thereafter he disclosed to Montezuma, "I am going after [Mooney] personally and trust that I shall add something to the volume of testimony against him and possibly knock him out. He was never anything else but a curse to the Indians."[46]

Convinced that Mooney was doing his best not only to defend but to encourage peyote eating, Zitkala-Ša and Pratt began a letter-writing campaign directed to government officials. Enlisting a host of missionary groups, IRA members, and Office of Indian Affairs employees, they effectively colluded to ban the ethnologist from the Oklahoma reservations where he did fieldwork.[47] The argument that a government employee was consciously attempting to thwart a congressional subcommittee was persuasive. Mooney received a demotion in the Bureau of Ethnology and a massive pay cut. Humiliated, he died of cardiac arrest three years later at age sixty, frustrated in his attempt to produce a definitive study on Peyotism.[48] Similar frustration greeted anti-peyote agitators over the next three years as proposed bans passed in the House but died in the Senate. Eventually, however, anti-peyote laws were adopted in thirteen states, influenced in part by Zitkala-Ša's lobbying of temperance and women's groups.[49] Her efforts in South Dakota were particularly notable. In 1920, she spoke at the Catholic Sioux Congress at Pine Ridge Reservation, denouncing the so-called Devil's root. Father Ketcham also spoke.[50] Three years later Zitkala-Ša brought twenty Sioux to testify against peyote before that state's legislature. On February 26, 1923, South Dakota adopted an anti-peyote law that criminalized possession, punishable by a five-hundred-dollar fine or one year in jail.[51]

Based on these events some scholars have understandably demonized Zitkala-Ša's anti-peyote campaign as a "holy war" to destroy Native religion or push for assimilation.[52] But based on all available evidence, Zitkala-Ša's motives for fighting peyote did not spring from either Catholicism or any secular assimilationist ideology. Instead, she remained deeply proud of her Sioux cultural heritage. Perhaps for this reason Zitkala-Ša saw peyote eating not as an indigenous practice, but as an outside influence on Plains Indians, whose first contact with the drug did not occur until the late nineteenth and early twentieth centuries.[53] The Ute experience with peyote, so closely connected to Lone Bear's obvious hucksterism and sexual exploitation of young girls, little resembled the religious aspects of its use among, for instance, the tribes of the Southwest.[54] Nonetheless, Zitkala-Ša can be faulted for not appreciating their religious ceremonies; to her, *Indian*

Zitkala-Ša posing for a photograph at the Catholic Sioux Congress, Holy Rosary Mission, Pine Ridge, South Dakota, 1920. (Courtesy of the Marquette University Archives, Bureau of Catholic Indian Missions Records, ID 00684)

Zitkala-Ša being interviewed by a Native reporter at the Catholic Sioux Congress, Holy Rosary Mission, Pine Ridge, South Dakota, 1920. (Courtesy of the Marquette University Archives, Bureau of Catholic Indian Missions Records, ID 10115)

culture certainly equated with traditional *Sioux* culture.[55] This fact resulted in a myopia concerning the implications of a peyote ban increasing government control on reservations, when such control should have been eliminated and should never have existed in the first place.

On a wider scale, Zitkala-Ša's motives for fighting peyote were—arguably and ultimately—in line with her declared purpose of guarding Indian interests in general. Despite her blindness to the dangers of federal control, Zitkala-Ša had good intentions. Just before the subcommittee hearings she wrote Parker: "I know I am hated by the Bureau and Peyote people but quite regardless of that, I must stand for what appears to me right."[56] Zitkala-Ša did honestly feel that peyote's spread had caused physical and societal harm on the Uintah Reservation. She opposed drug use in general, alcohol—the historical bane on many Indian reservations—included. Her desire to shield young women from sexual predation also clearly accounted for a large part of her anti-peyote campaign. That she enlisted so many women's organizations in her fight indicates her belief in women's power, channeled through the vein of progressive, first-wave feminism. One aspect of the anti-peyote campaign also remains highly compelling. After so many decades of destructive white encroachment, broken treaties, and massacres, Zitkala-Ša, a (female) Sioux Indian from Yankton, bent much of the U.S. government apparatus to *her* will, in a sharp reversal of historical tradition.

CHAPTER 10

FORGING A PLAN OF RESISTANCE

Zitkala-Ša's patriotic writings during World War I and her statements during her anti-peyote crusade might suggest that she had reconciled with
white America since the early 1900s. This was not the case. After 1917
Zitkala-Ša reforged her critique of U.S. society, building the foundations of
a proto–Red Power platform of resistance to white rule. Even while seeking
official aid on issues such as peyote, she highlighted the wrongs the U.S.
government had committed against Indians. In the *Washington Times* article
that ran before the peyote hearings, for instance, she unabashedly criticized
corrupt BIA officials for allowing white cattle ranchers, in collusion with
banks, to lease reservation lands for a pittance: "The trouble is that the
agents are so often political appointees, not selected for good character, but
as a reward for party work—and the Indian is the helpless victim of the
white man's cupidity." Zitkala-Ša's solution was based in her recent experience with women's groups. "I am desirous of having women sent in the capacity of agents to the Indians," she stated, "for I feel that in that case they
would give the red men fairer treatment."[1]

To Zitkala-Ša achieving fairer treatment meant abolition of the Indian
Bureau and granting of full U.S. citizenship to Indians. Because the SAI
had proved ineffectual, she increasingly turned to Christian women, who
affirmed her moral stances. With the support of the General Federation of
Women's Clubs, she plied the East Coast on a lecture tour, touting her husband's military service and displaying her beads and buckskin. Her message was simple: "If the Indian is good enough to fight for America, he is

good enough to be considered an American."[2] She had little trouble charming her hosts and the journalists sent to cover her appearances. Her arguments were however often lost on her white audiences, who focused on an engaging Sioux woman claiming to be a "direct descendent" of Sitting Bull. One reporter commented, "She has a striking face, strong features lit by splendid black eyes, a hint of dimples when she smiles and an abundance of blue-black hair. Delightfully simple she soon puts one at ease. What she has to say she gives with corresponding simplicity, and a directness that is satisfying. Watching her and listening to her comprehensive knowledge of both her race and ours, one silently acquiesces with her in her amused little observation 'the white man needs education as well as the Indian.'"[3] The reporter neglected to describe Zitkala-Ša's lecture, which undoubtedly called for overhauling federal Indian policy, granting U.S. citizenship to Indians, and recognizing the value of indigenous cultures and peoples. Little had changed in this respect since she delivered "Side by Side" more than two decades earlier. White society continued to objectify rather than understand Zitkala-Ša as an indigenous woman.

Though Zitkala-Ša had difficulty imparting her message in person and in the press, her written record in the *American Indian Magazine*, the SAI's most prominent outlet, remains unadulterated. In a series of articles she sketched what can be distilled into an early Red Power platform aimed at the defense and rejuvenation of Native cultures and societies. Its tenets were territorial primacy, citizenship (somewhat incongruous from a contemporary perspective), Indian Bureau abolition, cultural preservation, English learning for communication and self-defense, moral supremacy of indigenous peoples, and finally, retention of the Native-owned land base. In formulating her approach, Zitkala-Ša capitalized on two developments: the end of the Great War and the official democratic proclamations then in vogue. The first allowed more vociferous criticism of the government, the second, an opportunity to expose hypocrisy.

In 1919 Zitkala-Ša published "America, Home of the Red Man," which attempted to educate the white public by pointing out the irony of their perception of Indians. Zitkala-Ša related the story of her journey to South Dakota, the land where she was born, for the 1918 SAI conference. On the train she is "accosted" by a nosy traveler, a white man who has the audacity to call *her* a "foreigner." A series of images passes before her eyes: thousands of Indian soldiers on European battlefields, an impoverished Ute grandmother donating to the Red Cross, and a young Indian determined to serve despite his multiple battle wounds. These sacrifices are as unrecognized as the rights of the people who make them. The central question is,

"When shall the Red Man be deemed worthy of full citizenship if not now?" The stranger on the train is blind to these truths and uninterested in listening to Zitkala-Ša's exposition, encompassing everything from the history of the world's races to federal Indian policy. "America" she states, is "Home of the Red Man," who has the preeminent right to the nation. But unlike his fellow Americans, the Red Man "loves democracy" and "hates mutilated treaties."[4]

To bring further attention to the status of America's indigenous population, Zitkala-Ša drew parallels with European nations that were gaining independence in the aftermath of the war. As the Paris Peace Conference unfolded abroad, she noted in *AIM* how, due to U.S. intervention, the "little peoples are to be granted the right of self determination." What better time, then, to extend the franchise at home to the continent's original inhabitants? Indians were as deserving as the Europeans for whom they so bravely fought. Zitkala-Ša's claim for the Red Man was straightforward: "citizenship in the land that was once his own."[5] At present, "Paradoxical as it may seem," she explained, "the very people standing most in need of the aid and justice of the machinery of the law is debarred from the courts of America. Three-fourths of the Indian race being non-citizen, have no legal status, though a race that is good enough to fight and die for world democracy is surely worthy of full American citizenship and the protection of law under our constitution!"

Forcefully advocating citizenship was only one part of the equation. In addition, the BIA had to go. In *AIM*, Zitkala-Ša proclaimed the Indian Bureau the "love-vine strangling the manhood of the Indian race." Quite simply, it was preventing exercise of tribal sovereignty, personal freedom, fair hearing of legitimate claims, and all attempts at self-help.[6] Zitkala-Ša noted that, in an outright irony, during a recent speaking tour Montezuma and Eastman had been barred from entering reservations. The BIA "autocracy" was preventing Indian leaders from speaking with their people about democratic rights, while white "scum" and "riffraff" could enter Indian lands to homestead with impunity. This was "race discrimination" and "the rule of might of the old-world powers," the very things Indian soldiers had fought against.[7] Since American society had failed so spectacularly at democracy, one had to look farther back into history for inspiration.

In "The Coronation of Chief Powhatan Retold" (1919), Zitkala-Ša contrasted present and past events. She noted the recent arrival of Mrs. Woodrow Wilson in Europe. Three centuries earlier Pocahontas, "the first emissary of democratic ideas to caste-ridden Europe," had been received by the king and queen of England. The English colonists regarded Pocahontas's father,

Powhatan, one of the leaders of "the tribal democracies of the new world," as whimsical for his lack of interest in the "white man's articles of dress and decoration" and markings of "rank and power." Powhatan, with his higher system of values and "liberty loving soul," preferred "the gorgeous array of Autumn in that primeval forest where he roamed at will." Consequently, on the day he is to be crowned, he refuses to don the royal robes and accruements sent from across the ocean. Confusion reigns. The Englishmen, determined to carry out their king's orders, resort to trickery and physical power to make the chief kneel and receive the crown: "One leaned hard upon his shoulder to make him stoop a little and three stood ready to fix the royal gewgaw on his head." This forced subordination to a foreign culture was accompanied by a musket volley, which startled Powhatan and foreshadowed the destruction to come. "Are you come to trifle with me and to kill?" the chief asked.[8] The implicit answers on both counts are yes. Here, Zitkala-Ša reverses entrenched American narratives by designating democracy as an exclusively Indian virtue with roots in the Native world.

While asserting that Indian history rests on a higher moral plane, Zitkala-Ša also suggested that Natives should draw strength from indigenous religions. Though still a devout Catholic, she criticized the failures of Christianity and continued her public defense of Native religions in "An Indian Praying on the Hilltop" (1919). This ode to the Great Spirit affirmed the importance of ancestral beliefs while criticizing the hypocritical way Christianity was often wielded—"Poor in a land of plenty; friendless in a den of thieves. Without food and raiment; sick and weary of earth, these are the terrors of my dreams both night and day." But Zitkala-Ša insisted that no one could rob Natives of their God, who renews strength "like the eagle's" and gives hope for "the dawn of justice to the Indian."[9]

Finally, in her series of articles for the *American Indian Magazine* Zitkala-Ša declared that any renaissance of Indian culture and values was dependent on Indians defending their remaining land bases and all speaking with one voice. In an open letter to tribal leaders across America, she stressed that the time had come to "renew our efforts to speak English." English proficiency would aid communication among indigenous peoples of different nations and at last bring an end to the long history of whites taking advantage of Indians' lack of English literacy to cheat them out of their lands. Such lands, Zitkala-Ša noted with urgency, were being sold "too fast and without consideration for the future children of our race."[10]

Zitkala-Ša's anxiety over the loss of Indian land was more relevant than at any other time in American history. In 1906, the U.S. government had introduced fee patents under the Burke Act. The new policy erased the provision in the Dawes Act whereby the U.S. government held Indian allottees' properties in trust for twenty-five years before the owner was deemed "competent," and could sell the land. Initially, the issue of fee patents had been restricted. Then in 1914, Commissioner Sells enthusiastically endorsed a new project to make Indians independent of the BIA by allowing the legal sale of allotments. The change in the law opened the door to widespread graft. At Yankton, for instance, 75 percent of those who received fee patents relinquished their lands for short-term profit, which they spent unwisely. The result was deeper poverty. The Yankton superintendent complained that "land buyers, automobile agents and fakers of all kinds were busy almost day and night[. T]he most susceptible were given the most attention. Smooth toungues [sic] mixed bloods were employed and given a bonus for each deal made." Nonetheless, Sells accelerated the process. Under pressure from western congressmen eager to free up new land for agriculture, Sells issued a "declaration of policy" further liberalizing fee patents. Between 1917 and 1920 the BIA issued more than seventeen thousand, with devastating consequences. On many reservations up to 90 percent of Indians given fee patents sold off their property.[11]

Nevertheless, this issue was not the primary concern at the 1919 SAI conference. The gathering, held in Minneapolis, Minnesota, October 2–4, focused instead on gaining U.S. citizenship for Indians, a stance the Board of Indian Commissioners opposed.[12] Though they eagerly enabled the sale of Indian lands, they resolutely maintained that most Indians were not ready for the responsibilities of citizenship and still required "the Nation's guardianship." Regardless, the attendees at the SAI conference had cause for optimism. Just a few days prior, on September 27, Homer P. Snyder, representative from New York and chairman of the House Committee on Indian Affairs, had introduced a bill (H.R. 5007) that sought to grant citizenship to all indigenous peoples who had served in the military and received honorable discharges. The bill passed and was signed into law in November.[13] No surprise, then, that there was animated debate on the citizenship question and Indian Bureau abolition.[14] Thomas Sloan, in particular, made strong arguments. Acknowledging the sacrifice of veterans, he stated that "the parents who furnished Indian boys for soldiers should be entitled to citizenship."[15]

The 1919 conference had lighter moments. Attendees staged "The Conspiracy of Pontiac," a pageant written by President Charles Eastman. He, Zitkala-Ša, and Montezuma performed.[16] Eastman also gave an opening address that, like Zitkala-Ša's recent *AIM* articles, praised Indians for laying "the foundation of freedom and equality and democracy long before any white people came here" and for never stealing land or enslaving others.

"The day when an Indian becomes leader of this country," Eastman posited, "will be the day when civilization may come on a more stable foundation."[17]

Zitkala-Ša's speech was similar in tone. She deemed consciousness the "greatest gift in life," the one thing Indians could cling to in a rapidly changing world in which traditional ways had been rendered untenable. Building on Eastman's remarks, she insisted that the virtues transmitted through Indian ancestry and culture must be preserved. This was a challenge to be taken head-on. "Now we are meeting a civilization from a race that came from Europe," she asserted, "We have to meet it each day—there is no dodging, and it is not easy. It is going to take courage; it is going to test your strength. It is going to test your faith in the Greatest of All. It is going to be hard, but let us stand the test, true to the Indian blood. Let us do that. Let us teach our children to be proud of their Indian blood and to stand the test bravely." Zitkala-Ša went on to speak of her childhood in romantic terms: "I remember my mother. I was born in a teepee. I loved that life. It was beautiful, more beautiful than I can tell you." Yet her mother recognized that only white education could secure some kind of future for her daughter in the midst of overwhelming transition. Knowledge of white society was then, and continued to be, a crucial defense against encroachment. Indians therefore had to "continue speaking and claiming our human rights to live on this earth that God has made, so that we may think our thoughts and speak them—that we may have our part in the American life and be as any other human beings are."[18] This address was a call for sustaining indigenous cultures against the unavoidable attack of American society. Only by understanding one's enemy could one resist and create sovereign space for alternative values.

At this moment Zitkala-Ša had achieved the influence and public profile to promote her goals through the SAI—if the society could somehow be united and rejuvenated. Then, the unthinkable happened. Sloan, leader of the pro-Peyotism forces, challenged Eastman for reelection as president. Fearful that the "peyote-eaters," as she called them, were set to take the presidency, Zitkala-Ša spontaneously nominated her husband. Bonnin and Eastman both lost by a substantial margin. Zitkala-Ša was reelected to her posts, but instead of seeking compromise with the new leadership, she resigned from the organization, citing health problems.[19] Her disappointment must have been massive. She had come to the conference with very high hopes, writing to Montezuma beforehand that the gathering would certainly be "a humdinger."[20]

It was true that Zitkala-Ša was exhausted and in poor health. Around March she had contracted the flu, which in that era was often deadly.[21]

(Eastman's eldest daughter, Irene, had tragically died of the flu in October 1918.)[22] Her SAI work had also become too much for her to handle. "I am over-run with countless cases," Zitkala-Ša wrote to Montezuma in July, "I only wish I were more than one person, with only one pair of hands to take care of these matters, as they come. Would you believe that I have to rest sometimes when it becomes a physical impossibility to keep on? Right now, I have been too tired to relax; and suffer from sleeplessness. However, I am working on."[23] This stress was compounded by a white associate membership whom Zitkala-Ša felt was "divided in opinion about our work."[24] She had confided to Parker: "Pardon my comment that I am glad St. Peter has charge of the heavenly gate instead of our good active-Associate members whose bigotry would surely turn a vast majority of the Indian race away. In the meanwhile I shall implore St. Peter to be lenient with our Good Associate Members!!!!"[25]

Though often willing to do battle with others in the organization, Zitkala-Ša had long remained an enthusiastic and ambitious SAI believer. She had written to Montezuma in April 1919 that she hoped to "increase our subscriptions to the [American Indian] Magazine to a million!"[26] Before the conference she had, essentially by herself, been coping with a mailing list that numbered over 1,500.[27] Losing someone with this fierce level of commitment was a blow to the SAI, whether or not the membership appreciated it at the time. Eastman, deposed from the presidency, soon quit as well.[28]

Four more SAI conferences took place, each marked by dwindling attendance and increasing apathy. The final issue of the *American Indian Magazine* appeared in August 1920. The last meeting, in 1923, was organized by associate members in Chicago.[29] Montezuma, always the SAI firebrand, did not attend. Suffering from tuberculosis, he had moved to Arizona to spend the end of his life with his Yavapai relatives. He died shortly after.[30] A year before Zitkala-Ša had visited him and his wife while she was in Chicago on a lecture tour sponsored by the GFWC. It was a pleasant occasion and the last time they saw each other. Montezuma wrote to Pratt, "The other day, whom did I receive a telephone from, But Mrs. Bonnin. . . . You can imagine I was surprised for I imagine she had cut off with me. We made arrangement that she spend last Sunday with us. She came and we had a splendid visit."[31]

The SAI had no such happy reunion. The society had been entirely ineffective, marked by infighting and individual maneuvering.[32] But even sustained, unified action would have been of little consequence in that era. Much like the white stranger on the train in "America, Home of the Red Man," nobody was listening. For Zitkala-Ša personally, the SIA had served an important purpose, enabling her to rise to the forefront of the Indian rights movement and regain the visibility she had achieved at the start of the 1900s. She was not about to relinquish this status. At the 1919 conference, Zitkala-Ša stated her future intentions with one last dramatic flourish: "For myself, let me say if there is any Indian council in the United States that asks me to go there, in justice for the Indian, I will be there and I will not ask them to see that I will not go to jail."[33]

Following the disappointment of the 1919 SAI conference, the Bonnins considered their options. They ultimately decided to remain in the Washington area. Around this time Zitkala-Ša contacted former friends in East Coast publishing, endeavoring to relaunch her literary career.[34] The result was *American Indian Stories*, a compilation of her writings from 1900–1902, complemented by some new additions: "A Dream of Her Grandfather," "The Widespread Enigma Concerning Blue-Star Woman," and a forceful concluding essay, "America's Indian Problem." Published in 1921, the volume indicted white society for its treatment of indigenous peoples. By this time, Zitkala-Ša's attempts to enlighten the American public about the value of indigenous cultures had made some headway. In the 1920s textbooks used by pupils in New York; Washington, D.C.; and Virginia began to include stories from 1901's *Old Indian Legends*.[35] In 1921, Zitkala-Ša made personal appearances to address cultural misunderstandings, reading to young audiences from the book. One newspaper recorded that even after a two-hour wait, the children "sat enthralled while she talked to them."[36] *American Indian Stories* featured a testimonial from Helen Keller, who complimented *Old Indian Legends* for the "eternal wonder" it instilled in young children.[37] As welcome as such praise was, *American Indian Stories* would seek a much more political impact.

Vanessa Holford Diana writes that the chapters in *American Indian Stories* "are ordered in such a way as to represent growth towards an increasingly critical vision of the monocultural closemindedness with which U.S. Indian policy endorsed forced assimilation at government schools and oppressed Native Americans by relegating them to the status of wards of the state."[38] The book begins with the semiautobiographical series for the *Atlantic Monthly*, proceeding through the cultural reawakening and resistance of "Why I Am a Pagan" (renamed "The Great Spirit" and slightly edited to avoid overtly offending Christians), "The Soft-Hearted Sioux," "The Trial Path," and "A Warrior's Daughter."[39] "A Dream of Her Grandfather" and "The Widespread Enigma Concerning Blue-Star Woman" are placed before the final, overtly political "America's Indian Problem." The last three chapters add new dimensions to the narrative begun in Zitkala-Ša's childhood, reflecting her role as an activist and her increasing involvement with the General Federation of Women's Clubs through her citizenship campaign.

In the self-celebratory "A Dream of Her Grandfather," Zitkala-Ša receives a mysterious gift from her long-dead forbearer, a Sioux leader who once journeyed to Washington "in the hope of bringing about an amicable arrangement between red and white Americans." Decades later his granddaughter has followed his path, residing in Washington to "carry on his humanitarian work." One night she dreams that "a large cedar chest" is delivered to her door. She opens it to behold a vision of "a circular camp of white cone-shaped tepees, astir with Indian people." In the center a "village crier" adorned in feathers and riding a white pony calls. "Be glad! Rejoice! Look up, and see a new day is dawning! Help is near!" The granddaughter is "thrilled with new hope for her people."[40] This genuine need for "help" is revealed in "The Widespread Enigma Concerning Blue-Star Woman."

"Blue-Star Woman" is a much more complex work that exposes the consequences of Dawes Act allotment strategies in breaking up the Native land base and fomenting tribal disharmony. Blue-Star Woman is an elderly Sioux who, deprived of her "birthright" of land by the "white man's law," faces starvation. Two shorthaired Sioux dressed as "would-be white men" approach her and make a proposal. They can get her an allotment, but she will have to share half the spoils with them. This is an example of indigenous corruption born of white contact. Though Blue-Star Woman recognizes their treachery, she has little choice and reluctantly agrees to the scheme. The Indian Bureau superintendent subsequently allots another tribe's land to Blue-Star Woman. Their Chief, High Flier, protests in vain. He is arrested by a band of Indian police sent by the reservation superintendent. In jail High Flier has a remarkable vision of the Statue of Liberty brought to life by America's women, who are united in his people's cause. Buoyed by "the secret vision of hope," he serves his unjust sentence. But his release is tinged with irony. High Flier's son has been forced to conspire with the corrupt shorthair scoundrels in order to free him. The price: a half stake in his land. They hastily ink the Chief's thumb and present an allotment document. Sighing, the defeated old man presses his print onto the paper.[41]

"Blue-Star Woman" proposes that in the face of overwhelming government corruption and errant paternalism, only one force in America can achieve justice for the Indian. Much like the dynamic heroine Tusse in "A Warrior's Daughter," the women of the GFWC had to come to the rescue.[42] The final chapter of *American Indian Stories* addressed them directly.

"America's Indian Problem" recalls the original "hospitality of the American aborigine," who rescued the English colonizers in their first winter. Though America owes its very existence to the aid rendered by Natives, their kindness was quickly repaid with exploitation and thievery. Only conscientious female reformers can mend the situation with direct action and reciprocal generosity: "Now the time is at hand when the American Indian shall have his day in court through the help of the women of America." Then the "stain upon America's fair name" will be erased. One goal is paramount for the Indian: U.S. citizenship. Yet this step does not wipe the slate clean. Zitkala-Ša insists that broken treaties be "equitably settled" and a "constructive program" be created for Indian protection.[43] This call for action is the climax of *American Indian Stories*. The reader has seen Zitkala-Ša separated from her mother and forcibly divested of her Native culture and religion; and has learned of the wrenching upheavals of dislocation and white encroachment. The middle-class female reformer is left with a choice: ignore her country's crimes or constructively engage them. Some work to this effect was already underway. The western branches of the GFWC had been agitating for a broader national discussion of Indian issues, and of course, had been active in Zitkala-Ša's anti-peyote campaign.[44]

The real breakthrough came in June 1921, when Zitkala-Ša appeared as a guest speaker at the GFWC's biannual conference held in Salt Lake City. There she gave a speech detailing the difficulties afflicting indigenous peoples, very similar to "America's Indian Problem." She proposed that the BIA "be relieved of its practically unlimited autocratic supervision of an orderly people now kept prisoners on small remnants of land not shown on our maps." The bureau's "prolonged wardship," she added, was "not compatible with the idea of American freedom and American ideals, and contrary to the very constitution itself of the 'land of the free.'" The GFWC responded decisively by immediately resolving to "work for [Indian] citizenship rights [and] for the protection of their property" through a newly created National Indian Welfare Committee.[45] The committee, chaired by Stella Atwood, would both investigate injustices on reservations and lobby politicians in Washington.[46] Zitkala-Ša reportedly shed tears of gratitude. She remarked, "It has begun. Nothing now can stop it. We shall have help."[47] The *Federation News* later commented, "With Women Suffrage won, following a war of fifty years, standing organized women of America will now work for the enfranchisement of 'the first Americans,' who are still denied rights of citizenship and who as a subject people are kept as wards of the state under superintendents of practically unlimited powers."[48] The timing was fortuitous, for the situation required urgent attention.

In 1921 President Harding selected Albert B. Fall as secretary of the interior. A former senator from New Mexico, Fall was sympathetic to any legislation that involved the expropriation of Indian lands. That year Senator H. O. Bursum, also from New Mexico, authored a bill that would have transferred land from the state's resident Pueblos to white squatters. Fall endorsed it; reformers protested.[49] For Zitkala-Ša, Fall's actions likely underscored the immediacy of her two priorities: U.S. citizenship and abolition of the Bureau of Indian Affairs. Her pamphlet *Americanize the First American: A Plan of Regeneration* (1921) expounded on these steps toward self-determination, amounting to a seminal work of Red Progressivism.

Americanize the First American, its cover graced by a portrait of Zitkala-Ša framed by little stars and stripes, appeals to the "Womanhood of America." Their support is vital to resisting the "unscrupulous white men" who engineer bureaucratic oppression through the reservation system.[50] Directing her focus to the Sioux, Zitkala-Ša writes of the influenza epidemics and inadequate medical care that orphan many children. The fates of these vulnerable souls highlight the contrast between real and false guardianship, in a distinctly feminine vein. Whereas their natural parents would have seen to their needs, Indian children instead languish under a "wardship growing more deadly year by year." Invoking the cherished Victorian ideals of motherhood and religiosity, Zitkala-Ša underscores how the BIA system fails to uphold the universal virtues recognized by both Native and white women. "Indians love their children dearly," she writes, and "do not believe in corporal punishment." Progress, to female reformers, means the protection and education of youngsters. This belief establishes a common bond. Only women understand, through their higher spirituality, that children have a vital role in "solving the riddle of human redemption." Yet no progress will be made toward salvation if the "discrepancies in the meaning of American freedom" are allowed to reign unchecked. BIA sham paternalism must be fought with genuine maternalism to set the correct course.

Americanize the First American maps out the "constructive program" mentioned in "America's Indian Problem" in two circular charts, handwritten by Zitkala-Ša. The first is "What We Have," namely, "bureaucracy." The second is "What We Want," being "democracy," or "a government by the people." The first chart lists woefully little. Bureaucracy emanates from Washington through the Department of the Interior, the Bureau of Indian Affairs, reservation superintendents, and six thousand employees. This oversight severely restricts use of land and access to education. Land is either denied or "leased to White Cattle Men to the detriment of Indians," wasting its agricultural potential. Education is substandard compared to that received by whites and does not offer the opportunity for higher schooling. A final section, "Spiritual Welfare," mentions curtly that "missionaries are on Indian reservations." In contrast, "What We Want" outlines initiatives that emanate from a headquarters in Washington through an "Indian Citizens' Association," a "Reservation Executive Committee," and district and precinct offices presumably staffed by indigenous peoples. The multi-point plan suggests an agricultural program and farmers' association that discourages leasing, encourages crop rotation and animal husbandry, and establishes financial enterprises in the form of stock-company cooperative stores to expand and regulate business opportunities.

In line with progressive female organizations, *Americanize the First American* envisions the creation of a "Housekeepers' Club," intended to inculcate certain modern domestic values. At meetings women would read and discuss women's magazines and perfect "thrift habits" and home economics. In light of the enfranchisement of women in 1920, women would also study how best to vote in the "home, community, state and America." The club would be complemented by a "Parents' Association" intended to instill "the laws of morality" and "spiritual truths" and to guard against the menace of truancy. "Parents must realize," writes Zitkala-Ša, "that their children cannot compete with other children of America unless they are properly educated, and armed with school credentials and good references." In order to foster greater understanding and contact among reservation residents and white society, Zitkala-Ša also proposes a "Junior Red Cross League." This "army of Indian children" would work for community goals and establish contact with children throughout America and other countries to create "World Citizens." This is an international, cosmopolitan vision based in equal cultural exchange.[51]

Such aspects of *Americanize the First American*, as the title obviously connotes, suggest that it is an assimilationist document. To the degree that it advocates Indian participation in American and world affairs, it is. Yet the pamphlet equally promotes the preservation of Native religion and culture. The ultimate goal is unfettered existence outside of federal government control and the overwhelming influence of white society. Zitkala-Ša notes the need to study existing treaties, emphasizing self-defense. Her section "Spiritual Welfare" refers not to Christianity but to the Great Spirit. Taken together with the stress on tribal democracy and preservation of the land base, *Americanize the First American* is best seen as a program for self-determination rather than a blueprint for absorption. In Zitkala-Ša's scheme the potentially ameliorative aspects of white society serve Native peoples in their quest for regeneration, while engagement with the outer world brings advantages in the end. Only then can indigenous lands, values, and identities be protected and perpetuated. Significantly, Zitkala-Ša employs the same rhetoric she used in the early 1900s, insisting that under current conditions "Indians are virtual prisoners of war."

"Bureaucracy Versus Democracy," the pamphlet's final essay, spells out three essential demands for the Indian. First is "recognition by America as really normal and quite worth-while human beings" (particularly considering Indian sacrifices during World War I), "American citizenship for every Indian born within the territorial limits of the United States," and finally, "a democracy wheel whose hub shall be an organization of progressive Indian citizens" under the shelter of the U.S. Constitution. With such moves toward legal safeguards and self-government, the bane of America's bureaucratic machinery can be thrown off and indigenous peoples will be able to flourish once more, in accordance with their own traditions, as political equals.[52]

To Zitkala-Ša, then, citizenship—the most pragmatic and politically realistic option available to Indian activists—clearly meant self-protection and sovereignty.[53] The underlying implication of *Americanize the First American* is that the nation's original, legitimate inhabitants are the ones who best uphold the values of civilized democracy falsely preached by the invading hordes of "unscrupulous white men." This reversal of the American narrative is key to understanding the pamphlet's oppositional perspective. However, with no political recourse to exercise moral transformation, Native aspirations of democracy have been cruelly denied. To the members of the General Federation of Women's Clubs, this last aspect appeared compelling and relevant. They too had been refused political rights. Recently enfranchised after a long struggle and now poised to influence government policy on the national stage, America's Christian Sisterhood welcomed the message that only they could rectify the past sins of male oppressors. It was a persuasive call to arms.[54] The GFWC would prove a vital partner in facilitating Zitkala-Ša's future work.

CHAPTER 11

Oklahoma

With the support of the GFWC's two million members, Zitkala-Ša gained a larger platform on which to continue her agitation for Native causes into the 1920s.[1] In 1921, she began working closely with the organization as a lecturer and research agent for the National Indian Welfare Committee. In this capacity she traveled to California to investigate conditions there and raise awareness of the region's Indians. Just before Zitkala-Ša arrived, Berkeley professor Charles E. Chapman published *A History of California* (1921). Its opening chapter described the indigenous population: "The personal habits of the Californians were, to say the least, filthy. Their houses and they themselves were covered with vermin—which on occasion they would catch and eat! . . . As dried fish was sometimes an important article of the winter food supply it well be imagined that the odors of the home were none too inviting. Over some of their other private customs it is perhaps better to draw a veil! It is not surprising that many diseases followed in the wake of the filthy habits of the Californians." This was a curious example of biological revisionism. Chapman further stated that the peoples lived in "a state of upper savagery to that of lower barbarism." He capped the classification with a judgment typical of his time: "It can be seen that no civilized state might be expected to develop among the barbarous Californians. The only question was: How long could they postpone the inevitable conquest of the land by a capable people?" Chapman concluded in triumphant tones: "Yet they did not delay white settlement and conquest a single day, once the white man had overcome the obstacles of nature. This is indeed evidence of their insufficiency."[2]

In a series of articles for the *San Francisco Bulletin*, Zitkala-Ša reversed Chapman's thesis. She conjectured why her people had "fared so badly under the foremost democratic government of the world," coming to a much different conclusion—though it was, in fact, still related to race. "I used to wonder if it could be the pigment of the skin that was our offense," Zitkala-Ša wrote, "Yet, in nature, flowers of every hue abound. Sin could not be in color. When I began perusing the papers I was amazed at the crimes committed in large cities, brother against brother. Scarce could I believe the palefaces were killing one another, too. From this I reasoned it was not the Indian's dark skin that had brought on his unspeakable sorrows at the hands of heartless men, money crazed." White skin, then, was a marker of violence and inferiority. California's gold rush colonization offered proof, as did World War I. Reversing her public position of several years earlier, Zitkala-Ša termed the conflict "a monumental attempt at suicide by the Caucasian race."[3] Indian peoples, in contrast, had embodied the ideals of the Sermon on the Mount. Faced with white impulses to annihilate one another and amass material goods, Indians now had to "think and act together" for self-preservation.[4]

Directly after her West Coast sojourn, Zitkala-Ša took a tour of the southern states, speaking before women's clubs on Indian citizenship. Sponsored by the GWFC, she also lectured throughout Michigan, Iowa, and Ohio.[5] In 1922, Zitkala-Ša appeared at a ceremony celebrating the placing of a South Dakota memorial stone at the Washington Monument. There she recited a piece written for the occasion: "A Dakota Ode to Washington."[6] The schedule was intense. Between 1921 and 1927, Zitkala-Ša gave some four hundred public lectures.[7] During these years her husband also became increasingly involved in reform work. Released from military duty in August 1919, Bonnin enrolled in George Washington University Law School in 1921. Afterward, he supported the family by clerking for the law firm Munn, Anderson, and Munn, a job that provided valuable legal experience. Meanwhile, Bonnin began representing Indian claims before Senate and House Committees on Indian Affairs and undertaking a general review of past treaties, although there is no evidence he completed a law degree or took the bar exam.[8]

The early 1920s were a crucial time in the fight for Indian rights. The appointment of Fall as secretary of the interior was tremendously unpopular among reform groups. In 1922, Fall threw his support behind Bursum's bill that would divest the Pueblos of their communally owned land. He then

OKLAHOMA

decreed that reservations created by executive orders rather than formal treaties should be treated as "public lands." This ruling opened approximately 60 percent (twenty-two million acres) of Indian lands to exploitation of oil and gas resources. The IRA and GWFC objected strenuously, forming the American Indian Defense Association (AIDA)[9] "to secure to the American Indian just treatment from the government and people of the United States."[10]

The AIDA was headed by John Collier, a devoted activist who would eventually become commissioner of Indian affairs during the Roosevelt administration. The intense scrutiny on Fall was more than justified. In 1923, he resigned due to his starring role in the Teapot Dome scandal.[11] The Bursum Bill, meanwhile, was defeated.[12] Fall was replaced by Herbert W. Work. Work addressed reformers' criticisms by creating the Committee of One Hundred, charged with investigating the problems facing indigenous peoples. The committee included both indigenous and white reformers; Eastman, Roe Cloud, Parker, and Sloan were joined by World War I General John J. Pershing and perennial presidential contender William Jennings Bryan. In 1924 they endorsed the cessation of any legislation that would expropriate reservation lands set aside by executive order. In addition, they suggested improvements in health care and sanitation, the lifting of bans on religious and artistic expression, and the creation of a court of claims to settle outstanding tribal challenges.[13]

With Fall out of office, the AIDA turned its attention to Oklahoma, where the state's natural resources had become a blessing and a curse for indigenous peoples. Here, the greed of "heartless" white men, which Zitkala-Ša described in her California writings, was all too evident.[14] The Osage, residing on oil-rich lands, had accrued enormous wealth through selling leases at public auctions beginning in 1912. By 1916 their gas and oil royalties exceeded $8 million per annum. These monies were shared communally, so each member on the Osage tribal roll born before 1907 possessed a "headright" of more than $13,000 per year. One individual could inherit multiple headrights, making some families and individuals remarkably prosperous. National newspapers printed stories of lavish Osage spending on diamond-studded shoes and luxurious Pierce-Arrow automobiles. By the 1920s such notoriety had drawn unwanted attention from whites eager to find a way to exploit the tribe's oil wealth for their own gain. In 1921 federal legislation limited headright payments to "incompetent" adults. Local courts placed those Osages who spent too freely and incurred debts under the "guardianship" of white Oklahomans. Many guardians, predictably, enriched themselves with their wards' "surplus funds." Over the next three years six hundred whites managed to amass more than $8 million. Much worse, however, was the "Osage Reign of Terror," which commenced that year.[15]

On May 28, 1921, the body of an Osage woman, Anna Brown, was found at the base of a canyon with a bullet wound to the head. William K. Hale and his nephew Ernest Burkhart were found responsible. Hale had lived among the Osage for years, enriching himself through shady dealings and leases that often took advantage of his Indian neighbors. When Burkhart arrived from Texas he conspired with Hale to marry a full-blooded Osage, Mollie Kyle, then systematically have her family murdered to inherit their numerous headrights. Anna Brown was one of Kyle's sisters. Kyle's mother, Lizzie Q., was subsequently poisoned, while Kyle's other sister, Rita Smith, perished with her husband and servant soon after in an explosion. These deaths were followed by more than a dozen others connected with Hale and Burkhart's sinister machinations, which only ended in 1929 with their imprisonment. From 1921 to 1925, however, sixty Osages were documented as murdered for their wealth in similar circumstances.[16]

The Osage were not the only victims in Oklahoma. Numerous members of the Five Civilized Tribes—the Chickasaw, Creek, Choctaw, Seminole, and Cherokee—had for years been subjected to brutal thievery at the hands of white squatters and local government seeking oil profits. This compounded the grave wrongs the Five Civilized Tribes had experienced after Andrew Jackson's Indian Removal Act of 1830 began a long series of deadly marches westward along what is known as the "Trail of Tears." Once relocated alongside Plains peoples on twenty million acres declared Indian Territory by the U.S. government, the Five Tribes resolved to retain their independence from further white encroachment by forming small republics in which land was largely communally held. Unfortunately, in the late 1800s white ranchers recognized these lands as valuable for cattle grazing. As the nineteenth century waned, white interest was spurred on by the discovery of petroleum and mineral deposits. Beginning in the 1890s, the U.S. government forced the Dawes Act upon the Five Tribes in protracted negotiations underlined with the threat of violence. The ensuing allotments invited a flood of outsiders, among them all manner of speculators, or "grafters," who "managed" Indian properties. Between 1890 and 1907, almost a half million whites invaded Indian lands.[17]

When Oklahoma became a state in 1907, the federal government lifted all legal restrictions on tribal territories and transferred probate decisions from the Indian Bureau to local courts. These courts declared "all persons of one-half or more Indian ancestry to be incompetent to manage their own affairs" and appointed "guardians" to handle their legal dealings and property.[18] Estates could legally be distributed without a hearing in county court; only a judge's signature was needed.[19] The result was one of the most widespread abuses of human rights against indigenous peoples in the twentieth century. As Deborah Sue Welch states, "The graft and confusion that followed may have been unparalleled in American history."[20] Over the next fifteen years, scores of tribal members lost allotments to opportunists intent on appropriating valuable lands for themselves, in collusion with corrupt local officials, politicians, and businessmen. Determined to expose these crimes, Zitkala-Ša, AIDA attorney Charles H. Fabens, and long-time IRA activist Matthew K. Sniffen arrived in Oklahoma in November 1923.[21] Over five weeks, they interviewed victims and examined countless legal cases across six separate counties, publishing their findings in an IRA-financed pamphlet entitled *Oklahoma's Poor Rich Indians: An Orgy of Graft and Exploitation of the Five Civilized Tribes—Legalized Robbery* (1924). The Oklahoma injustices amply demonstrate why Zitkala-Ša so fervently advocated for U.S. citizenship and the protections it promised.

Oklahoma's Poor Rich Indians presents a harrowing portrait of what had long transpired in the state, revealing the extent to which officialdom foisted injustices on a people with no political rights. Its beginning details the rise of a class of about four thousand "professional guardians" who, by managing just a few estates, reaped fortunes. When oil was found on an Indian's land, an enterprising white would seek him or her out, file a petition to have the person declared incompetent, and request guardianship—usually submitted with a $500 bribe. Profits from leasing oil-rich lands went directly to these guardians, who, with the help of attorneys, tacked on exorbitant fees and administrative costs. In one instance a lawyer took $35,000 for services never rendered. Such arrangements became so lucrative that one of Oklahoma's biggest bootleggers quit the liquor business to take up guardianships. Because they were legal, guardianships held less risk. Yet the iniquity of guardianships paled in comparison to the violent crimes perpetrated against Native children.[22] As Angie Debo painstakingly detailed in *And Still the Waters Run* (1940), the "plundering of children" soon became "a lucrative and highly specialized branch of the grafting industry."[23] Every minor held an allotted estate, making orphans vulnerable prey for professional guardians. At risk of both kidnapping and rape, children were often left to fend for themselves on meager allowances once a guardian had tightened his court-mandated grasp. Some died of malnutrition.

It fell to Zitkala-Ša to relate the individual trials of those affected. Such cases were, as Fabens and Sniffen explained, "phases of our investigation that can be presented best by a feminine mind." Zitkala-Ša commenced with the case of a young lady named Millie Neharkey, the owner of oil-rich lands worth $150,000. On her eighteenth birthday Neharkey was abducted by a group of men associated with the Gladys Belle Oil Company. They first took her to Missouri, plied her with alcohol, and raped her repeatedly over the course of several days. The ringleader, Robert F. Blair, forced Neharkey to appoint him as her attorney. He hastily arranged the "sale" of her property to Gladys Belle for a mere $2,000. Zitkala-Ša spent time with Neharkey following her ordeal. The girl's descriptions of the rape left her "dumb." The courts eventually prosecuted Blair for malpractice and conspiracy. Neharkey survived and had some chance for retribution. Zitkala-Ša's next case history had none.

In Tulsa County a seven-year-old Choctaw girl, Ledcie Stechi, inherited twenty acres from her mother after the latter's untimely death. The girl resided with her grandmother in a ramshackle shelter in poverty that bordered on starvation. When oil was discovered on Stechi's land in 1921, Jordan Whiteman, owner of the First National Bank in Idabel, compelled the girl's uncle to relinquish legal guardianship to him. Whiteman allowed Stechi and her grandmother a credit of $15 a month at a local store while he enjoyed the profits of oil production. In 1922 he tried to sell part of her land, valued at $90,000, for $2,000, in the hope of accomplishing an illegal graft. Miraculously, the courts blocked his move and even increased Stechi's allowance to $200 a month. Whiteman did not honor the ruling. Near death, Stechi and her grandmother were taken in by an Idabel charitable organization. Zitkala-Ša painted the miserable scene: "The rich little Choctaw girl, with her feeble grandmother, came to town carrying their clothes, a bundle of faded rags, in a flour sack. Ledcie was dirty, filthy, and covered with vermin. She was emaciated and weighed about 47 pounds." After five weeks of treatment in the hospital, where for the first time in her life she received adequate sustenance, Stechi gained eleven pounds and recovered enough to attend the local Indian school. A mere twenty-four hours after she was enrolled, Whiteman appeared to take Stechi away. Her grandmother was forced to return to her shack in the hills. Stechi died a month later, likely poisoned by arsenic. A swarm of would-be guardians descended on the grandmother's home, vying to manage her newly inherited estate. The county court soon appointed a new guardian, disregarding the grandmother's protests. Zitkala-Ša warned, "She, too, will go the way of her grandchild, as sheep for slaughter by ravenous wolves in men's forms, unless the good people of America intervene immediately by remedial Congressional action."

During her time in Oklahoma, Zitkala-Ša attended county court to witness the ongoing legal travesties firsthand. On November 19 she sat in a courtroom to hear the case of an Osage woman, Martha Axe Roberts, who was attempting to rid herself of her present guardian, L. T. Hill. Roberts did not appear, but was represented by former Oklahoma congressman, T. A. Chandler. Even he could not protect her interests. Though Roberts had inherited an income of $15,000 per year, Hill denied its existence and instead made her periodic "loans" of just one or two dollars. When Roberts attempted to escape the situation with a move to her parents' home, Hill confiscated her car and every piece of furniture in her residence. Meanwhile, he placed a notice in the local newspaper warning creditors to reject any of her requests for funds. Soon thereafter Roberts's baby, a little more than year old, fell ill. Hill refused to pay for medical care and food, and the infant died. All this evidence of misconduct was stricken from the court record, replaced by "evidence" that Roberts was "crazy" and had "no sense of the value of money." The hearing concluded within a half hour with her case dismissed. The spectacle moved and disgusted Zitkala-Ša, compelling her to learn more. She visited Roberts in her parents' home and found her "perfectly sane." Roberts had merely been the victim of a system of legalized robbery that ensured "the Indian is legally bound and gagged."[24]

Oklahoma's Poor Rich Indians aimed to stimulate a congressional investigation that would dismantle the county court guardianship scheme and reinstate the lesser evil, Indian Bureau wardship. The effort was only marginally successful. Oklahoman members of Congress formally called for a congressional investigation and pledged to oust any judge who proved corrupt.[25] *Oklahoma's Poor Rich Indians* was introduced and read aloud before the subcommittee on Indian Affairs. Congress subsequently agreed to hold more hearings. *Outlook* magazine, which had featured Zitkala-Ša back in 1900, published an editorial that urged action.[26] The pamphlet's publication also impelled representatives of the Five Tribes, the Osage, and the Pawnee, to meet in Tulsa to form the Oklahoma Society of Indians, in an effort to protect their interests against guardianships. Internal disagreements and lack of any real political power doomed their efforts. After endorsing the call for an investigation, they disbanded.[27]

The promised congressional investigation to confirm the allegations in *Oklahoma's Poor Rich Indians* commenced almost a year later, in November 1924. But the findings greatly disappointed—and even derided—Zitkala-Ša, the AIDA, and the IRA. The investigation, held in Muskogee and led by chairman Homer P. Snyder, outright condemned *Oklahoma's Poor Rich Indians.* Snyder's opening statement dismissed the pamphlet entirely and Zitkala-Ša's contributions in particular: "We do not want hearsay evidence; we do not want long stories or legends about Indian lore or anything of that sort. We want specific cases and specific testimony." In reality, Snyder and Oklahoma Congressman Charles D. Carter, who initiated the hearings to silence criticism of his state, wanted a whitewash.[28] Before testimony even began, the congressional subcommittee went out of its way to express confidence in the Oklahoma court system. This tone prevailed. Debo writes, "During the whole proceedings the efforts of the committee to avoid discovering anything were unique even in Indian investigations."[29] A well-rehearsed cadre of oil company attorneys and local officials attacked Sniffen, contradicting his every statement and accusing him of manipulating the truth. Those who had cooperated with the original investigation, such as the superintendent of the Five Civilized Tribes, Shade Wallen, were publicly censured. The county courts under scrutiny for engineering the grafting schemes, meanwhile, were declared blameless. Snyder and his colleagues concluded that Zitkala-Ša, Fabens, and Sniffen had deliberately and dramatically exaggerated their claims and that Sniffen had essentially concocted evidence to validate his position within the IRA. Though the subcommittee admitted the existence of "unconscionable attorneys and persons who make it a profession to obtain appointments as guardians," they recommended no congressional action on the matter. Zitkala-Ša was invited to the Muskogee hearings. Acting on the advice of a GFWC attorney, she did not appear to avoid threats of libel.[30]

In the wake of Congress's refusal to act, many Oklahoma journalists and legislators responded. Newspapers denounced the subcommittee proceedings as a charade, while the state bar association condemned guardianships and even offered to aid in calling for another investigation.[31] Important legislation was proposed soon after. The Frye Bill, sponsored by Republican state senator E. M. Frye, sought to limit guardian compensation to $50 a month. Had it passed with that provision intact, many abuses might have been prevented. Instead, the bill passed in significantly modified form. Though it strictly limited compensation to $4,000 a year and capped attorneys' and auditing fees, local judges ignored or reinterpreted the new law. Consequently, guardians could still exceed compensation limits by claiming they had rendered "extraordinary services."[32] Ample room, therefore, remained for the same type of maneuvering that had cheated so many out of their properties and monies. Twenty-four guardians did face federal corruption charges in the wake of the hearings, but each settled out of court and circumvented legal repercussions. For the Osage some protection eventually came. In 1925, Congress passed a law that ensured only legitimate blood heirs could inherit Osage headrights.[33]

Despite the overall failure in Oklahoma, scholars have noted that Zitkala-Ša's efforts ultimately yielded beneficial results.[34] The Oklahoma findings in conjunction with the research presented by the Committee of One Hundred have been credited with inspiring an in-depth investigation into conditions on reservations, subsidized by John D. Rockefeller.[35] Its outcome was the 1928 Meriam Report (named after its director, the anthropologist Lewis Meriam), which prompted President Hoover to appoint two members of the IRA as commissioner and assistant commissioner of the BIA. More importantly, the Meriam Report led to substantial reform of federal Indian policy in the 1930s.[36]

Though her and her colleagues' efforts in Oklahoma produced little immediate change, Zitkala-Ša had cause for celebration in the summer of 1924, when Indians gained U.S. citizenship. In January 1924 a bill authored by Representative Snyder proposed granting citizenship certificates to Indians who requested them. In the Senate the progressive Wisconsinite Robert La Follette and Montanan Burton K. Wheeler amended the bill to extend citizenship without any such requirements. In May the Indian Citizenship Act (ICA) passed both houses and was signed into law soon after.[37] It read, "All non citizen Indians born within the territorial limits of the United States . . . are hereby, declared to be citizens of the United States: Provided That the granting of such citizenship shall not in any manner impair or otherwise affect the right of any Indian to tribal or other property."[38] Richard Henry Pratt died just weeks before the bill became law, missing what would have been the climax of his life's work.[39]

In a list of the major events and accomplishments of her life, written around 1929, Zitkala-Ša wrote, "Helped get Act through Congress granting citizenship to all Indians."[40] She had indeed played a supporting role. Historians generally conclude that war service provided the catalyst needed for progressive politicians to extend citizenship to 125,000 officially noncitizen Natives. Zitkala-Ša and other pro-citizenship reformers had a smaller but significant part in helping to formulate arguments and generate political interest in the issue.[41] The ICA, however, had serious drawbacks. States could still deny suffrage to Indians deemed unable to meet official requirements, which Arizona, Utah, and New Mexico did. This remained the case until after World War II.[42] Also, the act did not lift government restrictions on Indian lands or BIA control over reservations.[43] In light of these deficiencies, Zitkala-Ša would spend her remaining years trying to ensure that citizenship offered the protections it promised to "the first Americans." She would found her own Indian rights organization, the National Council of American Indians, to lead this fight and put her proto–Red Power platform into action.

CHAPTER 12

Princess Zitkala-Ša
and the National Council
of American Indians

Snyder's efforts to defame Zitkala-Ša at the Muskogee hearings did very little damage to her reputation. Instead, her Oklahoma investigation was reported in the *New York Times*, raising her profile even higher.[1] Throughout 1925 Zitkala-Ša gave many well-publicized lectures before women's groups, billed as "Princess Zitkala-Ša"—"directly descended from one of the greatest Indian chiefs of the past, Sitting Bull."[2] Her celebrity often interfered with her message. A newspaper article on a 1925 book fair recorded, "The princess, in Indian garb, was besieged by persons in the store. One woman wanted to know how she pronounced Hiawatha. There was a look of sadness in her eyes, for she is most interested in helping the Indians on the reservation. She exclaimed: 'They all want to know about me, but I would rather they would ask about the Indians.'"[3] Truthfully, the princess in her regalia may at times have been the cause of her audience's distraction. Yet in exhibiting elements of Native clothing at public appearances, Zitkala-Ša was acting within the tradition of female Indian activists, including Sarah Winnemucca (Paiute) and E. Pauline Johnson (Mohawk).[4] This approach remained effective with the women's groups Zitkala-Ša courted. Fortunately, her public speaking sometimes attracted much more serious attention to the causes she espoused.[5]

One article in particular, housed in the Gertrude and Raymond Bonnin Collection at Brigham Young University, shows that legitimate reportage did result from Zitkala-Ša's appearances. Her participation in a 1925 Illinois GWFC meeting, coming just two months after Snyder's denunciations

Zitkala-Ša in a publicity photograph. The image appeared in *American Indian Life* (July 1930), 21. (Manuscripts, Archives, and Special Collections Negative Files, 1970–2002, PC149. Box 4, Env. 83–155, Washington State University Libraries)

in Oklahoma, garnered lengthy coverage. The article opened with a mention of Zitkala-Ša's "special research work" in Oklahoma and accurately characterized her positions. She was quoted as saying that Natives were "a branch and part of the great human family" with "minds, hearts and souls, and beautiful thoughts." The newspaper also faithfully recorded her harsh words about the U.S. government: "In this great government at Washington, the Indians have suffered under the governmental machinery of the Indian Bureau, which has held them as wards. We send missionaries into foreign countries, even into Indian reservations, but one white sister suggested it would be more appropriate if some of our missionaries could be sent among the politicians at Washington. . . . Let us assist the Indian to regain the place he held, to recover his own self respect, which was his before he lost his rights and became a ward of the government." The ladies present "heartily applauded" Zitkala-Ša's speech, which also highlighted the fact that the Indian Citizenship Act was merely a step toward confronting many more challenges, abolition of the BIA first among them.[6]

In 1924 Zitkala-Ša joined the advisory board of the American Indian Defense Association, headed by John Collier.[7] Collier had begun his career in activism in New York, where he founded the National Community Center Association in 1917. The experience brought him into contact with many prominent intellectuals and reformers, including Mabel Dodge, a wealthy patron of the arts. When the community center movement collapsed in the wake of World War I, Collier moved to California. He briefly worked as a community organizer for the state legislature and as a teacher at San Francisco State College. On accepting an invitation from Dodge to visit her literary retreat in Taos, New Mexico, Collier encountered the Pueblos.[8] He quickly concluded that their "communal and ceremonial life [held] an answer to the problems of human society."[9] Unlike the IRA, which often showed little if any respect for Native traditions, Collier's AIDA rejected full assimilation and respected Indian religious freedoms.[10] Collier himself even supported Peyotism.[11]

Her role in the AIDA and strong friendship with Collier offered Zitkala-Ša another vital platform for agitation, but the Bonnins took actions independently, as well. In 1925 the Yankton Tribal Council employed Bonnin to deal with outstanding legal issues, in particular to protect the Yankton land base by challenging fraudulent allotments claimed by outsiders.[12] The Bonnins also sought to retain Yankton rights to the pipestone quarries, guaranteed by the treaty of 1858. When the Department of the Interior opened the quarries for outside exploitation in 1925, the Bonnins and lawyer Jennings C. Wise, representing the Yankton Sioux, sought a restraining order and sued to ensure continued access.[13] But Zitkala-Ša had greater ambitions: an intertribal union based on self-help and grassroots organizing—a new SAI, with herself at the helm.

On February 27, 1926, at age fifty, Zitkala-Ša founded the National Council of American Indians (NCAI).[14] All her life, whether in her writings, her community center work, or her involvement with the GFWC, she had emphasized her belief that women should lead the fight to redress the crimes of white men. In becoming NCAI president, Zitkala-Ša acted on this ideal. Bonnin, meanwhile, served as secretary, treasurer, and legal counsel. He had finished his law studies that year, though he never sought admission to the bar.[15] The Bonnins rented office space in the Bliss Building, the same edifice that housed the BIA and AIDA.[16] They meanwhile lived outside the city in what is now Lyon Park in Arlington County, Virginia. This was a good time for them financially. Bonnin's salary as a law clerk supported the NCAI office.[17]

The NCAI's dictum, "Help Indians Help Themselves in Protecting Their Rights and Properties," underscored its purpose in ensuring that the Indian Citizenship Act was meaningfully implemented.[18] Its original emblem was a camp of tepees resting peacefully on the rolling Dakota plains, meant to symbolize "universal brotherhood" among Indians.[19] The NCAI's funds derived from Zitkala-Ša's book royalties and public speaking fees, Bonnin's legal work, and occasional white donors.[20]

Zitkala-Ša's first order of business as NCAI president was petitioning Congress to enforce recently codified rights. The petition characterized the NCAI as "a constructive effort to better the Red Race and make its members better citizens of the United States." These aims could not be achieved until "the Indians are accorded the rights essential to racial self-respect and a spirit of loyalty to the United States." Zitkala-Ša explicitly linked her organization to the struggles of her ancestors. "A time there was," she wrote, "when the protest of our race against injustice was voiced in the war cries that rose from the primeval forest. No less audibly shall this protest resound through the hills and vales of our Fatherland, echoing the far-carrying appeals of justice and reason, never to be silenced until the pledge of the Nation, made to us by the Great Grandfather, and sealed by our blood on the fields of France, is redeemed."[21] This formal statement of opposition to decades of federal policy contained the hallmarks of a Red Power ideology rooted in organization, racial pride, assertion of rights, and determination to gain freedom and recognition. As if to emphasize this ideology, Zitkala-Ša appeared at the unveiling of a Sitting Bull statue in Washington on March 9, less than two weeks after the NCAI's founding.

"Members of the National Council of American Indians Take Part in Ceremony at Unveiling of Statue of the Great Sitting Bull," March 9, 1926, Washington, D.C. Zitkala-Ša is to the right of the statue. Raymond T. Bonnin is in the second row, far left. (Courtesy of L. Tom Perry Special Collections, Harold B. Library, Brigham Young University, Provo, Utah)

Senator Thomas F. Bayard, a Democrat from Delaware, sponsored the NCAI petition, which was written into the Congressional Record. Other politicians took note when, in November 1926, the NCAI helped unseat incumbent senators in South Dakota and Oklahoma who had been hostile to Indian interests. One of these was J. W. Harreld, of Oklahoma, who had been chairman of the Senate Committee on Indian Affairs during the most violent phase of his state's grafting of Indian property. He had done nothing to intervene.[22]

The same year Zitkala-Ša distributed *Representative William Williamson and the Indians,* a lengthy pamphlet criticizing that congressman's record on Indian issues. Specifically, Williamson had supported a bill allowing the imprisonment of Indians without due process, a bill seeking to divest reservations of oil lease monies, and a corrupt bridge project on Navajo land that Zitkala-Ša deemed "highway robbery." The pamphlet's closing lines declared, "The Time for Scaring Indians has Passed" and condemned "the Indian Bureau method of denouncing, frightening, and intimidating the Indian who attempts to stand for the rights of his people."[23] Unlike her lobbying efforts against the two incumbent senators, however, this attack was ineffective in preventing Williamson's reelection.

After the congressional elections of 1926, Interior Secretary Herbert Work commissioned the non-governmental Institute of Government Research to do a survey of reservation conditions.[24] That year, the Bonnins launched their own investigation. They traveled more than eleven thousand miles around Oklahoma and South Dakota, evidently mostly at their own expense, collecting information on the problems facing Indian reservations, information which was later presented to Congress.[25] When they were in Washington, they aided Indians in their relations with government departments and before congressional committees. In 1927, they again traveled eleven thousand miles, through California, Arizona, South Dakota, Minnesota, and Utah. These were hardly pleasure tours. The California-Arizona trip lasted sixteen days and was made with Senator Lynn J. Frazier, a clergyman named O. H. Bronson, the Colliers, and several academics. At one point the party traveled almost 1,500 miles in four days, despite being stuck in a sandstorm and passing one night lost in the desert. Luckily, they had only one flat tire and successfully "ran the last 100 Miles on four cylinders."

The conditions the Bonnins observed were distressing. In her report of this trip, Zitkala-Ša recorded that although Navajo schools and irrigation projects were going well, the hospitals were poor and alcoholism afflicted the Yuma Indians they visited: "Liquor is playing havoc at Yuma (poison alcohol): we witnessed a funeral of a boy just dead from wood alcohol. Drinkers are arrested and put to forced labor. Excellent plan to keep a supply of slavies." Yuma children also suffered from malnutrition due to the poor diet served in their boarding school. Parents were compelled to "sneak food in to their children." Making matters worse, "The Yuma prisoners eat with the children and use children's lavatory facilities." Zitkala-Ša also noted that tuberculosis was rampant and the tribe was being dispossessed of its lands. This last fact, she noted with sarcasm, was supposedly "all to the good, for it will 'assimilate' the Yumas."[26] In 1928, the Senate Committee on Indian Affairs appointed Raymond Bonnin to an investigatory role, charging him to visit reservations across the country in preparation for visiting delegations of senators.[27] This recognition was a boost to the NCAI's profile.

In 1912, Zitkala-Ša had written to Father Ketcham, "It is hard to stand helplessly by while we behold the graft carried on in the political game in

Washington, D.C. . . . The incentive to the political world is graft and not justice. Were I a man, I'd gather together all the Indian votes in our United States—then perhaps—my appeal for justice would have some consideration."[28] In 1927, the NCAI sought to do just this by creating an "Information Service Program" aimed at Indian voters.[29] This action represented a new strategy within the Indian reform movement based directly in the exercise of citizenship and voting rights. Zitkala-Ša hoped that by developing a voting bloc and becoming active in white governing bodies, Indians could influence policy on the local, state, and national levels. This plan never came to fruition, but the NCAI still became an effective force. In 1929, for instance, the Bonnins were able to clean up Indian Bureau corruption on the Cherokee Reservation in North Carolina.[30] In 1930, they helped to initiate Senate subcommittee hearings that exposed the use of corporal punishment in Indian schools in Arizona.[31]

The Bonnins also revived an idea Zitkala-Ša had suggested to Parker during their days in the SAI. In 1929 the NCAI began distributing the *Indian Newsletter*, directed at reservation populations.[32] Typewritten by Zitkala-Ša, the newsletter reflected the great diversity of interests the NCAI represented. One issue from 1930, for example, addressed the outstanding claims of the Ute, Sioux, Pueblo, Klamath, and Menominee tribes. The newsletters pointed out specific injustices, answered letters, summarized bills before Congress, informed readers of their rights, and encouraged organizing and solidarity. Zitkala-Ša also reminded readers of the vital importance of maintaining the indigenous land base. "Help one another to keep your lands," she exhorted, "Don't sell any of it if you can possibly keep from it."[33] Demand for the newsletter became greater than the NCAI could meet with its limited resources.[34] When not writing, lobbying, or testifying in Washington, the Bonnins made annual five-month trips across the country to address various issues in person, funded in part by the AIDA.[35] By 1932 the Bonnins had, by their own count, established fifty-seven NCAI "tribal lodges" across America.[36] Raymond Bonnin had also become heavily involved in gaining compensation for lost Ute lands in Colorado, working closely with lawyer and Indian rights activist Earnest L. Wilkinson.[37]

Central to all of the Bonnins' activities was support for the meaningful exercise of citizenship rights and opposition to the corrupt BIA system. Promoting these goals, Zitkala-Ša constantly returned to the shaming tactic of rhetorically contrasting American ideals with American Indian realities in order to gain sympathy and spur reform. In "What It Means to Be an Indian Today," written for the *Friends' Intelligencer* in 1929, she stressed the continuing gulf between indigenous peoples' official status and the injustices they endured—and the hypocrisy this evidenced. "I just received a letter from a Navajo Indian, a disabled war veteran who lies in hospital today," Zitkala-Ša began, "His Navajo people in Arizona were denied the ballot in this presidential year. There was no such discrimination made in citizenship when Indians were drafted for war service." But this veteran, like many Natives in the United States, was bound by a bureaucracy that denied any participation by its unwilling wards and stole from them at will. Zitkala-Ša noted that the Navajos had been robbed of $100,000 to build a tourist bridge across their lands. The monies, she contended, would have been better used for creating institutions of higher education. Yet even this small step forward would have constituted a luxury for a greater population that was so impoverished that, in the case of the South Dakota Sioux, they had been "reduced to eating horse flesh." Therefore: "To be and Indian today means . . . to be hungry, sick, and dying while still used for a national political football."[38]

Before white reformers, Zitkala-Ša used the same approach, combining strongly accusatory rhetoric with more conciliatory statements. In her speech at the 1928 conference of the Indian Rights Association, she drew on recent history to tout Indians' proven credentials, weaving a patriotic narrative that highlighted the hollowness of American ideals. After remarking, "The Indian's American citizenship has been dearly bought" through war service, Zitkala-Ša conjured an image of sacrifice permeated with bitter irony. "Positively," she announced, "no one on earth can honestly challenge the American Indian's loyalty to the Government of the United States, though this Government has waged more wars upon its Indian wards than any other nation against its own subordinate peoples." What was the reward? Government schools serving children "rotten meat, full of maggots, and spoiled flour which mice and cats had defiled," while elders sometimes died of starvation. In an ironic twist, "subordinate employees as well as the Indians are called 'disloyal' to the Government by their Superintendents when one of them dares to report existing evils." This dishonest practice, she argued, was the definition of injustice, as "any American citizen who can help to bring efficiency into the Federal machinery is 'loyal to the Government.'" There were two ways to look at the issue: either BIA employees were outright "incompetent" and warranted dismissal, or they were "criminals" whose deliberate "unChristian exploitation" caused "the ultimate destruction of helpless human beings—young and old." No matter which, a "housecleaning" was "imperative" on both patriotic and purely humanitarian grounds.[39]

The following year the Bonnins attended the thirty-fifth annual Friends of the Indian conference at Lake Mohonk, October 16–18, 1929. Zitkala-Ša, spontaneously asked to speak on "The Indian Side of the Question," delivered a long speech that explained the NCAI's aims and the need to help indigenous peoples help themselves. She concluded with a striking anecdote: "Someone has asked me when I was addressing an audience after this fashion: 'And are you a civilized Indian?' [The question garnered laughter from the crowd.] I told them I did not know, because civilization is a word that is very hard to define and to understand. I don't know what you mean by civilization. We send our little Indian boys and girls to school and when they come back talking English they come back swearing. There is no swear word in the Indian languages and I still haven't yet learned to swear." The audience applauded heartily.[40]

At times, however, Zitkala-Ša came very close to swearing when discussing the BIA. Soon after the onset of the Great Depression, the commissioner of Indian affairs granted superintendents emergency powers. In response, the NCAI put out a strongly worded press release, "Brutal Superintendents Are Triumphant," which accused superintendents of administering fatal beatings and being responsible for cases of starvation.[41] The same year Zitkala-Ša appeared before a Senate subcommittee investigating BIA corruption on the Flathead Reservation in Montana, prompted by claims in the *Washington Daily News* that officials were colluding with business interests to illegally develop the land's power resources. Zitkala-Ša charged that corrupt BIA officials intended to misappropriate perhaps more than $5,500 of Flathead monies.[42]

In 1933, the long struggle to abolish BIA control on reservations finally took a small step forward with the appointment of Collier as commissioner of Indian affairs. The Wheeler-Howard Act, also known as the Indian Reorganization Act (IRA), passed a year later, putting in place measures to encourage self-determination through tribal governments that had negotiating power. This "Indian New Deal," inspired by the recommendations of the Meriam Report, also put a halt to Dawes Act allotment schemes by supporting the merging of lands that could be managed cooperatively through tribal councils. Though the goals of the plan were not fully achieved due to legal restrictions and reluctance on the part of some allottees, more than two million acres were ceded to reservations. Indians also took advantage of the availability of new low-interest government loans.[43] Importantly, the act finally lifted the ban on traditional religious practices, including the Sun Dance ritual Zitkala-Ša had adapted into an opera.[44] These new measures constituted a sharp reversal from the era of assimilation, allotment, and off-reservation boarding schools. Indians would be appointed to the BIA. Native children would be schooled by day, on their reservations.[45] Collier and Zitkala-Ša had been allies for some time, working toward these ends. The two had had a major falling out in 1932 when the NCAI did not support Collier's petition against the previous commissioner of Indian affairs, C. J. Rhoads, but by the time Collier assumed the post in 1933 Zitkala-Ša was easily the best-known female Indian leader in the United States.[46] Consequently, Collier invited her to discuss policy plans for the Bureau of Indian Affairs.

For Zitkala-Ša the Indian Reorganization Act did not go far enough. In truth, Collier's endorsement of tribal autonomy was in many ways restricted. Under the Indian New Deal, Washington could still intervene to legally override local reservation policy, while new tribal constitutions were drawn up by white lawyers "based on Euro-American models and with no understanding of traditional native patterns of government and leadership." Most ruinously, the Indian Bureau system remained in place.[47] Zitkala-Ša deemed any scheme under BIA auspices unacceptable. Tension between her and Collier grew. After being passed over for inclusion in Collier's "brains trust," Zitkala-Ša turned from supporter to public critic.[48] When Collier attempted to reorganize Yankton in 1935 by enforcing new IRA provisions, the NCAI intervened to block him.

Though the Yankton Sioux were largely in favor of self-government (83 percent voted in favor of adopting the Indian Reorganization Act), the matter of a new constitution was a sticking point. The Bonnins and a man named Clement Smith, allied with full-blooded landowners who felt threatened by collusion between the BIA and those who had not yet been granted allotments, organized to persuade voters against a moderate, government-approved constitution similar to that of the nearby Pine Ridge and Rosebud Reservations. After their victory, the Bonnins submitted their own constitution to the Yankton Indian Office, along with a petition of support containing three hundred signatures (30 percent of the eligible electorate). The document sought to create an independent tribal council with legislative and veto power over even the secretary of the interior, while the council president would have the power to appoint employees on the reservation's government projects. After nine months of ostensible review, the Yankton Agency rejected it summarily. Graham D. Taylor points out that the constitution failed in some respects to account for further land distribution, while the lack of checks on the power of the council president could have created a system of political patronage. But the BIA likely rejected it over other issues.[49] The Smith-Bonnin constitution placed greater power in the hands of the elected council than in the bureau. Federal government opposition was also inevitable due to the constitution's underlying concept of real sovereignty, which included extending voting rights to tribal members living off-reservation. This broad version of democracy was intolerable. Debate over the new constitution continued for three years until Collier surrendered his effort to enact the government-approved constitution.[50] As a result of the impasse, Yankton held the status of a subagency under Rosebud until 1963.[51]

The 1935 clash at Yankton between Zitkala-Ša and the BIA was her last fight. Approaching age sixty, after many years of constant, stressful protest that failed to yield the results she desired, her health and finances began a rapid decline. Collier refused to pay the Bonnins for their liaison activities between Indian tribes and Congress, and with the country still in the midst of economic calamity, the NCAI membership fee, set at only $1.00 for individuals and $1.50 for tribal lodges, could not adequately sustain them or their activism. The NCAI office in Washington closed in 1934. All documents were moved to the Bonnins' home in Virginia. After 1935, the only significant income keeping the Bonnins afloat seems to have been furnished by their adopted son from Uintah, Oran Curry. As chairman of the Uintah-Ouray Ute Tribal Business Committee, Curry arranged for Bonnin to become the legal agent for the Uintah-Ouray Reservation.[52] By that time, Ohiya was faring much worse than his adopted brother. In his early thirties, married with four children, unemployed, and suffering from diabetes, he badly needed support.[53] Gertrude Bonnin's last years were not happy ones.

CHAPTER 13

THE FINAL DIARIES

In 1935 Zitkala-Ša wrote to her friend Elaine Eastman, who had complimented her on her life's work:

> I appreciate your genuine desire to give me credit for having tried to render
> service to the Red Race. But though it took a lifetime, the achievements are
> scarcely visible!!!
>   It is even a most strenuous effort to stand still and hold fast the small
> grounds that have been gained. I do not regret the try I made for I have
> learned many valuable inner lessons in the struggle . . . I have seen too
> many so-called Indian welfare people who are mere chameleons, ever re-
> flecting the "powers-that-be" right or wrong, and the Indian must be forced
> to conform to the whims of bureaucracy, ad infinitum! . . . It does not after
> all matter what person, or what political party is in office, the powers con-
> ferred upon them by Congress flow on unchanged. And the Indian is a
> veritable prisoner of war; there is no end of junketing trips at government
> expense "Investigating the Indian Bureau!" "Investigating Indian Reserva-
> tions!" Reports are piling up like Egyptian pyramids! . . . It is only a way of
> killing time.[1]

This letter reveals that, in private as in public, Zitkala-Ša remained adamant
that indigenous peoples were still "prisoners of war." Approaching old age,
she also felt the work she had done was largely in vain. Zitkala-Ša's final
diaries, kept between July 1935 and November 1937, tell the story of her last
years. Four themes dominate their contents: NCAI work, illness, family discord, and worry over financial privation.

The diaries begin on July 29, as Zitkala-Ša and Bonnin are driving across America. Passing through Ohio and Illinois, they reach the Menominee Reservation in Wisconsin on August 3, where they stop to "discuss matters," make the rounds to various meetings, and debate the "Indian question" late into the night with friends. Early on Zitkala-Ša writes, "Let nothing appear to you to be too difficult of accomplishment. Difficulties are the things that show what men are." She repeats this statement, followed by the injunction "Be cheerful" after a trying meeting with tribal members. This quaint maxim grows ever harder to follow. Even a visit to Chicago to see Ohiya and his family elicits a negative entry: "Chaos, worse than chaos reigned at the house." Chaos reigns as well on the Yankton Reservation when the Bonnins arrive there a few weeks later. They are drawn into a dispute with the Indian Bureau over the new constitution proposed under the Indian Reorganization Act, which has been "grossly misconstrued" by a BIA employee before a tribal assembly. Following a series of meetings and organizing efforts, the Bonnins leave for Utah and then Nevada's Pyramid Lake Paiute Indian Reservation. Once there, Zitkala-Ša takes copious notes on residents' reports of their situation.

The Nevada entries suggest an emotional desperation that resulted from documenting never-ending injustices. On September 6 and 7 Zitkala-Ša dictated requests for help from two elders. One, named Owyhee, had endured forced removal. He recounts, "In 1872 I was the Paiute Interpreter, when my people were moved away from Malhuer reservation. The survivors of this time are very few and the heirs are widely scattered. We desire your very able legal aid to present our claims against the government. . . . Distances are great—and money is scarce, so that it takes too much time to assemble all our heirs—therefore on their behalf some of us are acting for ourselves and including all proper claimants, in this letter to you, asking you if you will accept employment to handle our claims?"

The other, Councilman Jack Warwiall, tried to explain the tribe's current hardships. In contrast to Owyhee's tone of resignation, Warwiall expresses palpable frustration: "This res[ervation] was set aside for us. We live in peace—but in one way or another, it is being taken from us, land and water! Fish and fowls are gone: We will have no food—Hunting rights the state is trying to force us [to] conform with the state laws—We have laid down our guns. We have no income—our food is taken from us—cattle range is short—changing our old lives—the state calls it trespass."

These excerpts demonstrate the almost impossible mission of the NCAI. They are intermingled with scribbled accounts of the reservation's history and details of the government surveys that have dispossessed the indigenous

inhabitants: "Whites took best lands, Indians had no voice, unable to get
them out. Whites fail to pay leases. . . . Agents don't protect Indians against
white interlopers." This is all a recurring story that little can be done to
rectify. Yet the NCAI's presence is appreciated. Zitkala-Ša records one
tribesman's response to their visit: "You two are Indians. We are glad you
came to listen to us and to help us. Officials heretofore show no interest."
The details of subsequent meetings go on for pages.[2]

Zitkala-Ša's second diary begins on April 1, 1936. Then living in Virginia,
she and Bonnin have taken in their two eldest grandsons, Joseph and Raymie, due to Ohiya's struggle with diabetes, his difficulties finding work, and
his wife Elsa's own health problems. Zitkala-Ša starts the new diary in a
pensive mood, reflecting over the past ten years. Given her constant advocacy her conclusions are surprising: "Ten years have passed," she writes,
"and I have done nothing at all in all these years! Just a fretful milling
around in dense ignorance—that's all." Yet she is apparently not completely defeated: "There is no justification in permitting myself to become a
source of care or worry to anyone—The question is—'Then what?' For a
while I'll keep a daily record—to check on what I do—each day. Here goes!"
Zitkala-Ša falls ill soon after. She nevertheless presses on with her daily duties. Irritated by the rowdy behavior of Ohiya's "heedless boys," she writes:
"Prayed to know what the meaning of life is—Universal, impersonal?
Why?" In places, references to the Great Spirit are mixed with Christian-
influenced expressions.

Still occupied with NCAI business, Zitkala-Ša writes extensively on numerous bills, wrangling over the Yankton Constitution, dealings with the
subcommittee on Indian Affairs, and trips to see Collier, who never seems
to have time for her. The quarrelling boys and problems on Capitol Hill
bring on what sounds like chronic depression: "I am extremely nervous—
restless within—smothering sense—of things, about puts me out. There is
no use in trying to explain—even this much—as no one understands—or
cares." Her anxiety is compounded by financial worries. She regularly
wires Ohiya money to keep him afloat and searches for Bonnin's military
records, hoping to apply for a veteran's bonus, which thankfully they receive. Still, the couple must struggle to "dig up cash to pay milk bill." By
November 1936 they have been forced to take out a loan and, evidently, sell
one of their wedding rings. Ohiya, meanwhile, tries for a five-dollar-a-week
Works Progress Administration job that does not pan out. In September
things are so bad for him in Chicago that Zitkala-Ša suggests he and his
family come to Virginia.

Aggravations mount to the point where Zitkala-Ša breaks Sioux chil-
drearing traditions: "I struck Raymie on the back with a switch because he
was impudent when I corrected him. I am tired of playing policeman, disci-
plinarian to 'train' hard headed boys!" The boys had been doing badly in
school, particularly Raymie. In another incident, Zitkala-Ša slaps him for
his poor behavior. Later, Raymie surprises everyone when he gives his
grandparents a dollar for Christmas. Aware of his family's difficult financial situation, he had started secretly working in his school's cafeteria to
earn the money. Still, the misfortunes mount. Zitkala-Ša's health-related
"attack[s]" and "night sweat[s]," which occur with regularity, compound
her troubles—"Oh God may this absolutely be the last one!" Her son fares
no better: "Ohiya sick in bed [and] under doctor's care. Too sick to move to
hospital." There is "great joy," however, when Ohiya recovers enough to finally move into the Bonnins' home in February 1937. The same month Bonnin appeals to Collier for a reservation superintendency. He suggests
Yankton. Collier responds there is "no fund."[3]

In her last diary, recorded in a notebook issued by the Indian Service,
Zitkala-Ša writes mainly of Native issues. At its beginning she is once again
ill. Ohiya and family are still in Virginia, and he still has had no luck finding work. Zitkala-Ša records that with Bonnin's continuing legal help, the
Ute claim on coal proceeds from their land in Colorado has passed both
the House and Senate. But no sooner does she write this than President
Roosevelt vetoes the bill as "unjustified." Once again, the Bonnins have to
start over. This is where the diary ends.[4]

In 1950 the Utes were finally awarded $32 million in their ongoing law-
suit against the U.S. government.[5] That was much too late to bring any
emotional or financial benefit to the Bonnins. On January 25, 1938, Zitkala-
Ša's health failed irrevocably. After falling into a coma, she was admitted to
Georgetown Hospital, where she died the next day of cardiac dilation and
kidney disease, less than a month before her sixty-second birthday.[6] The
doctor who performed the autopsy listed her as "Gertrude Bonnin from
South Dakota—Housewife."[7] An obituary published in the *New York Times*
on January 28 was more laudatory. It summarized Zitkala-Ša's accomplishments as president of the NCAI and—once again—perpetuated the claim
that she was "a granddaughter of Sitting Bull." One of the last lines reads:
"Born on an Indian reservation, she became one of the champions of her
race, and frequently spoke on Indian history and *alleged* injustices Indians
have suffered."[8] Washington's *Evening Star* also ran a long obituary subti-
tled "Direct Descendent of Sitting Bull Won Fame for Aid Given Her

People." It praised Zitkala-Ša as one of the Indians' "staunchest friends" and "most diligent workers in their behalf."[9] The *Washington Post* also referred to Zitkala-Ša as a "direct descendant of Sitting Bull" in its obituary.[10] In many ways she was.

At a funeral service arranged by Wilkinson and longtime Mormon friends from Utah at Washington's church of Latter-day Saints, Collier eulogized Zitkala-Ša. "The Sioux and all Indians," he stated, "have lost a real leader."[11] Because of her husband's military service, Zitkala-Ša was buried in Arlington National Cemetery, alongside countless white soldiers who had fought in the name of Manifest Destiny. Inscribed on her tombstone is "Gertrude Simmons Bonnin—'Zitkala-Ša' of the Sioux Indians—1876–1938."[12] Ohiya Bonnin died a year later, in 1939, at age thirty-six, leaving Elsa a widow with four children. Ohiya's eldest son joined the Marines during World War II; Elsa moved back to Chicago, where Bonnin sometimes visited her when not working on the Ute claims. In 1940, Bonnin remarried. He and his new wife, an old friend who had also been widowed, moved to Arlington, Virginia. Bonnin died on September 24, 1942, after just a few weeks of illness. During this brief period he often spoke of returning to Utah and its natural beauty. He was buried with Zitkala-Ša at Arlington National Cemetery.[13]

In the spring of 1938, the year Zitkala-Ša died, the New York Light Opera Guild staged a revised version of *The Sun Dance Opera* under William Hanson's direction. Zitkala-Ša apparently took little interest in the revival. Not a word about the opera or Hanson can be found in her dairies.[14] It was likely just as well. Promoters advertised the plot's religious aspects as an "orgy."[15] Hanson claimed the opera was his alone, and Zitkala-Ša received virtually no credit as an artistic collaborator.[16] This omission foreshadowed Zitkala-Ša's quick but temporary disappearance from American history. Her life and work as a forerunner of Red Power can only now be fully appreciated.

Conclusion
Zitkala-Ša and Red Power

The Gertrude and Raymond Bonnin Collection at Brigham Young University contains two unpublished writings by Zitkala-Ša, "The Sioux Claims" (1923) and "Our Sioux People" (1923), that indisputably mark her as a forerunner of Red Power who asserted the moral, cultural, and religious superiority of Sioux over white civilization. In "Our Sioux People," a damning polemic against the U.S. government's colonial wars, Zitkala-Ša records how the Black Hills were "ceded under duress" in 1876. Since that time the Sioux, like many other indigenous nations, have been subjected to interference that has disrupted the "course of their evolution, determined by their own initiative, and according to their own philosophy." Even those sympathetic to the Indian cause have approached reform from the wrong standpoint. "Would-be friends," blinded by their own ethnocentrism, "know no other measure of progress than the degree of Caucasian domination over Indians." They wrongly label those Sioux who hold tightly to their culture the "most backward." On the contrary, they are "the more hopeful because of their reluctance to cast aside our native culture." This fact does not constitute any disadvantage that would thwart their success in white society. What prevents their success is the BIA, whose legacy is one of "absolute tyranny over America's aboriginal people, and a despoilation of his land and native culture."

Zitkala-Ša suggests that the bureau's machinations and dishonest dealings place Indians in a condition akin to slavery. Her critique is rooted in

189

the indigenous ideas in *Old Indian Legends*. "There is an old Sioux legend about Double-face," she explains, "a creature that had a face on both front and back of his head. It is told of him that he stole an Indian baby, and when the child cried from hunger he sang a lullaby to it,—while switching its little bare feet with a thorny rose bush." This image summarizes a federal policy that touts the virtues of education and assimilation, but does little more than repress Indian progress and appropriate their lands. In contrast, Harriet Beecher Stowe's villain in *Uncle Tom's Cabin*, Simon Legree, was infinitely more honest. "Legree, lashing Blackmen till their lacerated bodies were covered with blood," Zitkala-Ša notes, "was frank in his brutality and did not try to deceive by any pretence of humanitarianism. His hard face was single and not double." Nonetheless, the end result is the same: "cannibalism." Ironically, in the land of democracy, "the Sioux and other Indian tribes [not only are] denied a voice in and notification of federal actions involving their affairs, their land, their money, and schools for their children, but they are cut off from the world at large." They are denied the benefits of modern technology and knowledge, yet at the same time "are discouraged in the continuance of their own culture." Zitkala-Ša observes, "If a 'returned student' impelled either by love of his native dress, or by hard circumstances to fall back upon it, when the price of boots and a suit of clothes was not to be had, he is ostracized as having gone back to the blanket, as if he had committed a crime." Real crimes, however, are found within American expansionism.

Zitkala-Ša charges that as the U.S. enlarged westward it repeatedly failed on its own terms, both legal and moral, due to greed for Indian land and resources. When the Sioux successfully resisted, treaties made in "good faith" were quickly "trampled underfoot when the wild lust for gold stampeded white men across the plains to the Black Hills, into the country of the Sioux." Subsequent legislation has denied the Indians' rights to interpret the very documents that were supposed to ensure their freedom. In any other country such "treaty mutilation" would be "a serious affair." But because of white greed, the U.S. government made war on "the peaceful roaming Sioux." These actions amounted to a biblical sin that brought about an environmental Armageddon. War alone could not achieve the desired results. The Sioux were only "subdued by starvation," forced to surrender land that had been "filled with the stench of putrefying carcass of buffalo herds wantonly killed by paid sharp shooters, [an] outcome of [the] white man's broken promises to the Sioux weeping over little cold lifeless bodies in their weak arms, their little darlings dead from hunger and fever." This wicked deed done, "the Sioux were driven into small reservations, out of which they were never to go again without a pass,—never again as free men." If, instead, the westward push had "meant Americanization in the sense that the Indian's entity was to be recognized in the constitution of the United States, equal to other Americans," expansion would at least have been "in harmony with established custom of civilized races of the earth." Given the commonality of humanity, this should have been the inevitable course. "In spite of all efforts to segregate and differentiate the human family by color, and a sea of names," Zitkala-Ša emphasizes, "at heart they are all the same." All but the "Whiteman," who with "his Bible under one arm and gun powder under the other," has perpetrated atrocities that exclude him from any claim to true civilization.

Those whites who offer peace, meanwhile, are sorely misguided. The great irony of the reservation system is a Christian presence that seeks to uplift peoples in no need of moral or religious guidance. "Many devout missionaries," for instance, "have gone among the Sioux, teaching them the ten commandments." Zitkala-Ša characterizes the Sioux response: "You claim the Son of God came to the white man; and that it is His teachings you are bringing to us. They are good. We know them, but will you explain why the white men murdered the Son of God when he came to them? No Indian would have done that." Therefore, "good missionaries" have done little but make "the breaking of sacred promises by the Caucasian race" even more "incomprehensible." Missionary efforts would be better directed at Washington, for the Sioux express in thought and action the values preached by their subjugators. Key to this spiritual superiority is a lack of materialism. The Sioux believe that a man should "claim only what he used in his lifetime." Adherence to this principle has avoided "long battles over inherited riches that are waged by so-called 'civilized' races." Undergirding the Sioux worldview is an understanding of real freedom expressed by Sitting Bull: "They give us meat but they took away our liberty. I would rather live in a teepee and go hungry when game is scarce than give up my privilege as a free Indian." Such resistance is to be celebrated. But Indians "born in bondage" have now lost any recourse to the "democratic principles" that marked the past. "Who owned America before the white man came?" Zitkala-Ša asks, "And by what process has the ownership vested in the United States?" These would be "pertinent questions" in any "highly civilized nation" hoping to embody "the universal laws of justice."[1] America does not fit this description. It is the antithesis of civilization, religion, and democracy. The Sioux are the true standard-bearers of these ideals.

In "The Sioux Claims" and "Our Sioux People," we see Zitkala-Ša at her most nationalistic, most angry, and perhaps most candid. Some might charge that in these works Zitkala-Ša romanticizes the Sioux past or reconstructs the harmonious Eden whose state of grace expired with the coming of the white man, as she wrote of in "Impressions of an Indian Childhood." That is not the point here. What is important is how "The Sioux Claims" and "Our Sioux People" express Zitkala-Ša's ultimate perspective, so vastly dissimilar from the narrative preached within both the boarding school movement that educated her and the American civilizational discourses that her works subvert. Zitkala-Ša lived in a time when such open critiques would have been too politically provocative and would have alienated those she sought to sway. Though Zitkala-Ša's more diplomatically expressed criticism has been labeled assimilationist, her published work bears direct comparison to the ideas put forth by Indian activists in the late 1960s and 1970s, when the Native American civil rights movement emerged and gained national attention.

In 1972, the American Indian Movement's Trail of Broken Treaties march climaxed with a famous three-day occupation of the BIA headquarters. The "20-Point Indian Manifesto" that leaders presented there contained many of the same demands found in Zitkala-Ša's writings from the 1920s and 1930s. Red Power activists called for reviews of treaties, compensation for treaty violations, recognition of Indians' right to interpret treaties, restoration of millions of acres of lands, a new congressional committee on Indian relations, federal protection for offences committed against indigenous peoples, protection of cultural heritage, abolition of the BIA, improvements in standards of living, economic development, and education, and the right to establish nationwide Native organizations without U.S. government interference or control.[2] Zitkala-Ša articulated many of the same goals, or very similar ones, in *Americanize the First American*, her articles for the *American Indian Magazine*, and her concrete activism under the auspices of the SAI, GWFC, AIDA, and NCAI.

As a public intellectual, Zitkala-Ša shared the concerns of the Red Power era's leading Yankton Sioux literary voice, Vine Deloria, Jr., once head of another NCAI, the National Congress of American Indians.[3] In his 1969 manifesto *Custer Died for Your Sins*, Deloria engaged issues Zitkala-Ša had raised half a century before. He envisioned a regenerative platform in which "Indian people will not only be free to revitalize old customs, but also to experiment with new social forms." Moreover, he argued that through a "general policy of restitution of past betrayals," a true "renewal" for indigenous peoples could be "fully realized." This policy included federal "provisions for self-determination," strengthened by "a cultural leave-us-alone agreement" and the re-creation of "a viable land base for those Indian communities." Deloria's post-Progressive era formulation was much like his Yankton ancestor's, involving tribal corporations that would allow Indians to "achieve a prosperity not seen since the landing of the white man." Deloria, however, had the luxuries of freer expression and a more receptive audience that, prompted by the Vietnam War, was beginning to examine the American past and present. Zitkala-Ša had a more difficult task. She was largely barred from trumpeting such statements as "it is doubtful that any nation will ever exceed the record of the United States for perfidy" or "America has always been a militantly imperialistic world power eagerly grasping for economic control over weaker nations"—though she almost certainly would have agreed with those sentiments. Likewise, Zitkala-Ša could not unashamedly declare, without either making immediate conciliatory gestures or facing immediate negative consequences, that "one of the major problems of the Indian people is the missionary." Nor could she casually dub Christianity "the religion of the Easter Bunny" or defiantly state to her GWFC sisters, "There is not a single tribe that does not burn with resentment over the treatment it has received at the hands of an avowedly *Christian* nation."[4]

But reading Deloria's descriptions of the U.S. government's "program of cultural destruction" and his accusation that the coming of missionaries "shatter[ed] Indian societies and destroy[ed] the cohesiveness of the Indian communities," one cannot help but recall that Zitkala-Ša had said all these things decades earlier, in her critique of the boarding school movement, her story "The Soft-Hearted Sioux," and her denunciations of the BIA.

A second question is how Zitkala-Ša saw her identity. When Deloria put forth his candidacy for the presidency of the National Congress of American Indians, he distinguished "Indian Americans"—"an assimilated group"—from "American Indians"—a "definite and separate group" with a distinct identity. This characterization may well capture Zitkala-Ša's conception of the Indian's unique place in American society.[5] One of her unpublished, handwritten reports from the late 1920s, "Indian Affairs," opens with the statement, "I am an Indian." After detailing the many obstacles faced by indigenous peoples across the North American continent, Zitkala-Ša writes, "We are being exterminated."[6] "I am an Indian" and "We are being exterminated" are defining statements, which strikingly reveal both racial pride and the historical forces behind Zitkala-Ša's proto–Red Power platform.

Drawn-out comparisons could be made between Zitkala-Ša's and Deloria's positions, or between her goals of sovereignty and renewal and those of the many activist groups that protested during the American Indian civil rights movement.[7] One could also point to the less well-known struggles of the 1940s and 1950s, throughout which the National Congress of American Indians attempted to protect civil rights and fight tribal termination in the interest of self-determination. Or one could point to 1962's Declaration of Indian Purpose, an intertribal effort that called for preservation of indigenous cultures, restoration of the "right to self government," and territorial integrity "beyond the reach of predatory men."[8] This is not to suggest that the National Congress of American Indians, the American Indian Movement, Deloria, or any other figure or organization of the Red Power era took any inspiration from Zitkala-Ša's writings or protest. That this link has been so thoroughly broken remains unfortunate. Many scholars have focused on the differences between Zitkala-Ša, whom they call liminal or assimilationist, and the stances of later twentieth-century activists, rather than on the strong ideological consistencies. As for assimilationist interpretations of Zitkala-Ša, it is tempting to make the basic observation that as a young woman in Boston, she could very easily have made a socially advantageous marriage to any one of her long list of suitors: the Harvard man, the German violinist, the New Yorker from a wealthy family, or perhaps the well-known writer. Miss Gertrude Simmons could have stayed in white "civilization," written, played her violin, and performed her orations, or merely stayed comfortably at home, fulfilling the expectations of the Victorian Cult of True Womanhood. But for someone with her sense of justice and racial, cultural, and historical consciousness, this route to assimilation was as impossible as the task that she ultimately set for herself.

In order to understand Zitkala-Ša's place in American Indian history, we must appreciate how she struggled along the path of her forbearers against the policies of a government seeking imperialist expansion—a government that in her lifetime and on her ancestral lands had killed unarmed indigenous men, women, and children. That government's citizens largely acquiesced to, supported, or actively engaged in these means to accomplish the effective erasure of her people. As a woman whose culture, nation, and identity had been violently marginalized, Zitkala-Ša attempted to effect change. She fought the dispossession of Indians with every tool of white society she had mastered, enlisting other women in the fight. Throughout her life she argued for the superiority of indigenous (specifically Sioux)

cultures; the preservation of indigenous values, virtues, and religious beliefs; and the democratic right of tribal self-determination within the
United States on an equal footing with Euro-American society. These imperatives first revealed themselves in her semiautobiographical writings for
the *Atlantic Monthly* and culminated in her work in the National Council of
American Indians—where, unrestrained by any dominant association, she
attempted to organize a response to white control. Her writings, her activism, her perspective, her pride, and her call for sovereignty define Zitkala-
Ša's life and legacy as a forerunner of Red Power.

NOTES

Prologue

1. "The Oratorical Contest," *Earlhamite*, March 1896, 183–87; Zitkala-Ša, "The School Days of an Indian Girl," *Atlantic Monthly* 85 (February 1900), 193; W. C. Dennis to Cora Marsland, February 9, 1938, Gertrude Simmons Alumni Files, Lily Library, Earlham College, Richmond, Ind. The English Hotel and Opera House was one of Indianapolis's grandest structures, constructed in 1880 and demolished in 1948. See "Then and Now: English Hotel and Opera House, 120 Monument Circle," http://historicindianapolis.com/then-and-now -english-hotel-and-opera-house-120-monument-circle/ (accessed November 10, 2014).

2. Zitkala-Ša, "Side by Side," *Earlhamite*, March 16, 1896, 177–79.

3. Zitkala-Ša, "School Days of an Indian Girl," 194; "Oratorical Contest," 183.

4. See Paul H. Carlson, *The Plains Indians* (College Station: Texas A&M University Press, 1998), 5; Thomas Constantine Maroukis, *Peyote and the Yankton Sioux: The Life and Times of Sam Necklace* (Norman: University of Oklahoma Press, 2004), 8; and P. Jane Hafen, ed., introduction to *Dreams and Thunder: Stories, Poems, and* The Sun Dance Opera (Lincoln: University of Nebraska Press, 2001), xiv, for classifications. It should also be noted that today the term "Sioux" is no longer as widely accepted among speakers of Dakota, Nakota, and Lakota. "Sioux" is the name circuitously ascribed to this nation by their neighbors, the Ojibwas, who called them "Nadowe-is-iw-ug," or "Nadouessioux," which the French shortened to "Sioux." Other Euro-Americans later took up the word. See Maroukis, *Peyote and the Yankton Sioux*, 13. I use "Sioux" in this book because so many of the sources, Zitkala-Ša's as well, employ the term—meaning that considerable lexical dissonance would result from its abandonment.

5. Patrice Hollrah, " 'We Must Be Masters of Our Circumstances': Rhetorical Sovereignty and Political Resistance in the Life and Works of Zitkala-Ša," in *Old Lady Trill, the Victory Yell: The Power of Women in Native American Literature* (New York: Routledge, 2004), 27–28.

6. Barry M. Pritzker, *A Native American Encyclopedia: History, Culture, People* (Oxford: Oxford University Press, 2000), 340; Carlson, *Plains Indians*, 142, 146–62; Jeffrey Olster, *The Plains Sioux and US Colonialism from Lewis and Clark to Wounded Knee* (Cambridge: Cambridge

University Press, 2004), 77, 144; Thomas Powers, *The Killing of Crazy Horse* (New York: Knopf, 2010), 410–15.

7. Maroukis, *Peyote and the Yankton Sioux*, 21–23; Pritzker, *Native American Encyclopedia*, 295.

8. Jeffrey Myers, *Converging Stories: Race, Ecology, and Environmental Justice in American Literature* (Athens: University of Georgia Press, 2005), 111.

9. Carlson, *Plains Indians*, 175–79; Leon Speroff, *Carlos Montezuma, MD, A Yavapai American Hero: The Life and Times of an American Indian, 1866–1923* (Portland, Ore.: Arnica, 2005), 69–70.

10. Jerome A. Greene, *American Carnage: Wounded Knee, 1890* (Norman: University of Oklahoma Press, 2014), 96–102.

11. Carlson, *Plains Indians*, 179–82; Pritzker, *Native American Encyclopedia*, 330; Greene, *American Carnage*, xiii. Also see Bill Yenne, *Sitting Bull* (Yardley, Pa.: Westholme, 2008), 241–46, 270–74. The Indian Bureau had viewed Sitting Bull as a Ghost Dance instigator.

12. David Wallace Adams, *Education for Extinction: American Indians and the Boarding School Experience, 1875–1928* (Wichita: University Press of Kansas, 1995), 8–10. Also see Hazel W. Hertzberg, *The Search for an American Indian Identity: Modern Pan Indian Movements* (Syracuse, N.Y.: Syracuse University Press, 1971), 20. The names Office of Indian Affairs, Indian Office, Bureau of Indian Affairs, and Indian Bureau are often used interchangeably, although this government organ was officially called the Office of Indian Affairs until 1947, when its name was changed to Bureau of Indian Affairs. I use Bureau of Indian Affairs and Indian Bureau most frequently throughout this book because many of the primary sources, though dating from before 1947, employ these monikers. See C. L. Henson, "From War to Self-Determination: A History of the Bureau of Indian Affairs," www.americansc.org.uk /Online/indians.htm (accessed November 3, 2013).

13. Helen Hunt Jackson, *A Century of Dishonor: A Sketch of the United States Government's Dealings with Some of the Indian Tribes* (Boston: Roberts Brothers, 1885), 1.

14. Adams, *Education for Extinction*, 8–10.

15. Historical Society of Pennsylvania, Indian Rights Association Records, http://hsp.org /sites/default/files/legacy_files/migrated/findingaid1523ira.pdf (accessed October 5, 2012). The 1880s to 1934 (which marked the passage of the Indian Reorganization Act) is sometimes called the "assimilation period." See Robin DeRosa, "Critical Tricksters: Race, Theory, and *Old Indian Legends*," in *American Indian Rhetorics of Survivance: Word Medicine, Word Magic*, edited by Ernest Stromberg (Pittsburgh: University of Pittsburgh Press, 2006), 181.

16. Frederick E. Hoxie, *A Final Promise: The Campaign to Assimilate the Indians, 1880–1920* (Lincoln: University of Nebraska Press, 1984), 76.

17. Hertzberg, *Search for an American Indian Identity*, 21.

18. Richard Henry Pratt, "Origin and History of Work at Carlisle," *American Missionary* 37, no. 4 (1883): 110.

19. Paul Boyer et al., *The Enduring Vision: A History of the American People*, vol. 2, *Since 1865* (Boston: Houghton Mifflin, 2000), 482b.

20. Richard Henry Pratt, *Battlefield and Classroom: Four Decades with the American Indian, 1867–1904*, edited by Robert M. Utley (Lincoln: University of Nebraska Press, 1987), 24. For more explanation of Pratt's views on race see Jacqueline Fear-Segal, "Nineteenth-Century Indian Education: Universalism Versus Evolutionism," *Journal of American Studies* 33, no. 2 (August 1999): 323–41.

21. Hoxie records that the boarding school movement did not last very long because the U.S. government thought it too expensive to educate 40,000 Native children away from

home, in the East. Doing so would have required doubling the Indian Bureau budget. In the late 1880s and early 1890s on-reservation schools were established in the West at BIA agencies and other places with larger populations. They were staffed by civil servants and taught a uniform curriculum. Pratt was unhappy with these developments, convinced that keeping Indians in their natural surroundings or segregated on reservations would prevent their becoming civilized. As he put it, on-reservation schooling was "worse than no school at all." By the early 1890s, then, Pratt's ideas had become irrelevant in Washington, and though larger boarding schools like Carlisle and the Haskell Institute still existed, he no longer influenced government policy. Instead, the national Indian school program prevailed, thus lauded by the *Journal of Education*: "If every Indian child could be in school for five years, savagery would cease and the government support of Indians would be a thing of the past." See Hoxie, *Final Promise*, 60–67.

22. *Annual Report*, 1887, quoted in Dorothea M. Susag, "Zitkala-Ša (Gertrude Simmons Bonnin): A Power(full) Literary Voice," *Studies in American Indian Literatures* 5, no. 4 (1993): 16.

23. Richard Henry Pratt, *Origin of the Carlisle Indian Industrial School: Its Progress and the Difficulties Surmounted*, edited by Robert M. Utley (Carlisle, Pa.: Cumberland County Historical Society Publications, 1979), 9.

24. Paula Gunn Allen, ed., *Voice of the Turtle: American Indian Literature, 1900–1970* (New York: Random House, 1994), 116–17; Boyer et al, *Enduring Vision*, 481b; Alvin Josephy, Jr., *500 Nations: An Illustrated History of North American Indians* (New York: Knopf, 1994), 433–35; Peter Nabokov, *Native American Testimony: A Chronicle of Indian-White Relations from Prophecy to the Present* (New York: Viking Press, 1991), 220.

25. Brenda J. Child, *Boarding School Seasons: American Indian Families, 1900–1940* (Lincoln: University of Nebraska Press, 1998), 57. Considering such catastrophic events, it is hard not to note the irony permeating Commissioner of Indian Affairs Thomas J. Morgan's words in 1889. Speaking of the aims of boarding school education, he noted that "a fervent patriotism should be awakened in [students'] minds. . . . They should be taught to look upon the United States Government as their friend." This document is quoted in Ernest Stromberg, "Resistance and Mediation: The Rhetoric of Irony in Indian Boarding School Narratives by Francis La Flesche and Zitkala-Ša" in *American Indian Rhetorics of Survivance: Word Medicine, Word Magic*, edited by Ernest Stromberg (Pittsburgh, Pa.: University of Pittsburgh Press, 2006), 97.

26. See A. LaVonne Brown Ruoff, "Early Native American Women Authors: Jane Johnston Schoolcraft, Sarah Winnemucca, S. Alice Callahan, E. Pauline Johnson, and Zitkala-Ša," in *Nineteenth-Century American Women Writers: A Critical Reader*, edited by Karen L. Kilcup (Malden, Mass.: Blackwell, 1998), 99; Zitkala-Ša, "Impressions of an Indian Childhood," *Atlantic Monthly* 85 (January 1900): 46–47. I say "evidently tempted" by the apples because Zitkala-Ša may have used the fruits merely as a literary device in "Impressions of an Indian Childhood." Zitkala-Ša did however repeat the story in 1930 at the Lake Mohonk Conference. Whether this anecdote was part of her own mythology is open to debate. See *Report of the Thirty-Fifth Lake Mohonk Conference on the Indian* (Poughkeepsie, N.Y.: Lousing-Broas Printing for the Lake Mohonk Conference, 1930), 92–95. Susan Rose Dominguez's research shows that the date of Gertrude's arrival at White's was February 23, 1884, just a day after her supposed birthday of February 22 (born 1876). See Dominguez, "The Gertrude Bonnin Story: From Yankton Destiny to American History, 1904–1938" (Ph.D. diss., Michigan State University, 2005), 99. White's Residential and Family Services, meanwhile, provided the date February 14, 1884 (e-mail correspondence with author, January 26, 2015).

27. Susan Rose Dominguez, "Snapshots of Twentieth-Century Writers: Mary Antin, Zora Neal Hurston, Zitkala-Ša, and Anzia Yezierska," *Centennial Review* 41, no. 3 (1997): 551;

Dominguez, "Gertrude Bonnin Story," 147. During 1900–1902 Zitkala-Ša signed her correspondence to Carlos Montezuma "Zitkala-Ša," "Zitkala," or merely "Z." See her letters in the Montezuma Papers, Wisconsin Historical Society, Madison.

28. Approximately forty of the secondary sources listed in this volume's bibliography use the name Zitkala-Ša in either the title or the text, whereas Bonnin is used in only a handful. Recently, however, scholars appear to have swung in favor of Bonnin. Despite this trend, employing the Bonnin surname throughout this text would be highly impractical and at times would make it impossible to distinguish between Zitkala-Ša and her husband. Deborah Sue Welch also writes, "Given her life-long defense of the on-going viability of Indian cultural traditions, the selection [of the name Zitkala-Ša] seems appropriate. . . . I cannot judge what Zitkala-Ša's reaction would be to my choice. . . . However, I think it is as Zitkala-Ša, an American Indian leader, that she would have liked best to be remembered." This is a sound judgment. See Deborah Sue Welch, "Zitkala-Ša: An American Indian Leader, 1876–1938" (Ph.D. diss., University of Wyoming, 1985), ix.

29. Ruth Spack, *America's Second Tongue: American Indian Education and the Ownership of English, 1860–1900* (Lincoln: University of Nebraska Press, 2002), 145.

30. See Cathy N. Davidson and Ada Norris, eds., introduction to *American Indian Stories, Legends, and Other Writings* (New York: Penguin Books, 2003), xi–xxxv, for an account of Zitkala-Ša's life and achievements. For information on the GFWC, see Nancy F. Cott, *The Grounding of Modern Feminism* (New Haven, Conn.: Yale University Press, 1987), 23.

31. Scholars have produced numerous articles that focus on Zitkala-Ša's early writings; unfortunately, her later life and writings have received much less attention. The articles that pay serious attention to Zitkala-Ša's post-1902 works are Kevin Bruyneel, "Challenging American Boundaries: Indigenous People and the 'Gift' of U.S. Citizenship," *Studies in American Political Development* 18 (Spring 2004): 30–43; Vanessa Holford Diana, "Hanging in the Heart of Chaos: Bi-Cultural Limbo, Self-(Re)presentation, and the White Audience in Zitkala-Ša's *American Indian Stories*," *Cimarron Review* 121 (1997): 154–72; P. Jane Hafen, "Zitkala-Ša: Sentimentality and Sovereignty," *Wicazo Sa Review* 12, no. 2 (1997): 31–41; Charles Hannon, "Zitkala-Ša and the Commercial Magazine Apparatus," in *The Only Efficient Instrument: American Women Writers and the Periodical, 1837–1916*, edited by Aleta Feinsod Cane and Susan Alves (Iowa City: University of Iowa Press, 2001), 179–201; Hollrah, " 'We Must Be Masters of Our Circumstances' "; Julianne Newmark, "Pluralism, Place, and Gertrude Bonnin's Counternativism from Utah to Washington, D.C.," *American Indian Quarterly* 36, no. 3 (2012): 318–47; and Gary Totten, "Zitkala-Ša and the Problem of Regionalism," *American Indian Quarterly* 29, nos. 1–2 (2005): 84–123.

32. For "cultural ghost" commentary see D. K. Meisenheimer, Jr., "Regionalist Bodies/Embodied Regions: Sarah Orne Jewett and Zitkala-Ša," in *Breaking Boundaries: New Perspectives on Women's Regional Writing*, edited by Sherrie A. Inness and Diana Royer (Iowa City: University of Iowa Press, 1997), 115. This current of thought originated in Dexter Fisher [Alice Poindexter Fisher], "The Transformation of Tradition: A Study of Zitkala-Ša and Mourning Dove, Two Transitional American Indian Writers" (Ph.D. diss., City University of New York, 1979). Also see Mary Stout, "Zitkala-Ša: The Literature of Politics," in *Coyote Was Here: Essays on Contemporary Native American Literary and Political Mobilization*, edited by Bo Sholer (Philadelphia, Pa.: Coronet Books, 1984), 70–78. Other examples outside the field of Native studies include Laura Wexler, "Tender Violence: Literary Eavesdropping, Domestic Fiction, and Educational Reform," in *The Culture of Sentiment: Race, Gender, and Sentimentality in Nineteenth-Century America*, edited by Shirley Samuels (New York: Oxford University Press, 1992), 9–38; and Sidonie Smith, "Cheesecake, Nymphs, and We the People: Un/National Subjects about 1900," *Prose Studies* 17, no. 1 (1994): 120–40, both of which portray Zitkala-Ša

as somehow unwittingly half-Americanized. Finally, Nancy M. Peterson, in her more recent book, *Walking in Two Worlds*, writes of Zitkala-Ša's supposedly liminal character in a chapter tellingly entitled "Life in Limbo." See Peterson, *Walking in Two Worlds: Mixed-Blood Indian Women Seeking Their Path* (Caldwell, Idaho: Caxton Press, 2006), 159–79.

33. For explication see Davidson and Norris, introduction to *American Indian Stories*, xxiii–xxiv; Newmark, "Pluralism, Place, and Gertrude Bonnin's Counternativism," 318–47. For a very early critical, assimilationist interpretation, see James Sydney Slotkin, *The Peyote Religion: A Study in Indian-White Relations* (Glencoe, Ill.: Free Press, 1956), 47, 121. For later examples see William Willard, "The First Amendment, Anglo-Conformity and American Indian Religious Freedom," *Wicazo Sa Review* 7 (1991): 25–40. (Note that Willard is not a Zitkala-Ša detractor. See his "Zitkala-Ša: A Woman Who Would Be Heard!" *Wicazo Sa Review* 1 [1985]: 11–16. The article offers much scholarly praise for her lifetime of activism.) Also see Robert Allen Warrior, *Tribal Secrets: Recovering American Intellectual Traditions* (Minneapolis: University of Minnesota Press, 1995), 4, 10, 13–14; Thomas Constantine Maroukis, "The Peyote Controversy and the Demise of the Society of American Indians," *American Indian Quarterly* 37, no. 3 (Summer 2013): 159–80; Maroukis, *The Peyote Road: Religious Freedom and the Native American Church* (Norman: University of Oklahoma Press, 2010); Maroukis, *Peyote and the Yankton Sioux*; L. G. Moses, *The Indian Man: A Biography of James Mooney* (Urbana: University of Illinois Press, 1984), 192–205; and Scott Richard Lyons, "The Incorporation of the Indian Body: Peyotism and the Pan-Indian Public, 1911–1913," in *Rhetoric, the Polis, and the Global Village: Selected Papers from the 1998 Thirtieth Anniversary Rhetoric Society of America Conference* (Mahwah, N.J.: Lawrence Erlbaum Associates, 1999), 152. For the characterization of Mooney as the "champion of religious freedom," see Willard, "First Amendment," 30. Other assimilationist interpretations are found in Deborah Sue Welch, "Gertrude Simmons Bonnin (Zitkala-Ša)," in *The New Warriors: Native American Leaders since 1900*, edited by R. David Edmunds (Lincoln: University of Nebraska Press, 2001), 35–54; and to some degree, Welch, "Zitkala-Ša," 8, 71–72. For the most excoriating assimilationist interpretations, see Jace Weaver, "Splitting the Earth: First Utterances and Pluralist Separatism," in *American Indian Literary Nationalism*, edited by Jace Weaver, Craig S. Womack, and Robert Allen Warrior (Albuquerque: University of New Mexico Press, 2006), 2; Betty Louise Bell (Cherokee), "If This Is Paganism . . . Zitkala-Ša and the Devil's Language," in *Native American Religious Identity: Unforgotten Gods*, edited by Jace Weaver (Maryknoll, N.Y.: Orbis, 1998), 61–68.

34. Bicultural analyses include Hafen, "Zitkala-Ša"; Hollrah, "'We Must Be Masters of Our Circumstances'"; Amelia V. Katanski, *Learning to Write "Indian": The Boarding School Experience and American Indian Literature* (Norman: University of Oklahoma Press, 2005); Penelope Kelsey, "Narratives of the Boarding School Era from Victory to Resistance," *Atenea* 23, no. 2 (2003): 136 (Kelsey writes of Zitkala-Ša's "complex heritage"); Ruoff, "Early Native American Women Authors"; Ruth Spack, "Re-visioning Sioux Women: Zitkala-Ša's Revolutionary *American Indian Stories*," *Legacy: A Journal of American Women Writers* 14, no. 1 (1997): 25–42; Susag, "Zitkala-Ša (Gertrude Simmons Bonnin)"; Totten, "Zitkala-Ša and the Problem of Regionalism." Ruth J. Heflin, *I Remain Alive: The Sioux Literary Renaissance* (Syracuse, N.Y.: Syracuse University Press, 2000) also summarizes the bicultural perspective in her introduction (see esp. p. 9). For a feminist-inspired reading of Zitkala-Ša see in particular Margot R. Reynolds, "Mother Times Two: A Double Take on a Gynocentric Justice Song," in *Cultural Sites of Critical Interest: Philosophy, Aesthetics, and African American and Native American Women's Writings*, edited by Christa Acampora and Angela Cotton (New York: State University of New York, 2007), 171–90. Reynolds argues that the *Atlantic Monthly* series constitutes an attempt to "rework imperial, Christian-influenced patriarchy" (189). Davidson and Norris could also be counted in the bicultural school. They write, "Zitkala-Ša

did not live a dual or fractured life. Rather, she moved in, out, and between worlds." See their introduction to *American Indian Stories*, xiii. Also see Ron Carpenter, "Zitkala-Ša and Bicultural Subjectivity," *Studies in American Literatures* 16, no. 3 (2004): 1–27.

35. On the work and views of Red Progressives see Hertzberg, *Search for an American Indian Identity* (Hertzberg originated the term "Red Progressives"); Frederick E. Hoxie, *This Indian Country: American Indian Political Activists and the Place They Made* (New York: Penguin Press, 2012); Lucy Maddox, *Citizen Indians: Native American Intellectuals, Race, and Reform* (Ithaca, N.Y.: Cornell University Press, 2005). Warrior, with a more critical slant, writes of the Red Progressives' "integrationist legacy of post–Wounded Knee existence," calling them (including Zitkala-Ša) "Christian and secular assimilationist." "The purpose of these authors," Warrior notes, "was to gain sympathy from white audiences for the difficult, but to the authors necessary, process of becoming American citizens" (Warrior, *Tribal Secrets*, 7–8). For other works criticizing Zitkala-Ša's "assimilationist" activism see n. 33, above.

36. See Karen Redfield, "Inside the Circle, Outside the Circle: The Continuance of Native American Storytelling and the Development of Rhetorical Strategies in English," in *American Indian Rhetorics of Survivance: Word Medicine, Word Magic*, edited by Ernest Stromberg (Pittsburgh, Pa.: University of Pittsburgh Press, 2006), 151. Helen Jaskoski also observes that Native writers of this era were "always involved in a dynamic negotiation across many boundaries, barriers, gaps, and silences characterizing the emergent nation. Their understanding speaks to a profound faith in the possibility of language to overcome ignorance and hostility, as well as remarkable trust, which in the light of history may seem to have been misplaced, in the capacity of their audiences to be persuaded by rational argument and humane principles." See Helen Jaskoski, ed. *Early Native American Writing* (Cambridge: Cambridge University Press, 1996), xii. Vanessa Holford Diana also points to Zitkala-Ša's need to negotiate with and placate her white audiences while deploying criticisms. See Diana, "Hanging in the Heart of Chaos," and Hollrah, " 'We Must be Masters of Our Circumstances,' " for more on manipulation of the white audience. These two scholars discuss how Zitkala-Ša desired to influence early twentieth-century white American readers, who, imbued with all the prejudice, ethnocentrism, and nationalism of their era, demanded conciliatory gestures within the narrow national narrative and a heavy sprinkling of sugar coating, which she cleverly, tactically, and pragmatically utilized to sway opinion and resist, defy, and fight not only colonial assumptions in her writing, but also colonial policy through her activism. Also see Hannon, "Zitkala-Ša and the Commercial Magazine Apparatus," 179–201, regarding World War I. Katanski, quoting Warrior, writes of how Zitkala-Ša's work, like that of many Indian intellectuals of her era, "was guided by the political landscape they inhabited" (Katanski, *Learning to Write "Indian,"* 165). One could also point to p. 158, where Katanski writes that Zitkala-Ša often used "the masters' tools to dismantle the masters' house." Warrior, however, is less forgiving of Zitkala-Ša (Warrior, *Tribal Secrets*, 10). Indeed, to be heard at all, in her later activism Zitkala-Ša had to contend with the burden of the dominant, white discourses on civilization, religion, and nationhood, knowing full well that there was no return to traditional life on the Dakota plains. Her work therefore unavoidably contained forced, painful compromises and internal tensions impossible to resolve on a political level without demanding a white retreat to Europe. The inability to erase the Euro-American presence from the continent and the necessity to confront and engage the encroachers through negotiation meant that whether in denouncing the vicissitudes of Indian education and compulsory assimilation, or in urging the teaching of English and extension of U.S. citizenship to all indigenous peoples, Zitkala-Ša encountered both actual and rhetorical barricades that hemmed in her protest.

37. See Philip J. Deloria, "Four Thousand Invitations," *Studies in American Indian Literatures* 25 no. 2 and *American Indian Quarterly* 37, no. 3 [combined issue] (Summer 2013): 25–43. Deloria argues that although many SAI members could be considered assimilated, they just as equally "worked actively to preserve elements of Native cultures and societies from destruction." He adds that given their extraordinary commitment, and in light of new scholarship, "ranting about the supposedly assimilated Indians of the turn of the twentieth century seem[s] a little quaint" (26). Nonetheless, the assimilationist-bicultural debate over Zitkala-Ša's legacy has continued as recently as 2012, in Newmark, "Pluralism, Place, and Gertrude Bonnin's Counternativism." Here Newmark effectively criticizes Jace Weaver's assimilationist interpretation of Zitkala-Ša.

38. See Zitkala-Ša, *Americanize the First American: A Plan of Regeneration* (1921).

39. See, for instance, P. Jane Hafen, "A Cultural Duet: Zitkala-Ša and *The Sun Dance Opera*," *Great Plains Quarterly* 18, no. 2 (1998): 110. Hafen argues that in *The Sun Dance Opera* Zitkala-Ša sought to assert "the significance of Native cultures." Also, Carpenter writes that in the *Atlantic Monthly* series Zitkala-Ša "does not privilege Anglo or Yankton unilaterally." See Carpenter "Zitkala-Ša and Bicultural Subjectivity," 1. See Spack, "Re-visioning Sioux Women"; and Susag, "Zitkala-Ša (Gertrude Simmons Bonnin)" for other instances where Zitkala-Ša is represented as defending the validity and value of her culture.

40. Zitkala-Ša, *Americanize the First American*.

41. The working definition of proto–Red Power I offer is inclusive. In 1971 Alvin M. Josephy, Jr., wrote that Red Power meant "self-determination," specifically "the right of Indians to decide programs and policies for themselves, to manage their own affairs, to govern themselves, and to control their land and resources." Josephy elaborated,

> [Red Power] asserted angrily that Indian peoples were, and always had been, intelligent competent humans. Their history before the coming of the whites demonstrated that they managed their own affairs as well, if not better than, white men were now managing the affairs of the modern, non-Indian world. Indian societies, it stated, were usually just right for the conditions and environments of the individual peoples, who protected the environment and lived in harmony with nature and the cosmos. There was no reason to believe that the Indians on their own could not once again create— better and faster than any white man could make for them—societies that harmonized with the environments in which they existed. . . . Tribal lands, in this view, would be administered by and for Indians, with Indians controlling their own local governments, courts, funds, schools, and other public institutions. . . . [The aim was] the right of Indians to be free of colonialist rule and to run their own affairs, with security for their lands and rights. (Alvin M. Josephy, Jr., ed., *Red Power: The American Indians' Fight for Freedom* [New York: McGraw-Hill, 1971], 17–18.)

All of these themes resonate in Zitkala-Ša's work. Since 1971 use of the term "Red Power" has been debated. Bradley G. Shreve notes that "the words have been used in myriad ways"— sometimes referring to definitions like Josephy's, or to actions such as the occupation of Alcatraz and the BIA. Shreve argues that the term should be applied primarily to those who occupied Alcatraz, the "militants" of the American Indian Movement (AIM), and the National Indian Youth Council (NIYC), though not to members of the National Congress of American Indians (NCAI), who preferred lobbying tactics. See Shreve, *Red Power Rising: The National Indian Youth Council and the Origins of Native Activism* (Norman: University of Oklahoma Press, 2011), 6–8. Daniel M. Cobb, taking a more inclusive view of Indian activism generally, disagrees with the association of Red Power with the AIM, noting that the Yankton writer and activist Vine Deloria, Jr., used and popularized the term. See Cobb, *Native Activism in Cold War America: The Struggle for Sovereignty* (Lawrence: University Press of Kansas, 2008), 1–2, 135. Regardless of differences in method, Deloria, the activists of the late 1960s and 1970s, and the activists who came before them largely shared the ideology, demands, and goals Josephy sketched out in 1971. This biography is, in part, an attempt to show strong ideological consistencies between Zitkala-Ša's platform and that of Red Power, the issue of U.S. citizenship (the only possible route to legal protections in the early twentieth century) somewhat excepted.

1. The School Days of an Indian Girl

1. For Taté I Yóhin Win's approximate date of birth, see Yankton Sioux Tribe Agency Census, 1887, South Dakota State Archives, South Dakota State Historical Society, Pierre. Here she is listed as being sixty-one years old. However, the Yankton censuses are riddled with differing dates. She was perhaps born somewhat later because Gertrude was born in the mid-1870s, when by this reckoning Taté I Yóhin Win would have been around fifty and generally past childbearing years. On the other hand, Taté I Yóhin Win's obituary in the *Wagner Post* records her age as ninety. See *Wagner Post*, January 1, 1915, 5. For further information see Dominguez, "Gertrude Bonnin Story," 84. Regarding Yankton land loss, see Pritzker, *Native American Encyclopedia*, 340. For more on Zitkala-Ša's childhood, including translations of Taté I Yóhin Win's name, see Davidson and Norris, introduction to *American Indian Stories*, xiv–xv; Ruoff, "Early Native American Women Authors," 99; Speroff, *Carlos Montezuma, MD*, 206–207; and Welch, "Zitkala-Ša," 5–8.

2. Dominguez, "Gertrude Bonnin Story," 84.

3. Pritzker, *Native American Encyclopedia*, 340. The Yankton had previously ceded more than two million acres in 1830 and 1837, in what is now Iowa. They also owned 650 acres, the former Pipestone Reservation in present-day Minnesota. They sold this land to the U.S. government in 1929 for $333,000 but retained access to the quarry for pipe making. Also see Speroff, *Carlos Montezuma, MD*, 210. Speroff counts the precise size of the Yankton Reservation at 430,405 acres.

4. Dominguez, "Gertrude Bonnin Story," 84–85; The Yankton Sioux Tribe Agency Census of 1887 lists David Simmons as twenty-one years old then.

5. Spack, *America's Second Tongue*, 152.

6. Felker was listed as French in the 1900 Federal Census Indian Population Schedule for Greenwood, South Dakota, Wahehe Township, Charles Mix County, p. 315B. On the next page, David Simmons is listed as having been born in Missouri. For further information and the quotation about Felker being a "worthless fellow," see Dominguez, "Gertrude Bonnin Story," 85. Also see Zitkala-Ša, "Impressions of an Indian Childhood," 37–45.

7. Zitkala-Ša to Montezuma, July 1901, quoted in Speroff, *Carlos Montezuma, MD*, 226.

8. The Yankton Sioux Tribe Agency censuses are full of inconsistencies and errors. The census of 1887 lists Gertrude's age as 11; that of 1890 as age 14; the 1892 census lists Gertrude as born in 1877; the censuses of 1893–95 list Gertrude's age as 17, 18, and 19, respectively, corresponding to a birth year of 1876; the censuses of 1896–99, list her ages as 23, 24, and 25, with a birth year of 1873; the census of 1900 lists a birth year of 1876; whereas the 1901 census records a birth year of 1873. (e-mail correspondence with author, January 26, 2015). Skipping ahead, in the 1920 census Gertrude Simmons's birth date is listed as February 22, 1873, with a note that the date has been corrected from February 22, 1875. Here, Alfred O. Bonnin, Raymond T. Bonnin's brother, is listed in place of his son, Raymond Ohiya Bonnin, though the birth date of May 28, 1903, is correct. Such discrepancies may have been due to sloppiness

in data collection or estimations of unknown dates. The censuses are located in the South Dakota State Archives. Dominguez's research has shown that the Yankton Presbyterian Mission rolls initially listed Zitkala-Ša as Gertie Felker. By the time she went to White's, she was enrolled as Gertrude Simmons. Dominguez has also uncovered documentation that Gertrude was Ellen Simmons's tenth child. Zitkala-Ša gives her date of birth as February 22, 1876, in a *Washington Evening Star* article published on March 19, 1928. She states that she has the same birthday as George Washington. See Dominguez, "Gertrude Bonnin Story," 9, 21, 97, 99. Also, the *Indian Helper*, February 25, 1898, notes that "[Simmons] celebrates the 22nd, as the anniversary of her birth." Therefore, Zitkala-Ša did consider this her birth date. The date February 22 also appears in Zitkala-Ša, "Zitkala-Ša—Gertrude Bonnin" (1929?), manuscript in the Gertrude and Raymond Bonnin Collection, Perry Special Collections, Harold B. Lee Library, Brigham Young University, Provo, Utah. (The Bonnin Collection includes the NACI Records, 1926–1938.) Zitkala-Ša must have typed this list of her significant life accomplishments up to that point on her assumed birthday.

9. A mention of Felker's death is made in Dominguez, "Gertrude Bonnin Story," 85. Also see Zitkala-Ša to Montezuma, June–July 1901, Montezuma Papers. Zitkala-Ša does not speak of her biological father's death in any available source.

10. Dominguez, "Gertrude Bonnin Story," 85; Zitkala-Ša, "Impressions of an Indian Childhood," 38. Though the *Atlantic Monthly* series contains obvious inaccuracies, Dominguez's research corroborates these basic facts.

11. "Santee Student List," 47; Santee Normal Training School, Nebraska State Historical Society, Lincoln. At Santee the faculty taught the standard subjects—history, botany, English, geography, and music, along with Bible study. The Dakota language was not only permitted but taught. According to Elizabeth R. Gutch, there was also no corporal punishment. Instead, students were sent to their rooms for bad behavior. Industrial subjects were also stressed, such as homemaking for the girls, and blacksmithing and carpentry for the boys. See Elizabeth R. Gutch, "Study of Dakota Indian Students at the Santee Normal Training School," 4–5, Santee Normal Training School, Nebraska State Historical Society.

12. "Santee Normal Training School," Nebraska State Historical Society, RG2497.AM, www.nebraskahistory.org/libarch/research/manuscripts/organize/santee-school.htm (accessed September 7, 2014).

13. Dominguez, "Gertrude Bonnin Story," 101; "Divide and Conquer: The 'Indian Experiment' at Hampton Institute," http://xroads.virginia.edu/~cap/poca/poc_hamp.html (accessed December 23, 2014).

14. Zitkala-Ša, "Impressions of an Indian Childhood," 37–45.

15. Spack, *America's Second Tongue*, 144.

16. Ruoff, "Early Native American Women Authors," 99; Zitkala-Ša, "Impressions of an Indian Childhood," 46. As stated earlier, Zitkala-Ša's reference to apples may have been merely a literary device (see prologue n. 26).

17. Spack, *America's Second Tongue*, 152; Zitkala-Ša, "Impressions of an Indian Childhood," 46–47. Zitkala-Ša alludes to Taté I Yóhin Win's conversion to Christianity in one of her stories: "Like instantaneous lightning flashes came pictures of my own mother's making, for she, too, is now a follower of the new superstition." See Zitkala-Ša, "Why I Am a Pagan," *Atlantic Monthly* 90 (December 1902): 803. Further, Ellen Taté I Yóhin Win Simmons's funeral was held in the Presbyterian church in Greenwood. See her obituary in the *Wagner Post*, January 1, 1915, 5.

18. Josephy, *500 Nations*, 432.

19. Dominguez, "Gertrude Bonnin Story," 107.

20. Ibid., 106–109.

21. Zitkala-Ša, "School Days of an Indian Girl," 185. In "The Gertrude Bonnin Story," p. 99, Dominguez lists the exact date of Gertrude's arrival as February 23, 1884. White's Residential and Family Services provided the date February 14, 1884 (e-mail to author).

22. Zitkala-Ša, "School Days of an Indian Girl," 186.

23. Roumiana Velikova, "Troping in Zitkala-Ša's Autobiographical Writings, 1900–1921," *Arizona Quarterly* 51, no. 1 (2000): 63.

24. Zitkala-Ša, "School Days of an Indian Girl," 190.

25. Dominguez, "Gertrude Bonnin Story," 108.

26. See Zitkala-Ša, "School Days of an Indian Girl," 190, for a likely accurate depiction of White's rigid schedule.

27. "White's Institute, Indiana," in *Minutes from the Indiana Meeting of Friends*, 1892, quoted in Ruth Spack, "Dis/engagement: Zitkala-Ša's Letters to Carlos Montezuma, 1901–02," *MELUS: Journal of the Society for the Study of the Multi-Ethnic Literature of the United States* 26, no. 1 (2001): 192.

28. Zitkala-Ša, "School Days of an Indian Girl," 192. According to White's Residential and Family Services records, confirmed by Dominguez's research, Gertrude left White's on February 28, 1887. Dominguez, "Gertrude Bonnin Story," 99. (Date confirmed in e-mail to author, January 26, 2015.)

29. Dominguez, "Gertrude Bonnin Story," 109; "Santee Student List," 47. Santee Normal Training School, Nebraska State Historical Society. According to the list, Gertrude studied at Santee only in 1889.

30. Zitkala-Ša, "School Days of an Indian Girl," 190–92.

31. Dominguez, "Gertrude Bonnin Story," 99. Both Dominguez and White's Residential and Family Services give the date of Gertrude's second arrival as December 18, 1890 (e-mail to author, January 26, 2015).

32. *Wabash Plain Dealer*, June 26, 1885, quoted in Dominguez, "Gertrude Bonnin Story," 109. See p. 131 for citation.

33. Dominguez, "Gertrude Bonnin Story," 124, 109–10. This recruiting trip was one of two Gertrude made. The Yankton Sioux Tribe Agency Census of 1920 in the South Dakota State Archives, lists Raymond Telephause Bonnin's birth date as June 17, 1880.

34. Dominguez, "Gertrude Bonnin Story," 110–11; *Wabash Plain Dealer*, June 28, 1895, quoted in Dominguez, 111. For citation see p. 131.

35. Ibid., 111, 124.

36. Zitkala-Ša, "School Days of an Indian Girl," 192–93.

37. Dominguez, "Gertrude Bonnin Story," 116–17. Simmons addresses the Unthanks as "Aunt Sue" and Uncle Joe" in a letter written from Carlisle in 1898. See Simmons to Susan B. and Joseph T. Unthank, April 25, 1898, Susan B. Unthank Collection, Indiana State Library, Indianapolis. The letter reveals that Susan Unthank possessed a very expensive violin. Dominguez's research shows that Joseph T. Unthank made at least one donation to White's Institute. See Dominguez, "Gertrude Bonnin Story," 132.

38. See Dominguez, "Gertrude Bonnin Story," 116–23, for a description of Earlham. The first Indian student at Earlham was Arizona Jackson, who arrived in 1880. The first black student was a former slave named Osborn Taylor. See Thomas D. Hamm, *Earlham College: A History, 1847–1997* (Bloomington: Indiana University Press, 1997), 46. The speculation that the Unthanks paid Simmons's tuition and expenses at Earlham is based on Simmons's letter to Susan and Joseph Unthank, April 25, 1898, Unthank Collection. The letter makes clear the love and gratitude Simmons felt for the couple, and that she could rely on them for support.

39. "Record of Examinations of College Students" (1895–97), Gertrude Simmons Alumni Files. In the first term Simmons got five As. The second term she received two As and what

look to be two passes. In the third she completed only two courses—Latin and English composition—likely because she was first distracted by the oratory contest then hampered by illness.

40. Dominguez, "Gertrude Bonnin Story," 121–22. An Earlham alumnus, Chalmers Hadley, wrote of Zitkala-Ša: "For her graduation thesis she collected legends of her own tribe, translated them into Latin to meet college requirements and then re-wrote them in English for children, and their publication remains today a standard juvenile book." See Hadley, "Earlham," *Earlhamite*, June 1943, 14.

41. Hadley, "Earlham," 14. Zitkala-Ša also mentions her "slight" figure in "An Indian Teacher among Indians," *Atlantic Monthly* 85 (March 1900): 382.

42. Zitkala-Ša, "School Days of an Indian Girl," 193.

43. Hadley, "Earlham," 14.

44. See the following: *Earlhamite*, November 15, 1895, 61; "Music Recital," January 1, 1896, 108; March 1897, 187; "Personals and Locals," November 1, 1895, 47; "Halloween Party," November 1, 1895, 61; June 1896, 265; December 1895, 80.

45. "The Contest," *Earlhamite*, February 15, 1986, 139–41, 152. Oddly, "The Contest," while describing in detail all the other contestants' speeches, only included one line on Simmons's winning oration. Also see W. C. Dennis to Cora Marsland, February 9, 1938, Simmons Alumni Files. Dennis writes, "We naturally expected that as Seniors our class would sweep everything before it in the Oratorical Contest and to have this little Indian girl in the Freshman class beat our best was quite a surprise for us although I must say that I think we all took the defeat very nicely and supported her loyally when she went on to the State Contest."

46. Opal Thornburg, *Earlham: The Story of the College, 1847–1962* (Richmond, Ind.: Earlham College Press, 1963), 215. The senior's name was Eleanor Wood. After her victory the college held a three-day celebration.

47. W. C. Dennis, who was at the Indianapolis contest, recalled, "[Simmons] re-wrote her entire oration because she wished to talk upon the Indian question in the State Contest, and she had not expected to win in the College Contests her first year." Dennis to Marsland, February 9, 1938, Gertrude Simmons Alumni Files.

48. "Oratorical Contest," 183.

49. Zitkala-Ša, "School Days of an Indian Girl," 193.

50. "Oratorical Contest," 183–85.

51. "The College Orators," *Indianapolis News*, March 14, 1896. The reporter noted that for Simmons "there was less boisterousness of outburst than that which greeted the preceding speakers."

52. "Oratorical Contest," 185.

53. Zitkala-Ša, "Side by Side," 177–79. Among the scholars who have commented on "Side by Side," Welch characterizes it as an integrationist supplication to whites "to accept the Indian as fellow man, to afford him equal opportunities, [and] to live the Christian message of brotherhood." Welch, "Zitkala-Ša," 11. Dexter Fisher, meanwhile, sees in the speech a "pattern of ambivalence" that ends when Simmons "consents to the wisdom of learning the 'White Man's ways.'" Fisher, "Zitkala-Ša: The Evolution of a Writer," *American Indian Quarterly* 5, no. 3 (1979): 232–33. Betty Louise Bell most decisively labels "Side by Side" a "celebratory embrace of America and its paternalistic ambitions for the Indian." Bell, "If This Is Paganism," 63. Along the same lines, Thomas D. Hamm calls the speech "hardly a radical production." Hamm, *Earlham College*, 47. Lastly, Barbara Chiarello points out that whereas "Side by Side" appears to laud Christian brotherhood, in fact it does not and instead lauds Indian moral probity. Chiarello, "Deflected Missives: Zitkala-Ša's Resistance and Its (Un)

Containment," *Studies in American Indian Literatures* 17, no. 3 (2005): 4–6. Arguably, "Side by Side" shows Simmons's obvious resentment over the suffering American colonizers had wrought on her people and their appropriation of Indian ancestral lands. Despite the oration's final shift in tone and the allusions to Christianity as a civilizing force, "Side by Side" is a highly subversive text that resists far more than it conforms. The overly ingratiating conclusion, which speaks of Indians seeking the "White Man's ways" and adopting the "White Man's God" may have been honest, but may just as easily have been a ploy to curry favor with her white audience, who had just been treated to a reversal of their national and religious narratives. As Simmons makes plain, only the Indian has shown true fraternity. All her flattery of the United States is destabilized by her concurrent criticism that the young nation does not live up to its ideals, while the title "Side by Side" and the final lines regarding "our claim to a common country" may also be seen as arguing not for Indian assimilation but for participation on an equal footing. Regardless of how it is interpreted, the speech as a whole accomplishes a complete revision of the American perspective on the "Indian question." This type of sly criticism consistently marks Zitkala-Ša's later writings.

54. "Oratorical Contest," 185; "College Orators."

55. "College Orators."

56. Zitkala-Ša, "School Days of an Indian Girl," 194. Zitkala-Ša writes that when she took second place, "The evil spirit laughed within me when the white flag dropped out of sight, and the hands which furled it hung limp in defeat." Either this was a dash of fiction or the Butler boys in the top boxes had taken the "squaw" banner off its string and waved it while awaiting the decision. Dennis later wrote of having a different perspective on the "squaw" banner: "As I recollect, I did not think that [Simmons's] account of her experiences at Earlham was altogether fair in that she rather gave the impression that she was being put upon and, particularly, as I recollect it, she spoke of some of the things which happened at the State Contest as if students were attempting to persecute her because she was an Indian, when I think it was all good fun and just done to her as a contestant from a rival college and not as to an Indian." Nonetheless, in referring to Simmons as a "little Indian girl" earlier in the letter Dennis is obviously guilty of a similar lack of racial sensitivity, which was characteristic of his era. Simmons clearly did not interpret the "squaw" banner as a sporting gesture. Dennis to Marsland, February 9, 1938, Gertrude Simmons Alumni Files.

57. Thornburg, *Earlham*, 215.

58. The *Earlhamite* reported, "The successful contestant, Mr. Ewing, won a first, a second and a fourth grade on thought; one first and two seconds on delivery. The Indianapolis *Journal* bears the responsibility of the following quotation: 'Miss Simmons was given first place on thought by Prof. Cook, of Yale, and second place by Prof. Baker, of Harvard; Prof. Barkerville, of Vanderbilt, however, ranked her sixth on thought. This low grading, which was hardly deserved, is credited to the fact that Prof. Barkerville is a southern man, and Miss Simmons made reference to slavery as one of the blots on modern civilization. Miss Simmons was given two firsts on delivery.'" "Oratorical Contest," 185.

59. "College Orators"; "Oratorical Contest," 185.

60. "College Orators."

61. "De Pauw the Winner," *Indianapolis Journal*, March 14, 1896, quoted in Chiarello, "Deflected Missives," 7.

62. "At the College," *Earlhamite*, March 1896, 186–87.

63. *Earlhamite*, April 1896, 207.

64. Regarding *Anpao* the *Earlhamite* wrote, "Our editor-in-chief is a thoroughly professional man. Those thinking that the EARLHAMITE is the sole product of his massive intellect will be pleasantly surprised should a copy of the *Anpao* fall into their hands. Such is the

name of the publication which the happy association of such original personages as Chalmers Hadley, Okie Andrews and Gertrude Simmons at table has occasioned. Mr. Hadley is the figurehead, Miss Andrews the cartoon designer, and Miss Simmons the chief contributor." *Earlhamite*, May 1896, 255.

65. "Personals and Locals," *Earlhamite*, January 1, 1896, 109.

66. "Record of Examinations of College Students" (1895–97), Simmons Alumni Files. One of the Cs in the first term was for zoology. In the third term there is only one unintelligible mark, listed for Latin.

67. "A Ballad," *Earlhamite*, January 9, 1897. Another poem Simmons contributed after this period was "Iris of Life," printed in the *Earlhamite*, November 1898, 31.

68. See Speroff, *Carlos Montezuma, MD*, 208–209. Speroff, a medical doctor, posits that many of these symptoms may have been stress-related, as does Welch in "Zitkala-Ša," 12–14.

69. See Simmons to Susan and Joseph Unthank, April 25, 1898, Unthank Collection. In the letter Simmons mentions that she has become healthier and gained weight at Carlisle, but that she has not given up on college "for the sake of money-making."

70. Zitkala-Ša, "Indian Teacher among Indians," 381–82.

71. Spack, "Dis/engagement," 175. Though Zitkala-Ša eventually secured a teaching position, the *Indian Helper* reported she originally served as a clerk. *Indian Helper*, July 9, 1897. According to the *Earlhamite*, Zitkala-Ša began teaching in October. *Earlhamite*, October 1897, 19. Just before leaving Earlham she also sang Arditi's "The Dove" at the June 1897 commencement ceremony. *Earlhamite*, June 14, 1897, 286.

2. Carlisle and the Atlantic Monthly

1. Adams, *Education for Extinction*, 38–39; Speroff, *Carlos Montezuma, MD*, 44.

2. Fear-Segal, "Nineteenth-Century Indian Education," 326–27.

3. "Wants Indian Stories," *Indian Helper*, March 18, 1898, quoted in Spack, "Dis/Engagement," 176.

4. See Allen, *Voice of the Turtle*, 116–17; Boyer et al., *Enduring Vision*, 481b; Jessica Enoch, "Resisting the Script of Indian Education: Zitkala-Ša and the Carlisle Indian School," *College English* 65, no. 2 (2002): 117–41; Josephy, *500 Nations*, 434.

5. Luther Standing Bear, *My People the Sioux* (Lincoln: University of Nebraska Press, 1975), 133–34. Originally published 1928.

6. George E. Hyde, *Spotted Tail's Folk: A History of the Brule Sioux* (Norman: University of Oklahoma Press, 1961), 290–93.

7. Pratt, *Battlefield and Classroom*, 237–39.

8. *Indian Helper*, October 26, 1888, quoted in Enoch, "Resisting the Script of Indian Education."

9. Hyde, *Spotted Tail's Folk*, 290.

10. O. B. Super, "Indian Education at Carlisle," *New England Magazine* 18, no. 2 (1895): 220. Interestingly enough, East Coast periodicals that supported Carlisle's mission nevertheless at times expressed derision for its core values due to racism. In 1881 *Harper's New Monthly Magazine* published "Indian Education at Hampton and Carlisle." While endorsing the uplift of America's aboriginal population, the author conceded that the title might sound as odd to readers as "Education for Buffaloes and Wild Turkeys." Helen Wilhelmina Ludlow, "Indian Education at Hampton and Carlisle," *Harper's New Monthly Magazine* 62, no. 371 (April 1881): 659.

11. Standing Bear, *My People the Sioux*, 124, 157.

12. Hertzberg, *Search for an American Indian Identity*, 18.

13. Fear-Segal, "Nineteenth-Century Indian Education," 324.

14. Spack, "Dis/engagement," 181–82.

15. Richard Henry Pratt, "United States Indian Service, Training School for Indian Youths," *Report of the Commissioner of Indian Affairs*, 1881, quoted in Spack, "Dis/engagement," 182.

16. Spack, "Re-visioning Sioux Women."

17. Spack, "Dis/engagement," 182.

18. See *Indian Helper*, July 9, 1897, and August 6, 1897. In the first month Simmons also acted as the pianist for services in the school chapel. See *Indian Helper*, July 16, 1897. Unless otherwise noted, all further citations to the *Indian Helper*, *Red Man*, and *Red Man and Helper* that refer to Zitkala-Ša are taken from "Zitkala-Ša (aka Gertrude Simmons) at Carlisle," http://home.epix.net/~landis/zitkalasa.html (accessed August 8, 2011). Unfortunately, the Beinecke Rare Book and Manuscript Library at Yale University declined my request for scans of the originals.

19. Zitkala-Ša, "Indian Teacher among Indians," 384–85. There is also mention of David Simmons, called Dawée, having been fired from a clerkship at Greenwood in favor of a less dedicated white. While David Simmons apparently did work intermittently as an assistant issue clerk, it seems farming was his true profession. See Spack, *America's Second Tongue*, 152; Welch, "Zitkala-Ša," 8.

20. David Simmons received an allotment in 1892 and farmed there for the rest of his life. After allotment occurred (268,000 acres divided), the U.S. government took the remaining lands. See Welch, "Zitkala-Ša," 6, 21–23. Yankton did not accept allotment without protest. When the allotting agent appeared, tribal leaders ordered him to depart at once. After enforcement of the Dawes Act, a corrupt Yankton superintendent leased lands to white speculators who shared his "political faith" at eight to ten cents an acre, discounted from the going rate of twenty-five cents per acre. See Janet McDonnell, *The Dispossession of the American Indian: 1997–1934* (Bloomington: Indiana University Press, 1991), 22, 61–62. According to the South Dakota Land Patent Register in the Land Track Books, vol. 13, Gertrude Simmons received an eighty-acre allotment, which was later expanded to eighty-nine acres; Ellen Simmons received an allotment of 341 acres, and David Simmons received 160 acres. The Mix County Atlas, ca. 1889, shows that the adjoining allotments formed a square. Gertrude and Ellen Simmons were also given other plots nearby, adjoining those of members of the St. Pierre family. These allotments all fell within the Lawrence, Bryan, and Lone Tree townships. South Dakota State Archives.

21. Spack, *America's Second Tongue*, 152.

22. In the Yankton Sioux Tribe Agency Census, 1897, David is listed as thirty-one years old, his wife, Victoria, as twenty-five. The daughter, Irene, was five and Raymond was three. South Dakota State Archives.

23. Susag, "Zitkala-Ša (Gertrude Simmons Bonnin)," 13.

24. *Indian Helper*, September 27, 1897.

25. *Indian Helper*, October 15, 1897, October 29, 1897, April 1, 1898, and June 3, 1898.

26. Dominguez, "Gertrude Bonnin Story," 112.

27. *Indian Helper*, February 25, 1898.

28. Simmons to Susan and Joseph Unthank, April 25, 1898, Unthank Collection. This letter also mentions the school group portrait, "Faculty and Officers of Our School," taken for the *Indian Helper*. Simmons hopes to acquire a copy and send it to the Unthanks. The purpose of the letter, however, is to ask Susan Unthank if she will lend out her violin for a series of planned performances with the Carlisle Indian School Band: "I have promised to go

with a [*sic*] Carlisle Indian Band this fall (for six weeks) as violinist. I want to begin some most faithful practice right now. I know my playing would seem much better had I a good instrument. I know you have one. I cannot because of my very limited means pay a very high price for the use of any violin. Knowing that you know me and are interested in me I wondered if you would, through kindness, name me a sum within my reach—that is if you will loan me your violin from *now* till Nov[ember]. You know I would care for it with the tenderest [*sic*] kind of a [*sic*] devotion." Simmons adds: "This concert tour is to be a great thing as Capt. Pratt is back of it all."

29. *Indian Helper*, January 21, 1898.

30. Spack, *America's Second Tongue*, 160.

31. *Indian Helper*, July 1, 1898, August 12, 1898, and October 21, 1898.

32. Lone Bear became very friendly with Käsebier and wrote her letters until about 1912. See "Samuel Lone Bear, Sioux Indian," http://americanhistory.si.edu/collections/search /object/nmah_1005390 (accessed January 10, 2015).

33. Dominguez, "Gertrude Bonnin Story," 142–48. Regarding the Keiley photographs see Susan Close, *Faming Identity: Social Practices of Photography in Canada, 1880–1920* (Winnipeg, Manitoba: Arbeiter Ring, 2007), 113.

34. In a letter to Carlos Montezuma dated May 13, 1913, Zitkala-Ša writes, "I seem to be in a spiritual unrest. I hate this eternal tug of war between being wild or becoming civilized. The transition is an endless evolution—that keeps me in continual Purgatory." Montezuma Papers. Regarding the former portrait, in which Zitkala-Ša stands in profile, Barbara L. Michaels describes the pose as "an expression of yearning for the West." For more analysis see Close, *Faming Identity*, 112–14. The quotation by Michaels is on p. 114.

35. Dominguez, "The Gertrude Bonnin Story," 147. Dominguez also notes that Zitkanan (Red Bird) was the name of an Ihanktonwan leader from the 1800s. Dominguez, "Gertrude Bonnin Story," 21.

36. *Indian Helper*, September 2, 1898.

37. Dominguez, "Gertrude Bonnin Story," 148.

38. *Indian Helper*, October 21, 1898.

39. Dominguez, "Gertrude Bonnin Story," 149–50; Spack, *America's Second Tongue*, 146.

40. Dominguez, "Gertrude Bonnin Story," 150–52. Dominguez posits that Simmons likely resided in a boardinghouse while in Boston. See p. 163.

41. Ruth Spack, "Zitkala-Ša, *The Song of Hiawatha*, and the Carlisle Indian School Band: A Captivity Tale," *Legacy: A Journal of American Women Writers* 25, no. 2 (2008): 213–14.

42. *Indian Helper*, April 28, 1899.

43. Ibid., May 5, 1899.

44. Spack, "Zitkala-Ša, *The Song of Hiawatha*, and the Carlisle Indian School Band," 213–14.

45. Ellery Sedgwick, *The Atlantic Monthly, 1857–1909: Yankee Humanism at High Tide and Ebb* (Amherst: University of Massachusetts Press, 1994), 310–16.

46. Why Simmons, of Yankton-Nakota roots, chose the Lakota penname is unknown. The name Zitkala-Ša was also atypical in that it did not conclude with *win*, which in the Lakota dialect designates the person as female. For more on the name see Hollrah, "'We Must Be Masters of Our Circumstances,'" 27. Though Zitkala-Ša spoke Nakota and chose a Lakota name, she wrote in Dakota—perhaps because that was her native language or because Stephen Riggs's early Dakota orthography provided the easiest form of written expression. See Hafen, introduction to *Dreams and Thunder*, xiv. Complicating matters a bit further, though scholars usually identify Zitkala-Ša as Yankton-Nakota, she identified herself as Dakota. See, for instance, Zitkala-Ša, "The Sioux Claims" (1923), 1; "Our Sioux People" (1923), 11; Hafen, introduction to *Dreams and Thunder*, xiv.

47. Regarding the "political autobiography" see Beverly G. Six, "Zitkala-Ša (Gertrude Simmons Bonnin) (1876–1938)," in *American Women Writers, 1900–1945: A Bio-Bibliographical Critical Sourcebook*, edited by Laurie Champion (Westport, Conn.: Greenwood Press, 2000), 385. The quotation is attributed to Catherine Taylor; Meisenheimer, "Regionalist Bodies/Embodied Regions," 114–15. Also see Velikova, "Troping in Zitkala-Ša's Autobiographical Writings," 51. Velikova likewise characterizes the *Atlantic Monthly* series as a meld of autobiographical and political discourses. Also see Myers, *Converging Stories*, 111. Myers's research shows that in the five counties around the Pine Ridge and Rosebud Reservations, the number of Indians has actually increased by 350 percent between 1910 and 2000 to slightly more than thirty thousand. The neighboring white counties have seen a population decrease of 30 percent, now totaling around twelve thousand.

48. Sedgwick, *Atlantic Monthly, 1857–1909*, 310.

49. For more on these themes in Zitkala-Ša's work see Stromberg, "Resistance and Mediation," 95–109.

50. Rosanne Hoefel, "Writing, Performance, Activism: Zitkala-Ša and Pauline Johnson," in *Native American Women in Literature and Culture*, edited by Susan Castillo and Victor M. P. DaRosa (Porto, Portugal: Fernando Pessoa University Press, 1997), 110. One must, of course, also note Sarah Winnemucca's *Life among the Piutes: Their Wrongs and Claims* (1883). (*Piute* was the accepted spelling at the time.) Winnemucca's book was the first book/autobiography written and published by an indigenous woman. However, it was written with the help of an editor, Mary Mann, who helped overcome Winnemucca's "literary deficiencies." See Hoxie, *This Indian Country*, 150–51; editor's preface to *Life Among the Piutes: Their Wrongs and Claims* (Reno: University of Nevada Press, 1994).

51. Katanski, *Learning to Write "Indian,"* 159.

52. The following quotations from Zitkala-Ša, "Impressions of an Indian Childhood" are all in *Atlantic Monthly* 85 (January 1900): 37–47. Also see Agnes Picotte, foreword to *Old Indian Legends* by Zitkala-Ša (Lincoln: University of Nebraska Press, 1985), xv. Picotte claims that several incidents in the *Atlantic Monthly* series happened to other people. Katanski also argues that in the *Atlantic Monthly* series Simmons "meticulously constructed her identity as Zitkala-Ša." Simmons's later attempts to mold her public image as "Princess Zitkala-Ša," granddaughter of Sitting Bull, bolster this argument. Katanski, *Learning to Write "Indian,"* 114; Zitkala-Ša, "Princess Zitkala-Ša Center of Interest at Book Fair of Pen Women," *Washington Herald*, May 2, 1925. The newspaper's title is found in the Bonnin Collection.

53. See Martha J. Cutter, "Zitkala-Ša's Autobiographical Writings: The Problems of a Canonical Search for Language and Identity," *MELUS: Journal of the Society for the Study of the Multi-Ethnic Literature of the United States* 19, no. 1 (1994): 31–44; and Catherine Kunce, "Fire of Eden: Zitkala-Ša's Bitter Apple," *Studies in American Indian Literatures* 18, no. 1 (2006): 73–82, for more on biblical motifs in Zitkala-Ša's autobiographical essays.

54. For more analysis see Margaret A. Lukens, "The American Indian Story of Zitkala-Ša," in *In Her Own Voice: Nineteenth-Century American Women Essayists*, edited by Sherry Lee Linkon (New York: Garland, 1997), 143–45; Susan Bernardin, "The Lessons of a Sentimental Education: Zitkala-Ša's Autobiographical Narratives," *Western American Literature* 32, no. 3 (1997): 220–21. Bernardin states that Zitkala-Ša's recasting of her father as a Sioux warrior serves to preclude any notion that the author's impressive accomplishments can be attributed to her mixed ancestry.

55. See Spack, "Re-visioning Sioux Women"; Katanski, *Learning to Write "Indian,"* 117. For more on women in Sioux tradition see Margot R. Reynolds, "Mother Times Two," 171–90.

56. See Katanski, *Learning to Write "Indian,"* 217; Davidson and Norris, introduction to *American Indian Stories*, xxx.

57. The following quotations from Zitkala-Ša, "School Days of an Indian Girl" are all in *Atlantic Monthly* 85 (February 1900), 185–94.

58. See Mary Paniccia Carden, " 'The Ears of the Palefaces Could Not Hear Me': Languages of Self-Representation in Zitkala-Ša's Autobiographical Essays," *Prose Studies* 20, no. 1 (April 1997): 67. Carden refers to the ogling as the "colonizer's gaze." Also see Julianne Newmark, "Writing (and Speaking) in Tongues: Zitkala-Ša's *American Indian Stories*," *Western American Literature* 37, no. 3 (2002): 356. Regarding the telegraph poles, Newmark comments on how the young Gertrude "understood that the paleface had turned columns of wood into moaning, suffering entities."

59. See Katanski, *Learning to Write "Indian*," 120–21. Katanski writes that the hair-cutting scene depicts the truth behind boarding school before-and-after photographs, indicating not a civilizing, assimilative effect, but one that incites rebellion. Also see Pritzker, *Native American Encyclopedia*, 340. Pritzker notes that hair-cutting is associated with mourning in Nakota culture.

60. See Katanski, *Learning to Write "Indian*," 159. Katanski points out that this deathbed scene mirrors that of little Eva in *Uncle Tom's Cabin*—in that it is its opposite. Rather than the Bible signaling "transcendence," the book represents another deadly aspect of the "civilizing machine."

61. See Spack, *America's Second Tongue*, 157. Spack notes that "medical knowledge, so important to Lakota culture, was a source of power and respect for women. Lakota women who had visions might gain the power to cure and protect children through use of herbs and charms; these women formed the Women's Medicinal Cult, which gathered annually to prepare medicines for warriors. Even women who were not spiritualists had knowledge about every-day healthcare. Furthermore, their medical knowledge was so specific that that they could prepare medications and foods to treat distinct illnesses and conditions."

62. See Stromberg, "Resistance and Mediation," 105–106.

63. Carden, " 'The Ears of the Palefaces Could Not Hear Me,' " 67. Carden writes, "The banner, intended to render meaningless the speech that originates in an Indian woman's body, demonstrates that success wielding the white man's tools does not affect his formulation of her place in his culture."

64. The following quotations from Zitkala-Ša, "Indian Teacher among Indians," are all in *Atlantic Monthly* 85 (March 1900): 381–86.

65. For analysis see Newmark, "Writing (and Speaking) in Tongues," 337–38.

66. Zitkala-Ša's *Atlantic Monthly* series, though it did not change conventional thinking, did create a remarkable contrast. Both Patricia Okker and Barbara Chiarello note that the January 1900 issue of *Atlantic Monthly* that contained "Impressions of an Indian Childhood" featured another Indian story, Mary Johnston's serialized novel *To Have and To Hold*. Patricia Okker, "Native American Literatures and the Canon: The Case of Zitkala-Ša," in *American Realism and the Canon*, edited by Tom Quirk and Gary Scharnhorst (Newark: University of Delaware Press, 1994), 90; Chiarello, "Deflected Missives," 13–15. Its brave protagonists, Captain Ralph Percy and his dashing companion Diccon, are captured by a tribe of rabid savages who delight in the torture of innocent white explorers. In one scene that plays on the sexually salacious image of the "squaw," Diccon spontaneously molests one of his female captors: "Diccon . . . seized the Indian girl who brought him his platter of fish, and pulling her down beside him kissed her soundly, whereat the Indian girl seemed not ill pleased and the warriors laughed." Johnston's Chief is a scalp-toting monstrosity, "cruel and crafty beyond measure," whose "hideous" priests wear dead snakes in their hair. Crucially, she makes a clear delineation between white religious virtue and primitive degradation.

Percy narrates, "I strove for a courage that should be the steadfastness of the Christian, and not the vainglorious pride of the heathen." Mary Johnston, *To Have and to Hold, Atlantic Monthly* 85 (January 1900): 54–55. Unsurprisingly, the depictions of "savages" in *To Have and to Hold* impressed the critics immensely. One wrote, "The author's rare descriptive power does not fail her here: the picture of the wily Opechancanough, his body sleek with oil, glistening all over in the sunshine with powdered antimony, speaking fair words with a smiling face, while the inner devil looks through his cold snake eyes,—this is very fine." William E. Simonds, "Three American Historical Romances," *Atlantic Monthly* 85 (March 1900): 414. These popular racist stereotypes so enraptured readers that *To Have and to Hold* was credited with expanding the *Atlantic Monthly's* readership almost twofold. Okker observes that Zitkala-Ša's rendering of a small and helpless Sioux girl trembling in fear in front of "palefaces," then, constituted a radical departure from the typical narrative. Okker, "Native American Literatures and the Canon," 90.

67. Dexter Fisher, "The Transformation of Tradition: A Study of Zitkala-Ša and Mourning Dove, Two Transitional American Indian Writers," in *Critical Essays on American Literature*, edited by Andrew Wiget (Boston: G. K. Hall, 1985), 203.

68. "Persons Who Interest Us," *Harper's Bazar*, April 1900, 330.

69. Jesse W. Cook, "The Representative Indian," *The Outlook*, May 5, 1900, 80–83. Despite his withering contempt for aboriginal cultures, Cook was Zitkala-Ša's good friend for some time. He taught at Indian schools, including Carlisle, and was instrumental in convincing Carlos Montezuma not to sue her for losing an engagement ring he had given her. See Speroff, *Carlos Montezuma, MD*, 231–32. Cook's wife also chaperoned Zitkala-Ša on the Carlisle band's tour of the Northeast. See *Indian Helper*, March 23, 1900.

70. Elizabeth Luther Cary, "Recent Writings by American Indians," in *The Book Buyer* (New York: C. Scribner's Sons, 1902), 24–25. Earlham College's paper, the *Earlhamite*, reported on Zitkala-Ša's *Atlantic Monthly* writings as well, noting, "Miss Gertrude Simmons, who spent two years at Earlham a few years ago, and who is now a member of the Carlisle Indian School, is doing literary work which is very remarkable. The *Atlantic Monthly* contains a series of articles on Impressions of Indian Childhood, from her pen." *Earlhamite*, January 27, 1900, 109.

71. Bernardin, "Lessons of a Sentimental Education," 215.

3. Montezuma and the Rebellion

1. *Indian Helper*, February 2, 1900.

2. *Red Man*, February 1900, quoted in Enoch, "Resisting the Script of Indian Education."

3. Spack, "Dis/engagement," 186. Letters quoted in Spack, "Zitkala-Ša, *The Song of Hiawatha*, and the Carlisle Indian School Band," 214–15. Chamberlin's letter is dated March 9, 1900. Pratt's letter is dated March 20, 1900.

4. *Indian Helper*, March 9, 1900. For the size of the Carlisle band, see *Indian Helper*, March 30, 1900. That month the *Earlhamite* reported, "Miss Gertrude Simmons, who will be remembered by old Earlhamites, is soon to play the violin and recite 'Hiawatha,' at a literary club in Washington, at which President McKinley will preside." *Earlhamite*, March 1900, 117. The tour with Simmons was greatly delayed, perhaps because she had made the decision to move to Boston. Simmons's letter to the Unthanks indicated that the performances were originally planned for the fall of 1898. See Simmons to Susan and Joseph Unthank, April 25, 1898, Unthank Collection.

5. Quoted in Spack, "Zitkala-Ša, *The Song of Hiawatha*, and the Carlisle Indian School Band," 211–12.

6. *Red Man*, April 1900, quoted in Katanski, *Learning to Write "Indian,"* 160.

7. *Indian Helper*, March 30, 1900.

8. *Indian Helper*, March 23, 1900.

9. Spack, "Dis/engagement," 178.

10. *Indian Helper*, June 15, 1900.

11. Speroff, *Carlos Montezuma, MD*, 211.

12. Ibid., 1–2, 24–30, 90–96. Gentile "bought" Montezuma in 1871. Also see Spack, "Dis/engagement," 177–78, 185. Quote "honored guest" on page 177.

13. See, for instance, Super, "Indian Education at Carlisle," 229.

14. Hertzberg, *Search for an American Indian Identity*, 44.

15. "Zitkala-Ša in the *Atlantic Monthly*," *Red Man*, June 1900. This article was reprinted from the *Word Carrier*.

16. "Two Sides of Institution Life," *Red Man*, June 1900.

17. "Hunt for the South Side," *Red Man and Helper*, September 14, 1900. "Hunt for the South Side" downplayed the type of boarding school incidents recorded in the *Atlantic Monthly* series, yet admitted their potentially upsetting nature: "There are people like Zitkala Sa [sic], in her *Atlantic Monthly* articles a few months ago, who always insist upon sitting on the cold side of a hill. They have all sorts of experiences in life, happy as well as dull, but the remembrance of gloomy scenes and the dark pictures in life is alone retained. Those who make light of small trials and push them aside that sunshine and cheer may enter are the people who make the world worth living in. There is enough gloom in life as we go along from day to day, without treasuring up disagreeable experiences of the past." As a warning against such tendencies, "Hunt for the South Side" tells the story of a young girl who imbibes the godly insights of an older woman who is in bedridden with a broken leg. Rather than complain, the woman remains cheerful. Her little friend, on being sent to gather flowers, hunts everywhere but the sunny, south side of the hill. When the woman suggests she look there, the girl returns with a beautiful bouquet. "You were right," says the girl, "I had no idea that the south side made such a difference. The slope was half covered with the most beautiful blossoms, so big and deep colored. I'm going to put them in the pitcher beside you, so that you can reach your hands down deep into autumn and pretend you're picking them yourself." The older woman counters, "I should have to give up the memory of somebody who picked them for me," enabling the girl to understand the valor in a good deed well done and the value in appreciating others' efforts. The girl thinks a moment and answers: "Now I understand the difference. . . . You insist that you are living on the south side of life, and that you are getting every bit of sunshine there is, while most of us deliberately go and sit on the north side, and grumble because it is cold. . . . I've caught your secret now, and I'm going to sit in the sun. Then maybe I'll blossom." At that the "white face" smiles from the bed, and imparts a notable piece of wisdom: "And the best of it all is that there always is a south side, . . . the sun's side, and God's."

18. Zitkala-Ša to Montezuma, February 9, 1901, Montezuma Papers. This letter, sent from Roxbury, Massachusetts, and written when Zitkala-Ša was spending a Sunday in a cottage in the woods with several friends, is the only clue to how and when she and Montezuma met again after the Carlisle tour. It also reveals that Zitkala-Ša had already planned to return to Yankton to make her life. She writes, "I am expecting to teach next year in the government school in Yankton Agency S—D." She also writes, "By the time I come West—there will be two little books of mine in the press." One of the books she referred to was likely *Old Indian Legends*; the other obviously was never published.

19. Zitkala-Ša to Montezuma, February 9 and February 20, 1901, Montezuma Papers.

20. Zitkala-Ša, "The Soft-Hearted Sioux," *Harper's Monthly* 103 (October 1901): 505–508.

21. See Diana, "Hanging in the Heart of Chaos," 163–64; Redfield, "Inside the Circle, Outside the Circle," 154.

22. Zitkala-Ša to Montezuma, March 5 and March 17, 1901, Montezuma Papers.

23. See Spack, "Dis/Engagement," 188, 200.

24. *Red Man and Helper*, April 12, 1901, quoted in Fisher, "Zitkala-Ša," 230.

25. Zitkala-Ša to Montezuma, April 13, 1901, Montezuma Papers.

26. Zitkala-Ša to Montezuma, April 19, 1901, Montezuma Papers.

27. Zitkala-Ša to Montezuma, March 1901, quoted in Speroff, *Carlos Montezuma, MD*, 215–16.

28. Ibid., 215.

29. Zitkala-Ša to Montezuma, April 1901, Montezuma Papers.

30. Dominguez, "Gertrude Bonnin Story," 153.

31. Zitkala-Ša to Montezuma, April 19, 1901, Montezuma Papers.

32. Zitkala-Ša to Montezuma, March 1901, quoted in Speroff, *Carlos Montezuma, MD*, 215.

33. Spack, "Dis/engagement," 181.

34. Zitkala-Ša to Montezuma, April 19, 1901, Montezuma Papers.

35. Zitkala-Ša to Montezuma, June 1901, Montezuma Papers.

36. See Zitkala-Ša to Montezuma, February 20, 1901, Montezuma Papers. Zitkala-Ša writes that off-reservation schools are not superior to on-reservation schools.

37. Carlos Montezuma, "Indian Problem," quoted in Spack, "Dis/engagement," 185.

38. Zitkala-Ša to Montezuma, April 12, 1901, Montezuma Papers.

39. Zitkala-Ša to Montezuma, May 2 and May 7, 1901, Montezuma Papers.

40. Zitkala-Ša to Montezuma, May 13, 1901, Montezuma Papers.

41. Zitkala-Ša to Montezuma, April 19, 1901, Montezuma Papers.

42. Zitkala-Ša to Montezuma, May 28, 1901, Montezuma Papers.

43. Zitkala-Ša to Montezuma, May 30, 1901, Montezuma Papers.

44. Zitkala-Ša to Montezuma, June 1, 1901, Montezuma Papers.

45. Zitkala-Ša to Montezuma, June 1 and June 4, 1901, Montezuma Papers. The June 1 letter states, "I received a letter from my publisher asking me to write *another* volume of stories." Zitkala-Ša blamed her inability to finish the book on a pesky guest named Mr. Nichols. Zitkala-Ša to Montezuma, April 15, 1902, Montezuma Papers.

46. Zitkala-Ša to Montezuma, June 6, 1901, Montezuma Papers.

47. Zitkala-Ša to Montezuma, June–July 1901, Montezuma Papers.

48. Zitkala-Ša to Montezuma, June 20, 1901, Montezuma Papers.

49. Dominguez, "Gertrude Bonnin Story," 158; Zitkala-Ša to Montezuma, August 31, 1901, Montezuma Papers.

50. Zitkala-Ša to Montezuma, April 19, 1901, Montezuma Papers.

51. Zitkala-Ša to Montezuma, August 11, 1901, Montezuma Papers.

52. Zitkala-Ša to Montezuma, August 31, 1901, Montezuma Papers.

53. Zitkala-Ša to Montezuma, October 19, 1901, quoted in Speroff, *Carlos Montezuma, MD*, 228.

54. Dominguez, "Gertrude Bonnin Story," 100, 113, 174.

55. Bonnin's grandfather Joseph Picotte was a member of the American Fur Company. Bonnin's marriage to Emeline was his second. In 1863, he had married Philomene Darveaux in Canada. The union produced a daughter, but Bonnin was quickly widowed. The daughter remained in Canada with Joseph Bonnin's widowed mother when he left. Her married name was Corin Cummings. She eventually settled in Holyoke, Massachusetts. The second marriage to Emeline produced four sons and two daughters, both of whom died in childhood. See "Obituary of Joseph B. Bonnin," *Wagner Post*, January 8, 1915, 1. For

information on Raymond Bonnin's family history see also *Red Man and Helper*, June 13, 1902.

56. See Father Martin Kenel to Father William H. Ketcham, August 1, 1910, Bureau of Catholic Indian Missions Records, Raynor Memorial Libraries, Marquette University Archives, Milwaukee, Wisc. Kenel mentions that Bonnin was baptized as a child. Also see Zitkala-Ša to Richard Henry Pratt, July 9, 1909, Richard Henry Pratt Papers, Beinecke Rare Book and Manuscript Library, Yale University, New Haven, Conn. Zitkala-Ša mentions that Bonnin is not a "Church man." Also see Dominguez, "Gertrude Bonnin Story," 191.

57. See *Red Man and Helper*, June 13, 1902.

58. Zitkala-Ša to Montezuma, August 21, 1901, and June 23, 1902, Montezuma Papers.

59. Zitkala-Ša to Montezuma, September 4, 1901, Montezuma Papers.

60. See Spack, "Dis/engagement," 200. Spack states that *Old Indian Legends* was published in October 1901 in a trade edition, and in February 1902 as a textbook for schools. Hafen records that the book remained in print until 1950, then was resurrected thirty-five years later. See Jane Hafen, ed., introduction to *Iktomi and the Ducks and Other Sioux Stories* (Lincoln, Neb.: Bison Books, 2004), x. Regarding Angel DeCora Dietz's illustrations, see Hoefel, "Writing, Performance, Activism," 107. Angel DeCora Dietz, incidentally, left three thousand dollars to the SAI upon her death. See Zitkala-Ša to Montezuma, March 12, 1919, Montezuma Papers.

61. See Jeanne Smith, "'A Second Tongue': The Trickster's Voice in the Works of Zitkala-Ša," in *Tricksterism in Turn-of-the-Century American Literature: A Multicultural Perspective*, edited by Elizabeth Ammons and Annette White-Parks (Hanover, N.H.: University Press of New England, 1994): 47–48. Smith notes that Zitkala-Ša indicates "the primacy of Native Americans on American soil," hence "undermining the white reader's comfortable and usually unexamined sense of primacy and national citizenship." Also see Myers, *Converging Stories*, 111–38, for a larger discussion of *Old Indian Legends*. Myers discusses the book's narrative arc and argues for its significance as a critique of the American conservation movement. For more discussion also see DeRosa, "Critical Tricksters," 167–95.

62. Zitkala-Ša, "Old Indian Legends," in Davidson and Norris, *American Indian Stories*, 7, 27, 51.

63. Zitkala-Ša, "The Trial Path," *Harper's Monthly* 103 (October 1901): 127–31. Perhaps the fight between the two men for the grandmother's affections in "The Trial Path" mirrors the fight between Montezuma and Bonnin for Zitkala-Ša's affections.

64. For commentary see Totten, "Zitkala-Ša and the Problem of Regionalism," 95; Diana, "Hanging in the Heart of Chaos," 164.

65. Zitkala-Ša to Montezuma, October 19, 1901, quoted in Dominguez, "Gertrude Bonnin Story," 218. Zitkala-Ša added, "In a few days I shall return your ring to you." It is not clear that she did so. If she did, Montezuma sent it back before May 1902.

66. Zitkala-Ša to Montezuma, January 1, 1902, Montezuma Papers.

67. Zitkala-Ša to Montezuma, January 15, 1902, Montezuma Papers.

68. Zitkala-Ša to Montezuma, January 25, 1902, Montezuma Papers.

69. Zitkala-Ša to Montezuma, February 20, 1901, Montezuma Papers.

70. Zitkala-Ša to Montezuma, May 13, 1901, Montezuma Papers.

71. Zitkala-Ša, "The Indian District School: A Phase of Agency Life," *Boston Evening Transcript*, January 1902, quoted in Spack, "Dis/engagement," 186.

72. Zitkala-Ša to Montezuma, April 12, 1901, Montezuma Papers.

73. Zitkala-Ša to Montezuma, June 1901, Montezuma Papers.

74. Zitkala-Ša to Montezuma, April 3, 1901, Montezuma Papers.

75. Zitkala-Ša to Montezuma, April 1901, quoted in Spack, "Dis/Engagement," 181.

76. Zitkala-Ša to Montezuma, February 20, 1901, Montezuma Papers.
77. Dominguez, "Gertrude Bonnin Story," 193.
78. Zitkala-Ša to Montezuma, April 15, 1902, Montezuma Papers.
79. Zitkala-Ša to Montezuma, May 1, 1902, Montezuma Papers.
80. See Spack, "Dis/engagement," 190–91.
81. Zitkala-Ša to Montezuma, May 2, 1901, Montezuma Papers.
82. Zitkala-Ša, "A Warrior's Daughter," *Everybody's Magazine* 6 (April 1902): 132–40. See Diana, "Hanging in the Heart of Chaos," 163–64; and Spack, "Dis/engagement," 190–91, for more on "A Warrior's Daughter." This story also contains an antiracist element. A former slave has joined the Sioux after being taken captive in a raid against the enemy. His "unusual qualities" have endeared him to the tribe and he now lives freely outside the strictures of white control, having been "made a real man again."
83. In Diana's view the story allows its main character to define herself, free of the false restrictions imposed by societal norms and traditions, and the resulting mental and physical limitations ascribed to women in Victorian culture. See Diana, "Hanging in the Heart of Chaos," 163–64. Also see Paula Gunn Allen, ed., *Spider Women's Granddaughters: Traditional Tales and Contemporary Writing by Native American Women* (Boston: Beacon Press, 1989), 30. Allen (Laguna Pueblo and Métis) characterizes the story as a "vengeful little joke on the white women [Zitkala-Ša] spent so much time with."
84. The article from the *Tyndall Tribune* was reprinted in *Red Man and Helper*, June 13, 1902. Bonnin was twenty-two and Zitkala-Ša, twenty-six.
85. Zitkala-Ša to Montezuma, May 1, 1902, Montezuma Papers.
86. Zitkala-Ša to Montezuma, June 1902, Montezuma Papers.
87. Zitkala-Ša to Montezuma, June 23, 1902, Montezuma Papers.
88. Zitkala-Ša to Montezuma, July 10, 1902, Montezuma Papers.
89. See Speroff, *Carlos Montezuma, MD*, 231–32. As mentioned in chap. 2, n. 69, Jesse Cook was instrumental in persuading Montezuma not to sue. After Montezuma had a lawyer send Zitkala-Ša a letter in 1903, Cook convinced him that the act was foolish and would only damage his own reputation. Cook describes Zitkala-Ša as "a girl of moods and many minds."
90. Zitkala-Ša, "The Indian Dance: A Protest against Its Abolition," *Boston Evening Transcript*, January 25, 1902, 24. The "Indian Dance" had previously appeared in Santee's *Word Carrier* in 1901. The *Boston Evening Transcript* naturally gave the story more exposure. See Davidson and Norris, *American Indian Stories*, 267.
91. *Red Man and Helper*, August 22, 1902.
92. Zitkala-Ša, "Why I Am a Pagan," *Atlantic Monthly* 90 (December 1902): 801–803. Also see Katanski, *Learning to Write "Indian,"* 128. With reference to the "Christian pugilist," in the original text the word "Christian" is put within quotation marks, indicating how poorly the critic represented the values of his own religion. Also see Spack, "Dis/engagement," 193–94.
93. Diana, "Hanging in the Heart of Chaos," 161–62.
94. Zitkala-Ša to Montezuma, March 17, 1901, Montezuma Papers.
95. Zitkala-Ša to Montezuma, February 20, 1901, Montezuma Papers.
96. See Spack, *America's Second Tongue*, 162. Spack notes that "Why I Am a Pagan" may not be the thoroughly anti-Christian tract that it appears given Zitkala-Ša's later conversion. Instead, in *American Indian Stories* at least, it may be an indication of how "she rejected a Christianity that denigrated Native life." Also see Maddox, *Citizen Indians*, 143. Maddox writes that Zitkala-Ša used a "land-based philosophy" of "universal sympathy and respect" to criticize Christianity's focus on the afterlife and implicit rejection of both the present and the divinity of life on earth.

97. See R. Bonnin to Father William H. Ketcham, April 5, 1911, Bureau of Catholic Indian Missions. Here, Bonnin discusses his salary over several years in the Indian Service.

98. Zitkala-Ša, "Indian Teacher among Indians," 382.

4. Uintah

1. Zitkala-Ša's correspondence indicates that the Bonnins arrived in the winter of 1902. See, for instance, Zitkala-Ša to Father William H. Ketcham, January 5, 1911, Bureau of Catholic Indian Missions. Here, Zitkala-Ša writes, "I have lived among these people since the winter of 1902." Her typewritten chronology entitled "Zitkala-Ša–Gertrude Bonnin," also records that she moved to Utah in 1902. Bonnin Collection.

2. For information on Ute history see Virginia McConnell Simmons, *The Ute Indians of Utah, Colorado, and New Mexico* (Boulder: University of Colorado Press, 2000), 1–43, 50–60, 64, 86–87, 95–98, 117–18, 127–37, 207–25. For evidence that the Bonnins bought a claim during this period, see Zitkala-Ša to Father William H. Ketcham, May 25, 1910, Bureau of Catholic Indian Missions.

3. Speroff, *Carlos Montezuma, MD*, 233.

4. See Picotte, foreword to *Old Indian Legends*, xv. In "Zitkala-Ša–Gertrude Bonnin" Zitkala-Ša lists Ohiya's birthday as May 28, 1903, which corresponds with the date in the Yankton Census.

5. Welch, "Zitkala-Ša," 57, 59.

6. Simmons, *Ute Indians of Utah, Colorado, and New Mexico*, 208, 223.

7. Welch, "Zitkala-Ša," 57–59.

8. Speroff, *Carlos Montezuma, MD*, 232.

9. Davidson and Norris, introduction to *American Indian Stories*, xx.

10. Welch, "Zitkala-Ša," 57–58, 74.

11. "Brief History of Activities in Behalf of the American Indians: 1902–1932," 1, Bonnin Collection.

12. William Hanson, *Sun Dance Land* (Provo, Utah: J. Grant Stevenson, 1967), vi. Regarding the adoption of Oran Curry, see Dominguez, "Gertrude Bonnin Story," 185–87. Dominguez writes that Curry was likely adopted between 1905 and 1906.

13. See Zitkala-Ša to Arthur C. Parker, November 11 and December 14, 1916, Papers of the Society of American Indians (hereafter SAI Papers), Cornell University Library, Ithaca, N.Y. In the first letter Zitkala-Ša writes of Old Sioux being sick and living in a room in her home. In the second, she writes that he has lived with her for fourteen years.

14. "Obituary of Joseph B. Bonnin," 1. The obituary mentions that Emeline Bonnin suffered from "inflammatory rheumatism" for thirty years.

15. Hafen, introduction to *Dreams and Thunder*, xviii.

16. Davidson and Norris, introduction to *American Indian Stories*, viii.

17. Dominguez, "Gertrude Bonnin Story," 187; Zitkala-Ša to Charles S. Lusk, secretary, June 21, 1912, Bureau of Catholic Indian Missions.

18. Speroff, *Carlos Montezuma, MD*, 233.

19. Hafen, "Cultural Duet," 106.

20. Welch, "Zitkala-Ša," 72; Dominguez, "Gertrude Bonnin Story," 187. Regarding Zitkala-Ša's employment as a clerk in the Indian Service, see "Zitkala-Ša–Gertrude Simmons Bonnin," Bonnin Collection. She states that she was a clerk from 1907 to 1912 (likely off and on). Also see Zitkala-Ša's affidavit of May 27, 1912, held in the Bureau of Catholic Indian Missions. It states that she clerked at Uintah, earning $840 a year. The affidavit also states that she sold some of her land in South Dakota for $450.

21. Simmons, *Ute Indians of Utah, Colorado, and New Mexico*, 209.

22. See R. Bonnin to Father William H. Ketcham, April 5, 1911, Bureau of Catholic Indian Missions. In the letter Bonnin states that he resigned from the Indian Service in September 1909, even though he was earning $1,100 yearly.

23. Zitkala-Ša to Pratt, July 9, 1909, Pratt Papers. Zitkala-Ša writes with regard to the job offer, "Mr. Bonnin hesitated because he was not a 'Church man' but finally he accepted."

24. Ibid. This letter refers to previous letters in which the meeting in Philadelphia was planned, but it is difficult to determine how long they had been corresponding. Incidentally, Bonnin's April 5, 1911, letter to Ketcham (in the Bureau of Catholic Indian Missions) corroborates the Episcopalian coup and the troubles it caused him as superintendent.

25. Adams, *Education for Extinction*, 320–23. In exile from government service, Pratt was concentrating on public lecturing and writing to spread his views. After Pratt's departure from Carlisle, Commissioner of Indians Affairs Francis Luepp (appointed by Theodore Roosevelt in 1905) quickly directed changes. A Department of Native Arts was established, and Indian history was taught in a much more positive way. See Hertzberg, *Search for an American Indian Identity*, 17–18.

26. See the letter written by Whiterocks teacher Jennie Burton to Father William H. Ketcham, dated August 25, 1913, Bureau of Catholic Indian Missions. In it she complains of the Episcopalians' influence in the local community and over hiring and firing at the school.

27. See Kenel to Ketcham, August 1, 1910, Bureau of Catholic Indian Missions.

28. Dominguez, "Gertrude Bonnin Story," 192–93. The U.S. government had originally allowed the Catholic Church to found two missions in the Dakotas, one at Fort Yates, the other on Devil's Lake Reservation (now Spirit Lake). More were later established on other Sioux reservations.

29. Zitkala-Ša to Ketcham, May 25, 1910, Bureau of Catholic Indian Missions. The question of Zitkala-Ša's ultimate religious preference has been debated, likely due to her association with Mormonism, conversion to Catholicism, and interest in Christian Science later in her life. See Hafen, "Sentimentality and Sovereignty," 38; Davidson and Norris, introduction to *American Indian Stories*, xv; and Newmark, "Pluralism, Place, and Gertrude Bonnin's Counternativism," 344–45. Welch suggests that Zitkala-Ša's strongest ties were to Mormonism, and that she may have joined the church in secret. The only concrete evidence for this conclusion is that members of the Church of Latter-day Saints officiated at Zitkala-Ša's funeral, which Welch claims they would not usually do for a non-church member. But because Mormonism practices posthumous induction, Welch's speculation is not necessarily borne out. See Welch "Zitkala-Ša," 230, 273. Hafen, in contrast, contends that Zitkala-Ša practiced both Mormonism and Catholicism but considered "the Native cosmology" equally "legitimate." See Hafen, "Sentimentality and Sovereignty," 38. This conclusion appears sound in light of Zitkala-Ša's later public writings and statements, which often laud Native religions. The letters she wrote after returning to Utah, however, show that she considered Catholicism to be paramount. Yet, she never wavered in publicly criticizing aspects of Christianity she felt were inadequate or harmful and often had run-ins with the Episcopalians at Uintah. For her criticism of Christianity see, for instance, Zitkala-Ša, "The Indian's Awakening," *American Indian Magazine* 4 (January–March 1916): 57–59; Zitkala-Ša, "Heart to Heart Talk," *San Francisco Bulletin*, 1922. In her final diaries from July 21, 1935, to November 3, 1937 (Bonnin Collection), Zitkala-Ša, at one point at least, appears to give up all belief in any God. At other times she makes references to both Christianity and the Great Spirit.

30. Dominguez, "Gertrude Bonnin Story," 192, 198. Zitkala-Ša had also been impressed by a Catholic school she visited in June 1901, at Fort Totten. She wrote to Montezuma, "I

visited the Catholic school today. While the spirit of gentleness and kindness is a great good to the students I object to the suppression of individuality." Zitkala-Ša to Montezuma, June 4, 1901, Montezuma Papers.

31. Father Martin Kenel to Father William H. Ketcham, August 1, 1910, Bureau of Catholic Indian Missions. Kenel writes that Zitkala-Ša had worked as an issue clerk, a "position she filled to the satisfaction of all." Regarding the return to Utah, he writes, "In spring they left again in order to fulfill their claim conditions in Utah."

32. Zitkala-Ša to Ketcham, May 25, 1910; and Kenel to Ketcham, August 1, 1910, both in Bureau of Catholic Indian Missions. Kenel writes that the Bonnins had a claim in Utah before they arrived in Fort Yates.

33. Zitkala-Ša to Kenel, May 26, 1910, Bureau of Catholic Indian Missions.

34. Hafen, "Cultural Duet," 104.

35. T. Earl Pardoe, foreword to Hanson, *Sun Dance Land*, iii–iv. Hanson taught at Uintah Academy for fifteen years before moving on to Brigham Young University in 1924, where he spent thirty-three years.

36. Kenel to Ketcham, August 1, 1910, Bureau of Catholic Indian Missions.

37. Zitkala-Ša badly wanted to attend the Catholic Sioux Congress at Fort Yates. She wrote, "Oh, how I long to be at Fort Yates in June for the Indian Catholic Congress!" See Zitkala-Ša to Kenel, May 26, 1910, Bureau of Catholic Indian Missions.

38. Kenel to Ketcham, August 1, 1910, Bureau of Catholic Indian Missions.

39. Charles S. Lusk to Zitkala-Ša, August 6, 1910, Bureau of Catholic Indian Missions.

40. Lusk to Zitkala-Ša, August 31, 1910, Bureau of Catholic Indian Missions.

41. Zitkala-Ša to Ketcham, January 5, 1911, Bureau of Catholic Indian Missions.

42. Ketcham to Zitkala-Ša, January 17, 1911, Bureau of Catholic Indian Missions. Ketcham did write the bishop next day, enclosing Zitkala-Ša's letters and reminding him that "matters of this kind, when they are referred to this Bureau, cannot be ignored." Ketcham to Lawrence Scanlan, bishop of Salt Lake City, January 18, 1911, Bureau of Catholic Indian Missions.

43. Zitkala-Ša to Ketcham, January 29, 1911, Bureau of Catholic Indian Missions.

44. Ketcham to Zitkala-Ša, February 8, 1911, Bureau of Catholic Indian Missions.

45. Zitkala-Ša to Kenel, March 6, 1911, Bureau of Catholic Indian Missions.

46. Kenel to Ketcham, March 18 and March 24, 1911, Bureau of Catholic Indian Missions.

47. Zitkala-Ša to Kenel, March 25, 1911, Bureau of Catholic Indian Missions.

48. Zitkala-Ša to Lusk, June 21, 1912, Bureau of Catholic Indian Missions. Here, Zitkala-Ša writes of how she and her husband were treated almost like criminals when they had to move out of BIA housing and were forced to account for every item on a list of government property that they themselves had furnished.

49. Zitkala-Ša to Kenel, March 25, 1911, Bureau of Catholic Indian Missions. For unknown reasons Oran Curry is not mentioned as living with the Bonnins in this letter. Also see R. Bonnin to Ketcham, April 5, 1911, Bureau of Catholic Indian Missions. Here Bonnin states regarding the job offer in California, "At that time my business affairs were so unsettled that I could not avail myself of the pleasure of accepting."

50. Zitkala-Ša to Ketcham, April 5, 1911, Bureau of Catholic Indian Missions. It is possible that Father Martin died shortly after this date, though his date of death has been hard to uncover. An article in the *Indian Sentinel* (a Catholic publication) from 1923 explains that the small town of Kenel, North Dakota, was named after him and the Benedictine mission he established. See "Catholic Sioux Congress of South Dakota: Indian Hospitality and Faith," *Indian Sentinel* 3, no. 4 (October 1923): 147.

51. Ketcham to Zitkala-Ša, April 15, 1911, Bureau of Catholic Indian Missions.

52. Zitkala-Ša to Ketcham, April 22, 1911, Bureau of Catholic Indian Missions.
53. Zitkala-Ša to Ketcham, May 28, 1911, Bureau of Catholic Indian Missions.
54. Ketcham to Zitkala-Ša, June 6, 1911, Bureau of Catholic Indian Missions.
55. Zitkala-Ša to Ketcham, October 16, 1911, Bureau of Catholic Indian Missions.
56. Ketcham to Zitkala-Ša, November 21, 1911; Ketcham to Scanlan, November 21, 1911, Bureau of Catholic Indian Missions.
57. R. Bonnin to Ketcham, February 8, 1912, Bureau of Catholic Indian Missions.
58. Ketcham to R. Bonnin, February 21, 1912, Bureau of Catholic Indian Missions.
59. Zitkala-Ša to Ketcham, May 7/28, 1912, Bureau of Catholic Indian Missions. The letter appears to have been begun on May 7, then completed on May 28: on the typewritten letter, the latter date is handwritten under the typewritten May 7. At the letter's end, Zitkala-Ša also writes, "Therefore, Mr. Bonnin resigned to take effect May 27, 1912, which was yesterday."
60. McDonnell, *Dispossession of the American Indian*, 87–89.
61. Zitkala-Ša to Ketcham, May 7/28, 1912.
62. Lusk to Zitkala-Ša, June 14, 1912; chief clerk, Department of the Interior [signature illegible] to Lusk, June 15, 1912, Bureau of Catholic Indian Missions.
63. Zitkala-Ša to Lusk, June 21, 1912, Bureau of Catholic Indian Missions.
64. Lusk to Zitkala-Ša, December 12/18(?), 1912. Bureau of Catholic Indian Missions. (A typing error seems to have been made on the date, and it is unclear which one is correct.) Lusk writes, "It has just been decided that Mr. Bonnin is eligible for reinstatement in the Indian Office" and encourages him to apply. Zitkala-Ša to Ketcham, March 2, 1913, loc. cit., mentions that Bonnin was again working as a clerk.
65. Zitkala-Ša to Ketcham, August 28, 1912, Bureau of Catholic Indian Missions.

5. The Sun Dance Opera *and the Peyote "Menace"*

1. Hanson, *Sun Dance Land*, 78–80, 92.
2. Maddox, *Citizen Indians*, 197.
3. See Catherine Parsons Smith, "An Operatic Skeleton on the Western Frontier: Zitkala-Ša, William H. Hanson, and *The Sun Dance Opera*," *Women and Music* 5 (January 2001): 1–30, for a full account. As Smith points out, Hanson revised and expanded the score significantly for the opera's 1938 revival in New York. During the more than two decades since the original performance he clearly improved his skills as a composer, likely due to further study he undertook in Chicago in the 1920s. Afterward, he returned to take up a post at Brigham Young University in Provo. Also see Hafen, "Cultural Duet," 109.
4. William Hanson, *Sun Dance Land*, vi–vii, 62–114. Hanson also provides a quotation that may reveal the idiosyncrasy of Zitkala-Ša's Catholicism: "Our super controlled lives [referring to Natives] are constantly being helped and deterred by mystic beings, good or evil spirits, who also occupy the wonderland around us. Spirits of this wonderworld, sometimes our deceased relatives, or heroes of past mortal lives, come to us in visions or in controlled events. Old friends eagerly await the arrival of deceased humans at the Happy Hunting Grounds. Our forefathers live there" (114). This quotation is largely in keeping with Zitkala-Ša's public and private writings and general style of expression. Newmark's research has also revealed Zitkala-Ša's later interest in Christian Science and the Theosophy movement, as well as her interest in the Book of Mormon's accounts of Indians. See Newmark, "Pluralism, Place, and Gertrude Bonnin's Counternativism," 344–45. Returning to *Sun Dance Land*, other information of note includes R. Bonnin's original suggestion that the opera be based on the life of Old Sioux, or on Chipeta, the widow of Chief Ouray and an

important figure on the Uintah and Ouray Reservation at that time (74). In one compelling but very suspicious episode, Hanson records Zitkala-Ša telling an indigenous story about a great eagle—oddly, in the kind of broken English typical of a 1950s western (presumably to give an "authentic" feel). Toward the end she becomes too emotional to finish, and begins to weep. If true, this story might indicate the depth of her emotional connection to Sioux culture, but one is forced to look askance at Hanson's idiotic conjecture that the story's true meaning is that Old Sioux is Zitkala-Ša's father! *Sun Dance Land's* frustrating narrative is also hampered by Hanson's racist characterization of Old Sioux, who in addition to the misadventures detailed earlier, tries to blow out lightbulbs in the Vernal Opera House, after mistaking them for daylight then deciding they must be fire. "Me no savy" [sic], he sheepishly admits (78–79). Hanson's papers do contain a series of more plausible notes detailing the story of Old Sioux. They are used as source material in Dominguez, "Gertrude Bonnin Story." However, Hanson's account in *Sun Dance Land* appears so insulting, unreliable, and concocted as to defy credibility.

5. Hanson, *Sun Dance Land*, 2, emphasis added. Also see Hafen, "Cultural Duet," 103. Hafen writes that Zitkala-Ša undertook the project in order to "affirm her Sioux cultural identity and to engage the conventions of popular culture," while the well-meaning Hanson used the opera to express "his fondness for Indian peoples," but unconsciously perpetrated "artistic colonialism." Both Hafen and Catherine Parsons Smith (in "Operatic Skeleton on the Western Frontier") have noted tensions in the collaboration, specifically regarding each participant's motivations.

6. Joseph G. Jorgenson, *The Sun Dance Religion: Power for the Powerless* (Chicago: University of Chicago Press, 1972), 16–18.

7. Thomas E. Mails, *Sundancing: The Great Sioux Piercing Ritual* (Tulsa, Okla.: Council Oaks Books, 1998), 7, 13–14.

8. See Maroukis, *Peyote and the Yankton Sioux*, 20–21; Mails, *Sundancing*, 14.

9. Davidson and Norris, introduction to *American Indian Stories*, xx–xxi.

10. Jorgenson, *Sun Dance Religion*, 17–19, quotation on 7.

11. Smith, "Operatic Skeleton on the Western Frontier."

12. David Glassberg, *American Historical Pageantry: The Uses of Tradition in the Early Twentieth Century* (Chapel Hill: University of North Carolina Press, 1990), 84–85, quotation on 114.

13. Smith, "Operatic Skeleton on the Western Frontier."

14. Shari Huhndorf, "American Indian Drama and the Politics of Performance" in *The Columbia Guide to American Indian Literatures of the United States since 1945*, edited by Eric Cheyfitz (New York: Columbia University Press 2006), 308. The Omaha ethnologist Francis La Flesche also collaborated on an opera, *Da-o-ma*, with librettist Nelle Richmond Eberhart and composer Charles Wakefield Cadman beginning in 1908. The stormy collaboration lasted four years but the opera was never completed. See James W. Parins and Daniel F. Littlefield, Jr., introduction to *Ke-ma-ha: The Omaha Stories of Francis La Flesche* (Lincoln: University of Nebraska Press, 1998), xxxi–xxxii.

15. For accounts of *The Sun Dance Opera's* premiere and content see Susan Rose Dominguez, "Zitkala-Ša (Gertrude Simmons Bonnin), 1876–1938: (Re)discovering the Sun Dance," *American Music Research Journal* 5 (1995): 83–96; Hafen, "Cultural Duet"; Hafen, *Dreams and Thunder;* Smith, "Operatic Skeleton on the Western Frontier"; and Catherine Parsons Smith, "Composed and Produced in the American West, 1912–1913: Two Operatic Portrayals of First Nations Peoples," in *Opera Indigene: Re/presenting First Nations and Indigenous Cultures*, edited by Pamela Karantonis and Dylan Robinson (Burlington, Vt.: Ashgate, 2011), 187–207. Smith, in particular, thoroughly dissects the opera and details the differences between the

early version and the later version that was performed in New York City in 1938. By that time Hanson had expanded the opera to five acts and added the character of a jilted Shoshone maiden. Zitkala-Ša did not participate in the revival and the opera met with limited success. Interestingly, in the New York performance artists of indigenous descent played the leading roles, while the chorus was made up of whites. See Smith, "Operatic Skeleton on the Western Frontier." As an interesting aside the original version of *The Sun Dance Opera* featured music played on a traditional flute that Bonnin had given Zitkala-Ša to celebrate their wedding. See Hafen, "Cultural Duet," 104. Finally, "Winona" is the traditional Sioux name for the firstborn girl.

16. Hanson, *Sun Dance Land*, 82, 88–89, 177. Hanson is inconsistent on the size of the orchestra. On p. 82, he counts sixty musicians. On p. 177, he counts thirty. Also see the review of *The Sun Dance Opera* in *The Crisis* 8, no. 4 (August 1914): 162. It tells of a lecture on "the customs and legends" that inspired the opera.

17. N. L. Nelson, "Braves Aid in Indian Opera at Utah Presentation," *Musical America*, April 26, 1913, quoted in Smith, "Operatic Skeleton on the Western Frontier." Montezuma was not impressed with the ideas behind *The Sun Dance Opera*. He wrote a piece for the Chicago *Record Herald* criticizing the work for celebrating the past. There is apparently no recorded response from Zitkala-Ša. See Welch, "Zitkala-Ša," 118.

18. Dominguez declares the opera a "musical and cultural landmark" that reflects Zitkala-Ša's "dedication to Native traditions," but simultaneously acknowledges that placing the Sun Dance ceremony in an operatic context begs cultural misunderstanding. Even though *The Sun Dance Opera* featured "faithful borrowings from Native tribal cultures," conveying them through "a white cultural prism" is something that should perhaps be viewed "warily." See Dominguez, "Zitkala-Ša (Gertrude Simmons Bonnin)," 94. Smith meanwhile points out that the love triangle at the heart of the opera's plot is largely inauthentic, because men would not have taken part in the Sun Dance for the purpose of winning a bride. In Ute society fathers also did not give away their daughters to suitors, as marriage was viewed as an informal, often temporary arrangement. Ute women and girls not only had autonomy in the sexual realm, but they could also become shamans. Smith also suggests that the Utes may have been unhappy about participating in *The Sun Dance Opera* because they were likely performing for those who had quite recently stolen their land. She does not, however, comment on resentment the Utes might have felt at having to conform to a Sioux version of the ceremony, not their own. See Smith, "Operatic Skeleton on the Western Frontier." Along the same lines but offering a contrasting interpretation, Hafen suggests that "[Zitkala-Ša] and other Native participants may have been blind to the hazards of cultural appropriation, instead asserting their right to perform these dances, songs, and rituals in any venue." Albeit that if performed today the opera would "violate contemporary notions of artistic and tribal sovereignty and religious respect," Hafen argues it could be considered "a political gesture, as it demonstrated the viability of Sioux life and traditions." See Hafen, "Cultural Duet," 109.

19. Jorgenson, *Sun Dance Religion*, 19–23. The article in the *Denver Republican*, dated July 3, 1911, claimed that three hundred people took part in the Sun Dance. The article reveals what may have been a common dynamic: "The young braves who have attended different Indian schools throughout the country think themselves above the customs of their fathers and many refuse to go through the torturous labors of the sun dance." Those refusing to participate "were branded 'squaw men' and have been ruled out of the councils of the tribe." Only five years previously the Sun Dance had been kept secret, with only reservation officials observing. But as economic desperation prevailed, the Utes had become—at least according to the article—aware the potential economic benefit of their ceremony: "As the

spirit of money making invaded the reservation the Utes became more and more open with their dance and this year it was viewed by scores of soldiers from Fort Duchesne and by cowboys from miles around who were admitted at the rate of $1 apiece. The degeneration of the red men is not so complete, however, that they will allow pictures to be taken of their dance and before they could secure a place in the sacred area of the dance every visitor was searched for a camera." Whether the religious motivation had really been corrupted by money making can be questioned, as can the reporter's claim that the younger generation disapproved of the Sun Dance and had to be forced into participating. As Jorgenson points out, white prejudice often assumed that Indians who had attended boarding school happily threw off their old ways. Also, traditionally no one was forced to participate, though female shamans did encourage dancers to prepare and exert themselves for the betterment of the tribe.

20. Simmons, *Ute Indians of Utah, Colorado, and New Mexico*, 242–43.

21. See Hafen, "Zitkala-Ša," 38–39. Hafen suggests that Zitkala-Ša's goal may have been "elevating Native arts to the pinnacle of Western civilization—in this case, romantic opera."

22. Jorgenson, *Sun Dance Religion*, 23.

23. Omer C. Stewart, *Peyote Religion: A History* (Norman: University of Oklahoma Press, 1987), 178–80, 197, 201; Simmons, *Ute Indians of Utah, Colorado, and New Mexico*, 241. Stewart writes that "time has proved Sam Lone Bear to be lawless, immoral, exploitative, overbearing, acquisitive, and dishonest—a real scalawag. Among his sins were the exploitation of many young women and girls; the use of his position as a roadman and supplier of peyote to extract money and goods from peyotists; nonpayment of debts; the sale of cheap, ten-cent-store articles at inflated prices, claiming them to be possessed of magical properties; the performance of sleight-of-hand tricks in peyote meetings, claiming them to be manifestations of the supernatural; and just plain stealing and lying" (178).

24. See Zitkala-Ša to Arthur C. Parker, November 11, 1916, SAI Papers. Here, Zitkala-Ša gives a firsthand account.

25. Simmons, *Ute Indians of Utah, Colorado, and New Mexico*, 241–43.

26. Vittorio Lanternari, *The Religions of the Oppressed: A Study of Modern Messianic Cults*, trans. Lisa Sergio (New York: Mentor Books, 1963), 65–67. Peyote is a small, carrot-shaped cactus that grows primarily within and south of the Rio Grande Valley. Its round top, or "button," can be eaten raw, dried, or mixed into a tea. When ingested, the alkaloids—among them mescaline, anhaline, and lophophorine—cause physiological effects, including the sensation of levitation, visual and auditory hallucinations, and heightened powers of perception. Nausea is a possible side effect, though no long-term physiological damage results. The button is neither addictive nor classified as a narcotic.

27. Hesham R. El-Seedi et al, "Prehistoric Peyote Use: Alkaloid Analysis and Radiocarbon Dating of Archaeological Specimens of *Lophophora* from Texas," *Journal of Ethnopharmacology* 101, no. 3 (2005): 238.

28. Lanternari, *Religions of the Oppressed*, 66–67.

29. Weston LaBarre, *The Peyote Cult* (Norman: University of Oklahoma Press, 1989), 43–56.

30. Lanternari, *Religions of the Oppressed*, 67, 97–100.

31. Hertzberg, *Search for an American Indian Identity*, 311, 280–81.

32. Quoted in Stewart, *Peyote Religion*, 197. Exactly who this Standing Bear was is unclear. In a letter to Arthur C. Parker (November 11, 1916, SAI Papers) Zitkala-Ša mentions that Standing Bear was fifty-six years old when he came to Uintah. Therefore he could not have been either Oglala Chief Henry Standing Bear or the Oglala writer and intellectual Luther Standing Bear.

33. Simmons, *Ute Indians of Utah, Colorado, and New Mexico*, 241–42. Simmons also discusses Lone Bear's bad reputation and predilection for very young girls. She also records that the first Ute to use peyote was likely a man named Buckskin Charlie, who was introduced to the drug in the 1890s while visiting the Cheyenne and Arapahoe Reservation. He evidently never sought to broaden its use to his own people, however.

34. See Zitkala-Ša to Parker, November 11, 1916.

35. Lone Bear would travel for the rest of his days, sometimes returning to Utah. See Stewart, *Peyote Religion*, 178, 200–201; *Hearings before the Senate Subcommittee of the Committee of Indian Affairs of the House of Representatives on H.R. 2614, to Amend Sections 2139 and 2140 of the Revised Statutes and the Acts Amendatory thereof, and for Other Purposes* (Washington, D.C.: Government Printing Office, 1918), 125–28; Davidson and Norris, introduction to *American Indian Stories*, xxii; Newmark, "Pluralism, Place, and Gertrude Bonnin's Counternativism," 328. My use of "menace" is in reference to Zitkala-Ša's 1916 pamphlet *The Menace of Peyote*, which detailed what she saw as the "indiscriminate use" of the drug, its negative impact on infant mortality and crime rates, and the "moral and physical degeneracy" it encouraged. The General Federation of Women's Clubs subsidized its publication. See Zitkala-Ša, "Menace of Peyote," in Davidson and Norris, *American Indian Stories*, 241.

6. New Opportunities, New Trials

1. See Spack, "Dis/engagement," 201. Spack notes that Peter Iverson argues Zitkala-Ša had this delayed influence on Montezuma in the biography, *Carlos Montezuma and the Changing World of American Indians* (Albuquerque: University of New Mexico Press, 1982), 38.

2. Hertzberg, *Search for an American Indian Identity*, 32.

3. Speroff, *Carlos Montezuma, MD*, 333–34.

4. John W. Larner, "Society of American Indians," in *Native America in the Twentieth Century: An Encyclopedia*, edited by Mary B. Davis (New York: Garland, 1994), 603.

5. Hertzberg, *Search for an American Indian Identity*, 36. At the last minute Montezuma decided not to attend the first meeting because he felt the Indian Bureau was trying to influence the founding conference. See Speroff, *Carlos Montezuma, MD*, 333–34, 339.

6. "Society of American Indians," *Native American Encyclopedia*, http://nativeamerican encyclopedia.com/society-of-american-indians/ (accessed October 23, 2012).

7. Larner, "Society of American Indians," 604.

8. "Platform of the Third Annual Conference of the Society of American Indians," SAI Papers.

9. Larner, "Society of American Indians," 604.

10. Hertzberg, *Search for an American Indian Identity*, 93, 96.

11. Speroff, *Carlos Montezuma, MD*, 338.

12. Hertzberg, *Search for an American Indian Identity*, 37.

13. See "The Objects of the Society," a flyer in the SAI Papers.

14. Speroff, *Carlos Montezuma, MD*, 334.

15. Hertzberg, *Search for an American Indian Identity*, 40–41. Eastman was not initially allowed to attend to the survivors at Wounded Knee. Reservation authorities made him wait three days. For information on Eastman's early schooling, see Michael C. Coleman, "Motivations of Indian Children at Missionary and U.S. Government Schools," *Montana: The Magazine of Western History* 40 (Winter 1990): 30.

16. David Reed Miller, "Charles Alexander Eastman, The 'Winner': From Deep Woods to Civilization," in *American Indian Intellectuals*," edited by Margot Liberty (St. Paul, Minn.: West, 1978), 61–70.

17. Larner, "Society of American Indians," 603.

18. Welch, "Zitkala-Ša," 104; for more on women's contributions to the society, see 103–109.

19. Hoxie, *This Indian Country*, 231–32.

20. Hertzberg, *Search for an American Indian Identity*, 60–61, 65.

21. See Maddox, *Citizen Indians*, 193. The quotation is in a letter from Arthur C. Parker to J. N. B. Hewitt, dated August 30, 1913.

22. Laura Cornelius Kellogg's *Our Democracy and the American Indian: A Comprehensive Presentation of the Indian Situation as It Is Today* (Kansas City, Mo.: Burton, 1920) harshly criticized white society for its treatment of Natives and offered "a practical plan based on real values, with the singleness of purpose of bringing new life to a whole people" (10).

23. Deloria, "Four Thousand Invitations," 39; Speroff, *Carlos Montezuma, MD*, 239; Welch, "Zitkala-Ša," 130–31.

24. Speroff, *Carlos Montezuma, MD*, 234. Also see, for instance, Zitkala-Ša to Montezuma, June 23, 1913 (Montezuma Papers), in which she sends regrets at being unable to attend the 1913 SAI conference in Denver due to her many household duties.

25. Zitkala-Ša to Ketcham, October 4, 1913, Bureau of Catholic Indian Missions.

26. Zitkala-Ša to Ketcham, March 2, 1913, Bureau of Catholic Indian Missions.

27. Ketcham to Zitkala-Ša, March 11, 1913, Bureau of Catholic Indian Missions.

28. Zitkala-Ša to Ketcham, March 19, 1913, Bureau of Catholic Indian Missions.

29. See Zitkala-Ša to Ketcham, October 4, 1913, Bureau of Catholic Indian Missions.

30. Zitkala-Ša to Montezuma, May 13, 1913, Montezuma Papers.

31. Speroff, *Carlos Montezuma, MD*, 234, 399.

32. Zitkala-Ša to Montezuma, May 13, 1913, Montezuma Papers. The line, "I humbly beg your forgiveness for my gross stupidity of my former years—which was not relived by my misfortune to lose what I could not replace," appears to be an allusion to the lost engagement ring.

33. Zitkala-Ša to Montezuma, June 23, 1913, Montezuma Papers.

34. Ketcham to Zitkala-Ša, March 27, 1913, Bureau of Catholic Indian Missions.

35. Dominguez, "Gertrude Bonnin Story," 221.

36. Zitkala-Ša to Montezuma, June 23, 1913, Montezuma Papers.

37. The information on the Bonnins' marital difficulties is contained in Zitkala-Ša's letter to Ketcham, dated October 4, 1913, Bureau of Catholic Indian Missions. As for Mrs. Burton, she seems to have had a talent for irritating others. Zitkala-Ša *and* the Episcopalians disliked her. Both parties evidently took offense at her unsociable nature, and Zitkala-Ša complained that she dressed shabbily though she had enough money not to work. See the same letter.

38. Zitkala-Ša to Ketcham, October 4, 1913, Bureau of Catholic Indian Missions. Father Poirier was very intent on helping the Bonnins and spreading Catholicism among the Utes, though he knew funding considerations would make establishing a mission difficult. See Poirier to Ketcham, November 22, 1913, Bureau of Catholic Indian Missions.

7. In the Society of American Indians

1. Welch, "Zitkala-Ša," 94.

2. *Wagner Post*, January 1, 1915, 5. The obituary states that "the grandsons of the deceased acted as pallbearers for the occasion." It is not clear that Ohiya was one of them because the only surviving children mentioned in the obituary are David Simmons and Peter St. Pierre, the latter of which had been caring for his mother before her death.

Zitkala-Ša is not mentioned. A letter from Arthur C. Parker to Zitkala-Ša (November 5, 1915, SAI Papers) states, "I am in receipt of your registered parcel containing the papers relating to your claim to a share of your mother's property." Parker promises to "make a more detailed study of the case." No other correspondence available refers to the matter.

3. "Obituary of Joseph B. Bonnin," 1. After a service in Wagner's Masonic Hall, Bonnin's remains were taken to Greenwood for another service in the Episcopal church. Raymond Bonnin is mentioned in the obituary along with his three brothers and one half-sister.

4. Hanson, *Sun Dance Land*, 99–100. Hanson, revealing his prejudices, goes on to say, "Mr. Kneale was Uintah Indian Agent for many years, during which time considerable progress was made in better living and education of the red men. Many families located on their allotments and acquired modern habits of living. Some of the Utes continued their wanderlust habits and roamings, but the raids, the pilferings, and the lawlessness of the oldtimers were absent and forgotten. The presence of whiteman neighbors began to influence and convert the natives to the philosophy and ways of civilization. However, this was a slow process."

5. Zitkala-Ša, "A Year's Experience in Community Service Work among the Ute Tribe of Indians," *American Indian Magazine* 4 (October–November 1916): 307–308.

6. "Program for the Fifth Annual Conference of the Society of American Indians," SAI Papers. Arthur C. Parker invited President Wilson to attend the conference. Wilson (certainly through some underling) responded, asking Parker to "convey . . . my warm greetings to the conference and an expression of my very great interest in everything that affects the welfare and advancement of the American Indians." See President Woodrow Wilson to Arthur C. Parker, September 24, 1915, SAI Papers. Father Ketcham also received an invitation, as he did to the 1914 gathering. See Parker to Ketcham, February 2, 1914, and August 25, 1915, SAI Papers. Pratt was specifically asked to suggest topics for discussion at the conference. Parker proposed the theme of "Responsibility for the Red Man." See Parker to Pratt, April 23, 1915, SAI Papers. Also see Welch, "Zitkala-Ša," 94–95, 100.

7. "The Bulletin Board," *Quarterly Journal of the Society of American Indians* 4 (1915): 274.

8. "The Society of American Indians Fifth Annual Platform, Adopted at Lawrence Kansas, Oct. 2nd, 1915," SAI Papers.

9. Arthur C. Parker to Zitkala-Ša, August 10, 1915, SAI Papers.

10. Zitkala-Ša to Parker, August 18, 1915, SAI Papers.

11. Parker to Zitkala-Ša, August 23, 1915, SAI Papers.

12. Parker to Zitkala-Ša, November 5, 1915, SAI Papers. The letter also indicates there were already problems with Agent Kneale. Parker wrote, "Mr. Kneale may smile at your plan and give it a patronizing pat, but it is destined, I believe to become a power, that even he will be glad to recognize as an influence." Parker may have had too much faith in Kneale. Unfortunately, there is no letter by Zitkala-Ša on file in the SAI Papers that describes Kneale's behavior at this time.

13. Larner, "Society of American Indians," 604, quotation in Davidson and Norris, introduction to *American Indian Stories*, xxv.

14. Zitkala-Ša, "The Indian's Awakening," *American Indian Magazine* 4 (January–March 1916): 57–59.

15. Speroff, *Carlos Montezuma, MD*, 239. Zitkala-Ša's approach to the past certainly contrasted with that of Montezuma, who often proclaimed himself against what he termed "Indianism"; that is, looking to preserve indigenous cultures and languages. See Maddox, *Citizen Indians*, 121.

16. Zitkala-Ša to Parker, December 20, 1915, SAI Papers.

17. Zitkala-Ša to Parker, February 25, 1916, SAI Papers.

18. Zitkala-Ša to Parker, December 25, 1915, SAI Papers.

19. Ibid.

20. Zitkala-Ša to Parker, December 20, 1915, SAI Papers.

21. Willard, "First Amendment," 31.

22. Zitkala-Ša to Parker, December 25, 1915, SAI Papers.

23. Hertzberg, *Search for an American Indian Identity*, 151. Apparently the community center was repurposed because the need for clothing was less urgent when the weather improved in the spring.

24. Zitkala-Ša, "A Year's Experience in Community Service Work," 310.

25. Simmons, *Ute Indians of Utah, Colorado, and New Mexico*, 224–29.

26. See Zitkala-Ša, "Chipeta, Widow of Chief Ouray with a Word about a Deal in Blankets," *American Indian Magazine* 5 (July–September 1917): 168–70.

27. Zitkala-Ša to Parker, May 28, 1916, SAI Papers. Parker wrote back, promising to "endeavor to find out what became of the Ute matter" in Washington, but does not seem to have followed up. See Parker to Zitkala-Ša, June 7, 1916, SAI Papers. Zitkala-Ša's use of "Poor Lo" was in reference to Alexander Pope's "Essay on Man," line 99. It reads: "Lo, the poor Indian!" S. Alice Callahan (a descendent of Creek Indians) uses this phrase in her novel *Wynema: A Child of the Forest*, edited by A. LaVonne Brown Ruoff (1891; reprint, Lincoln: University of Nebraska Press, 1997), 52, 110.

28. Zitkala-Ša to Parker, June 20, 1916, SAI Papers.

29. Zitkala-Ša to SAI Vice President Estaiene DePeltquestangue, August 22, 1916, quoted in Maddox, *Citizen Indians*, 102.

30. Zitkala-Ša to Parker, August 15, 1916, SAI Papers.

31. Zitkala-Ša to Parker, June 20, 1916, SAI Papers. Parker agreed to the idea of a newsletter, though none was ever published. See Zitkala-Ša to Parker, December 28, 1916, SAI Papers. Here, Zitkala-Ša writes, "I am glad to learn of your plan for a simplified publication for reservation Indians."

32. Zitkala-Ša to Parker, February 25, 1916, SAI Papers. Zitkala-Ša expresses her respect for Parker in a letter to him dated December 21, 1916, SAI Papers. Congratulating him on his election to the SAI presidency, Zitkala-Ša writes, "No one is blessed with the clear vision; terse expression; and untrammeled composure, that you are. . . . you are the only one who can save the organization."

33. Zitkala-Ša, "A Year's Experience in Community Service Work," 310.

34. Speroff, *Carlos Montezuma, MD*, 239, 360; Hertzberg, *Search for an American Indian Identity*, 146–49.

35. See the program for the Sixth Annual Conference of the Society of American Indians, SAI Papers.

36. Hertzberg, *Search for an American Indian Identity*, 146–49.

37. Stewart, *Peyote Religion*, 198. In the summer of 1917, Zitkala-Ša also worked with Brosius to help pass the Gandy Bill. See Zitkala-Ša to Parker, June 11, 1917; Zitkala-Ša to Parker, June 13, 1917, SAI Papers.

38. Zitkala-Ša, "The Menace of Peyote," in Davidson and Norris, *American Indian Stories*, 241.

39. Zitkala-Ša, "The Red Man's America," *American Indian Magazine* 5 (January–March 1917): 64. Zitkala-Ša's artful condemnation of the disenfranchisement of Natives and their lack of freedom in the proverbial "Home of the Free" also spoke to the increasingly prominent issue of Indian citizenship among the reform community, discussed in later chapters. Note that Zitkala-Ša's mocking derision of American inequality, colonization, and hypocrisy, especially within the context of patriotic hymns, was becoming risky by the spring of 1917. See chapter 8, "In Washington at War."

40. "Indian Woman Has Accomplished Much for Uplift of Race," *Cedar Rapids Evening Gazette*, September 27, 1916, 3, quoted in Maddox, *Citizen Indians*, 149–50. The article also incorrectly stated that Zitkala-Ša was a graduate of Earlham and the Boston Conservatory of Music.

41. Davidson and Norris, introduction to *American Indian Stories*, xxvi.

42. Zitkala-Ša to Montezuma, December 10, 1916, Montezuma Papers.

43. Speroff, *Carlos Montezuma, MD*, 361–62.

44. Zitkala-Ša to Commissioner of Indian Affairs Cato Sells, November 14, 1916, SAI Papers.

45. Sells to Zitkala-Ša, December 1, 1916, SAI Papers.

46. Zitkala-Ša to Parker, November 27, 1916, SAI Papers. In this letter Zitkala-Ša added, with her customary humor, "Agent Kneale is not all one would wish of an executive but, we have to 'grin and bear it.' He is like all other agents, with a political drag. I must close my letter, as I seem unable to express myself only in slang phrases."

47. Zitkala-Ša to Parker, December 19, 1916, SAI Papers.

48. Hertzberg, *Search for an American Indian Identity*, 151.

49. Zitkala-Ša to Ketcham, January 29, 1917, Bureau of Catholic Indian Missions.

50. Zitkala-Ša to Parker, December 14, 1916, SAI Papers. Here, Zitkala-Ša mentions that her family lives in "one half of the house that Kneale lives in."

51. Zitkala-Ša to Ketcham, January 29, 1917, Bureau of Catholic Indian Missions. What is remarkable about this letter is that Zitkala-Ša, author of "Why I Am a Pagan," apparently had now decided that hell existed. From reading this letter and others that complain of the Episcopalians, it would also not be untoward to surmise that Zitkala-Ša's later critical statements on Christianity and Christians were motivated by such people. She apparently put Catholics in a different category, exonerating them from Christianity's detrimental effects on the indigenous population; she did the same with Native religions—approving of the Sioux Sun Dance, but condemning Peyotism. By 1917, Zitkala-Ša still had not managed to have a Catholic church established in Uintah. On February 8, 1917, Ketcham wrote her that the new bishop of Salt Lake, Bishop Glass, a "most zealous prelate," might finally help her. But the Bonnins soon moved and nothing came of it. The letter is held in the Bureau of Catholic Indian Missions.

52. Zitkala-Ša to Parker, December 14, 1916, SAI Papers.

53. Zitkala-Ša to Parker, November 11, 1916, SAI Papers.

54. Zitkala-Ša to Parker, December 14, 1916, SAI Papers. Incidentally, William Hanson claims that Old Sioux was buried in full regalia and headdress, but he apparently did not attend the funeral. See Hanson, *Sun Dance Land*, 93.

55. Parker to Zitkala-Ša, January 2, 1917, SAI Papers.

56. Zitkala-Ša to Parker, January 4, 1917, SAI Papers.

57. Zitkala-Ša to Parker, January 10, 1917, SAI Papers.

58. Correspondence between Zitkala-Ša and Parker indicates that the Bonnins arrived in Washington, D.C., in May. See Parker to Zitkala-Ša, May 14, 1917, addressed to Washington, and Zitkala-Ša to Parker, June 2, 1917, written from her new apartment in Washington. The decision to move may have been made in March. In a letter to Zitkala-Ša, dated March 27, 1917 (in the SAI Papers), Parker writes, "The news of your going on to Washington, D.C., is the best I have heard." Later correspondence between the two indicates that Ohiya was living with his parents in Washington. See, for instance, Parker to Zitkala-Ša, October 14, 1917, SAI Papers. An article in the *Friends' Intelligencer* also mentions that in Washington Zitkala-Ša's "husband and son of fourteen are with her for a time," suggesting either that Bonnin may have been soon to leave for military service or that Ohiya was still attending boarding school

for part of the year. The article also identifies Zitkala-Ša as "the granddaughter of the late Sitting Bull." See Marianna Burgess, "Zitkala-Ša (Red Bird)," *Friends' Intelligencer*, May 19, 1917, 313.

8. In Washington at War

1. Zitkala-Ša to Ketcham, February 26, 1917 (posted from Los Angeles), Bureau of Catholic Indian Missions.

2. See Newmark, "Pluralism, Place, and Gertrude Bonnin's Counternativism," 328.

3. Burgess, "Zitkala-Ša (Red Bird)," 313. Judging from her correspondence with Parker, Zitkala-Ša spent the beginning of February through much of March in California, apparently without her family. The trip was partly a vacation. See Parker to Zitkala-Ša, March 2, 1917, SAI Papers. Parker writes, "Let me have some word of encouragement from your California visitation. My hope is that you may have a needed rest." Also see Zitkala-Ša to Parker, March 2, 1917, SAI Papers.

4. See Dominguez, "Gertrude Bonnin Story," 240.

5. Speroff, *Carlos Montezuma, MD*, 362. Zitkala-Ša's SAI correspondence lists this address for the SAI headquarters. See, for instance, her letter to Pratt dated September 4, 1917, Pratt Papers.

6. For another account of the Zitkala-Ša–Baldwin dispute, see Welch, "Zitkala-Ša," 120–32.

7. Zitkala-Ša to Parker, June 2 and 6, 1917, SAI Papers.

8. See Speroff, *Carlos Montezuma, MD*, 239. Zitkala-Ša's suspicions of Father Gordon were so thoroughgoing that she initially refused orders to send him the SAI membership list. She wrote to Parker, "Father Gordon is not supporting this office; he does not even appreciate my sacrifice, to be here; and to be working as I am. Furthermore, he is liable to do mischief with these people who need to be conscientiously guided." Zitkala-Ša to Parker, June 28, 1917, SAI Papers.

9. Zitkala-Ša to Parker, June 28, 1917, SAI Papers. This letter contains a noteworthy complaint about Baldwin's failure to provide information and materials in a timely fashion: "I waited one week for her answer. (At this rate, we will set the world on fire, in the year 900,000)."

10. See, for instance, Zitkala-Ša to Parker, December 7, 1916, SAI Papers.

11. Zitkala-Ša to Parker, December 21, 1916, SAI Papers. Parker agreed, responding, "To divide the office [of secretary-treasurer] is killing the Society. At Lawrence it was insisted that this be done, but in practice the person responsible for the big work must have the cash in hand and momentarily know what is available. You are at present the real executive officer and working force. I am just the president with the general welfare at heart." Parker to Zitkala-Ša, January 2, 1917, SAI Papers.

12. Zitkala-Ša to Parker, January 10, 1917, SAI Papers.

13. Zitkala-Ša to Pratt, September 4, 1917, Pratt Papers.

14. Zitkala-Ša to Parker, June 2, 1917, SAI Papers. Zitkala-Ša reported, "Mrs. Baldwin said: 'I wish I could quit grinding every day; but if I did, I would land in the poor house.' This is impudence itself. I know how far my funds will carry me, in this free service for the Red Man; and I do not intend to land in the Poor House, either."

15. Zitkala-Ša to Parker, September 14, 1917, SAI Papers.

16. Zitkala-Ša to Parker, [September?] 1917, SAI Papers. This letter was likely enclosed with another letter to Parker dated September 19, 1917.

17. Zitkala-Ša to Parker, June 6, 1917, SAI Papers.

18. See Zitkala-Ša to Parker, January 9, 1918, SAI Papers. In this letter Zitkala-Ša expressed her gratitude for Parker's support: "Your generosity, in stating that the secretary's expenses were of the first importance; and should be paid before all others; and that you had so instructed, is only exceeded by your good looks."

19. See, for instance, Zitkala-Ša to Parker, June 21, 1917, and Parker to Zitkala-Ša, July 5, 1917, SAI Papers.

20. Quoted in Speroff, *Carlos Montezuma, MD*, 240.

21. David M. Kennedy, *Over Here: The First World War and American Society* (Oxford: Oxford University Press, 1980), 3–11.

22. Boyer et al., *Enduring Vision*, 663–67.

23. Speroff, *Carlos Montezuma, MD*, 416.

24. Kennedy, *Over Here*, 80.

25. Zitkala-Ša, "A Sioux Woman's Love for Her Grandchild," *American Indian Magazine* 5 (October–December 1917): 230–31.

26. Howard Zinn, *A People's History of the United States* (New York: HarperCollins, 1993), 134.

27. Kennedy, *Over Here*, 145–49.

28. See Thomas A. Britten, *American Indians in World War I: At Home and at War* (Albuquerque: University of New Mexico Press, 1997), 43–44; Maddox, *Citizen Indians*, 114. Estimates are that 50 percent of the Native population were citizens at this time.

29. Zitkala-Ša to Parker, June 20 1917, SAI Papers.

30. Zitkala-Ša to Parker, August 6, 1917, SAI Papers. Here, Zitkala-Ša inquires about Parker's military service: "Seneca, you are as brave as a Sioux! May the Great Spirit ever guard you and protect you! May you so realize His all-pervading Presence that no sense of hardships can crowd Him out of your consciousness, at any time."

31. Zitkala-Ša to DSP (Parker), November 23, 1917, SAI Papers. "DSP" was apparently short for "Dear Seneca President." The letter is signed "SS," or "Sioux Secretary." The letter also reveals that Zitkala-Ša had directly confronted the Commissioner of Indians Affairs about all-Indian regiments. She also attempted to take up the matter with the War Department but was "diverted." DSP and SS also appear on other letters around this time, such as SS to DSP, November 29, 1917, SAI Papers. Regarding Zitkala-Ša's comment about African Americans, Newmark's research shows that she tended to look down on uneducated whites and blacks. In a July 20, 1927, letter to R. Bonnin and Ohiya, Zitkala-Ša writes that on a train trip to Salt Lake City she encountered many "seedy" whites, and "perhaps these black folks were no worse than some of the dirty whites." She also expresses irritation that the blacks were wearing " 'Indian moccasins' (the kind usually sold to tourists by shop keepers) to lounge in!" Quoted in Newmark, "Pluralism, Place, and Gertrude Bonnin's Counternativism," 345.

32. Speroff, *Carlos Montezuma, MD*, 413–14.

33. Larner, "Society of American Indians," 604.

34. Britten, *American Indians in World War I*, 61. Incidentally, the son of SAI founding member Charles Alexander Eastman served in the war.

35. See Speroff, *Carlos Montezuma, MD*, 238; Dominguez, "Gertrude Bonnin Story," 239–40. Dominguez records that Bonnin only joined the SAI in that year, 1917. See Dominguez, "Gertrude Bonnin Story," 270. Also see "Testimonial Talk by Ernest L. Wilkinson at funeral service of Captain Raymond T. Bonnin," Bonnin Collection. In "Editorial Comment," *American Indian Magazine* 6 (July–September 1918): 113–14, Zitkala-Ša lauds the SAI's sacrifices.

36. Zitkala-Ša to Pratt, September 4, 1917, Pratt Papers.

37. Parker to Zitkala-Ša, July 5, 1917, SAI Papers. Here, Parker gives a monumental list of organizational tasks for Zitkala-Ša to complete in the run-up to the conference, including

writing fifty to one hundred Oklahoma Indians, sending a letter to everyone in the SAI membership, creating the program, inviting speakers, and reserving hotel space. The letter at least ends with a compliment: "The way you are working is a marvel and your loyal sacrifices and steadfast devotion is an inspiration to me."

38. Zitkala-Ša to Parker, September 19, 1917, SAI Papers.

39. Zitkala-Ša to My dear fellow-member, September 27, 1917, SAI Papers.

40. Speroff, *Carlos Montezuma, MD*, 362–63.

41. "Mrs. Bonnin Speaks," *Tomahawk*, December 6, 1917, 1.

42. Quoted in Speroff, *Carlos Montezuma, MD*, 363. Also see Hoxie, *This Indian Country*, 263. *Wassaja* was founded in 1916 and bore the subtitle "Let My People Go"—a reference to Montezuma's famous speech at the 1915 SAI conference in which he dramatically called for the abolition of the BIA. See Speroff, *Carlos Montezuma, MD*, 347–54. Zitkala-Ša subscribed to *Wassaja*. See Welch, "Zitkala-Ša," 147. Wassaja (Signaling, or Beckoning) was Montezuma's birth name. See Speroff, *Carlos Montezuma, MD*, 1.

43. See Britten, *American Indians in World War I*, 62. Parker's declaration of war was in part motivated by the fact that sixteen Onondagas had been participating in a German Wild West show in 1914. Some of the group were stranded in Essen, Germany, where they were verbally and physically assaulted by mobs as they tried to leave. In an odd (and today laughable) debacle some were arrested as Russian and Serbian spies. The incident angered both the Onondagas and the Oneidas, and declarations of war followed. Through their declaration, the Onondagas hoped also to strengthen their claims to tribal sovereignty. Also see Larner, "Society of American Indians," 604. Parker alludes to his spying in a letter to Zitkala-Ša: "Sometime, when the war is over, perhaps I will be able to tell you about my special work." Parker to Zitkala-Ša, July 11, 1918, SAI Papers.

44. Britten, *American Indians in World War I*, 177–78. As Britten records, neither bill protected Indian interests. Both insisted on "competency tests" and the forfeiture of communally owned property.

45. Zitkala-Ša, "Editorial Comment," *American Indian Magazine* 6 (July–September 1918): 113–14.

46. Zitkala-Ša, "Indian Gifts to Civilized Man," *American Indian* Magazine 6 (July–September 1918): 115–16.

47. Speroff, *Carlos Montezuma, MD*, 415. The main benefit of war participation was that the BIA, after discouraging Indian dances and celebrations during the war, relaxed the prohibition when soldiers returned. This became part of a rejuvenation of indigenous customs that allowed the young to experience repressed traditions and rituals for the first time. See Britten, *American Indians in World War I*, 149.

48. Hoxie, *This Indian Country*, 263. Montezuma's league called on "staunch Americans, lovers of liberty and haters of Prussian methods of government" to rally to his cause. He was supported by SAI luminaries Sloan and Eastman.

49. Speroff, *Carlos Montezuma, MD*, 420.

50. Ibid., 422.

51. Kennedy, *Over Here*, 85–86.

52. Quotations in Maddox, *Citizen Indians*, 192. Also see Speroff, *Carlos Montezuma, MD*, 420–27.

53. Zitkala-Ša to Parker, July 28, 1917, SAI Papers.

54. On organizational matters see Parker to Zitkala-Ša, April 8, 1918, and Zitkala-Ša to Parker, April 23 and May 10, 1918, SAI Papers. For the slogan quoted see Zitkala-Ša to "Dear fellow member," July 25, 1918, SAI Papers. Also see Hafen, introduction to *Dreams and Thunder*, xx, xxiv.

55. Zitkala-Ša to Parker, July 25, 1918, SAI Papers.

56. Zitkala-Ša to Parker, September 5, 1918, SAI Papers.

57. Speroff, *Carlos Montezuma, MD,* 242.

58. Parker to Zitkala-Ša, July 11, 1918, SAI Papers. Regarding organizational matters, Parker writes, "It is regretted that there are so few workers this year, and for whatever cause it may be. My own case is typical: throughout this year I shall be tied to imperative duties that will not even release me for the Conference."

59. Hertzberg, *Search for an American Indian Identity,* 175; Speroff, *Carlos Montezuma, MD,* 242.

60. Zitkala-Ša to Parker, October 3, 1918, SAI Papers. Here, Zitkala-Ša lists the newly elected SAI officers. Her name appears on the letterhead as "Secretary-Treasurer." (She must have had new stationery printed immediately.) Zitkala-Ša also writes that if Parker cannot continue as "Editor-General" of the *American Indian Magazine,* the attending SAI members at the conference have voted that she should replace him. Parker replied, "I am afraid it will be difficult for me to serve as Editor since the making up of a magazine is work that can only be done in one office." He suggested that Zitkala-Ša take the job. Referring to the removal of Baldwin from her post, Parker added, "It is splendid that you are now able to work without being hampered." Parker to Zitkala-Ša, October 14, 1918, SAI Papers.

61. Zitkala-Ša to Father Phillip Gordon, October 14, 1918, Montezuma Papers.

62. Zitkala-Ša to Montezuma, December 6, 1918, Montezuma Papers. Zitkala-Ša added, "Mrs. Baldwin lost the Cash Box last winter! it develops—I suppose—All's well that ends well!" These sentiments, along with those quoted in the chapter, were expressed in a handwritten postscript.

63. Zitkala-Ša wrote to Montezuma that she had wired many other SAI members, urging them to send telegrams to Wilson. Though she recognized the effort was likely futile, she agreed with Montezuma that "these wires could do no harm, and may do a great good for the Indian race." She also seemed to be laying plans for the BIA's abolition, suggesting that a bill be drafted stating that Indians would not lose any rights and separate nations would retain their monies once the agency was no more. "With these good ideas carefully worked out and drafted into a bill and urged upon the country and Congress at this psychological time, it does seem like we have more hope for the emancipation of the Red Man in America than ever before." See Zitkala-Ša to Montezuma, December 6, 1918, Montezuma Papers.

64. Zitkala-Ša, telegram to Wilson, November 25, 1918, Montezuma Papers. Unfortunately, the telegram had deteriorated significantly before it was copied onto microfilm. The only legible words are "[Presid]ent Wilson immediately we wish representation world . . . [conf]erence."

65. See Zitkala-Ša, "Editorial Comment," *American Indian Magazine* 6 (Winter 1919): 161–62. Britten also notes that Zitkala-Ša's push for Indian participation in the Paris Peace Conference might have inspired others. He writes, "Though unsuccessful, her actions may have prompted those taken a few years later by Iroquois leaders in Canada, who hoped that an appeal to the League of Nations and the International Court of Justice at The Hague might lead to improvements for the native peoples residing north of the United States. In December of 1923, the *New York Times* reported that a delegation of sixteen Arapahos from Wyoming had arrived in Paris to ask the League of Nations to intervene in their behalf with the United States government so that Native Americans 'might have the same rights and privileges as other Americans.'" Britten, *American Indians in World War I,* 168–69.

66. See Hertzberg, *Search for an American Indian Identity,* 175; Speroff, *Carlos Montezuma, MD,* 242.

67. Hoxie, *This Indian Country,* 264.

68. Britten, *American Indians in World War I*, 176.
69. Speroff, *Carlos Montezuma, MD*, 242, 363. Zitkala-Ša wrote to Montezuma regarding the closing, "Since the time I first read about the discontinuance of Carlisle, which came as a great shock to me, I regretted it deeply." Zitkala-Ša to Montezuma, August 26, 1918, Montezuma Papers. Zitkala-Ša also wrote to Frederic Paul Keppel, third assistant secretary of war, in an attempt to argue for Carlisle's continuance. Zitkala-Ša to Keppel, September 6, 1918, Montezuma Papers. Also see Zitkala-Ša, "Secretary's Report in Brief," *American Indian Magazine* 6 (July–September 1918): 122–24.

9. The Peyote Clash

1. Willard, "First Amendment," 30.
2. Hertzberg, *Search for an American Indian Identity*, 254.
3. Quoted in Willard, "First Amendment," 30.
4. Hertzberg, *Search for an American Indian Identity*, 127, 256.
5. Stewart, *Peyote Religion*, 198.
6. Parker to Zitkala-Ša, January 2, 1917, SAI Papers.
7. Zitkala-Ša to Parker, January 12, 1917, SAI Papers.
8. See Zitkala-Ša to Parker, November 11, 1916, SAI Papers. Zitkala-Ša waited at Kneale's office for an hour on the day the party went to Randlette but was unable to see him. She urged Parker to intervene by writing Commissioner Sells for help. In the letter she also, once again, calls the Utes a "benighted people" in need of guidance.
9. Zitkala-Ša to Parker, January 12, 1917, SAI Papers.
10. Zitkala-Ša to Parker, January 10, 1917, SAI Papers. The letter indicates that Zitkala-Ša even put her community center work on hold to continue her anti-peyote campaign. In December, Zitkala-Ša had told Parker a few weeks earlier that a bill banning peyote was about to pass the Utah State Legislature. "However," she wrote, "should the unforeseen take place; and the bill does not pass, it would not kill me. I would work a little harder for the next time." Zitkala-Ša to Parker, December 28, 1916, SAI Papers. The bill did pass. See Willard, "First Amendment," 31.
11. Zitkala-Ša to Parker, December 28, 1916, SAI Papers.
12. Zitkala-Ša, "Chipeta, Widow of Chief Ouray, 168–70. Like the gift of the shawls (see chapter 7), Chipeta's "wild rides" were not fiction. This was a reference to her role in preventing more bloodshed after the Meeker massacre. Zitkala-Ša reports McCook's response to her arguments much like she did in her letter to Parker: "When the Great White Father in Washington sent a letter to me telling me that whisky was bad, I stopped our people from its use. When the Great White Father sent a letter to me telling me that gambling was bad, I forbade our people to play cards. . . . Now the Great White Father has sent me no letter telling me peyote is bad. Therefore, as long as he permits its use, we will continue to use it."
13. See Tim Blevins, ed., *Extraordinary Women of the Rocky Mountain West* (Colorado Springs, Colo.: Pikes Peak: Pikes Peak Library, 2010), 20–21.
14. Maroukis, "Peyote Controversy," 177.
15. Moses, *Indian Man*, 200.
16. Welch, "Zitkala-Ša," 134–35; Zitkala-Ša to Parker, December 7, 1915; Zitkala-Ša to Parker, December 25, 1915, SAI Papers.
17. Willard, "First Amendment," 31; Burgess, "Zitkala-Ša (Red Bird)," 313; Maroukis, *Peyote Road*, 115–16.
18. Davidson and Norris, introduction to *American Indian Stories*, xxiii.
19. Zitkala-Ša to Parker, March 2, 1917, SAI Papers.

20. Parker to Zitkala-Ša, March 12, 1917, SAI Papers. This letter also reveals that Parker was considering ending publication of the *American Indian Magazine* due to lack of funds.

21. Speroff, *Carlos Montezuma, MD*, 240.

22. "Indian Woman in Capital to Fight Growing Use of Peyote Drug by Indians," *Washington Times*, February 17, 1918, 9.

23. Willard, "First Amendment," 29. Parker, in fact, called an emergency conference in Washington, D.C., on February 8–9, to discuss the "Important Indian legislation" in Congress. See Zitkala-Ša to My dear Fellow-member, January 31, 1918, SAI Papers.

24. Zitkala-Ša to Parker, February 19, 1918, SAI Papers.

25. Moses, *Indian Man*, 201–202, 1–18, 22–46, 81–85, 94–96, 160–61.

26. Anthony C. Wallace, "James Mooney (1861–1921) and the Study of the Ghost Dance Religion," in *James Mooney: The Ghost Dance Religion and the Sioux Outbreak of 1890*, edited by Anthony C. Wallace (Chicago: University of Chicago Press, 1970), vi–vii. Sherman Coolidge, a founding member of the SAI, assisted Mooney in his study of the Ghost Dance. See Speroff, *Carlos Montezuma, MD*, 337.

27. James Mooney to Marie Baldwin, December 8, 1914, SAI Papers. Mooney seems always to have had suspicions regarding the SAI. After the subcommittee hearings he wrote to Arthur Parker, claiming that "a large portion of the SAI is Indian only by remote ancestry." Mooney to Parker, October 31, 1918, Pratt Papers.

28. Spack, *America's Second Tongue*, 149.

29. Hertzberg, *Search for an American Indian Identity*, 23–24.

30. *Hearings on H.R. 2614*, 63, 66, 71–72.

31. See Willard, "First Amendment," 30, for this direct quotation; see also Moses, *Indian Man*, 198, 192–205. Moses also implies that Zitkala-Ša was essentially crazy or, in his words, "harried" by many "demons."

32. For discussions of Mooney's Catholicism and belief in similarities between Christianity and Native religions, see Moses, *Indian Man*, 4, 64, 91, 114.

33. *Hearings on H.R. 2614*, 63, 89, 111. Sloan stated, "The effect of the use of peyote among the Omahas has been to make a large number of drunkards decent, sober, honest men." He gave anecdotal cases in support. Ibid., 82–84.

34. Davidson and Norris, introduction to *American Indian Stories*, xxiii. Davidson and Norris have argued that Zitkala-Ša was likely aware of the "tribal mélange" she often donned for public appearances. They cite a letter from Zitkala-Ša to Parker, March 2, 1917, SAI Papers.

35. Moses, *Indian Man*, 200. Somewhat oddly, Welch portrays Mooney's attack as a successful humiliation that left Zitkala-Ša "severely shaken." The basis for this claim is unclear, as there is no evidence (particularly in the transcripts or ensuing congressional reports) indicating Mooney had been in the least victorious. Welch, "Gertrude Simmons Bonnin (Zitkala-Ša)," 45. Two days after Mooney's testimony Zitkala-Ša wrote Parker, "Mooney and [the Omaha ethnologist] Francis La Flesche are defending peyote!!!! Rather lame arguments they use." Zitkala-Ša to Parker, February 23, 1918, SAI Papers.

36. *Hearings on H.R. 2614*, 123–25. Why Zitkala-Ša became obsessed with the "orgy" issue is unclear. The Sun Dance, which she wholeheartedly supported, was often accompanied by pre- and extramarital sex. See Jorgenson, *Sun Dance Religion*, 23. Perhaps she was concerned about the consequences of venereal disease and pregnancy within a population that was already beleaguered by poverty and European viruses, or perhaps as a devout Catholic she disapproved of what she would have probably termed "fornication."

37. Willard, "First Amendment," 27; Stewart, *Peyote Religion*, 178, 195, 201.

38. *Hearings on H.R. 2614*, 124–30, 139, 141–47. Incidentally, when asked whether she was "on good terms" with the Utes, Zitkala-Ša remarked, "I love them; I do not hate them for anything harmful, but I want them saved, if possible." "Saved" was presumably not intended in a strictly religious sense—though in her letters to Ketcham Zitkala-Ša certainly used the word to denote conversion to Catholicism. Zitkala-Ša also mentioned the many warnings she had received about the physical harm she might court by fighting what she called "peyote agents." Undeterred, she insisted, "I would rather sacrifice one life, mine, than the whole of the Indian race." Ibid., 128–30.

39. "Prohibition of the Use of Peyote among Indians," *House Reports: 65th Cong., 2nd Sess. December 3, 1917–November 21, 1918* (Washington, D.C.: Government Printing Office, 1918), 23–26.

40. Zitkala-Ša to Pratt, May 21, 1918, Pratt Papers. The letter shows that Zitkala-Ša had become good friends with Pratt and his wife, spending evenings with the couple in the company of Elaine Eastman (who would later write a hagiography of Pratt). The letter ends. "I wish to thank you for that most enjoyable evening spent in your home. Mrs. Eastman and I had lots of fun going home. She put those big oranges into her coat pockets; one on each side and My! how they stuck out with every step she took."

41. Zitkala-Ša to President Wilson, June 22, 1918, SAI Papers.

42. Zitkala-Ša to Commissioner of Indian Affairs Cato Sells, June 29, 1918, SAI Papers.

43. Sells to Zitkala-Ša, June 31, 1918, SAI Papers.

44. Maroukis, *Peyote and the Yankton Sioux*, 131. Warrior notes that founding the Native American Church "managed to accomplish what the U.S. government was unwilling to allow politically and culturally: internal, self-determined adaptation to a new situation." See Warrior, *Tribal Secrets*, 12.

45. Zitkala-Ša to Pratt, January 29, 1919, Pratt Papers. She enclosed a letter from Mooney to Parker (October 31, 1918, Pratt Papers). It argued for peyote's legitimate use, saying that those within the SAI who testified against it were either ignorant and "not competent to judge" the health of the tribes or had never witnessed a ceremony.

46. Pratt to Montezuma, February 10, 1919, quoted in Moses, *Indian Man*, 211.

47. Willard, "First Amendment," 34–35. The American Indian Religious Freedom Act of 1978 gave full protection to the Peyote religion, among other indigenous religious practices. It was strengthened by the Religious Freedom Restoration Act of 1993 and further amendments in 1994 after the Supreme Court decision in *Employment Division, Department of Human Resources of Oregon v. Smith* (1990). See Randall P. Bezanson, *How Free Can Religion Be?* (Urbana: University of Illinois Press, 2006), 151–86.

48. Moses, *Indian Man*, 204–205, 218; Maroukis, *Peyote Road*, 57.

49. Maroukis, *Peyote Road*, 117–18. These states included Iowa (1924), New Mexico (1929), Wyoming (1929), Idaho (1935), and Texas (1937). Utah's anti-peyote law was repealed in 1935.

50. *Indian Sentinel* 2, no. 4 (October 1920): 172–73.

51. Maroukis, *Peyote and the Yankton Sioux*, 142. Zitkala-Ša also managed to achieve the ban in South Dakota despite the presence of the Native American Church, which was entirely unaware that an anti-peyote law was in the legislative works. See Stewart, *Peyote Religion*, 228.

52. For an assimilationist interpretation of the anti-peyote campaign see Slotkin, *Peyote Religion*, 47, 121. He describes Zitkala-Ša as "a marginal fusionist . . . violently opposed to Indian customs," who sought to "adopt the entire culture of the dominant group" in the hope of "social assimilation" through "White religious organizations." In rejecting everything

Indian and peyote specifically, he claims, Zitkala-Ša displayed true assimilationist lean-
ings, an obeisance to Victorian notions of morality and temperance, and a tacit admission of
white civilization's superiority. For later assimilationist interpretations see Willard, "First
Amendment"; Warrior, *Tribal Secrets;* Maroukis, "Peyote Controversy"; Maroukis, *Peyote
and the Yankton Sioux;* Moses, *Indian Man;* and Lyons, "Incorporation of the Indian Body."
The entrenched narrative of the Christian assimilationist Zitkala-Ša battling Mooney, the
"champion of religious freedom," is arguably a black-and-white rendering not borne out
by the record. Assuming that Zitkala-Ša's religious zeal and relationship with Ketcham
accounted for her quest to ban peyote would offer a neat conclusion. But her lack of interest in the religious aspects of the issue or in interpreting peyote consumption through a
Christian lens refute such interpretations. Granted, the Bonnins' letter to the IRA in 1916
did note that peyote encouraged the Utes to "reject the teachings of Church" (see Stewart,
Peyote Religion, 198), but this was perhaps more of generalization regarding sexual behavior than a call for conversion. Zitkala-Ša always seems to have had specific concerns
over this matter. Just as a simple religion-based analysis of Zitkala-Ša's anti-peyote stance
yields an unsound conclusion, so too does any analysis that puts Zitkala-Ša in the secular
assimilationist camp. Her reasons for fighting peyote use appear distinct from those of
her allies in the full assimilation camp, such as Pratt and the IRA, who saw a ban as just
another step in civilizing the savage. Scholars who defend Zitkala-Ša's alliance with Pratt
and former adversaries usually portray her anti-peyote campaign as a selective rap-
prochement. Such attempts to put a good face on what was in many respects an ugly situation appear to ignore the ring of paternalism and Victorian moral control emanating
from Zitkala-Ša's statements on peyote. Nonetheless, charges that her crusade constituted a ready capitulation to Euro-American civilization and rejection of indigenous cultures are unsubstantiated. See Davidson and Norris, introduction to *American Indian Stories,* xxiv. They characterize her actions as conciliation with a lesser evil, or a means to an
end, citing a piece of paper found in the Bonnin Collection, on which Zitkala-Ša wrote
over and over again a quotation by Abraham Lincoln: "I must stand with anybody that
stands right; stand with him while he is right and part with him when he goes wrong."
Also see Hollrah, "'We Must Be Masters of Our Circumstances,'" 43. Hollrah argues
Zitkala-Ša "sincerely believed that use of peyote would prevent American Indians from
fully participating in their own self-determination," though she admits Zitkala-Ša's requests for governmental control contradict this interpretation. Lastly, see Newmark,
"Pluralism, Place, and Gertrude Bonnin's Counternativism," 343. Newmark also rejects
the notion that Zitkala-Ša "sold out," arguing that she merely accepted "coexistence and
collaboration."

53. Willard, "First Amendment," 25. Also see Newmark, "Pluralism, Place, and Gertrude Bonnin's Counternativism," 328. Newmark's research corroborates this conten-
tion. In a 1917 anti-peyote speech delivered at the Sherman Institute in California (recorded in the *Sherman Bulletin,* April 4) Zitkala-Ša expressed the "perspective that peyote
is not native to Native people." Instead, it is brought to Indians by generically termed
"people" (ironically a fellow Sioux) who "tell them God has sent this to the Indian and
that it will give him visions. It does not give them visions like opium. Peyote is a deadly
poison."

54. Lanternari, *Religions of the Oppressed,* 66–67.

55. Welch writes of Zitkala-Ša's Sioux-centric conception of Indian culture in "Gertrude
Simmons Bonnin (Zitkala-Ša)," 44.

56. Zitkala-Ša to Parker, February 12, 1918, SAI Papers.

10. Forging a Plan of Resistance

1. "Indian Woman in Capital to Fight Growing Use of Peyote," 9.

2. "Urges Full Citizenship for Indians," *New Era–Lancaster*, March 29, 1918.

3. "Spirit of a Sioux Indian Woman, Zitkala-Ša Is Great Influence in Progress of Her Own Race," *New York Evening Post*, July 21, 1919.

4. Zitkala-Ša, "America, Home of the Red Man," *American Indian Magazine* 6 (Winter 1919): 165–66. The Ute grandmother's donation is factual. The seventy-five-year-old woman, named Pe-retta, gave five hundred dollars of her life savings (leaving only thirteen for herself), after hearing the reservation superintendent speak on the Red Cross. Commissioner Sells lauded her, and news of her selfless gift appeared in Indian periodicals. See Britten, *American Indians in World War I*, 137.

5. Zitkala-Ša, "Editorial Comment," *American Indian Magazine* 6 (Winter 1919): 161–62.

6. Zitkala-Ša, "Editorial Comment," *American Indian Magazine* 7 (Spring 1919): 5–9.

7. Zitkala-Ša, "Editorial Comment," *American Indian Magazine* 7 (Summer 1919): 61–63.

8. Zitkala-Ša, "The Coronation of Chief Powhatan Retold," *American Indian Magazine* 6 (Winter 1919): 179–80.

9. Zitkala-Ša, "An Indian Praying on the Hilltop," *American Indian Magazine* 7 (Spring 1919): 92.

10. Zitkala-Ša, "Letter to the Chiefs and Headsmen of the Tribes," *American Indian Magazine* 6 (Winter 1919): 196–97. In her address at the SAI annual conference in 1919, Zitkala-Ša also argued for learning English, not for purposes of assimilation, but for resistance and communication among disparate tribes that all had an interest in an intertribal organization that would fight to secure Native rights. In this sense, she said, English was a "convenience" just like, for example, "a coat." See Zitkala-Ša, "Address by the Secretary-Treasurer, Society of American Indians Annual Convention," *American Indian Magazine* 7 (Summer 1919), reprinted in Davidson and Norris, *American Indian Stories*, 213–18.

11. McDonnell, *Dispossession of the American Indian*, 87–110.

12. Hertzberg, *Search for an American Indian Identity*, 184. Also see Zitkala-Ša to My dear Fellow-Indian, August 21, 1919, SAI Papers. Here, Zitkala-Ša announces the conference dates, location, and theme: "American Citizenship for Indians."

13. Britten, *American Indians in World War I*, 176–78. Approximately 125,000 Natives lacked citizenship at this time. The *New York Times* printed the SAI's public statement on the law's passage: "A grateful government and people will not withhold from the Native American race full rights as free men under the constitution." See "Indian Citizenship," *New York Times*, January 12, 1919, quoted in ibid., 176.

14. Hertzberg, *Search for an American Indian Identity*, 187–88.

15. Hoxie, *This Indian Country*, 265.

16. Maddox, *Citizen Indians*, 51.

17. Hertzberg, *Search for an American Indian Identity*, 185.

18. Zitkala-Ša, "Address by the Secretary-Treasurer," 213–18.

19. Welch, "Zitkala-Ša," 162–64.

20. Zitkala-Ša to Montezuma, September 8, 1919, Montezuma Papers.

21. Zitkala-Ša to Montezuma, March 12, 1919, Montezuma Papers.

22. Zitkala-Ša to Montezuma, October 22, 1918, Montezuma Papers. Here, Zitkala-Ša writes, "Very sad news came today that Dr. Eastman's eldest daughter Irene died of the 'Flu' today. The Dr. has been in New Hampshire a week, being called there by her illness. Mrs. Eastman has just nursed her two daughters through an attack of the Flu; and was herself ill. I feel very sad for the bereaved family."

23. Zitkala-Ša to Montezuma, June 27, 1919, Montezuma Papers. The letter also answered Montezuma's recent criticisms that the SAI was doing too little to influence Congress, specifically regarding a recent appropriations bill that allowed the lease of Indian lands: "I am sure that you never meant to charge me with 'sitting in my office' indifferent to Congressional Acts. You must know in your heart, Dr. Montezuma, that I am and have been working too hard, for my own good but since workers are few; and the field calling for workers, great, I persevere. I am sure you appreciate my effort and you did not mean to discourage me by asking me, individually, to block Congress. You tell me to gather up 'forces' that are not in existence unless they are 'spirits.'"

24. Zitkala-Ša to Montezuma, October 22, 1918, Montezuma Papers.

25. Zitkala-Ša to Parker, May 21, 1919, SAI Papers.

26. Zitkala-Ša to Montezuma, April 28, 1919, Montezuma Papers.

27. Zitkala-Ša to Montezuma, September 8, 1919, Montezuma Papers. Zitkala-Ša wrote, "In the midst of conference work, I had to recheck and learn what names were lost, found them, over 1650 names and addresses. I had to prepare duplicate copies to send them. Now I am informed all the mailing is finished. But you remember clerical help is scarce in this town; and I had to work like a slave! With just one pair of hands, but luckily a giant determination to win out."

28. Hertzberg, *Search for an American Indian Identity*, 188. Upon leaving the SAI, Eastman criticized Sloan for making the organization "a political pressure group with patronage interests." See Raymond Wilson, *Ohiyesa: Charles Eastman, Santee Sioux* (Urbana: University of Illinois Press, 1983), 162.

29. Speroff, *Carlos Montezuma, MD*, 366–67. As SAI president, Sloan supported Harding for U.S. president, hoping to be nominated commissioner of Indian Affairs. It was a bold plan, but believing Indians to be in need of a civilizing force, Harding chose Charles H. Burke, a South Dakota congressman who had a paternalistic attitude toward Indians. See Hoxie, *This Indian Country*, 268.

30. Hoxie, *This Indian Country*, 268.

31. Quoted in Speroff, *Carlos Montezuma, MD*, 235.

32. See Maroukis, "Peyote Controversy," 159–80. Maroukis cites disagreement over the Peyote religion as a primary cause of the society's demise.

33. Quoted in Welch, "Zitkala-Ša," 165.

34. Ibid., 166–67.

35. Davidson and Norris, introduction to *American Indian Stories*, xiii, xxvii. Hayworth Publishing House, based in Washington, D.C., published *American Indian Stories*.

36. "Indian Legends Related: Zitkala-Ša Delights Audience of Children," *Savannah Morning News*, November 12, 1921, Bonnin Collection.

37. Quoted in Lukens, "American Indian Story of Zitkala-Ša," 153.

38. Diana, "Hanging in the Heart of Chaos," 156.

39. Interestingly, Hayworth printed two slightly different versions of *American Indian Stories* in 1921. In one, "Why I Am a Pagan" appears in its original form with its original ending: "If this is Paganism, then at present, at least, I am a Pagan." The second printing retitles the story "The Great Spirit," and concludes: "Here in a fleeting quiet, I am awakened by the fluttering robe of the Great Spirit. To my innermost consciousness the phenomenal universe is a royal mantle, vibrating with His divine breath. Caught in its flowing figures are the spangles and oscillating brilliants of sun, moon, and stars." Zitkala-Ša apparently decided either that the first version was unsuitable for a mainstream, Christian audience, or that the sentiments no longer accurately reflected her feelings. See Spack, *America's Second Tongue*, 162.

40. Zitkala-Ša, "A Dream of Her Grandfather," in *American Indian Stories*, edited by Davidson and Norris, 155–58. While "A Dream of Her Grandfather" can be judged self-celebratory, it contains a valuable message that Sioux women, in their capacity as cultural guardians, have carried on their nation's heritage. Spack argues the piece demonstrates that "as long as there is a female, the Sioux heritage can be preserved, especially if she is the descendant of a great male leader." See Spack, *America's Second Tongue*, 166.

41. Zitkala-Ša, "The Widespread Enigma Concerning Blue-Star Woman," in *American Indian Stories*, edited by Davidson and Norris, 159–82. Spack notes that this is one of the few times when Zitkala-Ša implicates her own people in the crimes perpetrated against them. This aspect of the story amounts to a rare admission that "the United States government depended on indigenous collaborators to diminish traditional power structures and thus subjugate Sioux communities." Spack, *America's Second Tongue*, 168. "Blue-Star Woman" was loosely based on the case of Ellen C. Bluestone, who petitioned for an allotment on the Yankton Reservation under highly questionable circumstances. Zitkala-Ša and her half-brother, David Simmons, attempted to block Bluestone's claim because Bluestone had lived most of her life at Standing Rock, had a white father, and admitted little connection to Yankton. The Yankton Tribal Council even voted to deny Bluestone's enrollment in the tribe. The BIA assistant commissioner E. B. Merritt, in particular, ignored all these protests, and Bluestone received her allotment. Zitkala-Ša and David Simmons were furious. See Welch, "Zitkala-Ša," 174–76.

42. Zitkala-Ša's appeal to the women of America parallels Winnemucca's entire career. Winnemucca, with her *Life Among the Piutes* and public speeches, also cultivated women's groups and sympathetic reformers, often highlighting the plight of Native peoples while reversing America's historical narratives and ideas of civilization. Winnemucca also appeared in Native dress. For a discussion of Winnemucca see Hoxie, *This Indian Country*, 150–80.

43. Zitkala-Ša, "America's Indian Problem," in *American Indian Stories*, edited by Davidson and Norris, 185–95. This essay also appeared in the GFWC magazine *Edict* in December 1921. See Dominguez, "Gertrude Bonnin Story," 251.

44. Welch, "Zitkala-Ša," 178.

45. See Dominguez, "Gertrude Bonnin Story," 252–54, quotations on 253–54.

46. Welch, "Zitkala-Ša," 179; Karen L. Huebner, "An Unexpected Alliance: Stella Atwood, the California Clubwomen, John Collier, and the Indians of the Southwest, 1917–1934," *Pacific Historical Review* 78, no. 3 (January 2009): 350.

47. Dominguez, "Gertrude Bonnin Story," 254; Welch, "Zitkala-Ša," 179.

48. Quoted in Dominguez, "Gertrude Bonnin Story," 252.

49. Hertzberg, *Search for an American Indian Identity*, 200–201.

50. All the following quotations are in Zitkala-Ša, *Americanize the First American*, 1–8. The subject of treaties, introduced in *Americanize the First American*, is later taken up in "The Sioux Claims" (1923), which is discussed in the conclusion. The unpublished polemical history dwells upon the loss of the Black Hills and the treaty violations that led up to the creation of the present reservation system.

51. "Cosmopolitan" is used here in reference to the critical paradigms laid out in Arnold Krupat's *Red Matters: Native American Studies* (Philadelphia: University of Pennsylvania Press, 2002), 1–23. In brief, Krupat divides Indian critical perspectives into nationalism, indigenism, and cosmopolitanism. Nationalists stress sovereignty, indigenists value a connection to the land and nature, and cosmopolitanists seek a greater connection to the world and Indians' rightful place within it. Interestingly, Zitkala-Ša's works at one time or another fulfill the criteria of each perspective, from the nationalism of "The Sioux Claims" and "Our

Sioux People" (see conclusion) to the indigenism of "Why I Am a Pagan" and the cosmopolitanism of *Americanize the First American*.

52. See Bruyneel, "Challenging American Boundaries," 35–36. Bruyneel has taken what could be termed a bicultural view of Zitkala-Ša's citizenship campaign. He comments that she presents two Americas: "the one to which indigenous people claim a long historical and cultural relationship and the one to which they presently seek political access." This dynamic, Bruyneel continues, "makes indigenous people distinct [and] articulates a deeper historical and cultural relationship to this land than can be claimed by those included in the US settler-state project." Although these comments specifically concern Zitkala-Ša's "Editorial Comment" in *American Indian Magazine* 6 (Winter 1919), they can be applied to *Americanize the First American*. From a contemporary perspective, advocating U.S. citizenship for Indians remains controversial. See Warrior, *Tribal Secrets*, 13–14. Warrior seems to implicate Zitkala-Ša in a wayward quest to gain citizenship rather than sovereignty. While this view is ideologically consistent with the anti-assimilationist position, in Zitkala-Ša's historical context citizenship can legitimately be viewed as a route to previously denied governmental protections, allowing for an assertion of Native rights. As John W. Larner argues, U.S. citizenship presented a solution for both assimilationists and those desirous of self-determination, because it enabled the "preservation of tribal polity and property." See Larner, "Society of American Indians," 604.

53. Although *Americanize the First American* does not make this claim explicitly, it is expressed in her unpublished "Our Sioux People." Zitkala-Ša writes, "The Red man claims his human rights. America is strong enough today, let us hope, to put into practice and into her legal records, her moral obligation to the Indian, so that hereafter the Indian shall have legal protection equal to any citizen of the United States." Zitkala-Ša, "Our Sioux People," 11, Bonnin Collection. Also see Katanski *Learning to Write "Indian,"* 165. Katanski writes of how Zitkala-Ša's work was subject to ideological boundaries due to her historical milieu.

54. Zitkala-Ša courted suffrage groups and certainly believed in their cause. See "Indian Woman to Be Speaker: Mrs. Gertrude Bonnin Will Discuss Her Race before Suffragists," *Washington Post*, June 2, 1918, 17. The article notes that her lecture will focus on "The Indian Woman of Today."

11. Oklahoma

1. Willard, "Zitkala-Ša," 13.

2. Charles E. Chapman, *A History of California: The Spanish Period* (New York: Macmillan, 1921), 11, 16–17, 19–20.

3. Zitkala-Ša, "California Indian Trails and Prayer Trees," *San Francisco Bulletin*, 1922. Reprinted in Davidson and Norris, *American Indian Stories*, 250–53. It is entirely possible that by now Zitkala-Ša privately regretted her vociferous support for Indian participation in the war effort. In a report written the same year she complained at length about how Pine Ridge Reservation residents had been abused in the name of patriotism during the war years. Specifically, Cato Sells, then commissioner of Indian Affairs, and E. B. Merritt, assistant commissioner, had forced them to sign contracts leasing their land for cattle ranching. The white ranchers not only violated the contract's requirement to fence their animals, but also refused to make promised lease payments. As a result, Zitkala-Ša writes, some Sioux starved due to destroyed crops and loss of cattle to the larger herds. Sells and Merritt took little interest in a Sioux delegate who protested against the situation. See Zitkala-Ša, "Our Sioux People," 4–5, Bonnin Collection.

4. Zitkala-Ša, "Heart to Heart Talk," *San Francisco Bulletin*, 1922. Reprinted in Davidson and Norris, *American Indian Stories*, 261–63. The successive articles, or chapters, were titled "California Indian Trails and Prayer Trees," "Lost Treaties of the California Indians," and "The California Indians of Today." "Heart to Heart Talk" came last. The pieces were later reprinted in the *California Indian Herald* and again as a pamphlet. The writings ruminate on white greed, white war, and the superiority of Indian spirituality. I do not discuss them in detail in the text to avoid redundancy. As in her writings from the early 1900s, Zitkala-Ša reverses racial and civilizational discourses by portraying whites and the societies they create as governed by base instincts. These themes are mostly repeated in the unpublished "The Sioux Claims" and "Our Sioux People" (from 1923) presented at length in the conclusion. The California writings are collected in Davidson and Norris, *American Indian Stories*. "Lost Treaties of the California Indians" outlined the history of white encroachment on the Pacific coast. In the first Zitkala-Ša writes that under treaties signed in the early 1850s purporting to secure seven and a half million acres of ancestral lands "for ever and ever," official representatives guaranteed "moneys, subsistence, clothing, supplies and educational advantages." The "first Californians" believed that any whites trespassing upon their land, when presented with the U.S. government's promise of territorial integrity on paper, would "leave them in peace." Instead, the tribes were overrun by "lawless gold seekers" who in their "delirium" brought death and discord. Laws forbade the sale of firearms and ammunition to Indians to discourage any attempt at the defense of their country, and those who dealt with government officials in good faith were forced to flee and hide. "The anguish of my Indian people," Zitkala-Ša records, "neither pen nor tongue can tell." The treaties were meanwhile returned to Washington, where they were archived by order of the Senate and kept undisclosed for a period of fifty years. These "lost" treaties, now finally made public, signify a duplicitous act that must be rectified by immediate government action. See Davidson and Norris, *American Indian Stories*, 254–57. "The California Indians of Today" describes the indigenous peoples' present situation, in which those who remain as "a small remnant of a noble race" are "bravely struggling for existence" in a mire of poverty, divestment, and "the diseases of the white man." Zitkala-Ša argues that if given the opportunity and necessary assistance, the California Indians will easily "equal the average American." She urges all Californians to support a bill pending before Congress that would finally settle outstanding indigenous claims against the U.S. government. If it is equitably adjudicated, "there will be no need to send destitute Indians to the almshouses, nor will there be a need to make them objects of charity." Achieving such justice is a simple question of "national honor." Davidson and Norris, *American Indian Stories*, 258–60. It appears that after the California writings were first published in the *San Francisco Bulletin*, Zitkala-Ša added some content to the versions that appeared in the *California Indian Herald*. The version of "Heart to Heart Talk" reprinted in *American Indian Stories, Legends, and Other Writings*, for instance, describes Zitkala-Ša's work in Oklahoma, which took place in 1923.

5. Zitkala-Ša, "Zitkala-Ša–Gertrude Bonnin," and "Brief History of Activities in Behalf of the American Indians," 3, Bonnin Collection.

6. Zitkala-Ša read the poem publicly on July 22, 1922. In "Dakota Ode" a young woman (presumably, Zitkala-Ša in her younger years) is chosen to represent the Seven Council Fires in Washington, D.C., by bringing the message of "brotherhood." The piece is, objectively, a self-congratulatory and offensive paean to the United States (e.g., Native peoples praise its founding with chants such as, "We venerate the memory of our great pale-face brother, Washington, the chiefest among guardians of spiritual fires—liberty and unity.") Given the occasion, the rhetoric is unsurprising, but one wonders if in this case Zitkala-Ša's

pandering to a white audience was excessive. Zitkala-Ša, "A Dakota Ode to Washington," in Davidson and Norris, *American Indian Stories*, 247–49, 267–68.

7. "Virginia Couple Devotes Lives to Indians," *Washington Post*, December 31, 1933, SM4. The article gives a summary of the Bonnins' lives and accomplishments.

8. Welch, "Zitkala-Ša," 180; Dominguez, "Gertrude Bonnin Story," 255–56; "Brief History of Activities in Behalf of the American Indians," 3–4; "Testimonial Talk by Ernest L. Wilkinson" Bonnin Collection. Wilkinson states that Bonnin entered law school in 1922, but his recollection may have been inaccurate. Dominguez writes, "Raymond T. Bonnin was enrolled as a 'special student' from 1921–1925. . . . It is not known if Raymond completed the course of legal study; he did not receive a law degree nor did he ever attempt to pass the Bar exam." See Dominguez, "Gertrude Bonnin Story," 256.

9. Hertzberg, *Search for an American Indian Identity*, 200–202; Huebner, "Unexpected Alliance," 337–66. Also of importance was the Leavitt Bill, or Dance Order, supported by Fall and the IRA, which proposed giving reservation superintendents the authority to stop any ceremony deemed improper. The AIDA strenuously opposed and defeated the Dance Order.

10. Britten, *American Indians in World War I*, 48.

11. Hoxie, *This Indian Country*, 269.

12. Hertzberg, *Search for an American Indian Identity*, 203.

13. Hertzberg, *Search for an American Indian Identity*, 202–204; Speroff, *Carlos Montezuma, MD*, 369–70.

14. Zitkala-Ša, "California Indian Trails and Prayer Trees," in Davidson and Norris, *American Indian Stories*, 252.

15. Terry P. Wilson, *The Underground Reservation: Osage Oil* (Lincoln: University of Nebraska Press, 1985), 122, 124, 127–29, 138–39; Margo Jefferson, "Books of the Times: Digging Up a Tale of Terror among the Osages," *New York Times*, August 31, 1994, www.nytimes.com/1994/08/31/books/books-of-the-times-digging-up-a-tale-of-terror-among-the-osages.html?pagewanted=all&src=pm (accessed December 11, 2014).

16. Wilson, *Underground Reservation*, 145–46; Jefferson, "Digging Up a Tale of Terror."

17. Angie Debo, *And Still the Waters Run: The Betrayal of the Five Civilized Tribes* (Princeton, N.J.: Princeton University Press, 1972), 3–31.

18. Willard, "Zitkala-Ša," 14.

19. Gertrude Bonnin, Charles H. Fabens, and Matthew K. Sniffen, *Oklahoma's Poor Rich Indians: An Orgy of Graft and Exploitation of the Five Civilized Tribes—Legalized Robbery* (Washington, D.C.: Office of the Indian Rights Association, 1924), 12.

20. Welch, "Zitkala-Ša," 183.

21. Dominguez records that Stella Atwood chose Zitkala-Ša for the Oklahoma investigation. The IRA paid her expenses plus a $150 honorarium. See Dominguez, "Gertrude Bonnin Story," 265.

22. Bonnin, Fabens, and Sniffen, *Oklahoma's Poor Rich Indians*, 1–23.

23. Debo, *And Still the Waters Run*, 103.

24. Bonnin, Fabens, and Sniffen, *Oklahoma's Poor Rich Indians*, 17–39. As Hollrah points out, Zitkala-Ša employs "the language of sentimentalism" in order to elicit greater "pathos" and "persuasive power"—particularly among female readers. To this end, Zitkala-Ša highlights cases in which defenseless women and girls are brutally victimized by men to make the case that only outside intervention can protect Oklahoma's most vulnerable Indians. Hollrah argues that this language is designed to appeal not only to female readers familiar with the dark side of masculinity, but also to notions of America's just and honorable foundations. Those who uphold American values must, as a moral imperative, intercede.

She points out that Neharkey is described not as a woman, but a "little girl" strikingly small, childlike, defenseless, and timid. As a "victim" whose "little body" had been "mutilated," her only hope rests in "the friends of humanity," or more specifically female reformers. Zitkala-Ša's re-creation of her rape heightens the urgency of the situation and the need for action. See Hollrah, " 'We Must Be Masters of Our Circumstances,' " 48–51.

25. Debo, *And Still the Waters Run*, 330–31.

26. Dominguez, "Gertrude Bonnin Story," 268.

27. Debo, *And Still the Waters Run*, 330–31.

28. Welch, "Zitkala-Ša," 190, 192.

29. Debo, *And Still the Waters Run*, 334.

30. Welch, "Zitkala-Ša," 190–93; Dominguez, "Gertrude Bonnin Story," 269.

31. Welch, "Zitkala-Ša," 192.

32. Debo, *And Still the Waters Run*, 331–32.

33. Wilson, *Underground Reservation*, 145–46. The law did not, however, affect inheritance rights of already married non-Indian spouses.

34. Marion E. Gridley, "Gertrude Simmons Bonnin: A Modern Progressive," in *American Indian Women* (New York: Hawthorne, 1974), 86.

35. Davidson and Norris, introduction to *American Indian Stories*, xxvii; Speroff, *Carlos Montezuma, MD*, 370.

36. Gridley, "Gertrude Simmons Bonnin," 86.

37. Hoxie, *This Indian Country*, 274.

38. Indian Citizenship Act, [H.R. 6355.] [Public Law No. 175.] Sixty-Eighth Congress. Sess. I. CHS.233, 1924. See House Report No. 222, Certificates of Citizenship to Indians, 68th Cong., 1st Sess., February 22, 1924. The legislation was sponsored by the same Representative Snyder so instrumental in derailing the course of justice at the Muskogee hearings.

39. Pratt was formally and extensively eulogized nine years later by Elaine Goodale Eastman, Charles Eastman's long-estranged wife. The last line of her hagiography *Pratt: The Red Man's Moses* reads, "And his soul goes marching on." Elaine Goodale Eastman, *Pratt: The Red Man's Moses* (Norman: University of Oklahoma Press, 1935), 272. The year 1924 also saw Chipeta's death. By that point she was almost eighty and completely blind. She was given a modest burial near her home according to Ute custom. She was later exhumed and buried next to her husband, Ouray. See Simmons, *Ute Indians of Utah, Colorado, and New Mexico*, 251–52.

40. Zitkala-Ša, "Zitkala-Ša–Gertrude Bonnin," Bonnin Collection.

41. Britten, *American Indians in World War I*, 179–81.

42. Hoxie, *This Indian Country*, 274.

43. Britten, *American Indians in World War I*, 177.

12. *Princess Zitkala-Ša and the National Council of American Indians*

1. "Charge Open Robbery of Indian Tribes: Investigators Demand Immediate Reform in Probate Law Administration in Oklahoma," *New York Times*, February 8, 1924.

2. "Women to Hear Indian Princess," *Indianapolis* [. . .] *Star*, February 21, 1924, Bonnin Collection. Unfortunately, the masthead of the newspaper is partially obscured on the photocopy available.

3. "Princess Zitkala-Ša Center of Interest at Book Fair of Pen Women," May 2, 1925, Bonnin Collection. The newspaper's title is not indicated on the clipping. Zitkala-Ša was a member of the National League of American Pen Women. See Davidson and Norris, introduction to *American Indian Stories*, xiii.

4. Hoxie, *This Indian Country*, 157; Charlotte Gray, *Flint and Feather: The Life and Times of E. Pauline Johnson, Tekahionwake* (Toronto, Ontario: HarperCollins, 2002), 154–61.

5. Given the nature of such events, the question naturally arises whether Zitkala-Ša's public image, based on the "drawing card" of Sioux ancestry, was somehow unseemly. From a modern perspective the vision of the "princess" Zitkala-Ša, dressed in buckskins and playing piano to a room of wealthy reformers, gives pause—for both its exploitation of white colonial curiosity and its almost shameless publicity seeking. There is, however, a strong basis for her self-characterization as Sitting Bull's granddaughter, even though Zitkala-Ša certainly knew that the white American public took her words literally, thinking her to be a blood relative of Sitting Bull. Given the purpose behind her obfuscation, the half-ruse can be appreciated as clever hoodwinking, though some scholars have characterized it as "selling out." Hafen characterizes Zitkala-Ša's public appearances as disingenuously "entrenched in an aboriginal persona." Hafen, introduction to *Dreams and Thunder*, xx. Spack also notes that as Sitting Bull's granddaughter, Zitkala-Ša "fed [her] era's hunger for an authentic Indian, most especially an Indian princess," and was hence "guilty" of "exoticizing of the Native woman." See Spack, *America's Second Tongue*, 169. Katanski argues (in reference to the *Atlantic Monthly* series) that Zitkala-Ša consciously and "meticulously constructed her identity" by, for example, remaking her father as a Sioux warrior. Princess Zitkala-Ša was certainly an extension of this manufactured public image. Katanski, *Learning to Write "Indian,"* 114. However, Fisher's claim that Zitkala-Ša's "own image of herself eventually evolved into an admixture of myth and fact, so that by the time of her death in 1938, she believed . . . that she was the granddaughter of Sitting Bull," conflates self-delusion with self-promotion and, perhaps, cultural practice. See Fisher, "Zitkala-Ša," 236. Susag explains that Zitkala-Ša's self-identification as *a* granddaughter of Sitting Bull was entirely legitimate. The Sioux called respected elders "grandfather," allowing Susag to argue that "Sitting Bull could have been Zitkala-Ša's grandfather because she revered him as a leader who until his death continued to fight for the territorial and cultural integrity of his people." Susag, "Zitkala-Ša (Gertrude Simmons Bonnin)," 16. It should also be remembered, as Harold Bloom writes, that Zitkala-Ša's clear penchant for "self-aggrandizement" was counterbalanced by the "selflessness" of her activism. Harold Bloom, "Zitkala-Ša," in *Native American Women Writers* (Philadelphia: Chelsea, 1998), 119. Even P. Jane Hafen, who is often critical of the way Zitkala-Ša represented herself and her culture, concedes that, "As an author, she transcribed oral tradition and experience, fiercely guarding her Indian identity and defying the aims of assimilist education." Hafen, introduction to *Dreams and Thunder*, xxiii.

6. Arietta Wimer Towne, "Mrs. Fowler Entertains Officers and Chairman at Her Home," *Oak Parker*, February 20, 1925.

7. Dominguez, "Gertrude Bonnin Story," 281.

8. Graham D. Taylor, *The New Deal and American Indian Tribalism: The Administration of the Indian Reorganization Act, 1934–45* (Lincoln: University of Nebraska Press, 1980), 12–13; Dominguez, "Gertrude Bonnin Story," 256–57.

9. Warrior, *Tribal Secrets*, 19–20.

10. Welch, "Zitkala-Ša," 196.

11. Hertzberg, *Search for an American Indian Identity*, 207.

12. Welch, "Zitkala-Ša," 204–206. One of the allotments investigated in 1925 was that of Ellen C. Bluestone (see chap. 10, n. 41).

13. "Indians Sue to Keep Pipestone Quarries," *Washington Post*, December 16, 1925, 26. This case was finally concluded when the Supreme Court ruled in 1927 that the Yankton deserved "just compensation" for the pipestone quarries. See Jennings C. Wise, *The Red Man*

in the New World Drama: A Politico-Legal Study with a Pageantry of American Indian History (Washington, D.C.: W. F. Roberts, 1931), 574–75.

14. Zitkala-Ša, "How the National Council of American Indians Came into Being and What of the Things It Is Trying to do through Organization," Bonnin Collection. Upon forming the NCAI Zitkala-Ša resigned from her position as research agent with the GFWC. See Dominguez, "Gertrude Bonnin Story," 269.

15. See "Brief History of Activities in Behalf of the American Indians," 4, Bonnin Collection. Also see Hafen, introduction to *Dreams and Thunder*, xxiii.

16. Speroff, *Carlos Montezuma, MD*, 244.

17. Dominguez, "Gertrude Bonnin Story," 277, 279. Also see Blanche Syfret McKnight, "Feminine Descendent of Sitting Bull Works for Her People," *Evening Star* [Washington], December 10, 1936. The article describes the Bonnins' home as "decorated with many Indian relics."

18. Zitkala-Ša's speech to the IRA conference in Atlantic City characterizes the NCAI as "based upon citizenship rights granted by Congress June 2, 1924." See "American Indian Problem: Address before the Indian Rights Association to Discuss the Report 'Problem of Indian Administration' by the Institute for Government Research—Atlantic City, December 14–15, 1928," 1, Bonnin Collection. In "How the National Council of American Indians Came into Being," she also describes the NCAI as dedicated to seeing that all indigenous peoples are "reunited under the rights of citizenship." The one-page, typewritten document is undated but is most likely from early 1926, Bonnin Collection.

19. See Zitkala-Ša, "How the National Council of American Indians Came into Being," Bonnin Collection. Here, Zitkala-Ša describes the NCAI's founding as a spontaneous occurrence at a regular meeting of tribal representatives in Washington, D.C. In a bout of false modesty and, likely, false reporting, she writes, "In electing officers, I was elected by acclamation. I tried to decline the honor, but they insisted upon my acceptance, and that I make it a success. I accepted the presidency." The position, however, entailed very real sacrifice: "For my service I receive no pay either directly or indirectly. I give my whole time to this work. In fact the work needs more help . . . It is humanitarian and it is necessary." Then, handwritten: "The Indians are poor. We lack funds. I have to do all my typing having no clerical assistance." Incidentally, Dominguez records that the NCAI logo "was replaced with a buffalo skull and pipe design in 1933." Dominguez, "Gertrude Bonnin Story," 286.

20. "Brief History of Activities in Behalf of the American Indians," 6, Bonnin Collection. Also see Hafen, introduction to *Dreams and Thunder*, xxi.

21. "Petition of the National Council of American Indians to the Senate" (1926), quoted in Wise, *Red Man in the New World Drama*, 571–73. Bruyneel notes that the juxtaposition of "racial self-respect" and "loyalty to the United States" indicates "a form of meaningful U.S. citizenship that does not remove from indigenous people their distinctive cultural, and by extension, political identity . . . that does not require surrendering a substantial foothold within indigenous communities." See Bruyneel, "Challenging American Boundaries," 36. For a full exploration of the forty-four-page petition, see Dominguez, "Gertrude Bonnin Story," 288–97. Dominguez also details Zitkala-Ša brief efforts to found an all-Indian Women's Orchestra in 1926 (pp. 197–99).

22. See Wise, *Red Man in the New World Drama*, 574. Wise explains that in the summer of 1926 the NCAI organized an Indian voting bloc. Also see Welch, "Zitkala-Ša," 203. The NCAI also lent its voice to anyone raising protests against the BIA. See "Calls Indian Bureau Unworthy of Trust: Dr. Emerson Asserts It Is Playing Politics Against the Life of Its Wards," *New York Times*, June 3, 1926. In this article condemning BIA cuts in appropriations for

"health work" on reservations, Zitkala-Ša is quoted in her capacity as president of the NCAI: "Mrs. Gertrude Bonnin (Zit-kala-Sa) [sic], President of the National Council of American Indians, a member of the Sioux tribe, declared that through the bureau's 'mismanagement' the Indians may all die in the poorhouses." Regarding the unveiling of the Sitting Bull statue see "Members of the National Council of American Indians Take Part in Ceremony at Unveiling of Statue of the Great Sitting Bull," March 9, 1926, Bonnin Collection.

23. Zitkala-Ša, *Representative William Williamson and the Indians* (Washington, D.C.: Allied Printing, June 1926), 3–14, Bonnin Collection.

24. Wise, *Red Man in the New World Drama*, 574. This survey produced the Meriam Report.

25. In "Zitkala-Ša–Gertrude Bonnin" (Bonnin Collection), Zitkala-Ša writes that the trip was made "at own expense." Also see Welch, "Zitkala-Ša," 210.

26. Zitkala-Ša, "Zitkala-Ša–Gertrude Bonnin," and untitled report on the California-Arizona trip, June 4, 1927, both in Bonnin Collection.

27. "Brief History of Activities in Behalf of the American Indians," 5, and "Zitkala-Ša–Gertrude Bonnin," both in Bonnin Collection.

28. Zitkala-Ša to Ketcham, August 28, 1912, Bureau of Catholic Indian Missions.

29. Dominguez, "Gertrude Bonnin Story," 287, 319, citing the NCAI pamphlet "Information Service for Indian Citizen Voters on Scattered Indian Reservations," (ca. 1927). It is unclear whether the program was successfully launched. Hertzberg (in *Search for an American Indian Identity*) deems the effort largely a failure.

30. "Brief History of Activities in Behalf of the American Indians," 5, Bonnin Collection. Also see Zitkala-Ša, "Zitkala-Ša–Gertrude Bonnin," Bonnin Collection.

31. "Indians' Charges to be Aired Today: Senate Committee Will Go into Stories of Brutality in the Reservation Schools," *New York Times*, May 23, 1930, 16.

32. "Brief History of Activities in Behalf of the American Indians," 5; Zitkala-Ša, "Zitkala-Ša–Gertrude Bonnin;" both in Bonnin Collection.

33. *Indian News Letter* 5, April 22, 1930, Peter Norbeck Papers, University of South Dakota, Vermillion.

34. "Brief History of Activities in Behalf of the American Indians," 5–6, Bonnin Collection.

35. Davidson and Norris, introduction to *American Indian Stories*, xxviii.

36. "Brief History of Activities in Behalf of the American Indians," 5–6, Bonnin Collection. "Virginia Couple Devotes Lives to Indians" records, contrary to the Bonnins' claims, that forty-nine tribes were in some way involved with the NCAI. This article also states that the organization had ninety "advisors of both red and white races" and represented almost all American Indians in one capacity or another.

37. "Testimonial Talk by Ernest L. Wilkinson," Bonnin Collection. Also see Hanson, *Sun Dance Land*, 120. According to Maroukis, during the early 1930s Zitkala-Ša very briefly attempted to resuscitate her anti-peyote campaign on the federal level by seeking the support of a U.S. senator. This hardly seems a full-on effort, and it met with no success. Maroukis, *Peyote Road*, 122.

38. Zitkala-Ša, "What It Means to Be an Indian Today," *Friends' Intelligencer*, January 19, 1929, 46–47, Bonnin Collection. In this article she also notes with fury that BIA superintendents willfully ignored suffering on reservations. The NCAI made a priority of exposing such behavior by government officers. See NCAI Press Release, "Brutal Superintendents Are Triumphant," May 19, 1930, Peter Norbeck Papers. Zitkala-Ša also gave a lecture entitled "What It Means to Be an Indian Today" at the annual convention of the Maryland League of Women Voters in May 1929. Dominguez, "Gertrude Bonnin Story," 280.

39. Zitkala-Ša, "American Indian Problem: Address before the Indian Rights Association to Discuss the Report 'Problem of Indian Administration' by the Institute for Government Research–Atlantic City, December 14–15, 1928," 1–3, 6, 11, Bonnin Collection. The IRA conference session in which Zitkala-Ša spoke focused on the recently released Meriam Report. See Dominguez, "Gertrude Bonnin Story," 301.

40. *Report of the Thirty-Fifth Lake Mohonk Conference on the Indian*, October 16–18 (Poughkeepsie, N.Y.: Lousing-Broas Printing for the Lake Mohonk Conference, 1930), 92–95.

41. "Brutal Superintendents Are Triumphant," Peter Norbeck Papers.

42. Welch, "Zitkala-Ša," 211.

43. Taylor, *New Deal and American Indian Tribalism*, 120–21.

44. Davidson and Norris, introduction to *American Indian Stories*, xliii.

45. Speroff, *Carlos Montezuma, MD*, 372–73.

46. Welch, "Zitkala-Ša," 219–22. By 1932 the relationship between Collier and Zitkala-Ša had become tense, as Collier's AIDA at times took actions without consulting the NCAI, in particular regarding the effort to publicly condemn the new BIA commissioner, C. J. Rhoads. The Bonnins supported Rhoads because he had tried to assist them in negotiations at Yankton. They also felt they had been regularly ignored by the AIDA and declined to support Collier, who was making a bid for commissioner—even though they received much financial support from the AIDA, which partially funded their yearly cross-county investigations.

47. Walter L. Williams, "Twentieth Century Indian Leaders: Brokers and Providers," *Journal of the West* 23, no. 3 (1984): 4.

48. Alison Bernstein, "A Mixed Record: The Political Enfranchisement of American Indian Women During the Indian New Deal," *Journal of the West* 23, no. 3 (July 1984): 13.

49. Taylor, *New Deal and American Indian Tribalism*, 100–101. The issue of a Yankton constitution had been fought over since 1931, with the Bonnins battling other factions for control of the tribal council. For a full account see Welch, Zitkala-Ša," 212–22. The original Yankton constitution of 1891, signed, incidentally, by David Simmons, gave all authority to the BIA. See Speroff, *Carlos Montezuma, MD*, 210.

50. Welch, "Zitkala-Ša," 223–28. Interestingly, Maroukis—critical of Zitkala-Ša's alleged assimilationist tendencies and anti-peyote lobbying—also notes that the main advantage of the Bonnins' constitution was its greater tribal autonomy. Maroukis, *Peyote and the Yankton Sioux*, 203.

51. Hafen, introduction to *Dreams and Thunder*, xxii.

52. Dominguez, "Gertrude Bonnin Story," 284, 311–14. Regarding Bonnin's role as legal agent, Dominguez writes that the secretary of the interior allowed him to take the job only on condition that he did not represent the Utes in any litigation or claims.

53. See "Circular Letter," May 9, 1935, Bonnin Collection. Ohiya's health and the Bonnins' family and financial situation are also described in Zitkala-Ša's diaries, kept from July 29, 1935, to November 3, 1937, Bonnin Collection.

13. The Final Diaries

1. Zitkala-Ša to Elaine Eastman, March 25, 1935, quoted in Welch, "Zitkala-Ša," 229.

2. Diary of Zitkala-Ša, July 29–October 7, 1935, Bonnin Collection. According to documents in the Bonnin Collection, Ohiya had previously tried to find work in Minneapolis as an expert mechanic after being trained in Washington, D.C. A letter of recommendation from the Indian Employment Service states, "Mr. Bonnin has very special training and comes with the highest possible commendations from the Bureau of Engineers in the District of

Columbia. He has the further advantage of a very special training in the operation and care of all kinds of office equipment such as typewriters, adding machines, mimeographs, addressographs, etc." The letter, dated May 9, 1935, also notes that Ohiya has four children ranging in age from one to twelve. See "Circular Letter," Bonnin Collection.

3. Diary of Zitkala-Ša, April 1, 1936–February 25, 1937, Bonnin Collection. Though this fact is not mentioned in the diary, Collier did at one point offer Bonnin a position as superintendent of the Mescalero Reservation in New Mexico. In the Bonnin Collection there is a letter from Bonnin to Collier, dated only "Oct" but likely written around this period, in which Bonnin declines the job. His rejection was a point of pride. Collier offered him a salary three hundred dollars less than agent vacating the position, with no relocation allowance. "Thus after careful consideration of all these facts," Bonnin writes with underlying sarcasm, "I have reached the conclusion that I cannot afford to accept your offer." The article "Virginia Couple Devotes Lives to Indians" notes, "In their house in Lyon Park [Virginia], Capt. Bonnin and Mrs. Bonnin live quietly, surrounded by exquisite examples of Indian arts and crafts, gifts from their people. They study and write constantly on behalf of the Indian, and never forget they are still Yankton Sioux."

4. Diary of Zitkala-Ša, August 2–November 3, 1937, Bonnin Collection.

5. Dominguez, "Gertrude Bonnin Story," 321. Dominguez also writes, "Bonnin's share went to his estate, which Wilkinson's firm administered." Wilkinson went on to become President of Brigham Young University (1949–1975)."

6. Register of the Gertrude and Raymond Bonnin Collection, 1926–1938.

7. Davidson and Norris, introduction to American Indian Stories, xxviii.

8. "Mrs. R. T. Bonnin, An Indian Leader," New York Times, January 28, 1938, emphasis added.

9. "Mrs. Bonnin Dies; Friend of Indians," Evening Star, January 26, 1938.

10. "Mrs. Bonnin, Sitting Bull Kin, Is Dead at 62," Washington Post, January 27, 1938, 26.

11. Davidson and Norris, introduction to American Indian Stories, xxviii. For the location of the funeral service see "Mrs. Bonnin's Rites," Evening Star, January 27, 1938. Collier is quoted in Dominguez, "Gertrude Bonnin Story," 316.

12. Speroff, Carlos Montezuma, MD, 246.

13. "Testimonial Talk by Ernest L. Wilkinson," Bonnin Collection; Register of the Gertrude and Raymond Bonnin Collection, 1926–1938. Wilkinson stated, "One of [Bonnin's] grandchildren is with the Marines in Hawaii; another is counting the days until about three months from now when he will become seventeen and can join the Navy." Bonnin's second wife was a Mormon from Utah and a longtime friend of the family whose husband, James B. Whittemore, died two days before Zitkala-Ša. Bonnin's funeral was held in a Mormon church. See Speroff, Carlos Montezuma, MD, 246, for a photograph of Zitkala-Ša and Bonnin's shared tombstone. Also see "Military Burial for R. T. Bonnin at Arlington Today," Washington Post, September 26, 1942, B11. Ohiya Bonnin was buried in Roosevelt City Cemetery, Roosevelt, Utah. See "Raymond Ohiya Bonnin," http://billiongraves.com/pages/records/index.php?record_id=1993269 (accessed November 9, 2014). Some sources claim Ohiya Bonnin predeceased his mother. See, for example, Gale J. Hardy, "Gertrude Simmons Bonnin," in American Women Civil Rights Activists: Biobibliographies of 68 leaders, 1825–1992 (Jefferson, N.C.: McFarland, 1993): 80. However, Wilkinson states, "The Captain and Mrs. Bonnin were blessed with a son, who unfortunately predeceased his father" (emphasis added). The faulty information in Hardy may have been taken from Sun Dance Land (112–13), where Hanson claims that Ohiya died before his mother. Given the book's general unreliability, the fact that Hanson was very elderly when he wrote it in the mid-1960s, and the

dates on the gravestone pictured on the billiongraves.com website, this claim can be discounted.

14. Hafen, introduction to *Dreams and Thunder*, xxiii. According to his unreliable memoir, just a week before *The Sun Dance Opera*'s New York premiere, Hanson heard news of Zitkala-Ša's death and traveled to Washington for her funeral. Along with this chronological impossibility, Hanson claims that Bonnin sent him a telegram revealing that his wife had died, and, all along, had been a Mormon. This part appears wholly disingenuous. Hanson also suggests that Zitkala-Ša had planned to attend the opera performances. Hanson, *Sun Dance Land*, 112–13.

15. Smith, "Operatic Skeleton on the Western Frontier."

16. Hafen, introduction to *Dreams and Thunder*, xxiii.

Conclusion

1. Zitkala-Ša, "Our Sioux People," 1–3, 10–19, 23, Bonnin Collection. The contents of "Our Sioux People" and "The Sioux Claims" are highly similar, in some cases identical. The writings were inspired by the Sioux Nation's decision to sue the U.S. government for treaty violations in an effort to gain $700 million in compensation for the Black Hills. The texts feature copious quotes from Sitting Bull, such as, "This is our country. The Great Spirit gave it to us when He placed us here in our own way," and "God Almighty made me an Indian but never a reservation Indian!" Zitkala-Ša also quotes Red Cloud's indignation over the absurdity of the Louisiana Purchase: "What right has France across the sea, to sell my land?" Why these writings were never published is unknown, because there are indications they were intended for public distribution. For instance, in "Our Sioux People," Zitkala-Ša appeals to reformers to remove "a bloody stain upon America's national honor for all time to come" (see pp. 13–15, 29, for the preceding quotations). In "The Sioux Claims," Zitkala-Ša also writes, "If America means to befriend oppressed people of the world, particularly those of our own continent, we, the Sioux nation, ask to be remembered. We seek justice, not charity" (16–17). However, these sentences seem like afterthoughts in the context of the whole works. Incidentally, after typing the word "cannibalism" in "Our Sioux People," Zitkala-Ša went back and placed a question mark over the word. Who knows whether she thought it was lexically inappropriate, too strong, or not strong enough? Finally, regarding the idea of integration on an equal footing, Katanski argues that Zitkala-Ša likely felt that Indians should have a right to choose among aspects of both cultures. She cites a passage from the *Atlantic Monthly* series in which Zitkala-Ša's mother "meant to give up her own customs for such of the white man's ways as pleased her, she made only compromises," a position that indicates the voluntary nature of alterations to lifestyle. Katanski adds, "Zitkala-Ša, too, is aware of the options available to her and chooses among them to please herself. . . . Although she and her family have adapted elements of European American culture into their lives, they have not simultaneously discarded Yankton or 'Indian' cultural markers and values." Katanski, *Learning to Write "Indian,"* 154–55. The same dynamic is alluded to in "Our Sioux People." Zitkala-Ša writes of the Pine Ridge Sioux's dedication to tradition, which does not necessarily preclude adaptation to new circumstances: "They will be quick to respond to any encouragement to save our native lore, songs, and ancient wisdom. This need not prevent them from a choice and acceptance of present day methods of gaining livelihood; or to acquire eventually, untethered American citizenship" (2).

2. Troy R. Johnson, *Red Power: The Native American Civil Rights Movement* (New York: Chelsea House, 2007), 9–10, 53–55. Also see Paul Chaat Smith and Robert Allen Warrior, *Like*

a Hurricane: The Indian American Movement from Alcatraz to Wounded Knee (New York: New Press, 1996), 153–68. For commentary on the 20 points, see Vine Deloria, Jr., and Clifford Lytle, *The Nations Within: The Past and Future of American Indian Sovereignty* (New York: Pantheon Books, 1984), 238–39. Zitkala-Ša explores the issue of treaty violations and compensation at length in "The Sioux Claims."

3. For a summary of Vine Deloria, Jr.'s, career see Hoxie, *This Indian Country*, 337–92.

4. Vine Deloria, Jr., *Custer Died for Your Sins: An Indian Manifesto* (New York: Macmillan, 1969), 264–66, 27, 52, 267, 28, 51, 101, 109, 50, 49, 102 (emphasis in the original).

5. Hoxie, *This Indian Country*, 342–43.

6. Zitkala-Ša, "Indian Affairs," 1, 7, Bonnin Collection. The full quotation, to give context, is: "In the 3rd paragraph of Mr. Merritt's 'Bulletin 12' he quotes President Jefferson which if followed would be what we Indians want but are not 'preserved in the occupation of our lands' nor are we encouraged in our progress toward becoming one with other Americans. We are retarded instead." With her pencil, Zitkala-Ša then crossed out "retarded" and replaced it with "being exterminated." Unfortunately, we do not know exactly when "Indian Affairs" was written. Only the fact that it was post-1928 is evident, as Zitkala-Ša refers to Hubert Work as the former secretary of the interior. His tenure ended that year.

7. Regarding the comparison between Zitkala-Ša and Deloria and specifically the latter's greater freedom of expression: Zitkala-Ša could obviously not title her works *Custer Died for Your Sins, God Is Red,* or *We Talk, You Listen.* Her historical milieu required titles more in the vein of *Please, Please Listen, and Try to Understand.* Still, the similarities between the two writers' works are compelling and cogent. I avoid belaboring them in the conclusion for purposes of concision. In *Behind the Trail of Broken Treaties* Deloria speaks of the viability of small populations existing as sovereign nations among larger states, drawing parallels between nations like Israel and Indian nations. Vine Deloria, Jr., *Behind the Trail of Broken Treaties: An Indian Declaration of Independence* (New York: Delacorte Press, 1974), 172, 183–86, 254–55. This idea is reminiscent of Zitkala-Ša's writings on the Versailles Peace Conference and her effort to have an Indian delegation included in order that their claims to nationhood and democracy would be recognized. Like Zitkala-Ša, Deloria also had an ambiguous relationship with Christianity, having graduated from a Lutheran school of theology. Yet he often criticized Christianity. See, for instance, Vine Deloria, Jr., *God Is Red* (New York: Grosset and Dunlap, 1973), 225–46. Sometimes a passage jumps out of Deloria's writing because Zitkala-Ša could have penned it, as does this one: "At present the visible poverty of Indian tribes veils the great potential of the Indian people from modern society. But in many ways the veil is lifting and a brighter future is being seen. Night is giving way to day. The Indian will soon stand tall and strong once more." Deloria, *Custer Died for Your Sins,* 241–42. Both Zitkala-Ša and Deloria had remarkable, biting wit and could employ sarcasm to great effect. In addition, Hoxie writes that as a professor at the University of Arizona, "Deloria focused the bulk of his intellectual energy on the two broad themes he had identified in *Behind the Trail of Broken Treaties* and *God Is Red:* spiritual renewal and political reforms that embraced the sovereignty of Native peoples within the United States." Hoxie, *This Indian Country,* 384. These two themes could be characterized as Zitkala-Ša's driving concerns. Referring to Deloria, Hoxie comments:

> From his first emergence into public life in 1964, Deloria had argued that American Indians should take advantage of every benefit they could derive from their status as citizens of the United States but that they should also never doubt the power that flowed from an indigenous heritage whose roots were far older than the nation's constitution or its laws and whose wisdom could not be contained in a single ceremony or shaman's aphorism. From the 1970s onward he advocated an open-ended process of

both cultural renewal and legal reform. . . . Native peoples should think of themselves as heirs to an immense heritage that propelled them, steadily and creatively, toward the twin goals of protecting and revitalizing Indian peoplehood. Only this constant striving could reinvigorate the nation's tribes, reignite their values, and truly restore the social and political bonds that had sustained them over the centuries. . . . His goal was nothing less than the continued survival of Indian people—and an Indian country—within the boundaries of the United States. (Hoxie, *This Indian Country*, 391–92)

This quotation could easily be retrofitted to describe Zitkala-Ša.
8. Cobb, *Native Activism in Cold War America*, 11–31, 52.

Selected Bibliography

Archives

Bureau of Catholic Indian Missions Records. Raynor Memorial Libraries, Marquette University Archives, Milwaukee, Wisc.

Bonnin, Gertrude and Raymond, Collection. L. Tom Perry Special Collections, Harold B. Lee Library, Brigham Young University, Provo, Utah.

Montezuma, Carlos, Papers. Wisconsin Historical Society, Madison.

Norbeck, Peter, Papers. University of South Dakota, Vermillion.

Pratt, Richard Henry, Papers. Beinecke Rare Book and Manuscript Library, Yale University, New Haven, Conn.

Society of American Indians Papers. Cornell University Library, Ithaca, N.Y.

Santee Normal Training School. Nebraska State Historical Society, Lincoln.

Simmons, Gertrude, Alumni Files. Lily Library, Earlham College, Richmond, Ind.

South Dakota State Archives. South Dakota State Historical Society, Pierre.

Unthank, Susan B., Collection. Indiana State Library, Indianapolis.

Works by Zitkala-Ša (Chronological Order)

"Side by Side." *Earlhamite*, March 16, 1896, 177–79.

"Impressions of an Indian Childhood." *Atlantic Monthly* 85 (January 1900): 37–47.

"The School Days of an Indian Girl." *Atlantic Monthly* 85 (February 1900): 185–94.

"An Indian Teacher among Indians." *Atlantic Monthly* 85 (March 1900): 381–86.

Old Indian Legends. Boston: Ginn & Co., 1901. Reprinted in *American Indian Stories, Legends, and Other Writings*, edited by Cathy N. Davidson and Ada Norris. New York: Penguin Books, 2003.

"The Soft-Hearted Sioux." *Harper's Monthly* 103 (October 1901): 505–508.

"The Trial Path." *Harper's Monthly* 103 (October 1901): 741–44.

"The Indian Dance: A Protest Against Its Abolition." *Boston Evening Transcript*, January 25, 1902, 24.

"A Warrior's Daughter." *Everybody's Magazine* 6 (April 1902): 346–52.

"Why I Am a Pagan." *Atlantic Monthly* 90 (December 1902): 801–803.

The Menace of Peyote. Pamphlet. 1916. Reprinted in Davidson and Norris, *American Indian Stories*, 239–41.

"The Indian's Awakening." *American Indian Magazine* 4 (January–March 1916): 57–59.

"A Year's Experience in Community Service Work among the Ute Tribe of Indians." *American Indian Magazine* 4 (October–December 1916): 307–10.

"The Red Man's America." *American Indian Magazine* 5 (January–March 1917): 64.

"Chipeta, Widow of Chief Ouray, with a Word about a Deal in Blankets." *American Indian Magazine* 5 (July–September 1917): 168–70.

"A Sioux Woman's Love for Her Grandchild." *American Indian Magazine* 5 (October–December 1917): 230–31.

"Mrs. Bonnin Speaks." *Tomahawk*, December 6, 1917, 1.

"Editorial Comment." *American Indian Magazine* 6 (July–September 1918): 113–14.

"Indian Gifts to Civilized Man." *American Indian Magazine* 6 (July–September 1918): 115–16.

"Secretary's Report in Brief." *American Indian Magazine* 6 (July–September 1918): 122–24.

"Editorial Comment." *American Indian Magazine* 6 (Winter 1919): 161–62.

"America, Home of the Red Man." *American Indian Magazine* 6 (Winter 1919): 165–67.

"The Coronation of Chief Powhatan Retold." *American Indian Magazine* 6 (Winter 1919): 179–80.

"Letter to the Chiefs and Headmen of the Tribes." *American Indian Magazine* 6 (Winter 1919): 196–97.

"Editorial Comment." *American Indian Magazine* 7 (Spring 1919): 5–9.

"An Indian Praying on the Hilltop." *American Indian Magazine* 7 (Spring 1919): 92.

"Editorial Comment." *American Indian Magazine* 7 (Summer 1919): 61–63.

"Address by the Secretary-Treasurer, Society of American Indians Annual Convention." *American Indian Magazine* 7 (Summer 1919): 153–57. Reprinted in Davidson and Norris, *American Indian Stories*, 213–18.

American Indian Stories. Washington, D.C.: Hayworth, 1921. Reprinted in Davidson and Norris, *American Indian Stories*.

"A Dream of Her Grandfather." Reprinted in Davidson and Norris, *American Indian Stories*, 141–42.

"The Widespread Enigma Concerning Blue-Star Woman." Reprinted in Davidson and Norris, *American Indian Stories*, 143–54.

"America's Indian Problem." Reprinted in Davidson and Norris, *American Indian Stories*, 155–60.

Americanize the First American: A Plan of Regeneration. Pamphlet. 1921.

"A Dakota Ode to Washington." Speech. 1922. Reprinted in Davidson and Norris, *American Indian Stories*, 247–49.

"California Indian Trails and Prayer Trees." *San Francisco Bulletin*, 1922. Reprinted in Davidson and Norris, *American Indian Stories*, 250–53.

"Lost Treaties of the California Indians." *San Francisco Bulletin*, 1922. Reprinted in Davidson and Norris, *American Indian Stories*, 254–57.

"The California Indians of Today." *San Francisco Bulletin*, 1922. Reprinted in Davidson and Norris, *American Indian Stories*, 258–60.

"Heart to Heart Talk." *San Francisco Bulletin*, 1922. Reprinted in Davidson and Norris, *American Indian Stories*, 261–63.

"Our Sioux People." Unpublished manuscript. 1923. Bonnin Collection.

"The Sioux Claims." Unpublished manuscript. 1923. Bonnin Collection.

Gertrude Bonnin, Charles H. Fabens, and Matthew K. Sniffen, *Oklahoma's Poor Rich Indians: An Orgy of Graft and Exploitation of the Five Civilized Tribes—Legalized Robbery.* Washington, D.C.: Office of the Indian Rights Association, 1924.

"How the National Council of American Indians Came into Being and What of the Things It is Trying to Do through Organization." 1926[?]. Announcement. Bonnin Collection.

Representative William Williamson and the Indians. Washington, D.C.: Allied Printing, June 1926. Pamphlet. Bonnin Collection.

"American Indian Problem: Address before the Indian Rights Association to Discuss the Report 'Problem of Indian Administration' by the Institute for Government Research—Atlantic City, December 14–15, 1928." Speech. Bonnin Collection.

"Indian Affairs." Unpublished manuscript. Circa 1929. Bonnin Collection.

"What It Means to Be an Indian Today." *Friends' Intelligencer,* January 19, 1929, 46–47.

"Zitkala-Ša—Gertrude Bonnin," February 22, 1929[?]. Bonnin Collection.

Diaries. July 21, 1935–November 3, 1937. Bonnin Collection.

Other Sources

Adams, David Wallace. *Education for Extinction: American Indians and the Boarding School Experience, 1875–1928.* Wichita: University Press of Kansas, 1995.

Allen, Paula Gunn, ed. *Spider Women's Granddaughters: Traditional Tales and Contemporary Writing by Native American Women.* Boston: Beacon Press, 1989.

———, ed. *Voice of the Turtle: American Indian Literature, 1900–1970.* New York: Random House, 1994.

Bell, Betty Louise. "If This Is Paganism . . . Zitkala-Ša and the Devil's Language." In *Native American Religious Identity: Unforgotten Gods,* edited by Jace Weaver, 61–68. Maryknoll, N.Y.: Orbis, 1998.

Bernardin, Susan. "The Lessons of a Sentimental Education: Zitkala-Ša's Autobiographical Narratives." *Western American Literature* 32, no. 3 (1997): 212–38.

Bernstein, Alison. "A Mixed Record: The Political Enfranchisement of American Indian Women During the Indian New Deal." *Journal of the West* 23, no. 3 (1984): 13–20.

Bezanson, Randall P. *How Free Can Religion Be?* Urbana: University of Illinois Press, 2006.

Blevins Tim, ed. *Extraordinary Women of the Rocky Mountain West.* Colorado Springs, Colo.: Pikes Peak Library, 2010.

Bloom, Harold. "Zitkala-Ša." In *Native American Women Writers,* 118–26. Philadelphia: Chelsea, 1998.

Boyer, Paul S., Clifford E. Clark, Jr., Neal Salisbury, Harvard Sitkoff, and Nancy Woloch. *The Enduring Vision: A History of the American People.* Vol. 2, *Since 1865.* Boston: Houghton Mifflin, 2000.

"Brief History of Activities in Behalf of the American Indians: 1902–1932." Bonnin Collection.

Britten, Thomas A. *American Indians in World War I: At Home and at War.* Albuquerque: University of New Mexico Press, 1997.

Bruyneel, Kevin. "Challenging American Boundaries: Indigenous People and the 'Gift' of U.S. Citizenship." *Studies in American Political Development* 18 (Spring 2004): 30–43.

Burgess, Marianna. "Zitkala-Ša (Red Bird)." *Friends' Intelligencer,* May 19, 1917, 313.

Callahan, S. Alice. *Wynema: A Child of the Forest.* Edited by A. LaVonne Brown Ruoff. Lincoln: University of Nebraska Press, 1997. First published 1891.

"Calls Indian Bureau Unworthy of Trust: Dr. Emerson Asserts It Is Playing Politics Against the Life of Its Wards," *New York Times,* June 3, 1926.

Carden, Mary Paniccia. " 'The Ears of the Palefaces Could Not Hear Me': Languages of Self-Representation in Zitkala-Ša's Autobiographical Essays." *Prose Studies* 20, no. 1 (April 1997): 58–76.

Carlson, Paul H. *The Plains Indians*. College Station: Texas A&M University, 1998.

Carpenter, Ron. "Zitkala-Ša and Bicultural Subjectivity." *Studies in American Literatures* 16, no. 3 (2004): 1–27.

Cary, Elizabeth Luther. "Recent Writings by American Indians." In *The Book Buyer*. New York: C. Scribner's Sons, 1902.

"Catholic Sioux Congress of South Dakota: Indian Hospitality and Faith." *Indian Sentinel* 3, no. 4 (1923): 147.

Chapman, Charles E. *A History of California: The Spanish Period*. New York: Macmillan, 1921.

"Charge Open Robbery of Indian Tribes: Investigators Demand Immediate Reform in Probate Law Administration in Oklahoma." *New York Times*, February 8, 1924.

Chiarello, Barbara. "Deflected Missives: Zitkala-Ša's Resistance and Its (Un)Containment." *Studies in American Indian Literatures* 17, no. 3 (2005): 1–26.

Child, Brenda J. *Boarding School Seasons: American Indian Families, 1900–1940*. Lincoln: University of Nebraska Press, 1998.

Close, Susan. *Faming Identity: Social Practices of Photography in Canada, 1880–1920*. Winnipeg, Manitoba: Arbeiter Ring, 2007.

Cobb, Daniel M. *Native Activism in Cold War America: The Struggle for Sovereignty*. Lawrence: University Press of Kansas, 2008.

Coleman, Michael C. "Motivations of Indian Children at Missionary and U.S. Government Schools." *Montana: The Magazine of Western History* 40 (Winter 1990): 30–45.

"The College Orators." *Indianapolis News*, March 14, 1896.

"The Contest." *Earlhamite*, February 1896, 139–41.

Cook, Jesse W. "The Representative Indian." *The Outlook*, May 5, 1900, 80–83.

Cott, Nancy F. *The Grounding of Modern Feminism*. New Haven, Conn.: Yale University Press, 1987.

Cutter, Martha J. "Zitkala-Ša's Autobiographical Writings: The Problems of a Canonical Search for Language and Identity." *MELUS: Journal of the Society for the Study of the Multi-Ethnic Literature of the United States* 19, no. 1 (1994): 31–44.

Davidson, Cathy N., and Ada Norris, eds. *American Indian Stories, Legends, and Other Writings*. New York: Penguin Books, 2003.

Debo, Angie. *And Still the Waters Run: The Betrayal of the Five Civilized Tribes*. Princeton, N.J.: Princeton University Press, 1972. First published 1940.

Deloria, Philip J. "Four Thousand Invitations." *Studies in American Indian Literatures* 25, no. 2 and *American Indian Quarterly* 37, no. 3 [combined issue] (Summer 2013): 25–43.

Deloria, Vine Jr. *Behind the Trail of Broken Treaties: An Indian Declaration of Independence*. New York: Delacorte Press, 1974.

———. *Custer Died for Your Sins: An Indian Manifesto*. New York: Macmillan, 1969.

———. *God Is Red*. New York: Grosset and Dunlap, 1973.

Deloria, Vine Jr., and Clifford Lytle. *The Nations Within: The Past and Future of American Indian Sovereignty*. New York: Pantheon Books, 1984.

DeRosa, Robin. "Critical Tricksters: Race, Theory, and *Old Indian Legends*." In *American Indian Rhetorics of Survivance: Word Medicine, Word Magic*, edited by Ernest Stromberg, 167–95. Pittsburgh, Pa.: University of Pittsburgh Press, 2006.

Diana, Vanessa Holford. "Hanging in the Heart of Chaos: Bi-Cultural Limbo, Self-(Re)presentation, and the White Audience in Zitkala-Ša's *American Indian Stories*." *Cimarron Review* 121 (1997): 154–72.

Dominguez, Susan Rose. "The Gertrude Bonnin Story: From Yankton Destiny to American History, 1904–1938." Ph.D. diss., Michigan State University, 2005.

———. "Snapshots of Twentieth-Century Writers: Mary Antin, Zora Neal Hurston, Zitkala-Ša, and Anzia Yezierska." *Centennial Review* 41, no. 3 (1997): 547–52.

———. "Zitkala-Ša (Gertrude Simmons Bonnin), 1876–1938: (Re)discovering the Sun Dance." *American Music Research Journal* 5 (1995): 83–96.

Eastman, Elaine Goodale. *Pratt: The Red Man's Moses.* Norman: University of Oklahoma Press, 1935.

El-Seedi, Hesham R., Peter A.G.M. De Smet, Olof Beck, Göran Possnert, and Jan G. Bruhn. "Prehistoric Peyote Use: Alkaloid Analysis and Radiocarbon Dating of Archaeological Specimens of *Lophophora* from Texas." *Journal of Ethnopharmacology* 101, no. 3 (2005): 238–42.

Enoch, Jessica. "Resisting the Script of Indian Education: Zitkala-Ša and the Carlisle Indian School." *College English* 65, no. 2 (2002): 117–41.

Fear-Segal, Jacqueline. "Nineteenth-Century Indian Education: Universalism Versus Evolutionism." *Journal of American Studies* 33, no. 2 (August 1999): 323–41.

Fisher, Dexter. "The Transformation of Tradition: A Study of Zitkala-Ša and Mourning Dove, Two Transitional American Indian Writers." In *Critical Essays on American Literature,* edited by Andrew Wiget, 202–11. Boston: G. K. Hall, 1985.

——— [Alice Poindexter Fisher]. "The Transformation of Tradition: A Study of Zitkala-Ša and Mourning Dove, Two Transitional American Indian Writers." Ph.D. diss., City University of New York, 1979.

———. "Zitkala-Ša: The Evolution of a Writer." *American Indian Quarterly* 5, no. 3 (1979): 229–38.

Glassberg, David. *American Historical Pageantry: The Uses of Tradition in the Early Twentieth Century.* Chapel Hill: University of North Carolina Press, 1990.

Gray, Charlotte. *Flint and Feather: The Life and Times of E. Pauline Johnson, Tekahionwake.* Toronto, Ontario: HarperCollins, 2002.

Greene, Jerome A. *American Carnage: Wounded Knee, 1890.* Norman: University of Oklahoma Press, 2014.

Gridley, Marion E. "Gertrude Simmons Bonnin: A Modern Progressive." In *American Indian Women.* New York: Hawthorne, 1974.

Hadley, Chalmers. "Earlham." *Earlhamite,* June 1943, 13–14, 20.

Hafen, P. Jane. "A Cultural Duet: Zitkala-Ša and *The Sun Dance Opera.*" *Great Plains Quarterly* 18, no. 2 (1998): 102–11.

———, ed. *Dreams and Thunder: Stories, Poems, and* The Sun Dance Opera. Lincoln: University of Nebraska Press, 2001.

———, ed. *Iktomi and the Ducks and Other Sioux Stories.* Lincoln, Neb.: Bison Books, 2004.

———. "Zitkala-Ša: Sentimentality and Sovereignty." *Wicazo Sa Review* 12, no. 2 (1997): 31–41.

Hamm, Thomas D. *Earlham College: A History, 1847–1997.* Bloomington: Indiana University Press, 1997.

Hannon, Charles. "Zitkala-Ša and the Commercial Magazine Apparatus." In *The Only Efficient Instrument: American Women Writers and the Periodical, 1837–1916,* edited by Aleta Feinsod Cane and Susan Alves, 179–201. Iowa City: University of Iowa Press, 2001.

Hanson, William. *Sun Dance Land.* Provo, Utah: J. Grant Stevenson, 1967.

Hardy, Gale J. *American Women Civil Rights Activists: Biobibliographies of 68 leaders, 1825–1992.* Jefferson, N.C.: McFarland, 1993.

Hearings before the Senate Subcommittee of the Committee of Indian Affairs of the House of Representatives on H.R. 2614 to Amend Sections 2139 and 2140 of the Revised Statutes and the Acts

Amendatory thereof, and for Other Purposes. Washington, D.C.: Government Printing Office, 1918.

Heflin, Ruth J. *I Remain Alive: The Sioux Literary Renaissance.* Syracuse, N.Y.: Syracuse University Press, 2000.

Hertzberg, Hazel W. *The Search for an American Indian Identity: Modern Pan-Indian Movements.* Syracuse, N.Y.: Syracuse University Press, 1971.

Hoefel, Rosanne. "Writing, Performance, Activism: Zitkala-Ša and Pauline Johnson." In *Native American Women in Literature and Culture,* edited by Susan Castillo and Victor M. P. DaRosa, 107–18. Porto, Portugal: Fernando Pessoa University Press, 1997.

Hollrah, Patrice E. M. "'We Must Be Masters of Our Circumstances': Rhetorical Sovereignty and Political Resistance in the Life and Works of Zitkala-Ša." In *Old Lady Trill, the Victory Yell: The Power of Women in Native American Literature,* 27–51. New York: Routledge, 2004.

Hoxie, Frederick E. *A Final Promise: The Campaign to Assimilate the Indians, 1880–1920.* Lincoln: University of Nebraska Press, 1984.

———. *This Indian Country: American Indian Political Activists and the Place They Made.* New York: Penguin Press, 2012.

Huebner, Karen L. "An Unexpected Alliance: Stella Atwood, the California Clubwomen, John Collier, and the Indians of the Southwest, 1917–1934." *Pacific Historical Review* 78, no. 3 (2009): 337–66.

Huhndorf, Shari. "American Indian Drama and the Politics of Performance." In *The Columbia Guide to American Indian Literatures of the United States since 1945,* edited by Eric Cheyfitz, 288–318. New York: Columbia University Press, 2006.

Hyde, George E. *Spotted Tail's Folk: A History of the Brule Sioux.* Norman: University of Oklahoma Press, 1961.

"Indian Legends Related: Zitkala-Ša Delights Audience of Children." *Savannah Morning News,* November 12, 1921.

"Indian Woman in Capital to Fight Growing Use of Peyote Drug by Indians." *Washington Times,* February 17, 1918, 9.

"Indian Woman to Be Speaker: Mrs. Gertrude Bonnin Will Discuss Her Race before Suffragists." *Washington Post,* June 2, 1918.

"Indians' Charges to Be Aired Today: Senate Committee Will Go into Stories of Brutality in the Reservation Schools." *New York Times,* May 23, 1930.

"Indians Sue to Keep Pipestone Quarries." *Washington Post,* December 16, 1925.

Jackson, Helen Hunt. *A Century of Dishonor: A Sketch of the United States Government's Dealings with Some of the Indian Tribes.* Reprint. Boston: Roberts Brothers, 1885. First published 1881.

Jaskoski, Helen, ed. *Early Native American Writing.* Cambridge: Cambridge University Press, 1996.

Johnson, Troy R. *Red Power: The Native American Civil Rights Movement.* New York: Chelsea House, 2007.

Johnston, Mary. *To Have and to Hold. Atlantic Monthly* 85 (January 1900): 54–66.

Jorgenson, Joseph G. *The Sun Dance Religion: Power for the Powerless.* Chicago: University of Chicago Press, 1972.

Josephy, Alvin M., Jr. *500 Nations: An Illustrated History of North American Indians.* New York: Knopf, 1994.

———, ed. *Red Power: The American Indians' Fight for Freedom.* New York: McGraw-Hill, 1971.

Katanski, Amelia V. *Learning to Write "Indian": The Boarding School Experience and American Indian Literature.* Norman: University of Oklahoma Press, 2005.

Kellogg, Laura Cornelius. *Our Democracy and the American Indian: A Comprehensive Presentation of the Indian Situation as it is Today.* Kansas City, Mo.: Burton, 1920.

Kelsey, Penelope. "Narratives of the Boarding School Era from Victory to Resistance." *Atenea* 23, no. 2 (2003): 123–37.

Kennedy, David M. *Over Here: The First World War and American Society.* Oxford: Oxford University Press, 1980.

Krupat, Arnold. *Red Matters: Native American Studies.* Philadelphia: University of Pennsylvania Press, 2002.

Kunce, Catherine. "Fire of Eden: Zitkala-Ša's Bitter Apple." *Studies in American Indian Literatures* 18, no. 1 (2006): 73–82.

LaBarre, Weston. *The Peyote Cult.* 5th ed. Norman: University of Oklahoma Press, 1989. First published 1935.

Lanternari, Vittorio. *The Religions of the Oppressed: A Study of Modern Messianic Cults.* Translated by Lisa Sergio. New York: Mentor Books, 1963.

Larner, John W. "Society of American Indians." In *Native America in the Twentieth Century: An Encyclopedia,* edited by Mary B. Davis, 603–604. New York: Garland, 1994.

Ludlow, Helen Wilhelmina. "Indian Education at Hampton and Carlisle." *Harper's New Monthly Magazine* 62, no. 371 (April 1881): 659–76.

Lukens, Margaret A. "The American Indian Story of Zitkala-Ša." In *In Her Own Voice: Nineteenth-Century American Women Essayists,* edited by Sherry Lee Linkon, 141–55. New York: Garland, 1997.

Lyons, Scott Richard. "The Incorporation of the Indian Body: Peyotism and the Pan-Indian Public, 1911–1913." In *Rhetoric, the Polis, and the Global Village: Selected Papers from the 1998 Thirtieth Anniversary Rhetoric Society of America Conference.* Mahwah, N.J.: Lawrence Erlbaum Associates, 1999.

Maddox, Lucy. *Citizen Indians: Native American Intellectuals, Race, and Reform.* Ithaca, N.Y.: Cornell University Press, 2005.

Mails, Thomas E. *Sundancing: The Great Sioux Piercing Ritual.* Tulsa, Okla.: Council Oak Books, 1998.

Maroukis, Thomas Constantine. *Peyote and the Yankton Sioux: The Life and Times of Sam Necklace.* Norman: University of Oklahoma Press, 2004.

———. "The Peyote Controversy and the Demise of the Society of American Indians." *American Indian Quarterly* 37, no. 3 (Summer 2013): 159–80.

———. *The Peyote Road: Religious Freedom and the Native American Church.* Norman: University of Oklahoma Press, 2010.

McDonnell, Janet. *The Dispossession of the American Indian: 1997–1934.* Bloomington: Indiana University Press, 1991.

McKnight, Blanche Syfret. "Feminine Descendent of Sitting Bull Works for Her People." [Washington] *Evening Star,* December 10, 1936.

Meisenheimer, D. K. Jr. "Regionalist Bodies/Embodied Regions: Sarah Orne Jewett and Zitkala-Ša." In *Breaking Boundaries: New Perspectives on Women's Regional Writing,* edited by Sherrie A. Inness and Diana Royer, 109–23. Iowa City: University of Iowa Press, 1997.

"Military Burial for R. T. Bonnin at Arlington Today." *Washington Post,* September 26, 1942.

Miller, David Reed. "Charles Alexander Eastman, The 'Winner': From Deep Woods to Civilization." In *American Indian Intellectuals,"* edited by Margot Liberty, 61–70. St. Paul, Minn.: West, 1978.

Moses, L. G. *The Indian Man: A Biography of James Mooney.* Urbana: University of Illinois Press, 1984.

"Mrs. Bonnin Dies; Friend of Indians." [Washington] *Evening Star,* January 26, 1938.

"Mrs. Bonnin, Sitting Bull Kin, Is Dead at 62." *Washington Post,* January 27, 1938.

"Mrs. Bonnin's Rites." [Washington] *Evening Star,* January 27, 1938.

Myers, Jeffrey. *Converging Stories: Race, Ecology, and Environmental Justice in American Literature.* Athens: University of Georgia Press, 2005.

Nabokov, Peter. *Native American Testimony: A Chronicle of Indian-White Relations from Prophecy to the Present.* New York: Viking Press, 1991.

NCAI. "Brutal Superintendents Are Triumphant." Press Release, May 19, 1930.

———. *Indian Newsletter.* April 22, 1930.

Newmark, Julianne. "Pluralism, Place, and Gertrude Bonnin's Counternativism from Utah to Washington, D.C." *American Indian Quarterly* 36, no. 3 (2012): 318–47.

———. "Writing (and Speaking) in Tongues: Zikala-Ša's *American Indian Stories.*" *Western American Literature* 37, no. 3 (2002): 335–58.

Okker, Patricia. "Native American Literatures and the Canon: The Case of Zitkala-Ša." In *American Realism and the Canon,* edited by Tom Quirk and Gary Scharnhorst, 87–101. Newark: University of Delaware Press, 1994.

Olster, Jeffrey. *The Plains Sioux and U.S. Colonialism from Lewis and Clark to Wounded Knee.* Cambridge: Cambridge University Press, 2004.

"The Oratorical Contest." *Earlhamite,* March 1896, 183–87.

Parins, James W., and Daniel F. Littlefield, Jr. Introduction to *Ke-ma-ha: The Omaha Stories of Francis La Flesche.* Lincoln: University of Nebraska Press, 1998.

"Persons Who Interest Us." *Harper's Bazar,* April 1900, 330.

Peterson, Nancy M. *Walking in Two Worlds: Mixed-Blood Indian Women Seeking Their Path.* Caldwell, Idaho: Caxton Printers, 2006.

Picotte, Agnes. Foreword to *Old Indian Legends* by Zitkala-Ša, xi–xviii. Lincoln: University of Nebraska Press, 1985.

Powers, Thomas. *The Killing of Crazy Horse.* New York: Knopf, 2010.

Pratt, Richard Henry. *Battlefield and Classroom: Four Decades with the American Indian, 1867–1904,* edited by Robert M. Utley. Lincoln: University of Nebraska Press, 1987.

———. "Origin and History of Work at Carlisle." *American Missionary* 37, no. 4 (1883): 108–11.

———. *Origin of the Carlisle Indian Industrial School: Its Progress and the Difficulties Surmounted,* edited by Robert M. Utley. Carlisle, Pa.: Cumberland County Historical Society Publications, 1979. First published 1908.

"Princess Zitkala-Ša Center of Interest at Book Fair of Pen Women." *Washington Herald,* May 2, 1925.

Pritzker, Barry M. *A Native American Encyclopedia: History, Culture, People.* Oxford: Oxford University Press, 2000.

"Prohibition of Use of Peyote among Indians." In *House Reports: 65th Cong., 2nd Sess. December 3, 1917–November 21, 1918.* Washington, D.C.: Government Printing Office, 1918.

Redfield, Karen. "Inside the Circle, Outside the Circle: The Continuance of Native American Storytelling and the Development of Rhetorical Strategies in English." In *American Indian Rhetorics of Survivance: Word Medicine, Word Magic,* edited by Ernest Stromberg, 149–64. Pittsburgh, Pa.: University of Pittsburgh Press, 2006.

Report of the Thirty-Fifth Lake Mohonk Conference on the Indian. October 16–18. Poughkeepsie, N.Y.: Lousing-Broas Printing for the Lake Mohonk Conference, 1930.

Review of *The Sun Dance Opera. The Crisis* 8, no. 4 (1914): 162.

Reynolds, Margot R. "Mother Times Two: A Double Take on a Gynocentric Justice Song." In *Cultural Sites of Critical Interest: Philosophy, Aesthetics, and African American and Native*

American Women's Writings, edited by Christa Acampora and Angela Cotton, 171–90. New York: State University of New York, 2007.

Ruoff, A. LaVonne Brown. "Early Native American Women Authors: Jane Johnston Schoolcraft, Sarah Winnemucca, S. Alice Callahan, E. Pauline Johnson, and Zitkala-Ša." In *Nineteenth-Century American Women Writers: A Critical Reader*, edited by Karen L. Kilcup, 81–111. Malden, Mass.: Blackwell, 1998.

Sedgwick, Ellery. *The Atlantic Monthly, 1857–1909: Yankee Humanism at High Tide and Ebb.* Amherst: University of Massachusetts Press, 1994.

Shreve, Bradley G. *Red Power Rising: The National Indian Youth Council and the Origins of Native Activism.* Norman: University of Oklahoma Press, 2011.

Simmons, Virginia McConnell. *The Ute Indians of Utah, Colorado, and New Mexico.* Boulder: University of Colorado Press, 2000.

Simonds, William E. "Three American Historical Romances." *Atlantic Monthly* 85 (March 1900): 408–14.

Six, Beverly G. "Zitkala-Ša (Gertrude Simmons Bonnin) (1876–1938)." In *American Women Writers, 1900–1945: A Bio-Bibliographical Critical Sourcebook*, edited by Laurie Champion, 383–87. Westport, Conn.: Greenwood Press, 2000.

Slotkin, James Sydney. *The Peyote Religion: A Study in Indian-White Relations.* Glencoe, Ill.: Free Press, 1956.

Smith, Catherine Parsons. "Composed and Produced in the American West, 1912–1913: Two Operatic Portrayals of First Nations Peoples." In *Opera Indigene: Re/presenting First Nations and Indigenous Cultures*, edited by Pamela Karantonis and Dylan Robinson, 187–207. Burlington, Vt.: Ashgate, 2011.

——. "An Operatic Skeleton on the Western Frontier: Zitkala-Ša, William F. Hanson, and *The Sun Dance Opera*." *Women and Music* 5 (January 2001): 1–30.

Smith, Jeanne. " 'A Second Tongue': The Trickster's Voice in the Works of Zitkala-Ša." In *Tricksterism in Turn-of-the-Century American Literature: A Multicultural Perspective*, edited by Elizabeth Ammons and Annette White-Parks, 46–60. Hanover, N.H.: University Press of New England, 1994.

Smith, Paul Chaat, and Robert Allen Warrior. *Like a Hurricane: The Indian American Movement from Alcatraz to Wounded Knee.* New York: New Press, 1996.

Smith, Sidonie. "Cheesecake, Nymphs, and We the People: Un/National Subjects about 1900." *Prose Studies* 17, no. 1 (1994): 120–40.

Spack, Ruth. *America's Second Tongue: American Indian Education and the Ownership of English, 1860–1900.* Lincoln: University of Nebraska Press, 2002.

——. "Dis/engagement: Zitkala-Ša's Letters to Carlos Montezuma, 1901–1902." *MELUS: Journal of the Society for the Study of the Multi-Ethnic Literature of the United States* 26, no. 1 (2001): 173–204.

——. "Re-Visioning Sioux Women: Zitkala-Ša's Revolutionary *American Indian Stories.*" *Legacy: A Journal of American Women Writers* 14, no. 1 (1997): 25–42.

——. "Zitkala-Ša, *The Song of Hiawatha*, and the Carlisle Indian School Band: A Captivity Tale." *Legacy: A Journal of American Women Writers* 25, no. 2 (2008): 211–24.

Speroff, Leon. *Carlos Montezuma, M.D., A Yavapai American Hero: The Life and Times of an American Indian, 1866–1923.* Portland, Ore.: Arnica, 2005.

"Spirit of a Sioux Indian Woman: Zitkala-Ša Is Great Influence in Progress of Her Own Race." *New York Evening Post*, July 21, 1919.

Standing Bear, Luther. *My People the Sioux.* Lincoln: University of Nebraska Press, 1975. First published 1928.

Stewart, Omer C. *Peyote Religion: A History*. Norman: University of Oklahoma Press, 1987.

Stout, Mary. "Zitkala-Ša: The Literature of Politics." In *Coyote Was Here: Essays on Contemporary Native American Literary and Political Mobilization*, edited by Bo Sholer, 70–78. Philadelphia, Pa.: Coronet Books, 1984.

Stromberg, Ernest. "Resistance and Mediation: The Rhetoric of Irony in Indian Boarding School Narratives by Francis La Flesche and Zitkala-Ša." In *American Indian Rhetorics of Survivance: Word Medicine, Word Magic*, edited by Ernest Stromberg, 95–109. Pittsburgh, Pa.: University of Pittsburgh Press, 2006.

Super, O. B. "Indian Education at Carlisle." *New England Magazine* 18, no. 2 (1895): 224–40.

Susag, Dorothea M. "Zitkala-Ša (Gertrude Simmons Bonnin): A Power(full) Literary Voice." *Studies in American Indian Literatures* 5, no. 4 (1993): 3–24.

Taylor, Graham D. *The New Deal and American Indian Tribalism: The Administration of the Indian Reorganization Act, 1934–45*. Lincoln: University of Nebraska Press, 1980.

"Testimonial Talk by Ernest L. Wilkinson at funeral service of Captain Raymond T. Bonnin." Bonnin Collection.

Thornburg, Opal. *Earlham: The Story of the College, 1847–1962*. Richmond, Ind.: Earlham College Press, 1963.

Totten, Gary. "Zitkala-Ša and the Problem of Regionalism." *American Indian Quarterly* 29, nos. 1–2 (2005): 84–123.

Towne, Arietta Wimer. "Mrs. Fowler Entertains Officers and Chairman at Her Home." *Oak Parker*, February 20, 1925.

"Urges Full Citizenship for Indians." *New Era–Lancaster*, March 29, 1918.

Velikova, Roumiana, "Troping in Zitkala-Ša's Autobiographical Writings, 1900–1921." *Arizona Quarterly* 51, no. 1 (2000): 49–64.

"Virginia Couple Devotes Lives to Indians." *Washington Post*, December 31, 1933.

Wallace, Anthony C. "James Mooney (1861–1921) and the Study of the Ghost Dance Religion." In *James Mooney: The Ghost Dance Religion and the Sioux Outbreak of 1890*, edited by Anthony C. Wallace, v–xxi. Chicago: University of Chicago Press, 1970.

Warrior, Robert Allen. *Tribal Secrets: Recovering American Intellectual Traditions*. Minneapolis: University of Minnesota Press, 1995.

Weaver, Jace. "Splitting the Earth: First Utterances and Pluralist Separatism." In *American Indian Literary Nationalism*, edited by Jace Weaver, Craig S. Womack, and Robert Allen Warrior, 1–89. Albuquerque: University of New Mexico Press, 2006.

Welch, Deborah Sue. "Gertrude Simmons Bonnin (Zitkala-Ša)." In *The New Warriors: Native American Leaders since 1900*, edited by R. David Edmunds, 35–54. Lincoln: University of Nebraska Press, 2001.

———. "Zitkala-Ša: An American Indian Leader, 1876–1938." Ph.D. diss., University of Wyoming, 1985.

Wexler, Laura. "Tender Violence: Literary Eavesdropping, Domestic Fiction, and Educational Reform." In *The Culture of Sentiment: Race, Gender, and Sentimentality in Nineteenth-Century America*, edited by Shirley Samuels, 9–38. New York: Oxford University Press, 1992.

Willard, William. "The First Amendment, Anglo-Conformity and American Indian Religious Freedom." *Wicazo Sa Review* 7 (1991): 25–40.

———. "Zitkala-Ša, a Woman Who Would Be Heard!" *Wicazo Sa Review* 1 (1985): 11–16.

Williams, Walter L. "Twentieth Century Indian Leaders: Brokers and Providers." *Journal of the West* 23, no. 3 (July 1984): 3–6.

Wilson, Raymond. *Ohiyesa: Charles Eastman, Santee Sioux*. Urbana: University of Illinois Press, 1983.

Wilson, Terry P. *The Underground Reservation: Osage Oil.* Lincoln: University of Nebraska Press, 1985.

Wise, Jennings C. *The Red Man in the New World Drama: A Politico-Legal Study with a Pageantry of American Indian History.* Washington, D.C.: W. F. Roberts, 1931.

"Women to Hear Indian Princess." *Indianapolis* [. . .] *Star.* February 21, 1924.

Yenne, Bill. *Sitting Bull.* Yardley, Pa.: Westholme, 2008.

Zinn, Howard. *A People's History of the United States.* New York: HarperCollins, 1993.

INDEX

Page references to illustrations are in italic *type. All books, articles, short stories, poems, pamphlets, speeches, orations, announcements, and unpublished manuscripts listed as main entries are by Zitkala-Ša unless otherwise indicated.*

"Address by the Secretary-Treasurer, Society of American Indians Annual Convention" (speech), 239n10

"America, Home of the Red Man" (article), 151–52, 156

American Indian Defense Association (AIDA), 14, 169, 175–76, 192, 244n9; founding of, 165; and John Collier, 14, 165, 175, 249n46; and NCAI, 179, 249n45; in Oklahoma, 14, 165, 167; and Zitkala-Ša, 175

American Indian Magazine (*AIM*), 13, 156; and Zitkala-Ša, 105–106, 113–14, 124–25, 127–28, 130, 134, 151–54, 192, 234n60

American Indian Movement (AIM), 16, 192, 194, 203n41

American Indian Stories (book), 13, 14, 157–59, 218n96, 240n39

Americanize the First American (pamphlet), 13, 192, 241–42nn50–53; analysis of, 160–62

American Protective League, 124, 129

"America's Indian Problem" (article), 157–60, 241n43

Arlington, Va., 126, 176, 188

Arlington National Cemetery, 188

Atlantic Monthly, 12, 19, 37, 45–46, 49, 61, 107, 157, 195, 214n70, 215n17; and Bliss Perry, 37; depictions of American Indians in, 37,

213–14n66; and Zitkala-Ša's "Impressions of an Indian Childhood" in, 37, 40–41, 199n26; and Zitkala-Ša's "An Indian Teacher among Indians, in, 37, 42–43; and Zitkala-Ša's "The School Days of an Indian Girl" in, 37, 41–42; and Zitkala-Ša's "Why I Am a Pagan" in, 62–63, 107, 205n17, 281n92

Atwood, Stella (GFWC activist), 159, 244n21

Bad Hand (Bonnin's adoptive grandfather). *See* Old Sioux (aka Bad Hand, Bonnin's adoptive grandfather)

Baker, Fred A. (BIA clerk), 100–101

Baldwin, Marie: background of, 96; dispute with Zitkala-Ša, 120–22, 130, 231n9, 231n14, 234n60, 234n62; in SAI, 96, 111, 120–22, 130, 231n14, 234n60, 234n62, 236n27; views of, 120, 132

"Ballad, A" (poem), 27

Battle of the Greasy Grass (Little Big Horn Creek), 8

Big Foot, 9

bison, 8, 65, 81–82. *See also* buffalo

Black Hills (Paha Sapa), 7, 8, 189, 190, 241n50, 251n1

Blair, Robert F. (Okla. "guardian"), 168

Blood Clot Boy (Sioux avenger), 57

Bluestone, Ellen C. (allottee at Yankton), 241n41, 246n12

boarding schools, 18, 28, 49, 51, 94, 95, 96, 115, 126, 198–99n21, 213n59, 225n19, 230n58; creation of, 10; description of, 11, 41, 50, 199n25; reform of, 181; Zitkala-Ša's critique of, 12, 19–21, 41–43, 51, 54, 63, 98, 178, 192–93. *See also* Uintah Boarding School

Board of Indian Commissioners, 9, 70, 103, 132, 133, 137, 154

Bonnin, Alfred O. (Raymond T. Bonnin's brother), 204n8

Bonnin, Elsa (Ohiya Bonnin's wife), 186, 188

Bonnin, Emeline (*née* Picotte) (Raymond T. Bonnin's mother), 56, 67, 216n55, 219n14

Bonnin, Gertrude Simmons. *See* Zitkala-Ša (Gertrude Simmons, Gertrude Simmons Bonnin)

Bonnin, Joseph (Zitkala-Ša's grandson), 186

Bonnin, Joseph Barnebe (Raymond T. Bonnin's father), 56, 102, 216n55, 228n3

Bonnin, Raymie (Zitkala-Ša's grandson), 186–87

Bonnin, Raymond Ohiya, 183, 204n8, 227n2, 230n58, 232n31; birth of, 13, 66, 219n4; and burro incident, 116–17; death of, 188, 250n13; education of, 98; in final diaries of Zitkala-Ša, 185–87; qualifications of, 249–50n2; and Zitkala-Ša, 13, 66, 72–73, 83, 96–98, 101, 115–18

Bonnin, Raymond Telephause, 12–13, 74, 79, 102–103, *177*, 204n8, 228n3, 230n58, 232n31, 250n3, 251n14; background of, 21, 56, 216–17n55; and BIA, 12, 64, 67, 72–73, 76–77, 96, 99–100, 116–17, 126, 220n22, 222n64; and burro incident, 116–17; and Catholicism, 56; and courtship of Zitkala-Ša, 56–57, 217n63; death and funeral of, 188, 250n13; in final diaries of Zitkala-Ša, 185–87; and John Collier, 187, 250n3; law studies of, 164, 176, 244n8; legal work of, 164, 175–76; and Marie Baldwin, 121; marital troubles with Zitkala-Ša, 97–101; military service of, 126, 164; in NCAI, 176, 17, 182–83; possible recruitment by Zitkala-Ša, 21; second marriage of, 188, 250n13; and Senate Committee on Indian Affairs, 173; and *The Sun Dance Opera*, 222n4, 223n15; as Uintah school superintendent, 68–69, 220n24; views of, 80; wedding of, 61, 218n84

Boston, Mass., 5, 12, 34, 35–37, 43, 48, 50, 54, 64, 67, 194, 211n40, 214n4, 216n45

Brigham Young University, 71, 85, 173, 189

Brosius, S. M. (IRA activist), 112, 133, 229n37

Brown, Anna (Osage victim), 166

buffalo, 19, 78, 190. *See also* bison

Buffalo Bill Cody's Wild West Show, 34, 82; and Samuel Lone Bear, 34, 89; and Sitting Bull, 8

Bureau of Catholic Indian Missions, 70, 72, 77, 78, 120

Bureau of Indian Affairs (Indian Bureau, Indian Office), 9, 69, 97, 103, 128, 158, 160, 166, 169, 171–72, 176, 181–82, 192, 198nn11–12; and Carlos Montezuma, 93, 111–12, 114, 127–29, 226n5, 233n42; and Charles Eastman, 95; and conflicts with Zitkala-Ša, 67, 73, 76, 99–100, 115, 126, 149, 182–83; 247n22; and fee patents, 154; and criticisms of Zitkala-Ša, 109–10; 118–19, 122, 150, 152, 159–60, 175, 180–81, 189, 193; and employment with Zitkala-Ša, 69–70, 219n20, 221n31; and Marie Baldwin, 96, 120, 122; occupation of, 192, 203n41; and peyote, 132, 136; and Raymond T. Bonnin, 12, 64, 67, 72–73, 76–77, 96, 99–100, 116–17, 126, 220n22, 222n64; and Richard Henry Pratt, 69, 94; and SAI, 111–12, 131, 154; at Uintah, 66, 71, 73, 109–10, 115; and views on Zitkala-Ša, 16, 111–12, 120, 129, 151, 234n63; and World War I, 125;

Bureau of Investigation (BOI), 124, 129

Burke Act, 76, 153

Burkhart, Ernest (Okla. conspirator), 166

Bursum, Holm Olaf (U.S. sen., R.-N.M.), 160, 164

Bursum Bill, 164–65

Burton, Jennie (Whiterocks teacher), 99, 227n37

"California Indians of Today, The" (article), 243n4

"California Indian Trails and Prayer Trees" (article), 243n4

Carlisle Indian Industrial School, 12, 44, 91, 94, 144, 199n21, 214n69; in *Atlantic Monthly*, 37, 42–43; and Carlos Montezuma, 49; closure of, 131; conditions at, 30; curriculum of, 31; founding of, 10, 28; and Luther Standing Bear, 30; philosophy of, 10, 29–31, 209n10; and Richard Henry Pratt, 10, 23, 28, 30–31, 42–43, 69, 220n25; and Samuel Lone Bear, 89; and Spotted Tail, 30; and Zitkala-Ša (Gertrude Simmons), 12, 27, 37, 46, 61, 206n37, 210n28, 235n69; and Zitkala-Ša as employee of, 31–34, and Zitkala-Ša criticism of, 42–43, 54

Carlisle Indian School Band, 46–8, 210n28

Carter, Charles D. (U.S. rep., D-Okla. [Chickasaw]), 127

Cary, Elizabeth Luther (literary critic), 44

Catholicism: and the Catholic Church, 70, 72, 73; and Catholic school, 96, 98; and James Mooney, 140, 236n32; and Raymond T.

Bonnin, 56; and Zitkala-Ša, 13, 70, 73, 75, 85, 101, 143, 146, 153, 220n29, 222n4, 227n38, 237n38

Catholic Sioux Congress, 69, 71; and Zitkala-Ša, 146, 221n37

Century of Dishonor, A (book by Helen Hunt Jackson), 9

Chamberlin, Joseph Edgar (Boston literary figure), 37, 46

Chapman, Asa C. (BIA clerk), 97, 100–101

Cheyenne, 8–9, 14, 138, 226n33

Chicago, Ill., 49–50, 53–56, 59–61, 64, 89, 97–98, 156, 185–86, 188, 222n3

Chipeta, 89, 222n4; background of, 66, 235n12; death of, 245n39; and meeting with Zitkala-Ša, 133–34; protests of, 109, 135; and Sun Dance, 88; and Zitkala-Ša article on, 134–35

"Chipeta, Widow of Chief Ouray with a Word About a Deal in Blankets" (article), 134–35

Christianity, 11; and Carlisle, 29–31; and IRA, 9–10, 132; and James Mooney, 138, 140–41, 145; and Peyotism, 91; and Zitkala-Ša, 42–43, 51, 62–63, 85, 107, 135, 143, 218n92, 218n96. *See also* Catholicism

Church of Jesus Christ of Latter-day Saints, 71; and Zitkala-Ša, 68, 188, 220n29

citizenship, 10, 94, 125, 127–28, 154, 171, 204n41, 239n13, 242,52; and SAI, 126, 131, 154; and Zitkala-Ša, 13, 16, 127–28, 130–31, 150–52, 158–60, 162, 164, 167, 171–72, 175–76, 179–80, 202n36, 229n39, 242n52, 247n18, 247n21, 251n1. *See also* Indian Citizenship Act

Collier, John, 14; in AIDA, 165, 175, 249n46; background of, 175; as commissioner of Indian Affairs, 181–83, 250n3; and Raymond T. Bonnin, 187, 250n3; and Zitkala-Ša, 175, 178, 182–83, 188, 249n46

Colton, Don (Utah state sen., R.), 136

Committee of One Hundred, 165, 171

Committee on Public Information (CPI), 123–24

Cook, Jesse W. (Carlisle teacher), 44, 214n69, 218n89

Coolidge, Sherman (SAI activist), 26, 236n26

Cornelius Kellogg, Laura (SAI activist), 95–96, 227n22

"Coronation of Chief Powhatan Retold, The" (article), 152–53

Crazy Horse, 8

Creel, George (CPI head), 123–24

Cult of True Womanhood, 31, 61. *See also* domesticity

Curry, Oran (Bonnin's adoptive son), 219n49; adoption of, 67, 219n12; on anti-peyote trip,

133; as chairman of the Uintah-Ouray Ute Tribal Business Committee, 183

Custer, George Armstrong, 7–8, 79, 124

Dagenett, Charles E. (SAI activist), 94, 132

Daiker, Fred H. (BIA chief of law and order), 132

"Dakota Ode to Washington, A" (oration), 164, 243–44n6

Dawes Severalty Act, 8, 10, 32, 76, 154, 158, 166, 181, 210n20

Day, Fred Holland (photographer), 36

Debs, Eugene V. (socialist leader), 129

Deloria, Vine, Jr., 16, 192–94, 204n41, 252n7

Dennis, W. C. (Earlham alumnus), 207n45, 208n56

Department of the Interior, 9, 82, 87, 160, 175

DePeltquestangue, Estaiene (SAI activist), 110

Devil's (now Spirit) Lake Reservation, 54, 220n28

Dietz, Angel DeCora (artist, SAI activist, Carlisle superintendent), 57, 217n60

Dodge, Mabel (patron), 175

domesticity, 53, 98, 194. *See also* Cult of True Womanhood

Dragon, Utah, 88–89, 116, 133–34, 142

"Dream of Her Grandfather, A" (short story), 157–58, 241n40

Duncan, John (Ute chief), 91

Earlham College, 3, 11–12, 21–24, 26, 42, 137–38, 206n38, 208n56

Earlhamite, 23, 26–27

Eastman, Charles Ohiyesa Alexander, 144, 165; background of, 94–95; death of daughter Irene, 156, 239n22; at peyote hearings, 137, 143; and SAI, 15, 95, 130, 154–56, 240n28; and World War I, 232n34, 233n48; and Wounded Knee, 94, 226n15

Eastman, Elaine Goodale: death of daughter Irene, 156, 239n22; and Richard Henry Pratt, 144, 245n39; and Zitkala-Ša, 144, 184, 237n40, 245n39

English Opera House and Hotel, 3, 6, 23, 197n1

Espionage Act, 124, 129

Fabens, Charles E. (AIDA lawyer), 167–68, 170

Fall, Albert B. (secretary of the Interior), 160, 164–65, 244n9

Fanciulla del West, La (opera by Puccini), 83

fee patents, 76, 153–54

Felker (Zitkala-Ša's biological father), 18, 204n6, 205nn8–9

Five "Civilized" Tribes, 166, 170

Flathead Reservation, 181

Fort Duchesne, Utah, 66, 75, 88, 96, 101–103, 107–108, 116, 118, 225n19
Fort Totten, N.Dak., 54–55
Fort Yates, N.Dak., 69, 71, 75, 220n28, 221n32, 221n37
Frazier, Lynn J. (U.S. sen., R-N.Dak.), 178
Friends' Intelligencer, 119, 179, 230–31n58, 248n38
Friends of the Indian, 10, 180. *See also* Indian Rights Association (IRA)
Frye, E. M. (Okla. state sen., R.), 170
Frye Bill, 170

Gandy, H. L. (U.S. rep., D.-S.Dak.), 112, 136
Gandy Bill, 112–13, 229n37
General Federation of Women's Clubs (GFWC), 150, 158, 162; creation of Indian Welfare Committee, 159; founding of, 13; and Zitkala-Ša, 14, 156, 159, 162–63, 170, 176, 241n43, 247n14
Gentile, Carlos (Montezuma's surrogate father), 49, 215n12
Ghost Dance, 8, 87, 91, 138, 144, 198n11, 236n26
Ginn & Company, 12, 50, 55, 67
Gladys Belle Oil Company, 168
Gordon, Phillip (Catholic priest, SAI activist): in SAI, 111, 120; and Zitkala-Ša, 120, 130, 231n8
Grant, Ulysses S., 9, 95
Great Sioux Reservation, 7
Great Spirit (Wakan Tanka), 81, 91, 106, 186, 232n30
"Great Spirit, The" (revised version of "Why I Am a Pagan"), 240n34
Greenwood, S.Dak., 18, 56, 102, 204n6, 205n17, 210n19, 228n3
Gruenberg, Eugene (violinist), 35–36

Hadley, Chalmers (Earlham alumnus), 207n40, 209n64; description of Gertrude Simmons (Zitkala-Ša), 22–23
Hale, William K. (Okla. conspirator), 166
Hampton Institute, 18–19, 95, 209n10
Hanson, William F., *84*; and Albert H. Kneale, 102, 228n4; background of, 71, 221n35; and Ohiya Bonnin, 250n13; and Old Sioux, 230n54; and *Sun Dance Land*, 78–79, 81, 223n4; and *The Sun Dance Opera*, 13, 71, 78, 80–81, 83, 188, 222n3, 223n5, 224nn15–16, 251n14; and Zitkala-Ša, 13, 71, 78–81, 188, 222–23n4, 250nn13–14
Harper's Bazar, 44
Haskell Institute, 11, 56, 67, 75, 91, 199n21
Hayden, Carl (U.S. sen., D.-Ariz.), 127, 136
"Heart to Heart Talk" (article), 243n4
Herbert, Victor (composer), 83

Hill, L. T. (Okla. "guardian"), 169
"How the National Council of American Indians Came into Being" (announcement), 247nn18–19
Hyslop, John (Mormon rancher), 117–18

Iktomi (spider fairy), 57
"Impressions of an Indian Childhood" (short story), 37, 40–41, 199n26
"Indian Affairs" (unpublished manuscript), 193, 252n6
Indiana State Oratorical Contest (1896), 3, 23–26, 42, 207n45
Indian Bureau. *See* Bureau of Indian Affairs (Indian Bureau, Indian Office)
Indian Citizenship Act (ICA), 171, 175–76, 245n38. *See also* citizenship
"Indian Dance, The: A Protest Against Its Abolition" (short story), 62, 64, 218n90
Indian Helper, 29–30; and Zitkala-Ša (Gertrude Simmons), 32, 34, 45, 205n8, 209n71, 210n18
Indian New Deal. *See* Indian Reorganization Act
Indian Office. *See* Bureau of Indian Affairs (Indian Bureau, Indian Office)
"Indian Praying on the Hilltop, An" (poem), 153
Indian Removal Act, 166
Indian Reorganization Act (IRA), 181–82, 185
Indian Rights Association (IRA), 9–10, 103, 138, 165, 171, 175, 244n9; and Oklahoma, 167, 169–70; and peyote, 112–13, 132–33, 146; and Zitkala-Ša, 13, 113, 133, 180, 238n52, 244n21, 247n18, 249n39
"Indian's Awakening, The" (poem by Zitkala-Ša), 105–107, 111
"Indian Teacher among Indians, An" (short story), 37, 42–43
Indian Welfare Committee, 159, 163
Iya (camp eater), 57

Jackson, Andrew, 166
Jackson, Helen Hunt, 9
Johnson, E. Pauline (Mohawk writer), 173

Käsebier, Frederick (Gertrude Käsebier's son), 34
Käsebier, Gertrude (photographer), 34, 36, 89, 211n32
Keiley, Joseph (photographer), 34
Keller, Helen, 157
Keller, Marie (Carlos Montezuma's wife), 97
Kenel, Martin (Catholic priest), 221n50; and William H. Ketcham, 71, 73–74; and Zitkala-Ša, 70–74, 221n31

Ketcham, William H. (Catholic priest, director Bureau of Catholic Indian Missions), 146, 221n42; and Martin Kenel, 71, 73–74; and peyote, 114, 137; and Raymond T. Bonnin, 220n24, 221n49; and Zitkala-Ša, 70–78, 80, 96–101, 115–16, 178, 230n51, 238n52
Kinney, J. F. (BIA agent), 11
Kneale, Albert H. (Uintah superintendent), 228n12, 235n8; and burro incident, 116–17; character of, 102, 110, 228n4, 230n46; and Chipeta, 109; and community center, 102, 117; and peyote, 134; and Ute grazing lands, 117–18; wife of, 107, 115–17; and Zitkala-Ša, 102, 110, 117–18, 134, 228n12, 230n46, 235n8
Kyle, Mollie (Osage victim), 166

La Flesche, Francis, 223n14, 236n35
La Follette, Robert (U.S. sen., R./Prog.-Wisc.), 171
Leupp, Francis Ellington (commissioner of Indian Affairs), 68
Life Among the Piutes (autobiography by Sarah Winnemucca), 212n50, 241n42
Lincoln, Abraham, 65, 238n52
Little Big Horn Creek, 8
Lone Bear, Samuel, 90, 226n35; background of, 88–89; character of, 91, 142, 225n23, 226n33; and Gertrude Käsebier, 34, 211n32; and peyote, 89, 91, 133, 142; and Zitkala-Ša, 142, 146
Longfellow, Henry Wadsworth, 22, 46, 48
"Lost Treaties of the California Indians" (article), 243n4
Lusk, Charles S. (Bureau of Catholic Indian Missions secretary), 72, 76, 222n64
Lyon Park, Va., 176, 250n3

Madoniawaybay (Sioux) (Zitkala-Ša's houseguest), 130
Marshall, Thomas (Gertrude Simmons's [Zitkala-Ša's] fiancé), 21, 32, 50; death of, 37; engagement of, 34–35
Martin, Jewell D. (Uintah superintendent), 99–101
McCook, John (Ute chief): background of, 89; and peyote, 89, 133–34; and Zitkala-Ša, 133–35, 235n12
McKenzie, Fayette Avery (SAI founder), 93–94
McKinley, Ida Saxon, 48
McKinley, William, 48, 214n4
Menace of Peyote, The (pamphlet), 113, 226n35
Menominee Reservation, 185
Meriam, Lewis (anthropologist), 171
Meriam Report, 14, 171, 181, 249n39

Merritt, E. B. (Yankton superintendent), 241n41, 242n3, 252n6
Mohonk, Lake (New Paltz, N.Y.), 132–33, 180, 199n26
Montezuma, Carlos, 48; background of, 49; and BIA abolition, 120, 127–28; at Carlisle, 48–49; death of, 156; and Richard Henry Pratt, 49, 146, 156; and SAI, 93, 111–12, 114, 127, 130–31, 154, 156, 226n5; views on education, 49, 54, 59–60; and Wassaja, 127, 129, 233n42; wife Marie Keller, 97; and World War I, 128–29, 131; and Zitkala-Ša, 12, 63–64, 101, 107, 111–12, 114, 130–31, 152, 155, 211n34, 226n1, 234n63, 235n69, 240n23; and Zitkala-Ša break-up, 61–62, 214n69, 218n89; and Zitkala-Ša engagement ring, 57, 61–62, 214n69; and Zitkala-Ša's last meeting with, 156; and Zitkala-Ša reconciliation, 97–99; and Zitkala-Ša romance, 50–62, 215n18; and Zitkala-Ša's The Sun Dance Opera, 224n17
Mooney, James (Smithsonian ethnologist), 13–14, 139, 142; background of, 137–38; and campaign against Zitkala-Ša, 146; Catholicism, 140, 236n32; death of, 146; and Native American Church, 145; peyote testimony of, 138–41; and Richard Henry Pratt; 143, 146; and SAI, 138, 236n27; scholarly views of, 201n33, 238n52; and Zitkala-Ša, 141, 143, 145–46, 236n35, 237n45
Mormonism, 220n29
Mormons, 65–66, 68, 71, 188, 109, 220n29, 222n4

National Congress of American Indians (NCAI), 192–94, 203n41
National Council of American Indians (NCAI), 14, 172, 184, 187, 192, 195, 247n14, 248n22; aims of, 176, 181, 247n18; and "Brutal Superintendents Are Triumphant," 181, 248n38; closure of, 183; emblem of, 176, 247n19; founding of, 176, 247n19; information service program of, 179, 248n29; investigations by, 178, 181, 185–86; and John Collier, 178, 182, 249n46; membership fee of, 183; newsletter of, 179; petition of, 176–77; and pipestone quarries, 175, 246n13; tribal lodges of, 179, 248n36; and Yankton, 182, 186
Native American Church, 145, 237n44, 237n51
Natoma (opera by Victor Herbert), 83
Navajo, 14, 91, 141, 177–78, 180
Neharkey, Millie (Okla. victim), 168, 245n24
Nelson, N. L. (BYU professor), 85–87
Nevin, Arthur (composer), 83
New Paltz, N.Y., 103, 132

Očeti Šakówin (Seven Council Fires), 7, 243n6
Office of Indian Affairs. *See* Bureau of Indian
   Affairs (Indian Bureau, Indian Office)
Oklahoma, 127, 138, 145–46, 169–71, 177; and
   AIDA, 14, 165, 167; guardianships in, 165–67;
   history of, 166–67; and Zitkala-Ša, 14, 167–69,
   173–74, 178
Oklahoma's Poor Rich Indians (pamphlet by
   Charles H. Fabens, Matthew K. Sniffen, and
   Gertrude Simmons Bonnin [Zitkala-Ša]),
   167–70, 244–45n24
Old Double Face (Sioux legend), 57, 190
Old Indian Legends (book), 12, 14, 56–57, 190,
   215n18, 216n45, 217nn60–61
Old Sioux (aka Bad Hand, Bonnin's adoptive
   grandfather), 67, 72–73, *86*; death of, 116,
   230n54; illness of, 213n13; in *Sun Dance
   Land*, 79, 223n4; in *The Sun Dance Opera*, 85,
   222n3
Onondagas, 127, 233n43
Osage, 165–66, 169, 171
Osage Reign of Terror, 166
Ouray (Northern Ute chief), 65–66, 89, 134–35,
   222n4, 245n39
"Our Sioux People" (unpublished manuscript),
   16, 189–92, 242n53, 242n3, 243n4, 251n1
Outlook, The, 44, 169

pageants, 82–83
Paha Sapa. *See* Black Hills (Paha Sapa)
Paiute, 8, 91, 173, 185
Paris Peace Conference, 130–31, 152, 234n65
Parker, Arthur C., *104*; and *American Indian
   Magazine*, 127, 234n60; background of, 95;
   and Cato Sells, 103–104; and Committee of
   One Hundred, 165; and Indian regiments,
   124–25; military service of, 126–27, 232n30;
   and peyote, 132–33, 136, 236n23; and SAI, 15,
   94–95, 113, 124–25, 127, 130, 228n6, 228n12,
   232n30, 232n37; 234n58, 234n60; and World
   War I, 124–25, 233n43; and Zitkala-Ša, 111,
   179; Zitkala-Ša California correspondence,
   136; and Zitkala-Ša/Marie Baldwin dispute,
   120–23; Zitkala-Ša Uintah correspondence,
   103–105, 107–10, 115–18, 133–34, 228n2,
   229n27, 229nn31–32, 235n8, 235n10; Zitkala-Ša
   Washington correspondence, 120–22, 125,
   129–30, 137, 149, 156, 230n58, 231n3, 231n8,
   232–33n37, 234n58, 234n60, 236n35
Perry, Bliss (*Atlantic Monthly* editor), 37
peyote, 91; and Arthur C. Parker, 132–33, 136,
   236n23; and Cato Sells, 145; and Charles
   Eastman, 137, 143; congressional report
   on, 144; hearings on, 136, 138–44; and IRA,
   112–13, 132–33, 146; and James Mooney,

138–41; and John McCook, 89, 133–34; and
   Richard Henry Pratt, 112, 143–46, 238n52;
   and SAI, 13, 87, 95, 112, 127, 131–32, 137, 155,
   240n32; and Samuel Lone Bear, 89, 91, 133,
   142; scholarly interpretations of anti-peyote
   campaign, 237–38n52; and Thomas L.
   Sloan, 137, 141, 236n33; at Uintah, 89, 91,
   108, 112, 131, 133–34, 142, 149, 226n33; in
   Washington Times, 136–37; and William H.
   Ketcham, 114, 137; and Zitkala-Ša, 13–14, 92,
   108, 117, 120, 150, 155; Zitkala-Ša campaign
   against, 108, 112–13, 119, 133–36, 144–49, 159,
   226n35, 236n33, 238n38, 248,n37; Zitkala-Ša
   at peyote hearings, 136, 141–43, 237n38.
   See also Peyote religion (Peyotism)
Peyote religion (Peyotism), 91, 132, 137,
   140–41, 146, 155, 175, 230n51, 237n47, 240n32
Picotte, Joseph (Raymond T. Bonnin's
   grandfather), 56, 216n55
Pine Ridge Reservation, 8–9, 19, 21, 82, 91, 95,
   98, 133–34, 146, 182, 212n47, 242n3, 251n1
pipestone quarries,7, 17, 83, 175, 246n13
Pocahontas, 152
Poia (opera by Arthur Nevin), 83
Powder River, 7–8
Powhatan, 152–53
Pratt, Richard Henry, 12–14, *29*, 32, *33*, 66, 94,
   112, 129, 220n25, 245n39; in *Atlantic Monthly*,
   42–43; background of, 10, 28, 30; and Carlos
   Montezuma, 49–50, 54, 156; death of, 171;
   dismissal from Carlisle, 69; campaign
   against James Mooney, 144–46; and Joseph
   Edgar Chamberlin, 46; and peyote, 112,
   238n52; at peyote hearings, 143–44; and
   SAI, 94, 112, 228n52; views of, 10–11, 28–30,
   199n21, 238n52; and Zitkala-Ša conflicts,
   44, 46, 51–52, 54, 57, 61–62; and Zitkala-Ša
   friendship, 68–69, 121, 126, 133, 137, 144,
   211n28, 237n40
Progressive era, 15, 193
Puccini, Giacomo, 83
Pueblo, 14, 91, 160, 175, 179
Pyramid Lake Paiute Indian Reservation, 185

Q., Lizzie (Osage victim), 166
Quakerism, 21, 64
Quakers, 4–5, 9, 11, 22, 137

Red Cloud (Oglala chief), 7, 251n1
Red Man, 45–46, 49–50, 210n18
Red Man and Helper, 50–51, 210n18, 215n17
"Red Man's America, The" (article), 113, 124,
   128, 229n39, 239n4
Red Power, 16, 63, 150, 172, 189, 192, 194–95,
   203–204n41

Red Progressives, 15, 96, 202n35
Representative William Williamson and the Indians (pamphlet), 177–78
Rhoads, C. J. (commissioner of Indian Affairs), 182, 249n46
Richmond, Ind., 11, 21, 26, 137
Roberts, Martha Axe (Okla. victim), 169
Roe Cloud, Henry (SAI activist), 94, 132, 165
Roosevelt, Franklin Delano, 165, 187
Roosevelt, Theodore, 109
Rosebud Reservation, 8–9, 98, 182–83, 212n47
Royer, Daniel F. (BIA agent), 8

Salt Lake City, Utah, 68, 72, 85, 88, 159, 232n31
Santee Normal Training School, 18, 21, 26, 51, 95, 205n11, 218n90
Scanlan, Lawrence (bishop of Salk Lake City), 72, 75, 96, 221n42
"School Days of an Indian Girl, The" (short story), 37, 41–42
Schurz, Carl (secretary of the Interior), 124
Sedition Act, 124
Selective Service Act, 124–25
Sells, Cato (commissioner of Indian Affairs), 101, 103–104, 109, 239n4, 242n3; and fee patents, 154; and peyote, 145; and World War I, 124–25; and Zitkala-Ša, 115, 145, 235n8
Seven Council Fires (Očeti Šakówin), 7, 243n6
Sheridan, Philip (U.S. gen.), 8
Sherman Institute, 119, 238n53
"Side by Side" (oration), 3–6, 11, 23, 25–26, 42–43; scholarly analysis of, 207–208n53
Simmons, David (Zitkala-Ša's half-brother), 56, 210n20, 227n2; in *Atlantic Monthly* series, 210n19; background of, 18–19, 204n4, 204n6; and Bluestone case, 241n41; family of, 32, 55, 210n22; profession of, 32, 210n19; and Yankton constitution, 249n49
Simmons, Ellen. *See* Taté I Yóhin Win (Ellen Simmons)
Simmons, Gertrude. *See* Zitkala-Ša (Gertrude Simmons, Gertrude Simmons Bonnin)
Simmons, John Haysting (Ellen Taté I Yóhin Win Simmons's second husband), 17–18
Simmons, Victoria (David Simmons's wife), 32, 55, 210n22
Sioux, 14, 16, 18, 58, 70, 80, 95, 115, 138, 160, 179–80, 188; culture of, 18; etymology of, 197n4; history of, 7–9, 19, 31–32; in "Our Sioux People" and "The Sioux Claims" by Zitkala-Ša, 189–92, 251n1; and peyote, 91, 146; and Sun Dance, 81–82, 85, 87; women of, 40–41, 213n61
"Sioux Claims, The" (unpublished manuscript), 189, 192, 241n50, 243n4, 251nn1–2

"Sioux Woman's Love for Her Grandchild, A" (poem), 124, 128
Sirawap, Dick (Lone Bear's friend at Uintah), 89
Sitting Bull: and Buffalo Bill Cody's Wild West Show, 8; and Ghost Dance, 198n11; killing of, 9, 21; and Old Sioux, 67, 79; quotes by, 191, 251n1; resistance of, 8; Zitkala-Ša's identification with, 13, 136, 151, 173, 176, 187–88, 212n52, 231n58, 246n5, 247n17, 248n22
Sloan, Thomas L. (SAI activist): background of, 94–95; and Committee of One Hundred, 165; and peyote, 137, 141, 236n33; in SAI, 154–55, 240nn28–29; and World War I, 233n48
Smith, Clement (Yankton resident), 182
Smith, Rita (Osage victim), 166
Smithsonian (Bureau of Ethnology), 137–38, 146
Sniffen, Matthew (IRA activist), 167–68, 170
Snyder, Homer P. (U.S. rep., R.-N.Y.): and Indian citizenship, 154, 171, 245n38; in Oklahoma, 170; and Zitkala-Ša, 170, 173
Society of American Indians (SAI), 15, 138, 151, 176, 179; aims of, 94; and Arthur C. Parker, 15, 94–95, 113, 124–25, 127, 130, 228n6, 228n12, 232n30, 232n37; 234n58, 234n60; and BIA abolition, 111–12, 114, 127, 131; and Carlos Montezuma, 15, 93, 111–12, 114, 127, 130–31, 154, 156, 226n5; and Charles Eastman, 15, 95, 130, 154–56, 240n28; and citizenship, 131, 154; demise of, 156–57; factionalism of, 111, 115, 131, 165; founding of, 93; and Marie Baldwin, 96, 111, 120–22, 130, 231n14, 234n60, 234n62, 236n27; membership of, 94–95; 1915 conference of, 103; 1916 conference of, 111–12; 1917 conference (cancelled) of, 126; 1918 conference of, 129–30; 1919 conference of, 154–55; and peyote, 13, 87, 95, 112, 127, 131–32, 137, 155, 240n32; and Richard Henry Pratt, 94, 112, 228n52; and World War I, 123–24, 126–28; and Zitkala-Ša, 13, 96–97, 101, 105–106, 111, 119, 126, 136, 150; Zitkala-Ša as secretary of, 114, 118–19, 120–22, 126, 128, 131, 150–51; Zitkala-Ša as secretary-treasurer of, 123, 130; Zitkala-Ša's anti-peyote campaign in, 113, 136, 145; Zitkala-Ša's ideas for, 103, 107, 109–10, 115; Zitkala-Ša's resignation from, 156–57; Zitkala-Ša at conferences of, 103, 111–13, 129–30, 154–57; Zitkala-Ša and Uintah SAI chapter, 108
Society of American Indians Quarterly Journal, 94, 103; name change of, 105; and Zitkala-Ša, 105

"Soft-Hearted Sioux, The" (short story), 51, 62–63, 157, 193
Song of Hiawatha, The (poem by Henry Wadsworth Longfellow), 22, 46, 214n4
Spotted Tail (Oglala chief), 30
"squaw" banner, 6, 24–25, 42, 208n56
Standing Bear, 91, 133–34, 225n32
Standing Bear, Henry (Oglala chief), 94, 225n32
Standing Bear, Luther (Oglala chief), 30, 225n32
Standing Rock Reservation, 8, 241n41; and Zitkala-Ša, 13, 61, 69–70
Steadman, William H. (Carlos Montezuma's guardian), 49
Stechi, Ledcie (Okla. victim), 168
Stowe, Harriet Beecher, 190
St. Pierre, Henry (Ellen Taté I Yóhin Win Simmons's son), 17–18
St. Pierre, Peter (Ellen Taté I Yóhin Win Simmons's son), 17–18, 227n2
St. Pierre, Pierre (Ellen Taté I Yóhin Win Simmons's first husband), 17
suffrage: Indian, 171; women's, 25, 159
Sun Dance, 13, 83, 85, 138, 224n18; bans on, 69, 82, 181; at Uintah, 88–89, 224–25n19; and Zitkala-Ša, 70–71, 80, 181, 230n51, 236n36
Sun Dance Land: and Albert H. Kneale, 102, 228nn4; and Old Sioux, 79, 223n4, 230n54; and *The Sun Dance Opera*, 79–81; unreliability of, 78, 222–23n4, 224n16, 250–51nn13–14; and Zitkala-Ša, 80, 222n4
Sun Dance Opera, The, 13, 71, 96–98; and Carlos Montezuma, 224n17; creation of, 78–80; discussion of, 82–83, 87–88; premiere of, 78, 83, 101; review of, 85–87; revival in 1938 of, 188, 222n3, 251n14; revivals of, 85, 101; scholarly interpretations of, 87, 223n15, 224n18; synopsis of, 83

Tasunkakokipapi (Oglala chief), 7
Taté I Yóhin Win (Ellen Simmons): in *Atlantic Monthly*, 40–43; birth of, 204n1; and Christianity, 19, 205n17; death and funeral of, 102, 227n2; early life of, 17–18, 55; at Yankton, 18–19, 21, 32, 48, 56; and Zitkala-Ša, 21, 41–42, 56, 60, 64, 227–28n2
Teapot Dome Scandal, 165
Tillman, John N. (U.S. rep., D.-Ark.), 143
Trail of Broken Treaties, 192
Trail of Tears, 166
Treaty of Fort Laramie (1868), 7
"Trial Path, The" (short story), 51, 57, 157, 217n63
tribal mélange, 136, 141, 236n34

Trueblood, Edwin P. (Earlham professor), 26
Twenty-point Indian Manifesto, 192, 252n2

Uintah and Ouray Reservation (Uintah), 13, 64–66, 72–73, 87, 96, 99, 101–103, 115, 121, 183, 223n4, 225n32, 230n51; conditions on, 66, 78–79; irrigation project on, 109; peyote on, 89, 91, 108, 112, 131, 133–34, 142, 149, 226n33; Zitkala-Ša's description of, 71, 75
Uintah Boarding School, 66–67, 75; Episcopalian takeover, 68–69; and Zitkala-Ša, 67
Uintah Valley Reservation, 65
Uncle Tom's Cabin (novel by Harriet Beecher Stowe), 115
Unthank, Joseph T. (Zitkala-Ša's Quaker "uncle"), 22, 27, 32, 206nn37–38, 210n28, 214n4
Unthank, Susan B. (Zitkala-Ša's Quaker "aunt"), 21–22, 27, 32, 206nn37–38, 210n28, 214n4
Utes, 13–14, 117–18, 179, 228n4; history of, 65–66, 109, 187; and Raymond T. Bonnin, 67, 179, 187–88; and Sun Dance, 70–71, 80, 87–88, 224–25n19; and *The Sun Dance Opera*, 78, 83, 224n18; and Zitkala-Ša, 67–68, 100, 111, 114, 119, 135, 142; and Zitkala-Ša and Catholicism, 70–72, 75, 101; and Zitkala-Ša and community center, 102, 107; and Zitkala-Ša's views on, 70–72, 75, 108, 235n8

Vernal, Utah, 68, 71, 78, 83, 85

Wabash, Ind., 11, 19, 21, 24, 27, 32
Wakan Tanka. *See* Great Spirit (Wakan Tanka)
Wallen, Shade (superintendent of the Five Civilized Tribes), 170
"Warrior's Daughter, A" (short story), 60–61, 157–58, 218nn82–83
Washington, D.C., 13, 28, 48, 59, 69–70, 73, 76–77, 96, 100–101, 110, 118–22, 126, 136, 137, 167–59, 161, 175–76, 178–79, 183, 187–88, 199, 214n2, 230n58, 235n12, 240n35, 243n4, 247n19, 249n2, 251n14
Washington, George, 164, 205n8
Wassaja (Carlos Montezuma's journal), 127, 129, 233n42
Whiteman, Jordan (Okla. "guardian"), 168
Whiterocks, Utah, 66, 68, 72, 75–76, 88, 96, 99, 108–109
White's Manual Labor Institute, 11, 19–21, 23, 31, 56; in *Atlantic Monthly*, 12, 19, 41, 206n26; and Zitkala-Ša (Gertrude Simmons), 19–21, 199n26, 205n8, 206n28, 206n31

"Why I Am a Pagan" (short story), 61–63, 107, 157, 205n17, 218n92, 218n96, 230n51, 240n39, 242n51
"Widespread Enigma Concerning Blue-Star Woman, The" (short story), 157–58, 241n41
Wilkinson, Ernest L. (lawyer, activist), 179, 188, 250n5, 250n13
Williamson, William (U.S. rep., R.-S.Dak.), 177–78
Wilson, Woodrow, 123, 130–31, 144, 228n6, 234nn63–64
Winnemucca, Sarah (Paiute activist), 173, 212n50, 241n42
Wise, Jennings C. (lawyer, activist), 175
Women's Christian Temperance Union, 108, 136
Women's National Indian Association, 9
Word Carrier, 26, 51, 63, 215n15, 218n90
Work, Herbert W. (commissioner of Indian Affairs), 165, 178
World War I, 15, 123, 165, 175; and Arthur C. Parker, 124–27; and Carlos Montezuma, 127–29; and Indian regiments, 124–25; and Indians, 128, 233n47; and Raymond T. Bonnin, 126; and SAI, 126; and Zitkala-Ša, 125–29, 150, 162, 232n31
World War II, 171
Wounded Knee massacre, 9, 15, 21, 43, 69, 87, 95, 226n15
Wovoka, 8

Yankton Reservation, 3, 7, 12, 18–21, 27, 31–32, 40, 42, 48–50, 53, 55–56, 60, 62, 83, 149, 154, 175, 182–83, 185, 187, 210n20, 215n18, 241n41, 249n46
Yankton Sioux, 6, 14; constitution of, 186, 249n49; and fee patents, 154; hiring of Raymond T. Bonnin, 175; history of, 7, 17; and Indian Reorganization Act, 182–83; and NCAI, 182–83; and pipestone quarries, 7, 17, 83, 175, 246n13; society of, 18, 32, 80
"Year's Experience in Community Service Work among the Ute Tribe of Indians, A" (article), 111
Yuma, 178

Zitkala-Ša (Gertrude Simmons, Gertrude Simmons Bonnin): 20, 29, 33, 35, 36, 38, 39, 47, 84, 112, 147, 148, 174, 177; and AIDA, 175; and Albert H. Kneale, 102, 110, 117–18, 134, 228n12, 230n46, 235n8; and *American Indian Magazine*, 105–106, 113–14, 124–25, 127–28, 130, 134, 151–54, 192, 234n60; anti-peyote campaign of, 108, 112–13, 119, 133–36, 144–49, 159, 226n35, 236n33, 238n38, 248n37; and

Arthur C. Parker, 111, 179; and Arthur C. Parker/Marie Baldwin dispute, 120–23; Arthur C. Parker California correspondence, 136; Arthur C. Parker Uintah correspondence, 103–105, 107–110, 115–18, 133–34, 228n2, 229n27, 229n31, 229n32, 235n8, 235n10; Arthur C. Parker Washington correspondence, 120–22, 125, 129–30, 137, 149, 156, 230n58, 231n3, 231n8, 232–23n37, 234n58, 234n60, 236n35; in *Atlantic Monthly*, 37, 40–43, 62–63, 107, 199n26, 205n17, 281n92; birth and birth date of, 6, 18, 199n23, 204–205n8; and BIA (Bureau of Indian Affairs, Indian Bureau, Indian Office) conflicts with, 67, 73, 76, 99–100, 115, 126, 149, 182–83; 247n22; and BIA criticism by, 109–10, 118–19, 122, 150, 152, 159–60, 175, 180–81, 189, 193; and BIA employment of, 69–70, 219n20; 221n31; and BIA in view of, 16, 111–12, 120, 129, 151, 234n63; in Boston, 12, 34–37, 43, 48, 54, 211n40; in California, 163–64, 191–20, 136, 163–64,, 178, 231n3, 238n53; and Carlisle (Indian Industrial School), 12, 27, 37, 46, 61, 206n37, 210n28, 235n69; at Carlisle, 31–34, 42–43, 46; as Carlisle employee, 31–34; and Carlisle Indian School Band, 46–8, 210n28; Carlisle under criticism by, 42–43, 54; and Carlos Montezuma, 12, 63–64, 101, 107, 111–12, 114, 130–31, 152, 155, 211n34, 226n1, 234n63, 235n69, 240n23; and Carlos Montezuma break-up, 61–62, 214n69, 218n89; and Carlos Montezuma engagement ring, 57, 61–62, 214n69; and Carlos Montezuma last meeting, 156; and Carlos Montezuma reconciliation, 97–99; and Carlos Montezuma romance, 50–62, 215n18; Carlos Montezuma and *The Sun Dance Opera*, 224n17; at Catholic Sioux Congress, 146, 221n37; and Catholicism, 13, 69–70, 73, 75, 85, 101, 143, 146, 153, 220n29, 222n4, 227n38, 237n38; and Cato Sells, 115, 145, 235n8; childhood of, 18–20; and Chipeta, 133–35; and Christianity, 42–43, 51, 62–63, 85, 107, 135, 143, 218n92, 218n96; and Church of Jesus Christ of Latter-day Saints, 68, 188, 220n29; and citizenship, 13, 16, 127–28, 130–31, 150–52, 158–60, 162, 164, 167, 171–72, 175–76, 179–80, 202n36, 229n39, 242n52, 247n18, 247n21, 251n1; critique of boarding schools, 12, 19–21, 41–43, 51, 54, 63, 98, 178, 192–93; critique of white civilization, 4–6, 12, 14, 26, 40–43, 57, 59–61, 64, 150, 164, 151–53, 189–92, 202n36, 207–208n53, 217n61, 218n82, 243n4, 251n1; death and funeral of, 187–88; descriptions of, 22–23, 26, 46, 80, 151; diaries of, 184–87; at Earlham, 11–12, 22–23, 26–27,

Zitkala-Ša *(cont.)*
206n38, 207n40, 208n56, 208–209n64,
209nn66–67, 209n71; in *Earlhamite*, 23, 26–27,
208n58, 208–209n64; 209n67, 209n71, 214n70,
214n4; and Elaine Goodale Eastman, 144,
184, 237n40, 245n39; and Ellen C. Bluestone,
241n41, 246n12; and Felker, 18, 204n6, 205n8,
205n9; at Fort Totten, 54–55, 220–21n30; and
Frederick Käsebier, 34; and Fred Holland
Day, 36; and Gertrude Käsebier, 34, 36, 89,
211n32; and GFWC, 14, 156, 159, 162–63,
170, 176, 241n43, 247n14; illnesses of, 23, 27,
122, 155–56, 187, 209n68; at Indiana State
Oratorical Contest, 3–6, 23–26; and *Indian
Helper*, 32, 34, 45, 205n8, 209n71, 210n18,
214n69; and IRA, 13, 113, 133, 180, 238n52,
244n21, 247n18, 249n39; and Indian women's
orchestra, 247n21; and James Mooney, 141,
143, 145–46, 236n35, 237n45; James Mooney
campaign against by, 146; and John Collier,
175, 178, 182–83, 188, 249n46; and John
McCook, 133–35, 235n12; and Joseph Edgar
Chamberlin, 37, 46; and Joseph Keiley, 34;
land ownership by, 32, 61, 210n20; land
purchases by, 70, 76; lecture tours of, 13, 108,
113, 120, 150–51, 156, 163–64, 173, 248n38;
and Marie Baldwin, 120–22, 130, 231n9,
231n14, 234n60, 234n62; and Martin Kenel,
70–74, 221n31; and Mormonism, 220n29;
musical abilities of, 21, 23, 35–36, 46, 78–79,
98–99, 201n18; name of, 6, 12, 55–56, 205n8,
211n46; and National Council of American
Indians (NCAI), 14, 176–79, 181–87, 247n18,
247n19, 247–48n22, 248n29, 248, 36, 248n38,
249n46; objectification of by press, 15, 26,
151; and Ohiya Bonnin, 72–73, 83, 96–98, 101,
115–18; Ohiya Bonnin birth, 13, 66, 219n4;
and Ohiya Bonnin burro incident, 116–17;
Ohiya Bonnin education, 98; Ohiya Bonnin
in final diaries, 185–87; in Oklahoma, 14,
167–69; and Old Sioux, 67, 72–73, 116; and
Oran Curry, 219n49; Oran Curry adoption,
67, 219n12; and Oran Curry on anti-peyote
trip, 133; and Paris Peace Conference,
130–31, 152, 234n65; and peyote, 13–14, 92,
108, 117, 120, 150, 155; at peyote hearings,
136, 141–43, 237n38; and Phillip Gordon,
120, 130, 231n8; and proto-Red Power
platform, 16, 63, 15–53, 176, 194, 203n41; and
Quakerism, 21, 64; Raymond T. Bonnin
courtship of, 56–57, 217n63; Raymond T.
Bonnin in final diaries of, 185–87;
Raymond T. Bonnin marital troubles with,
97–101; Raymond T. Bonnin as possible
recruit of, 21; in *Red Man*, 45–46, 49–50; in

Red Man and Helper, 50–51, 215n17; and
Richard Henry Pratt conflicts, 44, 46, 51–52,
54, 57, 61–62; and Richard Henry Pratt
friendship, 68–69, 121, 126, 133, 137, 144,
211n28, 237n40; and SAI, 13, 96–97, 101,
105–106, 111, 119, 126, 136, 150; SAI
anti-peyote campaign by, 113, 136, 145; SAI
ideas by, 103, 107, 109–10, 115; SAI
resignation by, 156–57; as SAI secretary,
114, 118–19, 120–22, 126, 128, 131, 150–51; as
SAI secretary-treasurer, 123, 130; at SAI
conferences, 103, 111–13, 129–30, 154–57; and
SAI Uintah chapter, 108; and Samuel Lone
Bear, 142, 146; at Santee Normal Training
School, 21; scholarly interpretations of, 14,
132, 146, 200n32, 201n33, 201n34, 238–39n52,
242n52; scholarly interpretations of and
news reports on anti-peyote campaign,
136–37, 237–38n52; and Sitting Bull, 13, 136,
151, 173, 176, 187–88, 212n52, 231n58, 246n5,
247n17, 248n22; and *Society of American
Indians Quarterly Journal*, 105; and "squaw"
banner, 6, 24–25, 42, 208n56; at Standing
Rock, 69–70; and Sun Dance, 70–71, 80, 181,
230n51, 236n36; in *Sun Dance Land*, 80, 222n4;
and Taté I Yóhin Win (Ellen Simmons), 21,
41–42, 56, 60, 64, 227–28n2; and *The Sun
Dance Opera*, 13, 71, 83, 96–98; and *The Sun
Dance Opera* creation, 78–80; and *The Sun
Dance Opera* premiere, 78, 83, 101; and *The
Sun Dance Opera* review, 85–87; and *The Sun
Dance Opera* revivals, 85, 101, 188, 222n3,
251n14; and *The Sun Dance Opera* scholarly
interpretations, 87, 223n15, 224n18; and
Thomas Marshall, 21, 32, 50; and Thomas
Marshall death, 37; and Thomas Marshall
engagement, 34–35; and tribal mélange, 136,
141, 236n34; at Uintah, 66–77, 79, 96–97,
99–102, 107–111, 115–18, 133–34, 136; and
Uintah Boarding School, 67; and Utes, 67–68,
100, 111, 114, 119, 135, 142; and Utes and
Catholicism, 70–72, 75, 101; and Utes and
community center, 102, 107; Utes as viewed
by, 70–72, 75, 108, 235n8; and Vine Deloria,
Jr., 16, 192–94, 252–53n7; in Washington, D.C.,
119–22, 125–26, 129–30, 141–46, 157, 176–78;
wedding of, 61, 218n84; at White's Manual
Labor Institute, 19–21, 199n26, 205n8, 206n28,
206n31; and William F. Hanson, 13, 71, 78–81,
188, 222n4, 222–23n4, 250n13, 250n14; and
William H. Ketcham, 70–78, 80, 96–101,
115–16, 178, 230n51, 238n52; and World War I,
125–29, 150, 162, 232n31; at Yankton, 18–21,
32, 40, 42, 48, 56, 60–64. *See also entries for
individual works by Zitkala-Ša*